CAST IRON

The Ultimate Cookbook

13-Digit ISBN: 978-1-60433-888-1
10-Digit ISBN: 1-60433-888-1

This book may be ordered by mail from the publisher. Please include $5.99 for
postage and handling. Please support your local bookseller first!
Books published by Cider Mill Press Book Publishers are available at special
discounts for bulk purchases in the United States by corporations, institutions,
and other organizations. For more information, please contact the publisher.

Cider Mill Press Book Publishers
"Where good books are ready for press"
PO Box 454
12 Spring Street
Kennebunkport, Maine 04046
Visit us online!
cidermillpress.com

Typography: Adobe Garamond, Brandon Grotesque, Lastra, Sackers English Script

Printed in China
3 4 5 6 7 8 9 0

CAST IRON

The Ultimate Cookbook

RACHAEL NARINS

CIDER MILL PRESS

BOOK
PUBLISHERS
KENNEBUNKPORT, MAINE

CONTENTS

INTRODUCTION

What makes a person want to write about cast-iron cookware, anyway? For one thing—as mentioned time and time again in this book—it's a timeless, versatile, eco-friendly tool for anyone who likes to cook.

When we're young and learn to cook—assuming you too learned to cook at a young age—cast iron is daunting. We are too weak to lift it, so it is left to the adults in the house. Maybe you—like me—grew up watching Sunday pancakes being cooked and expertly flipped in the pan your grandmother used, or maybe you watched someone tend to freshly caught fish as they sizzled in a perfectly seasoned cast-iron skillet that sat over a campfire. Or maybe you also spent chilly winter afternoons in a wooden cabin, après-ski, warming up by a cast-iron stove, waiting patiently for the hot chocolate to be cool enough to take a sip.

Such memories drive us to cherish something, to pursue learning more about it, and to find a community that appreciates the timeless and the beautifully made.

The other incredible aspect of cast iron is how it's used by people almost everywhere in the world. In this book, you'll find recipes that call for specialized cast iron from places like Japan, South Africa, and Denmark, as well as the United States, Latin America, and India. In its various forms, cast-iron cookware is a strong and versatile tool that is used and loved by people from all walks of life, no matter where they live. In many ways, cast-iron cookware is the melting pot of the world, literally and figuratively.

There's more to life than cast-iron cookware and the food that can be prepared in it, but to a curious mind, it can be a fascinating and inexhaustible topic. For me, this book was a way to delve a little bit deeper and to explore the world through a unique lens. Take some time with this book and you'll see how incredibly varied the recipes are, and how they represent almost every corner of the planet. It's a trip around the world without having to leave your kitchen.

A CAST IRON OVERVIEW

According to Los Alamos National Laboratory, iron is the fourth most common element in the Earth's crust by weight. People have utilized this abundance to make tools, including cookware, for thousands of years.

A tomb in Luhe Distirct in Jiangsu, an eastern coastal province in China, is where the world's earliest known cast-iron artifacts have been discovered. Those date to the early fifth century BCE, and over the course of the next two centuries all manner of cast-iron tools were made and used across China. Mass production of iron and cast-iron tools became so important that the Han state was permitted a monopoly on iron production in 117 BCE. From China, foundries spread across Central Asia and Europe.

To create cast-iron tools and cookware, iron is melded with steel and additional chemicals. This process raises the carbon levels, creating an incredibly strong material. To form a pan, the molten metal is poured into a single-use mold made of clay and sand. That's what puts the "cast" in cast iron. The sand in the mold is what creates a rough surface. The inside of the pan is then smoothed out before being sold. (See the Industry Insiders chapter for more on how cast-iron cookware is made.)

Until stoves and ovens became common, most cooking was done on open fires outdoors or in an indoor hearth or fireplace. In either situation, a cauldron was used, either by being placed directly on the flames or coals or by being suspended over them, which led to the development of round and three-legged pots. When flat-topped stoves started appearing in homes, skillets and other flat-bottomed cookware were developed.

In seventeenth-century Holland, foundry techniques were refined (hence the likely origin of the colloquial name "Dutch oven") and many pots, pans, and kettles were exported to England and the rest of Europe. In the early eighteenth century, Englishman Abraham Darby visited Holland to study the cast-iron production process; when he returned home, he founded the Bristol Iron Company in 1708 and patented a method of sand-casting pans in hollow molds using set patterns for mass production. This new method lowered the cost of pans, meaning they could be sold for less than brass cookware, allowing more people access to them. Soon enough, Darby's products were being shipped internationally, including across the Atlantic Ocean to the colonies.

SUGAR KETTLES

A sugar kettle, also known as a syrup kettle, is recognizable to most of us now as a firepit or a water fountain. Maybe even as a chic koi pond. They're used that way today because they're a conversation piece and just plain work well, plus you can leave them to fend against the elements without worrying. They're so heavy there's almost no chance one would be taken in the night. In the past, though, these cast-iron vessels were used on plantations for boiling sugarcane juice to extract sugar, one of the most important crops in the early history of the United States.

The large, wide shape allowed for maximum evaporation as the sugarcane boiled down into sugar over a live fire in a series of kettles—in what was called a Jamaica train—that were stirred constantly for hours by slaves. Cast iron made the kettles incredibly durable and able to withstand the extremely high temperatures of boiling sugar. The vessels were also inefficient, however, since the heat could not be regulated while the juice cooked.

As a result of the longevity of cast iron, you can see a large collection of antique sugar kettles on a visit to the Whitney Plantation, a slavery museum in Wallace, Louisiana, or at almost any other former sugar plantation. Antique sugar kettles are often sold at auctions or by collectibles dealers. While a new kettle may cost around $2,000 (plus shipping!) a collectible can go for many more thousands.

THE TRY-POT
AND *MOBY-DICK*

The try-pot was a large-scale cast-iron vessel used by whalers. Set over a heat source, a try-pot would be used to render oil from whale blubber as well as from penguin meat. This work was primarily done on land, but, by the eighteenth century, whaling ships were outfitted with try-works. Furnaces built onboard were mounted with these pots in order to let the ships stay out at sea for longer periods of time. Herman Melville dedicated a chapter of *Moby-Dick* to this innovation, and, as with everything in this literary masterpiece, his meditation on these structures makes them about much more than rendering blubber, as the excerpt below makes clear.

Leslie Adkin, photographer, "Relics of old whaling days; try-pots, used to render down the blubber, in valley at back of Wharekohu Bay." 26 February 1921; North Island, New Zealand. Gift of G. L. Adkin family estate, 1964. Museum of New Zealand Te Papa Tongarewa (A.005928).

CHAPTER 96. The Try-Works.

Besides her hoisted boats, an American whaler is outwardly distinguished by her try-works. She presents the curious anomaly of the most solid masonry joining with oak and hemp in constituting the completed ship. It is as if from the open field a brick-kiln were transported to her planks.

The try-works are planted between the foremast and mainmast, the most roomy part of the deck. The timbers beneath are of a peculiar strength, fitted to sustain the weight of an almost solid mass of brick and mortar, some ten feet by eight square, and five in height. The foundation does not penetrate the deck, but the masonry is firmly secured to the surface by ponderous knees of iron bracing it on all sides, and screwing it down to the timbers. On the flanks it is cased with wood, and at top completely covered by a large, sloping, battened hatchway. Removing this hatch we expose the great try-pots, two in number, and each of several barrels' capacity. When not in use, they are kept remarkably clean. Sometimes they are polished with soapstone and sand, till they shine within like silver punch-bowls. During the night-watches some cynical old sailors will crawl into them and coil themselves away there for a nap. While employed in polishing them—one man in each pot, side by side—many confidential communications are carried on, over the iron lips. It is a place also for profound mathematical meditation. It was in the left hand try-pot of the Pequod, with the soapstone diligently circling round me, that I was first indirectly struck by the remarkable fact, that in geometry all bodies gliding along the cycloid, my soapstone for example, will descend from any point in precisely the same time.

Removing the fire-board from the front of the try-works, the bare masonry of that side is exposed, penetrated by the two iron mouths of the furnaces, directly underneath the pots. These mouths are fitted with heavy doors of iron. The intense heat of the fire is prevented from communicating itself to the deck, by means of a shallow reservoir extending under the entire enclosed surface of the works. By a tunnel inserted at the rear, this reservoir is kept replenished with water as fast as it evaporates. There are no external chimneys; they open direct from the rear wall. And here let us go back for a moment.

It was about nine o'clock at night that the Pequod's try-works were first started on this present voyage. It belonged to Stubb to oversee the business.

"All ready there? Off hatch, then, and start her. You cook, fire the works." This was an easy thing, for the carpenter had been thrusting his shavings into the furnace throughout the passage. Here be it said that in a whaling voyage the first fire in the try-works has to be fed for a time with wood. After that no wood is used, except as a means of quick ignition to the staple fuel. In a word, after being tried out, the crisp, shriveled blubber, now called scraps or fritters, still contains considerable of its unctuous properties. These fritters feed the flames. Like a plethoric burning martyr, or a self-consuming misanthrope, once ignited, the whale supplies his own fuel and burns by his own body. Would that he consumed his own smoke! for his smoke is horrible to inhale, and inhale it you must, and not only that, but you must live in it for the time. It has an unspeakable, wild, Hindoo odor about it, such as may lurk in the vicinity of funereal pyres. It smells like the left wing of the day of judgment; it is an argument for the pit.

By midnight the works were in full operation. We were clear from the carcase; sail had been made; the wind was freshening; the wild ocean darkness was intense. But that darkness was licked up by the fierce flames, which at intervals forked forth from the sooty flues, and illuminated every lofty rope in the rigging, as with the famed Greek fire. The burning ship drove on, as if remorselessly commissioned to some vengeful deed. So the pitch and sulphur-freighted brigs of the bold Hydriote, Canaris, issuing from their midnight harbors, with broad sheets of flame for sails, bore down upon the Turkish frigates, and folded them in conflagrations.

The hatch, removed from the top of the works, now afforded a wide hearth in front of them. Standing on this were the Tartarean shapes of the pagan harpooneers, always the whale-ship's stokers. With huge pronged poles they pitched hissing masses of blubber into the scalding pots, or stirred up the fires beneath, till the snaky flames darted, curling, out of the doors to catch them by the feet. The smoke rolled away in sullen heaps. To every pitch of the ship there was a pitch of the boiling oil, which seemed all eagerness to leap into their faces. Opposite the mouth of the works, on the further side of the wide wooden hearth, was the windlass. This served for a sea-sofa. Here lounged the watch, when not otherwise employed, looking into the red heat of the fire, till their eyes felt scorched in their heads. Their tawny features, now all begrimed with smoke and sweat, their matted beards, and the contrasting barbaric brilliancy of their teeth, all these were strangely revealed in the capricious emblazonings of the works. As they narrated to each other their unholy adventures, their tales of terror told in words of mirth; as their uncivilized laughter forked upwards out of them, like the flames from the furnace; as to and fro, in their front, the harpooneers wildly gesticulated with their huge pronged forks and dippers; as the wind howled on, and the sea leaped, and the ship groaned and dived, and yet steadfastly shot her red hell further and further into the blackness of the sea and the night, and scornfully champed the white bone in her mouth, and viciously spat round her on all sides; then the rushing Pequod, freighted with savages, and laden with fire, and burning a corpse, and plunging into that blackness of darkness, seemed the material counterpart of her monomaniac commander's soul.

So seemed it to me, as I stood at her helm, and for long hours silently guided the way of this fire-ship on the sea. Wrapped, for that interval, in darkness myself, I but the better saw the redness, the madness, the ghastliness of others. The continual sight of the fiend shapes before me, capering half in smoke and half in fire, these at last begat kindred visions in my soul, so soon as I began to yield to that unaccountable drowsiness which ever would come over me at a midnight helm.

But that night, in particular, a strange (and ever since inexplicable) thing occurred to me. Starting from a brief standing sleep, I was horribly conscious of something fatally wrong. The jaw-bone tiller smote my side, which leaned against it; in my ears was the low hum of sails, just beginning to shake in the wind; I thought my eyes were open; I was half conscious of putting my fingers to the lids and mechanically stretching them still further apart. But, spite of all this, I could see no compass before me to steer by; though it seemed but a minute since I had been watching the card, by the steady binnacle lamp illuminating it. Nothing seemed before me but a jet gloom, now and then made ghastly by flashes of redness. Uppermost was the impression, that whatever swift, rushing thing I stood on was not so much bound to any haven ahead as rushing from all havens astern. A stark, bewildered feeling, as of death, came over me. Convulsively my hands grasped the tiller, but with the crazy conceit that the tiller was, somehow, in some enchanted way, inverted. My God! what is the matter with me? thought I. Lo! in my brief sleep I had turned myself about, and was fronting the ship's stern, with my back to her prow and the compass. In an instant I faced back, just in time to prevent the vessel from flying up into the wind, and very probably capsizing her. How glad and how grateful the relief from this unnatural hallucination of the night, and the fatal contingency of being brought by the lee!

Look not too long in the face of the fire, O man! Never dream with thy hand on the helm! Turn not thy back to the compass; accept the first hint of the hitching tiller; believe not the artificial fire, when its redness makes all things look ghastly. Tomorrow, in the natural sun, the skies will be bright; those who glared like devils in the forking flames, the morn will show in far other, at least gentler, relief; the glorious, golden, glad sun, the only true lamp—all others but liars!

By the mid-eighteenth century, foundries had been established in the American colonies, and the Dutch oven, also known as a "bake kettle" and "bake oven," was commonplace. Originally, Dutch ovens stood on three legs, which allowed them to be set over a heat source, and some versions had longer legs than others. The tight-fitting lids produced the "oven" effect, which was conducive to all types of food being cooked in the vessel, from stews and soups to loaves of bread. One Dutch-oven innovation included a flat, lipped lid that allowed hot coals to be placed on top of the cookware.

In 1836, the J. Harriman Company secured a patent for a cast-iron cookstove, and so began a long line of US patents for cast-iron cookware and related tools, accessories, and implements. In 1842, S. C. Riley patented the invention of a "certain new and useful improvement in uten-

sils to be used with cooking-stoves of various kinds, but which are furnished with oval or elongated holes or openings in the top plate for the admission of kettles, stewpans, and other articles usually employed with such stoves." By the late nineteenth century, storied cast-iron cookware makers like Griswold, Lodge, and Wagner were producing cookware that was thinner and lighter than what we are accustomed to today, thanks to virgin ore mined from regions like Erie, Pennsylvania, and Sidney, Ohio.

The number of cast-iron patents secured into the twentieth century is dizzying: Waffle Iron, Gridiron, Corn Cob Baking Pan, Improved Egg Pan and Cake Baker, Cake Griddle, Egg Fryer, and many more. The following pages feature early approved cast-iron patent designs along with descriptions about what made each creation patent-worthy.

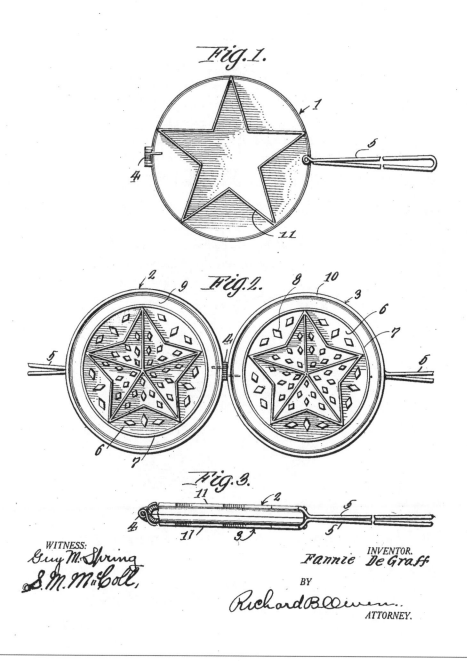

F. DE GRAFF.
WAFFLE IRON.
APPLICATION FILED APR. 19, 1919.

1,336,734.

Patented Apr. 13, 1920.

Fig.1.

Fig.2.

Fig.3.

WITNESS:
Guy M. Spring
S. M. McColl

INVENTOR.
Fannie De Graff

BY

Richard B. Owen
ATTORNEY.

WAFFLE IRON

"Another objective is to construct a waffle iron which is designed to be lifted bodily and turned with very little exertion."

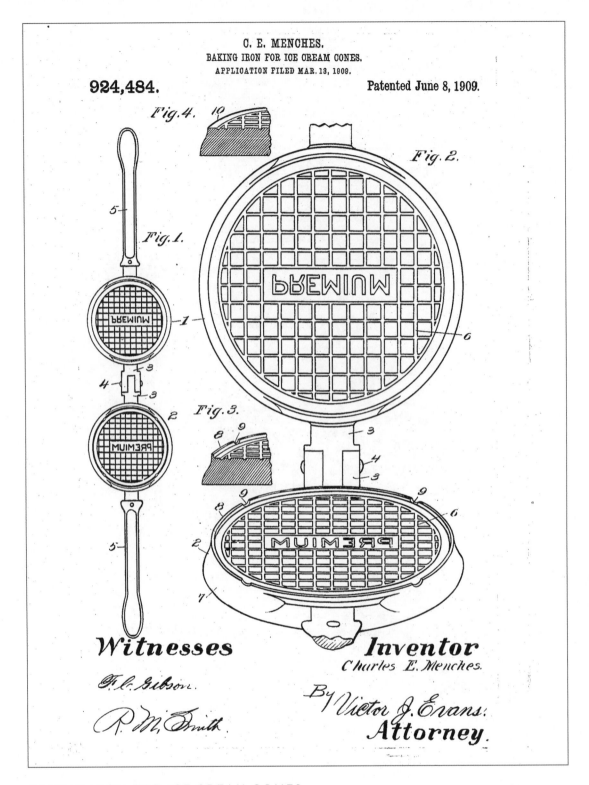

C. E. MENCHES.
BAKING IRON FOR ICE CREAM CONES.
APPLICATION FILED MAR. 13, 1909.

924,484.

Patented June 8, 1909.

Fig.4.

Fig.2.

Fig.1.

Fig.3.

Witnesses

F. C. Gibson.

R. M. Smith.

Inventor
Charles E. Menches.

By Victor J. Evans.
Attorney.

BAKING IRON FOR ICE CREAM CONES

"The object of the invention being to provide a baking iron of the class described which will properly confine the batter and form each one with a smooth, finished marginal edge, avoiding the usual irregular zig-zag edges now so common, and imparting to the waffle or cake a neat and finished appearance."

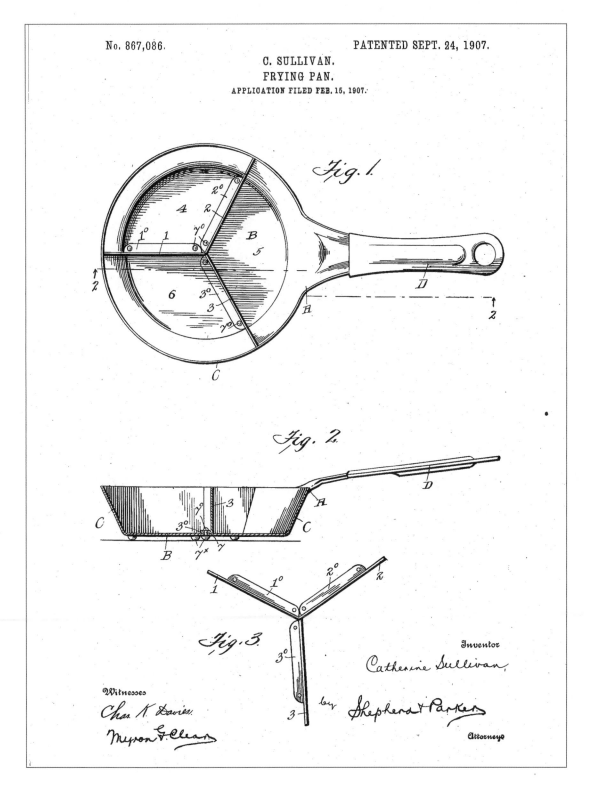

No. 867,086.

PATENTED SEPT. 24, 1907.

C. SULLIVAN.
FRYING PAN.
APPLICATION FILED FEB. 15, 1907.

Fig. 1.

Fig. 2.

Fig. 3.

Inventor
Catherine Sullivan,
by Shepherd & Parker
Attorneys

Witnesses
Chas. K. Davies.
Myron G. Clean

FRYING PAN

"This invention relates to an attachment for the ordinary frying pan, and is in the nature of a series of division walls or partitions, creating a number of compartments within the pan in order that a number of different commodities may be cooked therein without mixing."

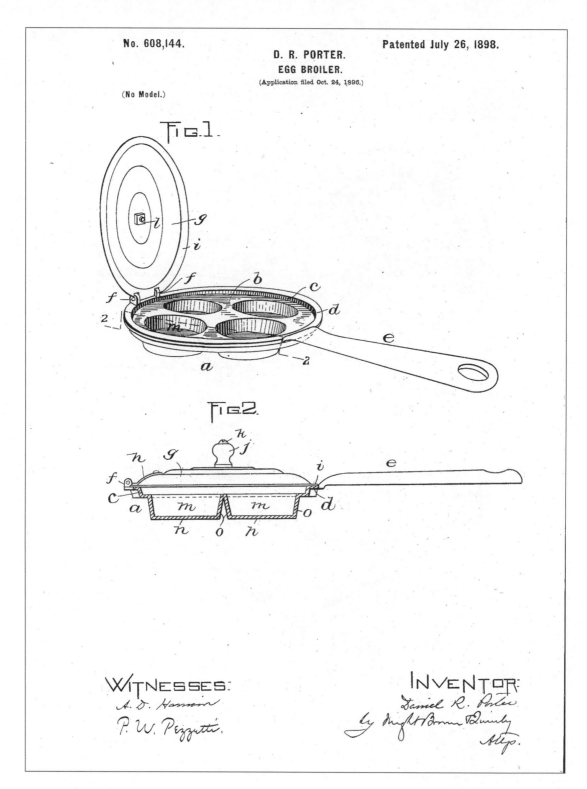

No. 608,144.

D. R. PORTER.
EGG BROILER.
(Application filed Oct. 24, 1896.)

Patented July 26, 1898.

(No Model.)

Fig.1.

Fig2.

WITNESSES:
A. D. Hanson
P. W. Pezzetti.

INVENTOR:
Daniel R. Porter
by Knight Brown Quinby
Attys.

EGG BROILER

"This invention has for its object to provide a cooking utensil adapted to fry eggs in a satisfactory manner without the necessity of turning the eggs during the frying operation."

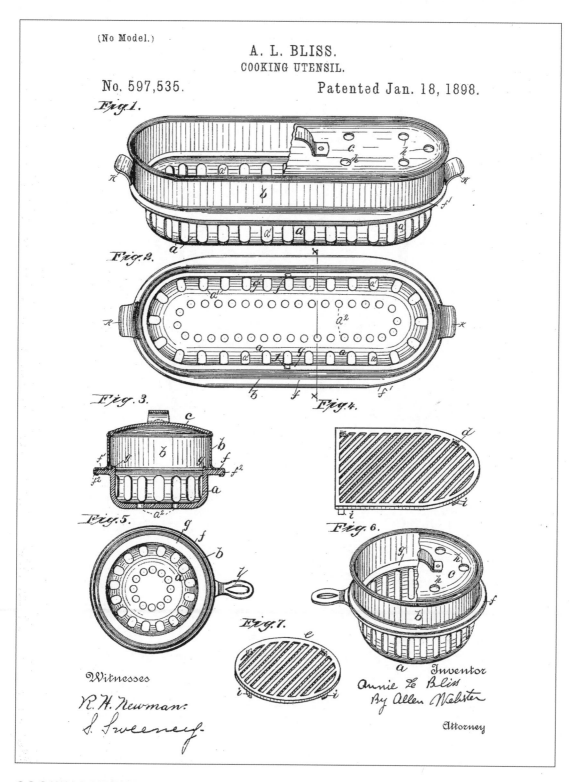

(No Model.)

A. L. BLISS.
COOKING UTENSIL.

No. 597,535.

Patented Jan. 18, 1898.

Fig. 1.

Fig. 2.

Fig. 3.

Fig. 4.

Fig. 5.

Fig. 6.

Fig. 7.

Witnesses
R. H. Newman.
S. Sweeney.

Inventor
Annie L. Bliss
By Allen Webster
Attorney

COOKING UTENSIL

"My device is so constructed and arranged that when a fire is kindled in it and the utensil is properly disposed on the stove the smoke, gases, and other products of combustion will be carried downwardly into the stove or range and thus up the chimney, thus avoiding the objections arising when these products escape into the room."

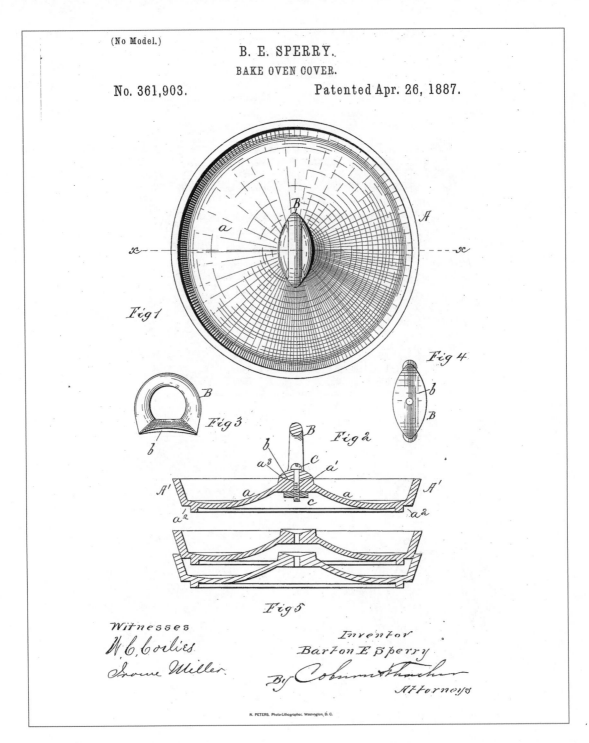

N. PETERS. Photo-Lithographer, Washington, D. C.

BAKE OVEN COVER

"Heretofore in bake-oven covers of this description it has been customary to cast the handle and body of the cover in a single piece, so that in packing the covers for storage or shipment it is impossible to nest them, owing to the projecting handles, and a large amount of space is thereby taken up. In my improvement it will readily be seen that when it is desired to pack the covers it is only necessary to remove the handles, when the bodies can be nested, fitting one within the other . . . and thereby taking up a minimum of space, while at the same time the arrangement is extremely compact and will stand rough handling."

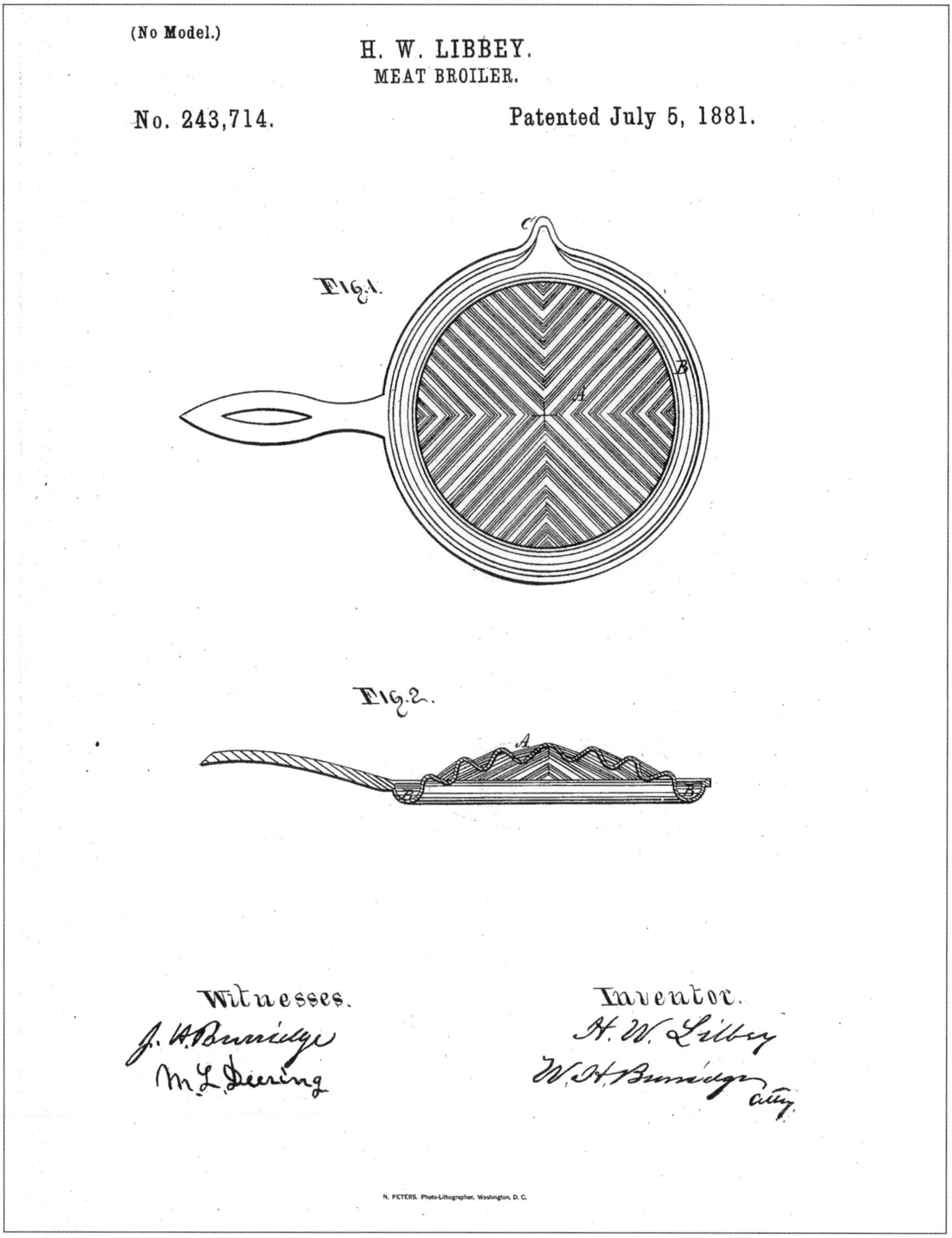
(No Model.)
H. W. LIBBEY.
MEAT BROILER.
No. 243,714.
Patented July 5, 1881.
Fig. 1.
A
B
C
Fig. 2.
A
B
B
Witnesses.
J. H. Burridge
M. L. Deering
Inventor.
H. W. Libbey
W. H. Burridge atty.
N. PETERS. Photo-Lithographer. Washington, D. C.

MEAT BROILER

"The object of this improved broiler is to broil meat over coals of fire without allowing the meat to come in direct contact with the fire or the smoke and flames thereof, and thereby avoid smoking and burning of the meat and at the same time obtain the flavor peculiar to meat cooked upon an ordinary gridiron with wood coals, and without losing the juices thereof, which, when the meat is broiled upon an open gridiron, are lost by falling through the space between the bars into the fire."

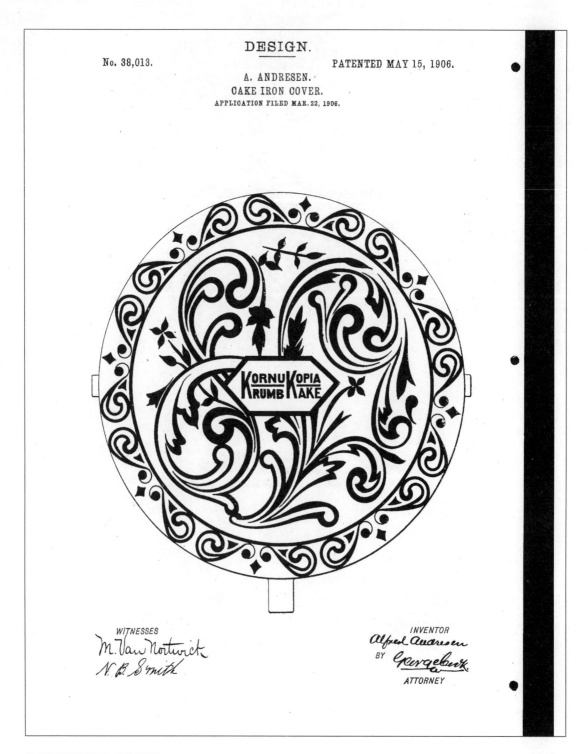

CAKE IRON COVER

This ornate design by Alfred Andresen & Co. in Minneapolis, Minnesota, created specifically to appeal to the region's Scandinavian population, graced a Griswold-made wafer iron; the arabesque pattern would be pressed into the batter and baked into the surface of the finished confection.

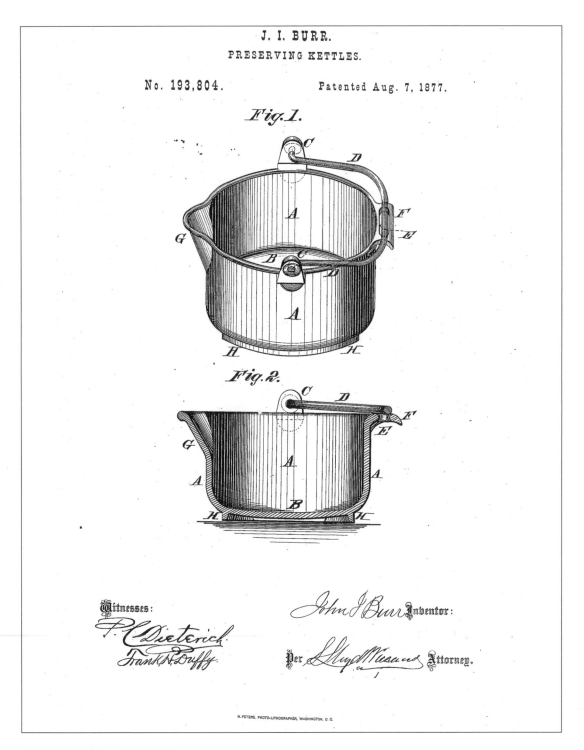

N. PETERS, PHOTO-LITHOGRAPHER, WASHINGTON, D. C.

PRESERVING KETTLES

"The nature of my invention consists in forming upon a preserving-kettle provided with a bail, hinged or otherwise flexibly attached or jointed thereto, a lip or spout for pouring, and opposite to the lip or spout a handle, for the purpose of tilting the kettle when suspended by the bail and pouring from the spout, which handle is looped, for a twofold purpose—first, to afford a better hold in tilting the kettle, and, second, to expose such a large part of its surface for radiation of heat relatively to the small section at its points of junction with the body of the kettle that it will not become inconveniently hot to the hand."

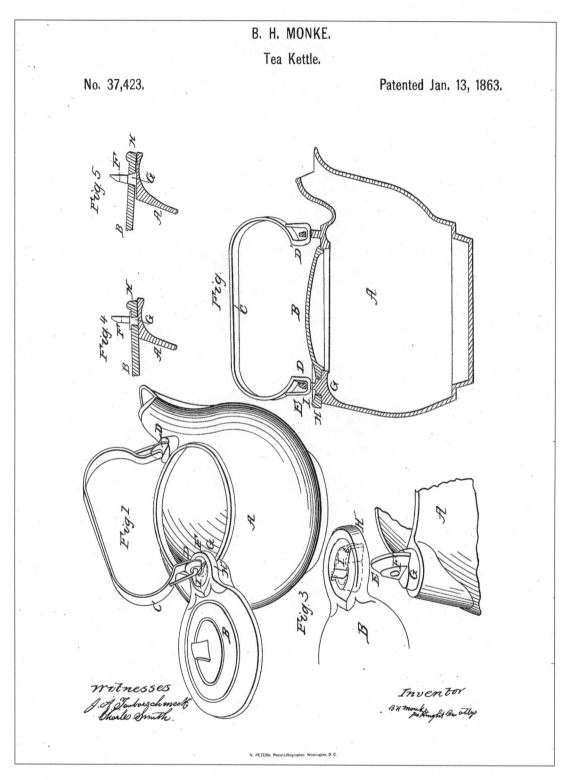

TEA KETTLE

"My invention relates to a form of tea kettle or other bailed and covered hollow ware having a swing-lid pivoted to a peculiarly-shaped ear, and secured by the bail, which ear may be a part of the kettle-casting itself."

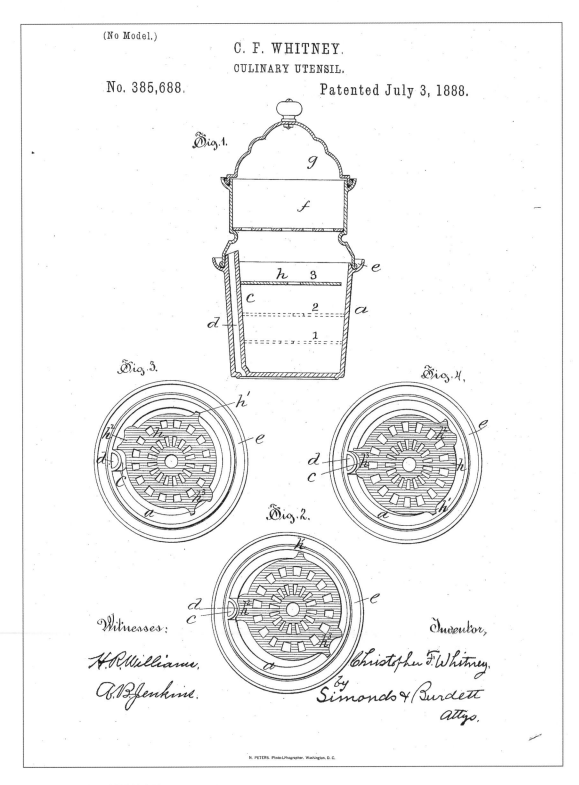

(No Model.)

C. F. WHITNEY.
CULINARY UTENSIL.

No. 385,688.

Patented July 3, 1888.

Fig. 1.

Fig. 3.

Fig. 4.

Fig. 2.

Witnesses:
H. R. Williams.
A. B. Jenkins.

Inventor,
Christopher F. Whitney,
by
Simonds & Burdett
Attys.

N. PETERS. Photo-Lithographer. Washington, D. C.

CULINARY UTENSIL

"The object of my invention is to provide a kettle with means for providing a chamber of varying capacity in the upper part of the kettle for the reception of articles to be steamed; and to this end my improvement consists in the combination of a kettle having on the inside a vertical flange with an adjustable disk having on its edge a plural number of bearing points or projections and one or more peripheral sockets."

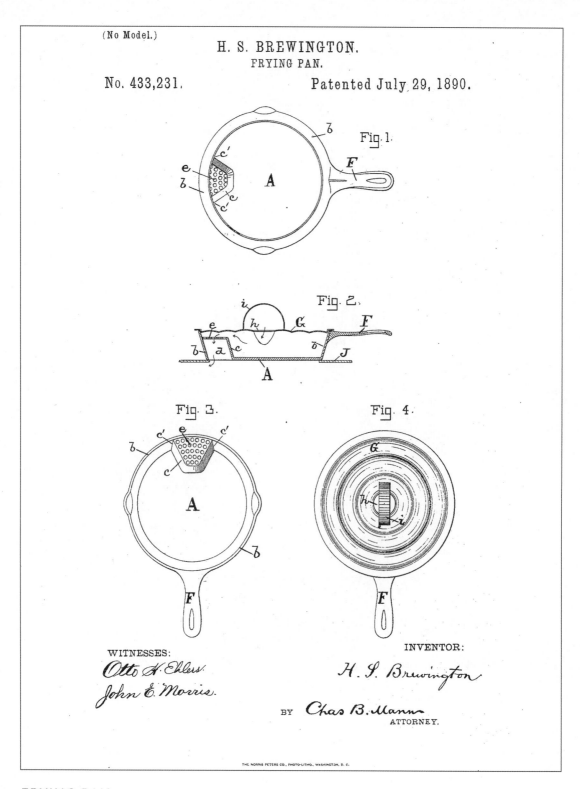

FRYING PAN

"This invention relates to an improvement in frying-pans; and its objective is to provide an improved construction, whereby to allow the fumes and smoke arising from cooking to pass from the pan directly through the stove and into the chimney."

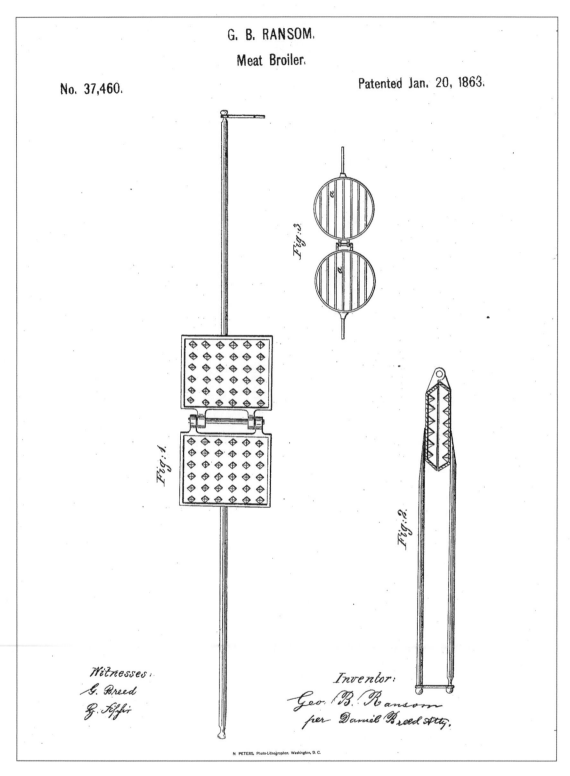

MEAT BROILER

"My improvement in meat-broilers consists of two shallow pans fitting together, so that one may serve as a cover to the other, both pans being provided with a series of pyramids to prevent the meat from coming in contact with the bottom of the pans, in order to completely enclose the meat while broiling and to prevent it from frying."

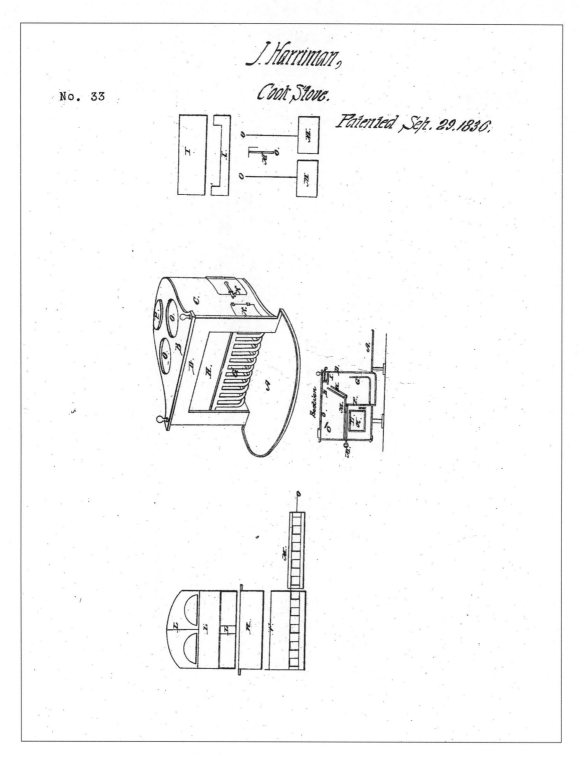

COOK STOVE

"New and useful improvements in the manner of constructing a Franklin Stove for cooking and other purposes, and that the following is a full and exact description of the construction and operation of the said stove as improved by me. This stove is to be made of cast iron, except the oven, which is to be made of sheet iron."

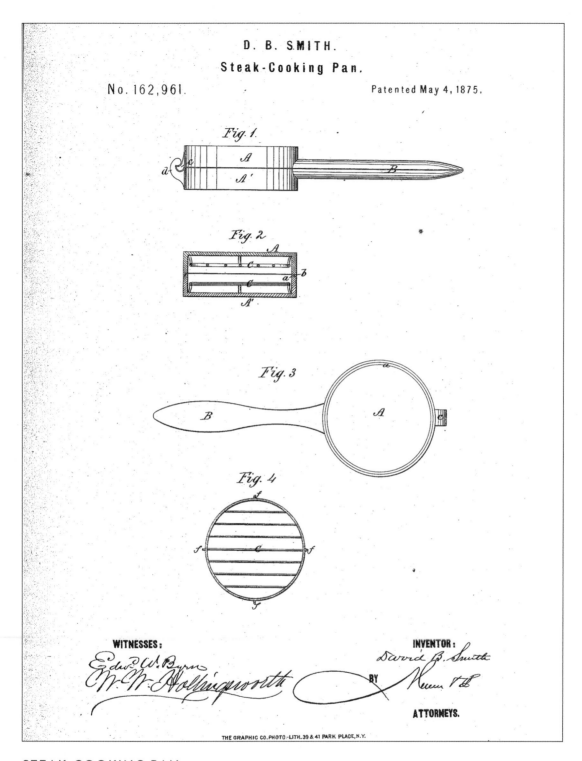

D. B. SMITH.
Steak-Cooking Pan.

No. 162,961.

Patented May 4, 1875.

Fig. 1.

Fig. 2.

Fig. 3.

Fig. 4.

WITNESSES:
Edwd W. Byrn
W. W. Hollingsworth

INVENTOR:
David B. Smith
BY

ATTORNEYS.

THE GRAPHIC CO.PHOTO-LITH.39 & 41 PARK PLACE, N.Y.

STEAK-COOKING PAN

"The object of this invention is to provide an improved arrangement for broiling steak and other meats, by means of which all of the flavor and juice of the meat are preserved, the tendency to burn obviated, and the meat cooked free from ashes and without the taste of smoke imparted thereto. It consists in two symmetrically-shaped pans, having extended handles, one of the said pans being made with a recess or depression at its edge, and the other with a corresponding lip, which, when the pans are placed together, insure a tightly-closed chamber."

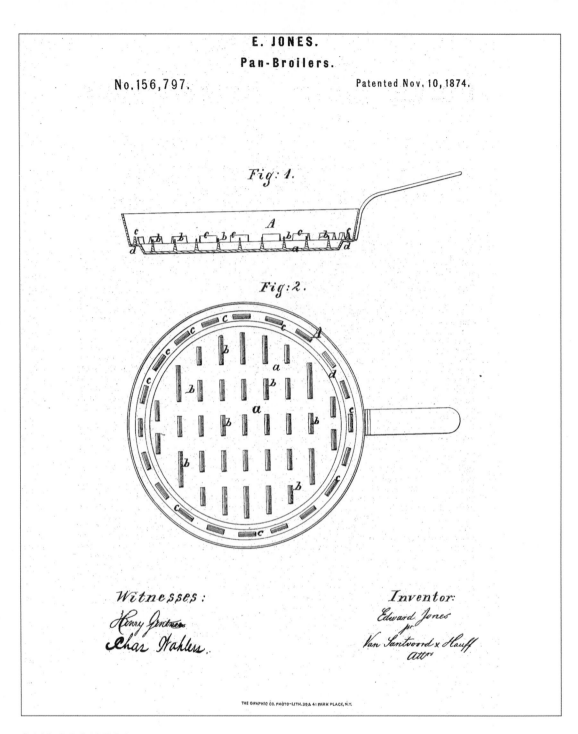

E. JONES.

Pan-Broilers.

No. 156,797.

Patented Nov. 10, 1874.

Fig: 1.

Fig: 2.

Witnesses:

Henry Gentman

Chas Wahlers.

Inventor:

Edward Jones

pr

Van Santvoord & Hauff

Attys

THE GRAPHIC CO. PHOTO-LITH. 39 & 41 PARK PLACE, N.Y.

PAN-BROILERS

"My invention has for its object to improve upon that class of pan-broilers the bottoms of which are provided with hollow cones or corrugations, which support the meat to be broiled; and my invention consists in a pan-broiler which is provided with a raised rim or flange, upon which is located a series of teeth or ribs, arranged circumferentially thereon, while the bottom proper of said pan is provided with a series of teeth, the arrangement being such that if a piece of meat is placed upon the teeth or ribs, and the pan placed into the hole of a stove or range, the heat radiating from its bottom will also strike that portion of the meat which is supported by the circumferential teeth or ribs, and thereby the operation of broiling meat of any kind is materially facilitated."

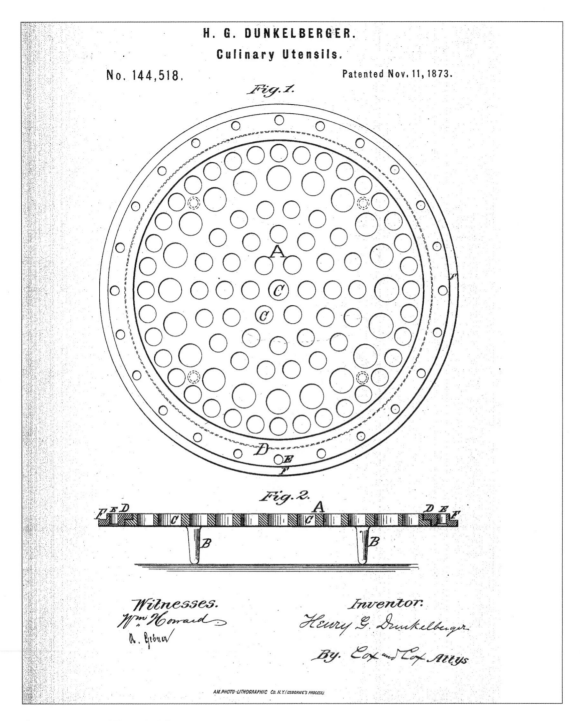

CULINARY UTENSILS

"My invention relates to a new and useful improvement in culinary utensils. Its objective is to provide a convenient utensil for cooking articles of food, whereby the cooking may be accomplished without danger of the food being burned by coming in contact with the bottom of the vessel employed, and especially to provide a utensil that may be adapted to vessels of different sizes."

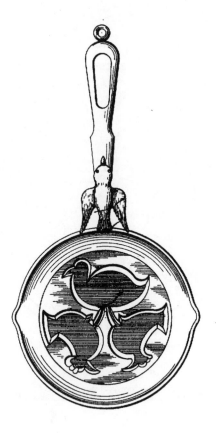

FRYING PAN

The bird theme here is not only found in the pan but on the handle as well.

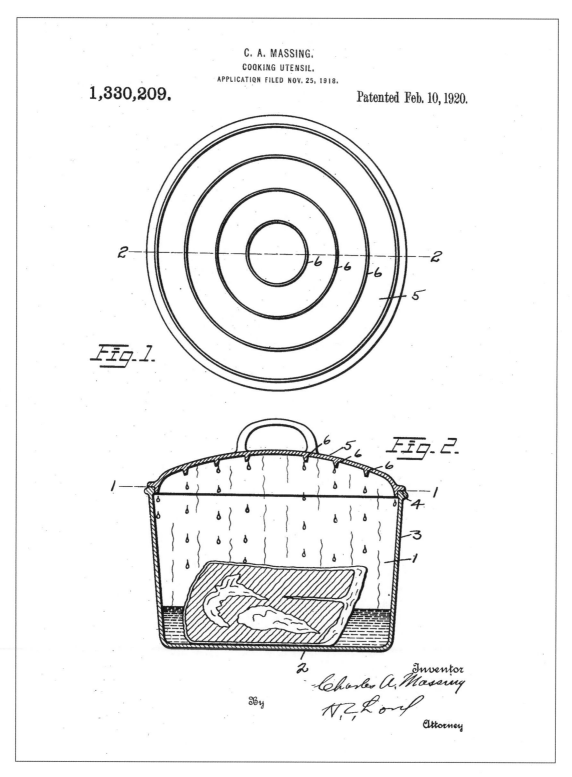

C. A. MASSING.
COOKING UTENSIL.
APPLICATION FILED NOV. 25, 1918.

1,330,209.

Patented Feb. 10, 1920.

Fig.1.

Fig.2.

Inventor
Charles A. Massing

By

Attorney

COOKING UTENSIL (SELF-BASTING LID)

"The invention relates to what is commonly called a Dutch oven used for roasting meats and other materials."

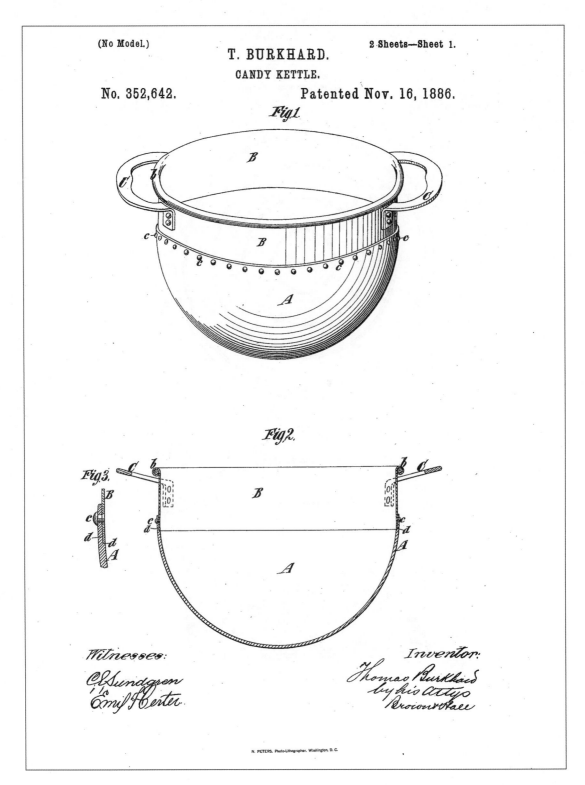

T. BURKHARD.

CANDY KETTLE.

No. 352,642.　　　　Patented Nov. 16, 1886.

Fig 1.

Fig 2.

Fig 3.

Witnesses:

Inventor:

Thomas Burkhard
by his Attys
Brown & Hall

CANDY KETTLE

"A new and useful improvement in Candy-Kettles of which the following is a specification. The kettles heretofore employed for cooking candy have been made of copper or have had copper bottoms, and great care has to be exercised in their use, as they will burn at a temperature of about 300, and by being once burned the copper undergoes some change, which will cause it always afterward to impart

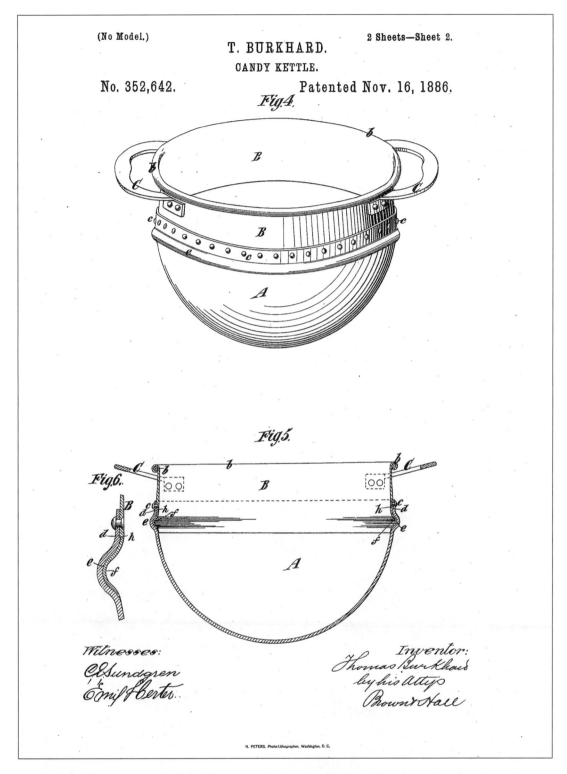

T. BURKHARD.

CANDY KETTLE.

No. 352,642.

Patented Nov. 16, 1886.

Fig.4.

Fig.5.

Fig.6.

Witnesses:
C. I. Sundgren
Emil Herter.

Inventor:
Thomas Burkhard
by his Attys
Brown & Hall

a burned taste to the candy cooked in it, even though the candy may not be overheated. I have discovered that if a kettle which has its surface with which the candy comes in contact of cast-iron or cast-steel be employed for cooking candy the kettle will not, after being overheated, impart a burned taste to candy subsequently cooked in it."

After World War II, the availability of lightweight stainless steel and aluminum drove cast iron out of favor. While some of the major manufacturers stopped production altogether, their high-quality pans remained in circulation and today are considered collectible. One maker, Lodge, came to dominate the market, but there are also small artisan foundries making new pans every day (see the Industry Insiders chapter). Those modestly sized companies are making a big difference. Since the mid-2000s, sales of new cast-iron pans in the United States have increased by more than 225 percent.

To anyone who enjoys cooking, a cast-iron pan is a thing of beauty: the form, the weight, the possibilities, the commitment that comes with owning it, and the knowledge that each pan is either already a part of history or has the potential to be. Each pot and pan is a work of art, as proven by every person who has ever decoratively displayed their cookware. In the end, you may choose cast iron because it is practical, inexpensive, expensive, utilitarian, a work of art, a collectible, an heirloom, or an item you intend to pass down to future generations.

To love something as perfectly imperfect as a cast-iron pan is a way to connect with something bigger: the love of good food, made well. And this is evidenced in all the different types of cast-iron cookware made and utilized the world over. Popular shapes are flat pans with no sides, grill pans, and griddles. Those aren't all, though. Cast-iron pans have been designed for specific recipes: everything from the round Danish puffed pancakes, aebleskiver, to the Japanese takoyaki, or octopus fritters, and India's tava flatbreads.

CAST-IRON COOKWARE THE WORLD OVER

3-LEGGED DUTCH OVEN

A 3-legged cast-iron camping pot has a lip on the lid that allows you to pile hot coals on top to create an oven effect while cooking outdoors. Through trial and error, this can quickly become your favorite cooking vessel. Use it for soup, sukiyaki, goulash, stew, chili, or, if you're ambitious, bread. It's also a fun conversation piece if you want to work it into your home decor. And don't forget to fill it with apples around Halloween!

AEBLESKIVER

A Danish aebleskiver pan has 7 deep wells to make round, puffed pancakes. The pan itself can be used for other recipes but is ideally suited for the tradional holiday treat that gives the pan its name. You can also use it for fritters or small donuts, baking up cupcake batter, or making pastry-wrapped

fruit dumplings. In a fun twist, this pan is also used in Thailand for a coconut-milk pancake called *khanom krok*.

CAST-IRON STOVE

The ultimate in cast-iron cookware accessories has to be a full cast-iron kitchen stove. The first cast-iron cookstoves were manufactured in the early 1600s in Lynn, Massachusetts. The ability of the stove to withstand heating and cooling made it desirable. The 5-plate or jamb-style stove was perfected in 1728 in Germany, and these stoves, which were sometimes very ornate, became quite popular in Europe. From there, Ben Franklin created the Pennsylvania Fireplace around 1740, which became the standard for the next 200 years, surging in popularity after the American Civil War. Cast-iron kitchen stoves started being replaced with steel-construction gas ranges in the early 1900s. Today, you can still find antique stoves for your home. If you plan on installing one, it is critical to consult with a contractor regarding dimensions and ventilation. There are also several brands, including AGA, Carron, and Lacunza, that still make enameled cast-iron ranges fit for every lifestyle.

BALTI

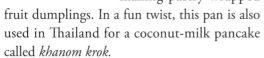

Indian *balti* curries are made in a bowl-shaped pot with straight sides and two loop handles, similar to a wok. The name of the recipe comes from the name of the pan it is cooked in, which loosely translates to "bucket." The elegantly designed pot is also frequently used as a tabletop serving dish, either family-style or individually.

BASTIBLE

Soda bread wasn't invented by the Irish, but it is most commonly associated with them because Ireland's climate is only conducive to growing wheat that is low in gluten when processed into flour. Soda bread, along with pretty much everything else, was cooked in a bastible, an Irish cast-iron pot that could be hung over the fire from a crane or placed directly on the coals.

BISCUIT PAN

A beautiful collectible, the 7-well biscuit pan is not just for fluffy biscuits: you can also make popovers, muffin tops, and crisp-edged brownies in it. We also love making individual puff-pastry pies (sweet and savory) in this versatile pan.

BREAD IRON

Also known as a an "oat-cake warmer" or "harnen stand," blacksmiths in rural Ireland made these eye-catching pieces in the eighteenth and nineteenth centuries. They were used to dry bread and oat-cakes after they were baked. When not in use, they were hung on the wall, doubling as a decorative piece.

CALDERA

The *caldera* is a wide, deep pot with a lid that is used in Puerto Rican cooking. It can be used at home on a stove or over a campfire. Today most *caldera* pans are made of steel, but the classic, collectible styles are all cast iron. It's ideal for making chicken and rice, bean stew, or a pot roast.

COMAL

In Mexico, and in Central and South America, these griddles are used mostly to cook tortillas and arepas. They are also used for more general food preparation, from toasting spices to searing meat.

CORNSTICK PAN

Made by Lodge, and used almost exclusively for making corncob-shaped, golden corn bread, this is one of the most beloved cast-iron pan shapes, even though its utility is limited. Most corn bread recipes that are written for 10-inch skillets will make the right amount to fill this 7-well pan. They come pre-seasoned and, like all cast-iron pieces, get better with frequent use as the seasoning gets stronger.

CREPE PAN

French crepe pans are wide and flat with a slightly sloped edge. The sloping sides and the weight of the cast iron make flipping crepes easier than in any other type of pan. They are also great for making omelettes and quesadillas and for dry-roasting garlic. As with most other cast-iron pans, these are also made in steel, but seeking out real cast iron makes all the difference—so long as the weight doesn't bother you.

DISCADA

Also referred to as a "plow disc" and "cowboy wok," these 22- to 24-inch cast-iron discs are said to have been used in fields that were tilled by implements of the very same shape being pulled behind tractors. Sharing a name with a meat-heavy Mexican dish from the northern part of the country, this cookware was popularized in the American Southwest. Some historians connect the expansion of the American railroad system to this innovation: many of the laborers laying track were Chinese, and they were looking for something like a wok (though a wok is much thinner and better suited for flash frying).

FLUTED TUBE PAN

The fluted tube pan is most commonly used to make the Bundt-style cakes popular in Eastern European Jewish cuisine, but it can also be used to make kugel or savory dishes. Its shape is based on a gugelhupf mold. The word "Bundt" is trademarked by Nordic Ware.

FONDUE POT

The caquelon, a glazed ceramic pot with a thick handle, is the traditional fondue vessel. Over time, as this cheesy Swiss delicacy has become popular the world over, a wide array of fondue pots have been developed from enamel-coated steel to electric, and, of course, cast iron. In fact, there is an entire range of cast-iron fondue pots, though enameled ones look the most like the caquelon.

GAMASOT

A gamasot is a very large, traditional Korean pot used to cook rice, stewed soybeans, and myriad other dishes. Originally made of bronze, *gamasot* (or just *sot*) are wide and deep and have a rounded lid. They are designed with three tabs so the pot can be suspended in a hole cut into the top of a box-shaped coal-burning oven.

HAGAMA

This cast-iron pot reaches back to the early seventeenth century in Japan and remains in use today because of its simple efficacy in cooking rice.

JAMBALAYA POT

The rice dish cooked in this pot is synonymous with Louisiana and reflects the ethnic diversity of the New Orleans port. Is its origin West African jollof or Spanish paella? Sometimes it is red, other times brown (as a result of not using tomatoes). No matter the style, this is a one-pot riot of veggies, sausage, chicken, and seafood.

KADAI

This bowl-shaped pan, sometimes referred to as an "Indian wok," can handle any and all stir-frying duties. In India, however, it is traditionally only used for deep frying.

KAZAN

This Central Asian cookware is part cauldron, part Dutch oven; it comes in an array of sizes, though traditionally it is used for preparing recipes for large groups of people. Some *kazan* are set on tripods over a fire; in some places, a hole is dug in the ground, a fire is lit in the hole, and then the vessel is placed over the aperture.

KOREAN GRILL PAN

Korean cast-iron grill pans are designed to be used on a tabletop burner in a communal setting. The convex shape allows fat from beef, pork, or chicken to drip down the channels, gathering in the well at the bottom. The fat is then easily poured off thanks to a small spout. Reserved fat can be used for cooking or as a quick and easy way to enrich soup.

OVAL GRATIN

Once only used by restaurants to cook individual servings, the oval gratin is now popular in home kitchens. Either in a large or a single-portion size, the shape is ideal for cooking a small fish or long vegetables such as carrots and leeks. It's also a beautiful way to present mac and cheese or roasted beets.

PIE IRON

Don't let the name fool you. Popular with outdoorsy types in Midwestern states like Illinois, Minnesota, and Wisconsin, this open-fire cooking tool isn't really about pie. Rather, it's more like a handheld oven with two square hinged pans, inside of which you can cook eggs and make grilled cheese sandwiches.

PIZZA PAN

There is nothing more perfect than a cast-iron pan for a deep-dish pizza. That said, sometimes you want the regular thin-crust style, and a cast-iron pizza pan is one way to go. Even when it's well-seasoned, you will want to make sure to sprinkle it with cornmeal before you add your dough, sauce, and toppings. The pan will give you a nice blistered and crispy crust.

PLANCHA

A workhorse of Spanish cuisine, this thick slab of cast iron is ideal for searing vegetables, seafood, and thin cuts of meat. It can be placed over a heat source, from a range to a grill, but using open fire will add a welcome touch of smokiness.

PLETT

A *plett* pan is used to make traditional little Swedish pancakes. It typically has 7 shallow wells and a short handle with a loop so that it can be hung on a hook, promoting that *hygge* feeling. The short, straight sides of each well make it slightly difficult to season evenly, so you need to oil it before use, even if it appears to be well-seasoned.

POTJIE

Outside of cities in South Africa, the lidded *potjie* pot has been used for hundreds of years over open fires, replacing more traditional clay pots. The name is Afri-

kaans and means "small pot." There are lots of recipes that can be made in the *potjie*, but ultimately, it is about layering. Protein is put in first, with vegetables, liquid, and seasonings placed on top, allowing the meat to stew and the vegetables to steam. There is a great recipe for braised lamb made in a *potjie* on page 313, but you can also make Crab & Okra Soup (page 458), Hungarian goulash, or Irish lamb stew in one, if you're outdoors and feeling inspired.

RICE POT
The even heat distribution afforded by cast iron makes it an ideal material for cooking rice.

SAGANAKI
Best known as a pan-fried Greek cheese dish, this style of appetizer is named after the pan it is cooked in; hard cheeses, like kefalotyri or halloumi, are dredged in flour, seared, and then hit with a squeeze of lemon.

TAMAGOYAKI SKILLET
Tamagoyaki is a Japanese rolled omelette that's served for breakfast or lunch and is sometimes used in sushi. These pans can be used for any food preparation, but to make the perfect *tamagoyaki*, you need a square pan.

TAGINE
This cone-shaped baking dish originated in North Africa and was made of terra-cotta. An enameled cast iron base is far better suited for browning recipe ingredients.

TAVA
Indian *tava* pans are flat or convex disks of cast iron with one or two handles that are typically wooden. They're used for making flatbreads like dosa or paratha over an open flame or on a cooktop. While classically these would be made from iron, today they are more likely to be steel. Netherton Foundry, located in Shropshire, England, makes a very upscale version for the UK market.

TETSUBIN
As the sober choreography of the Japanese tea ceremony makes clear, the Japanese take tea seriously. So it stands to reason that this is more than just a kettle in which you boil water for tea. Because of the cast iron, a *tetsubin* will mineralize and soften water, making for a sweeter, smoother tea. Yes, you need to care more for a cast-iron kettle since water and iron do make for rust, but, just like a well-seasoned skillet, if you love tea, a cared-for *tetsubin* will make you love tea even more.

TWO-SIDED GRILL/ GRIDDLE
Two-sided grill/griddle pans sit over two burners on a cooktop and are incredibly versatile. They can be used for cooking larger quantities of pancakes, quesadillas, steaks, burgers, and more. Although it stretches over two burners, keep in mind that it gets hotter in the areas directly over the flame. Some higher-end stoves (like by French maker Lacanche) even come with cast-iron grill/ griddle plates set into in the center of the cook-

top, which should be treated the same as a free-standing one, and seasoned periodically.

WAFFLE IRON

It's hard to imagine a time before the electric waffle iron, but there was one. You can transport yourself to that era with a stove-top cast-iron waffle iron pan. It's not just effective on the stove, you can have a terrific time putting it right into the fireplace. And don't limit yourself to waffles! These are ideal for brownies—or go really wild and try it with falafel. Just make sure it is well-seasoned and use a little additional fat to make sure everything comes out in one piece.

WEDGE PAN

This fun 8-well pan was designed for corn bread. It's almost even better for scones, though. Or try classic yellow cake or cupcake batter. You'll have no trouble finding dozens of uses for this beautiful conversation piece.

WOK

To stir-fry is to quickly sear your food in a round-bottom wok in very hot oil. But that is not all you can do in this pan. Chinese cast-iron woks are relatively thin and come to temperature relatively quickly. You can also use the wok as a stockpot, deep fryer, or even a stove-top smoker (see page 465).

A FEW NOTES ABOUT THE RECIPES IN THIS BOOK

This is a book in which every recipe has been written to be made in cast-iron cookware. There are no delicate French sauces and other things that require subtle and very gentle temperature control. The beauty of cast iron is the heat, and that's what these recipes reflect. That doesn't mean you can't make everything in a regular skillet, though; you'll just get slightly different results.

Timing is also important in these recipes. We all want recipes for the super-fast dinner that gets on the table in 5 minutes with no dishes to wash, but those are few and far between—or more commonly known as salad or frozen food. You may not always have the time to cook, but when you do, slow down and really let the flavors develop. Look at what you're cooking and ask yourself: Is that brown enough? Is it cooked through? It really does make a difference.

Almost every recipe that includes spicy peppers will include the note "or to taste," since you are going to know best about your own heat tolerance. Just remember, you can always add more but it's pretty tricky to take ingredients out, so go slow and taste.

Speaking of seasoning, the single most important seasoning, when it comes to making things taste good, is salt. In this book most of the recipes will direct you to use it "to taste" because that makes the most sense. Remember, you can always add more, but you can't take it out.

When a recipe calls specifically for kosher salt, make sure to use that. Don't substitute table salt (this is especially true for the Salt-Crusted Lamb with Lemon-Herb Dressing on page 301). Table salt grains are finer and therefore a teaspoon is, by weight, much more salt than a teaspoon of large crystal kosher salt. These recipes were all tested with Diamond Crystal Kosher Salt. The shape and weight of the crystals are ideal: they're basically hollow and easy to crush by hand when seasoning your food.

The handles of your cast-iron pots and pans will get hot. Always—always—use something to protect yourself from getting burned, and never use a wet cloth to pick up a hot pan, as the moisture transfers heat. If you have to walk away from a hot skillet, drape a cloth over the handle (away from the flames) so no one else gets burned either.

Use a thick, dry cloth, pot holder, or oven mitt when you're touching hot cookware. (We know, this is not a news flash; think of it more as a gentle reminder.) You can also purchase a rubber or leather sleeve that fits over the handle. These need to be removed when you put the pan in the oven, obviously. They also need to be cleaned periodically.

The simple beauty of cast-iron pans makes them a stunning addition to your table, too. That said, never place a hot pan directly onto any wooden, marble, cloth, or plastic surface. Have a trivet or thick cloth on hand to prevent scorching or stains.

Last but not least, we all drop things at times. It happens. But when it happens with cast iron, you really don't want to try and catch it. (Same goes for your knives. Never try to catch a falling knife.) Just jump out of the way and take a deep breath. It's all good, and no part of you will be burned or broken. Except maybe your smile, but you can get that back.

BREAKFAST

*S*ometimes breakfast is as simple as grabbing a piece of fruit and running out the door. But other times we want, or really need, to sidle up to the stove and take a few minutes to make something that is worth lingering over. In other words, a real meal. In this chapter, you can choose from recipes that span the globe, bouncing from a classic Chinese Congee (see page 102) to a soul-soothing, healthy Whole Grain Porridge (see page 75) and an elaborate San Francisco breakfast of yore, the Hangtown Fry (see page 105).

No matter what you pick to get your day started off on the right foot, you can proceed knowing that, thanks to your well-seasoned cast iron, cleanup will be easy—meaning you won't come home to a sink full of dishes (assuming you're on top of the dishes from the previous night, of course).

BLUEBERRY SCONES

YIELD: 4 TO 6 SERVINGS / ACTIVE TIME: 30 MINUTES / TOTAL TIME: 50 MINUTES

These are delicious whenever you eat them, but they're especially good about 15 minutes after you take them out of the oven, slathered with butter.

1. Preheat the oven to 400°F. Position a rack in the middle of the oven.

2. In a large bowl, whisk together the flour, sugar, baking powder, baking soda, and salt. Add the butter pieces and mix with an electric mixer until just blended, or mix with a fork so that the dough is somewhat crumbly.

3. Stir in the orange zest and milk, and gently fold in the blueberries, being careful not to overmix.

4. With flour on your hands, transfer the dough to a lightly floured surface. Form the dough into a circle about ½-inch thick. With a long knife, cut the dough into 12 wedges.

5. Butter a 10-inch cast-iron skillet, then place the scone wedges in the skillet in a circle, leaving some space between the pieces. Bake for 20 to 25 minutes, or until golden.

6. If desired, sprinkle with some additional sugar when just out of the oven.

VARIATIONS: Substitute fresh cranberries for the blueberries or use a blend of ½ cup blueberries and ½ cup cranberries. You can also substitute ½ cup dried cherries or dried sweetened cranberries for the blueberries.

TIP: Blueberries split when cooked and their juices can get a little messy. If you want a neater-looking scone, you can use dried blueberries. Reduce the amount used by about half, though, as their flavor is also more concentrated.

INGREDIENTS:

- 3   CUPS ALL-PURPOSE FLOUR
- ⅓   CUP SUGAR, PLUS MORE FOR SPRINKLING
- 2½   TEASPOONS BAKING POWDER
- ½   TEASPOON BAKING SODA
- 1   TEASPOON SALT
- 1½   STICKS OF UNSALTED BUTTER, CHILLED AND CUT INTO PIECES
- 1   TABLESPOON ORANGE ZEST
- 1   CUP WHOLE MILK OR HALF-AND-HALF
- 1   CUP FRESH BLUEBERRIES

STICKY BUNS

YIELD: 6 SERVINGS / **ACTIVE TIME:** 1 HOUR AND 30 MINUTES / **TOTAL TIME:** 2 HOURS

These take a bit of preparation time, but the result is worth it. Your family or friends will wake up to the smell of these baking, and soon you'll have a kitchen full of people happily waiting for these to come out of the oven.

1. Preheat the oven to 375°F.

2. Lightly dust a flat surface with flour. Spread the frozen biscuit dough out in rows of 4 biscuits each. Cover with a kitchen towel and let sit for about 30 minutes, until the dough is thawed but still cool.

3. While dough is thawing, toast the pecans. Spread the pieces on a cookie sheet and bake for about 5 minutes, stirring the pieces with a spatula about halfway through. Be sure not to overcook. Allow to cool. Put the pieces in a bowl and add the cinnamon and nutmeg, stirring to coat the nuts with the spices.

4. Sprinkle flour over the top of the biscuit dough and then press it out to form a large rectangle (approximately 10 by 12 inches). Spread the softened butter over the dough.

5. Sprinkle the brown sugar over the butter, then the seasoned nuts. Roll the dough with the butter, brown sugar, and nuts in it, starting with a long side. Cut into 1-inch slices and place in a lightly greased 10-inch cast-iron skillet.

6. Place in the oven for about 30 to 35 minutes, until the rolls in the center are cooked through. Remove from the oven and allow to cool.

7. Make the glaze by mixing the confectioners' sugar, half-and-half, and vanilla. Drizzle over the warm rolls and serve.

VARIATION: Substitute toasted walnut or almond pieces instead of the pecans for a nuttier, earthier flavor.

INGREDIENTS:

ALL-PURPOSE FLOUR, FOR DUSTING

1 (26.4 OZ.) PACKAGE OF FROZEN BISCUITS

½ CUP CHOPPED PECANS

1 TEASPOON GROUND CINNAMON

¼ TEASPOON NUTMEG

4 TABLESPOONS UNSALTED BUTTER, SOFTENED

¾ CUP FIRMLY PACKED LIGHT BROWN SUGAR

1 CUP CONFECTIONERS' SUGAR

3 TABLESPOONS HALF-AND-HALF

½ TEASPOON VANILLA EXTRACT

CINNAMON COFFEE CAKE

YIELD: 6 TO 8 SERVINGS / **ACTIVE TIME:** 1 HOUR AND 30 MINUTES / **TOTAL TIME:** 2 HOURS

Cinnamon is not only wonderfully fragrant, it is also a natural antioxidant and anti-inflammatory and helps to fight infection.

1. Preheat the oven to 325°F.

2. To make the cake, whisk together the flour, sugar, baking soda, salt, and cinnamon in a large bowl. Add the butter and mix with a handheld mixer until blended.

3. In a small bowl, whisk together the eggs, vanilla, and buttermilk. Pour into the flour mixture and blend on high speed until the batter is light and fluffy. Pour the batter into a greased, 10-inch cast-iron skillet.

4. To make the topping, whisk together the flour, sugars, cinnamon, and salt in a bowl. Add the softened butter and combine to form a crumbly dough.

5. Sprinkle the topping over the cake in the skillet. Put the skillet in the oven and bake for 45 minutes, until a knife inserted in the middle comes out clean. Allow to cool for about 10 minutes before serving.

INGREDIENTS:

FOR THE CAKE
- 1¾ CUPS ALL-PURPOSE FLOUR
- ⅔ CUP SUGAR
- ½ TEASPOON BAKING SODA
- ¼ TEASPOON SALT
- ¼ TEASPOON GROUND CINNAMON
- 1 STICK OF UNSALTED BUTTER, SOFTENED
- 2 EGGS
- 1 TEASPOON VANILLA EXTRACT
- ¾ CUP BUTTERMILK

FOR THE TOPPING
- 1 CUP ALL-PURPOSE FLOUR
- ½ CUP GRANULATED SUGAR
- ½ CUP DARK BROWN SUGAR
- ½ TEASPOON CINNAMON
- ¼ TEASPOON SALT
- 6 TABLESPOONS UNSALTED BUTTER, SOFTENED

ROSEMARY & BLACK PEPPER SCONES

YIELD: 4 TO 6 SERVINGS / ACTIVE TIME: 30 MINUTES / TOTAL TIME: 50 MINUTES

While these are a bit savory for an early breakfast, they are a hit for brunch, when they can very nicely complement a simple omelette and a Mimosa made with fresh orange juice.

1. Preheat the oven to 400°F. Position a rack in the middle of the oven.

2. In a large bowl, whisk together the flour, baking powder, baking soda, and salt. Add the butter pieces and mix with an electric mixer until just blended, or mix with a fork so that the dough is somewhat crumbly.

3. Stir in the rosemary, black pepper, and milk or half-and-half, being careful not to overmix.

4. With flour on your hands, transfer the dough to a lightly floured surface. Form the dough into a circle about ½-inch thick. With a long knife, cut the dough into 12 wedges.

5. Butter a 12-inch cast-iron skillet, then place the scone wedges in the skillet in a circle, leaving some space between the pieces. Bake for 20 to 25 minutes, or until golden.

INGREDIENTS:

3 CUPS ALL-PURPOSE FLOUR, PLUS MORE FOR DUSTING

2½ TEASPOONS BAKING POWDER

½ TEASPOON BAKING SODA

1 TEASPOON SALT

1½ STICKS OF UNSALTED BUTTER, CHILLED, AND CUT INTO PIECES

1 TABLESPOON DRIED ROSEMARY

1 TABLESPOON FRESHLY GROUND BLACK PEPPER

1 CUP WHOLE MILK OR HALF-AND-HALF

CHEDDAR & JALAPEÑO SCONES

YIELD: 4 TO 6 SERVINGS / **ACTIVE TIME:** 30 MINUTES / **TOTAL TIME:** 50 MINUTES

The spiciness of jalapeño livens up any meal. For an added kick of flavor, split the cooked scones in half and put a spoonful of sour cream and some sliced avocado in the middle.

1. Preheat the oven to 400°F. Position a rack in the middle of the oven.

2. In a large bowl, whisk together the flour, baking powder, salt, and black pepper. Add the butter pieces and mix with an electric mixer until just blended, or mix with a fork so that the dough is somewhat crumbly.

3. Stir in the cheese, jalapeño, and milk, being careful not to over-mix.

4. With flour on your hands, transfer the dough to a lightly floured surface. Form the dough into a circle about ½-inch thick. With a long knife, cut the dough into 12 wedges.

5. Place the wedges in a circle in a lightly greased 12-inch cast-iron skillet, leaving some space between the pieces.

6. Brush with the beaten egg. Bake for 20 to 25 minutes, or until golden.

VARIATION: Ramp up the heat by substituting Pepper Jack cheese for the cheddar, or substitute a serrano pepper for the jalapeño.

INGREDIENTS:

- 2 CUPS ALL-PURPOSE FLOUR, PLUS MORE FOR DUSTING
- 1 TEASPOON BAKING POWDER
- ½ TEASPOON SALT
- 1 TEASPOON FRESHLY GROUND BLACK PEPPER
- 4 TABLESPOONS UNSALTED BUTTER, CHILLED, CUT INTO PIECES
- ¾ CUP GRATED SHARP CHEDDAR CHEESE
- ½ CUP SLICED OR CHOPPED JALAPEÑO PEPPER
- ½ CUP WHOLE MILK
- 1 EGG, BEATEN WITH A LITTLE MILK

CORNMEAL CREPES

YIELD: 6 SERVINGS / ACTIVE TIME: 40 MINUTES / TOTAL TIME: 1 HOUR AND 20 MINUTES

These crepes put a French twist on the traditional johnnycake. You can fill them with almost anything, but they're particularly wonderful with fruit and real maple syrup.

1. Sift the cornmeal, flour, salt, and cinnamon into a bowl.

2. Place the milk, cream, eggs, and 3 tablespoons of the butter in another bowl and beat until combined. Add the wet mixture to the dry mixture, stir to combine, and let stand for 30 to 40 minutes.

3. Place the remaining butter in a 10-inch cast-iron skillet and warm over medium heat. Stir the batter and pour about ⅓ cup into the skillet. Tilt and swirl the pan so that a thin layer of the batter covers the entirety of it.

4. Cook until the edges of the crepe start to lift away from the pan and turn slightly golden. Turn the crepe over and cook for another 20 to 30 seconds. Transfer cooked crepes to a plate and cover. If the skillet becomes too dry, add butter as needed.

INGREDIENTS:

¾   CUP FINELY GROUND CORNMEAL

1¼   CUPS ALL-PURPOSE FLOUR

1   TEASPOON SALT

1   TEASPOON CINNAMON

1¾   CUPS WHOLE MILK

¼   CUP CREAM

3   EGGS

4   TABLESPOONS MELTED UNSALTED BUTTER, PLUS MORE AS NEEDED

FRENCH TOAST

YIELD: 4 TO 6 SERVINGS / ACTIVE TIME: 20 MINUTES / TOTAL TIME: 40 MINUTES

The secret to great French toast is the choice of bread and the amount of egg mixture that saturates the bread. If you use a basic sandwich bread, you won't need as much egg mixture. If you use an egg-based bread like challah, or a sourdough bread, you'll need more egg mixture, as these kinds of bread are denser. They will also need to sit in the egg mixture longer. As you'll need to adjust the recipe for the type of bread you're using, make sure to have some extra eggs and milk on hand.

1. In a mixing bowl, combine the eggs, milk, vanilla, and nutmeg (if desired).

2. Place the slices of bread in a baking dish. Pour the egg mixture over the bread, shaking the pan to distribute evenly. Flip the pieces of bread a couple of times to coat both sides with the mixture.

3. Heat 2 tablespoons of the butter in a 10-inch cast-iron skillet over medium-high heat. Add 2 slices of bread to the pan and cook until golden brown on each side, 2 to 3 minutes a side. Transfer the cooked pieces to a warm plate or keep warm in the oven while you cook the additional pieces.

4. Serve with maple syrup or jam.

VARIATION: If you want to make gluten-free French toast, just use gluten-free bread. It's as simple and delicious as that. You'll want one that's got some density to it and minimal crust.

INGREDIENTS:

6   EGGS

1   CUP WHOLE MILK

½   TEASPOON VANILLA EXTRACT

    PINCH OF NUTMEG (OPTIONAL)

6   THICK-CUT SLICES OF BREAD

4-6   TABLESPOONS UNSALTED BUTTER

    MAPLE SYRUP, FOR SERVING (OPTIONAL)

    JAM, FOR SERVING (OPTIONAL)

BANANAS FOSTER FRENCH TOAST

YIELD: 4 TO 6 SERVINGS / **ACTIVE TIME:** 10 MINUTES / **TOTAL TIME:** 10 MINUTES

The ultimate pairing of decadent breakfast and sweet, boozy dessert, this combination of two classics is sure to win over everyone.

1. Preheat the oven to 200°F and place an ovenproof dish in it. Heat a 12-inch cast-iron skillet over medium-high heat and melt 1 tablespoon of butter per batch of French toast.

2. In a bowl, add the eggs, sugar, heavy cream, cinnamon, vanilla, and salt and stir to combine. Dunk the slices of bread in the batter to cover both sides. Cook the bread in batches for 1 minute per side, or until a light brown crust forms. Remove from the pan and keep warm in the oven.

3. Place the skillet over medium-high heat and start to prepare the bananas Foster. Add the stick of butter and the brown sugar.

4. Once the butter and sugar are melted, add the bananas to the pan and cook for 3 minutes. Shake the pan and use a spoon to cover the bananas with the sauce.

5. Pull the pan away from the heat and add the rum. Using a long match or lighter, carefully light the rum on fire. Place the pan back over the heat and shake the pan until the flames are gone.

6. Add the cream. Stir to blend and pour over the French toast. Sprinkle with powdered sugar and serve.

TIP: When adding alcohol to hot pans, make sure you pull them away from heat before adding the alcohol. This will help you avoid potential fires and injuries.

INGREDIENTS:

FOR THE FRENCH TOAST

3 TABLESPOONS UNSALTED BUTTER

8 EGGS

2 TABLESPOONS SUGAR

½ CUP HEAVY CREAM

1 TABLESPOON CINNAMON

1 TABLESPOON VANILLA EXTRACT

PINCH OF SALT

1 LOAF OF BRIOCHE, CUT INTO 10 TO 12 SLICES

FOR THE BANANAS FOSTER

1 STICK OF UNSALTED BUTTER

½ CUP LIGHT BROWN SUGAR, PACKED

3 BANANAS, SLICED

¼ CUP DARK RUM

½ CUP HEAVY CREAM

POWDERED SUGAR, FOR TOPPING

PECAN-CRUSTED MAPLE FRENCH TOAST

YIELD: 4 SERVINGS / ACTIVE TIME: 20 MINUTES / TOTAL TIME: 40 MINUTES

What better to do with leftover crusty bread than soak it in some fresh eggs and cream, sizzle it up in some butter, and encase it in pecans and maple syrup? Enjoying it with strong coffee and thick-sliced bacon, that's what!

1. Preheat the oven to 200°F and place an ovenproof serving dish in it.

2. In a small bowl, combine the eggs, heavy cream, and ½ cup of the maple syrup. Whisk to thoroughly combine, or use an immersion blender.

3. Put the bread in a dish and cover with the egg mixture. Let the bread soak up the egg mixture for about 20 minutes, turning halfway so both sides can soak.

4. Place the chopped pecans, cinnamon, and nutmeg in a shallow dish and stir before spreading out across dish. Dip each slice of soaked bread into the pecan-spice mixture, making sure every slice is covered on both sides.

5. Warm a 10-inch cast-iron skillet over medium heat. Add 2 tablespoons of the butter and, as it melts, tilt the pan to coat it evenly. When the butter is heated but not browned, add 4 slices of the pecan-crusted bread. Allow to cook for about 4 minutes, then flip. Drizzle the pieces with maple syrup while they're cooking on the other side, and after another 4 minutes or so, flip them again so the side with the maple syrup gets cooked for about 1 minute.

6. Transfer the cooked pieces to the serving dish in the oven. Repeat the cooking process for the remaining slices of bread.

7. Before serving, warm the remaining maple syrup (and some additional syrup) in a microwave-safe container for 30 seconds. Test the warmth. You don't want to over-warm it, just take the chill out. Serve the French toast with maple syrup.

TIP: The sugar in the maple syrup will also caramelize on the skillet as long as the heat is kept on medium, which will toast the sugar without burning it.

INGREDIENTS:

- 4 EGGS
- ½ CUP HEAVY CREAM
- ¾ CUP ALL-NATURAL MAPLE SYRUP, PLUS MORE TO TASTE
- 8 SLICES OF SLIGHTLY STALE THICK-CUT BREAD
- 2 CUPS PECANS, FINELY CHOPPED
- 1 TEASPOON CINNAMON
- 1 TEASPOON NUTMEG
- 4 TABLESPOONS UNSALTED BUTTER

SKILLET APPLE PANCAKE

YIELD: 4 TO 6 SERVINGS / **ACTIVE TIME:** 30 MINUTES / **TOTAL TIME:** 1 HOUR

Make this the morning after you go apple picking. It's a great way to use up some of the apples and get your day off to a great start.

1. Preheat the oven to 425°F.

2. In a large bowl, whisk together the eggs, milk, sugar, vanilla, and salt. Add the flour and whisk to combine. Set the batter aside.

3. Place a 12-inch cast-iron skillet over medium-high heat and add the butter, tilting the pan to thoroughly coat the bottom. Add the apple slices and top with the cinnamon, nutmeg, and ginger. Cook, while stirring, until apples begin to soften, about 5 minutes. Add the brown sugar and continue to stir while cooking for an additional few minutes, until the apples are very soft. Pat the cooked apples along the bottom of the skillet to distribute evenly.

4. Pour the batter over the apples, coating them evenly. Transfer the skillet to the oven and bake for about 20 minutes, until the pancake is browned and puffy. Sprinkle with confectioners' sugar when fresh out of the oven, if desired. Serve immediately.

VARIATION: To make a gluten-free version of this recipe, just substitute the ¾ cup of flour with ¾ cup Gluten Free All-Purpose Baking Flour from Bob's Red Mill and add 1 teaspoon of xanthan gum. Mix together before whisking into your wet ingredients.

INGREDIENTS:

- 4   EGGS
- 1   CUP WHOLE MILK
- 3   TABLESPOONS SUGAR
- ½   TEASPOON VANILLA EXTRACT
- ½   TEASPOON SALT
- ¾   CUP ALL-PURPOSE FLOUR
- 4   TABLESPOONS UNSALTED BUTTER
- 2   APPLES, PEELED, CORED, AND SLICED THIN
- ¼   TEASPOON CINNAMON
-   DASH OF GROUND NUTMEG
-   DASH OF GROUND GINGER
- ¼   CUP LIGHT BROWN SUGAR
-   CONFECTIONERS' SUGAR, FOR SPRINKLING (OPTIONAL)

DAVID EYRE'S PANCAKE

YIELD: 4 SERVINGS / **ACTIVE TIME:** 30 MINUTES / **TOTAL TIME:** 30 MINUTES

This recipe was run in the *New York Times* years ago and has quite the following. It's more of a popover than a traditional pancake, but it's a delicious tribute to writer and editor David Eyre.

1. Preheat the oven to 425°F.

2. In a bowl, combine the flour, milk, eggs, and nutmeg. Beat lightly; leave the batter a little lumpy.

3. Melt the butter in a 12-inch cast-iron skillet and, when very hot, pour in the batter.

4. Transfer the skillet to the oven and bake for 15 to 20 minutes, until golden brown.

5. Sprinkle with the sugar, return briefly to the oven, then remove. Sprinkle with lemon juice and serve with your favorite jam.

INGREDIENTS:

- ½ CUP ALL-PURPOSE FLOUR
- ½ CUP WHOLE MILK
- 2 EGGS, LIGHTLY BEATEN
- PINCH OF NUTMEG
- 4 TABLESPOONS UNSALTED BUTTER
- 2 TABLESPOONS CONFECTIONERS' SUGAR
- JUICE OF ½ LEMON
- JAM, FOR SERVING

WHOLE GRAIN PORRIDGE

YIELD: 4 SERVINGS / **ACTIVE TIME:** 5 MINUTES / **TOTAL TIME:** 30 MINUTES

This dish is all about mastering the method and then tweaking to make it your own. Try this recipe as suggested, and then take all of the liberties you can think of, swapping in any grain, dried fruit, and milk that you want.

1. Place all of the ingredients, other than the Granny Smith apple and the almonds, in a cast-iron Dutch oven.

2. Bring to a gentle simmer and cover. Cook, while stirring occasionally to prevent the porridge from sticking to the bottom, for 20 minutes.

3. Remove the porridge from heat and ladle into warm bowls. Peel the apple and grate it over each bowl. Top with the chopped almonds and serve.

INGREDIENTS:

- 1 CUP BUCKWHEAT GROATS
- 1 CUP STEEL-CUT OATS
- 2 TABLESPOONS FLAX SEEDS
- 2 TEASPOONS CINNAMON
- 1 CUP CHOPPED DRIED FRUIT (APPLES, APRICOTS, PINEAPPLE, DATES, ETC.)
- 2 CUPS WATER
- 2 CUPS ALMOND MILK
- 1 GRANNY SMITH APPLE, FOR GARNISH
- ¼ CUP CHOPPED ALMONDS, FOR GARNISH

GRANDMA GOODRICH'S GRITS

YIELD: 8 TO 10 SERVINGS / **ACTIVE TIME:** 15 MINUTES / **TOTAL TIME:** 45 MINUTES

Thelma Goodrich hailed from Dallas, Texas, and she always made this simple dish for special occasions. She passed it on to her granddaughter, Briana Chalais, who says it remains the most popular dish at her family gatherings. Once you try it, you'll see why. The beauty of cast iron is on full display here, as it lends the bottom a gorgeous burnish.

1. Preheat the oven to 425°F.

2. Place the water in a saucepan and bring to a boil. While stirring constantly, slowly add the grits. Cover, reduce the heat to low, and cook, while stirring occasionally, until the grits are quite thick, about 5 minutes. Remove from heat.

3. Place the eggs, butter, and milk in a bowl, season with salt and pepper, and stir to combine. Stir the cooked grits into the egg mixture, add three-quarters of the cheese, and stir to incorporate.

4. Pour the mixture into a greased cast-iron baking dish or skillet, place in the oven, and bake for 30 minutes. Remove, sprinkle the remaining cheese on top, and return the grits to the oven. Bake until the cheese is melted and the grits are firm, about 15 minutes. Remove from the oven and let cool slightly before cutting into squares and serving.

INGREDIENTS:

4   **CUPS WATER**

1   **CUP QUICK-COOKING GRITS**

2   **LARGE EGGS**

4   **TABLESPOONS UNSALTED BUTTER, AT ROOM TEMPERATURE**

¾   **CUP WHOLE MILK**

   SALT AND PEPPER, TO TASTE

1   **LB. CHEDDAR CHEESE, GRATED**

PEANUT BUTTER & BACON OATS
with FRIED EGGS

YIELD: 4 TO 6 SERVINGS / ACTIVE TIME: 5 MINUTES / TOTAL TIME: 20 MINUTES

Peanut butter, bacon, and eggs in oats? It may sound crazy at first, but the saltiness of the crispy bacon, the texture added by the peanut butter, and the creaminess of the egg yolk work really well together, creating a brand-new take on oatmeal.

1. Cook the bacon in a 10-inch cast-iron skillet over medium heat. Remove the bacon from the pan and use the bacon fat to fry the eggs.

2. When the eggs have been fried, remove them from the pan and set aside. Wipe remaining grease from the pan with a paper towel. Add oats, water, and salt and cook over medium heat for 7 to 10 minutes, or until oats are the desired consistency.

3. While the oats are cooking, chop the bacon. Add the bacon and peanut butter to the oatmeal and stir to combine.

4. Top each portion with a fried egg and serve.

INGREDIENTS:

6	SLICES OF THICK-CUT BACON
6	EGGS
2	CUPS OATS
6	CUPS WATER
1	TABLESPOON KOSHER SALT
¼	CUP PEANUT BUTTER OF YOUR CHOICE

BREAKFAST TACOS

YIELD: 6 SERVINGS / ACTIVE TIME: 10 MINUTES / TOTAL TIME: 1 HOUR

Tacos are the best thing ever, and when you can start your day off with them, that's a double win. The add-ons are what make this the ultimate post-party breakfast, since a large crowd can tailor their breakfast to their liking.

1. Heat the oil in a 12-inch cast-iron skillet over medium heat. In a separate bowl, mix together the eggs, spices, and cilantro.

2. Add the egg mixture to the skillet and scramble until eggs are cooked through.

3. Serve with warm tortillas, Pico de Gallo, Guacamole, and other toppings of your choice.

PICO DE GALLO

Combine all of the ingredients in a bowl. Refrigerate 1 hour before serving to let the flavors mingle.

GUACAMOLE

Place all of the ingredients in a small bowl, mash to combine, and set aside.

INGREDIENTS:

- 2 TABLESPOONS VEGETABLE OIL
- 8 EGGS
- 1 TABLESPOON CHILI POWDER
- 1 TABLESPOON CUMIN
- ½ TABLESPOON ADOBO SEASONING
- 1 TABLESPOON DRIED OREGANO
- 2 TABLESPOONS CHOPPED CILANTRO
- 6 CORN TORTILLAS (SEE PAGE 169), WARMED
- PICO DE GALLO (SEE RECIPE), FOR SERVING
- GUACAMOLE (SEE RECIPE), FOR SERVING
- TOPPINGS OF CHOICE, FOR SERVING

PICO DE GALLO

- 4 ROMA OR PLUM TOMATOES, DICED
- 1 JALAPEÑO PEPPER, DICED
- ½ CUP CHOPPED RED ONION
- ¼ CUP CHOPPED CILANTRO LEAVES
- ZEST AND JUICE OF ½ LIME
- SALT, TO TASTE

GUACAMOLE

- FLESH FROM 2 RIPE AVOCADOS
- 2 TABLESPOONS CHOPPED CILANTRO
- 2 TABLESPOONS MINCED RED ONION
- ZEST AND JUICE OF ½ LIME
- 1 TABLESPOON MINCED JALAPEÑO PEPPER (OPTIONAL)
- SALT, TO TASTE

HUEVOS RANCHEROS

YIELD: 4 SERVINGS / ACTIVE TIME: 25 MINUTES / TOTAL TIME: 40 MINUTES

Y ou can make this a one-dish meal by cutting the tortillas into ½-inch pieces and frying them. Once they've crisped up, spoon the beans and butter over them, pressing them into the bottom of the skillet to brown. Break the eggs over the beans and cover so that the eggs start to set. Cook for about 2 minutes. Take off the lid, cover with cheese, and serve.

1. Heat the oil in a 10-inch cast-iron skillet over medium-high heat. Fry the tortillas, one at a time, until firm but not crisp. Transfer cooked tortillas to a plate lined with a paper towel, and separate with paper towels while cooking.

2. Put the beans and butter in a bowl and heat in the microwave for about 1 minute, stirring halfway through.

3. Fry the eggs in the skillet over easy and, once nearly cooked, sprinkle with cheese so that the cheese melts.

4. Place a crispy tortilla on a plate, top with the beans and eggs, and serve hot with the salsa, jalapeños, and cilantro.

INGREDIENTS:

2 TABLESPOONS VEGETABLE OIL

4 CORN TORTILLAS (SEE PAGE 169)

½ LB. BLACK OR REFRIED BEANS

1 TABLESPOON UNSALTED BUTTER

4 EGGS

½ CUP GRATED SHARP CHEDDAR CHEESE

½ CUP COTIJA OR GRATED MONTEREY JACK CHEESE

½ CUP FRESH SALSA, FOR SERVING

JALAPEÑO PEPPERS, SLICED, FOR SERVING

FRESH CILANTRO, CHOPPED, FOR SERVING

STEAK & PEARL ONION FRITTATA

YIELD: 6 SERVINGS / ACTIVE TIME: 10 MINUTES / TOTAL TIME: 25 MINUTES

Frittatas are traditionally enjoyed at breakfast, but this one is hearty enough to work any time of day. Serve this with an arugula-and-red onion salad for a quick on-the-go lunch if you find yourself pressed for time.

1. Preheat oven to 400°F. Place a 10-inch cast-iron skillet over medium-high heat and add the olive oil. Once the pan is hot, add the pearl onions, salt, and pepper and cook until onions start to caramelize, about 5 to 7 minutes.

2. While the onions are cooking, place the eggs, cream or half-and-half, salt, and pepper in a bowl and scramble until combined.

3. Add the steak to the pan with the onions and cook until steak is cooked through, about 2 to 3 minutes. Add the butter and parsley and stir until the butter is melted. Sprinkle the cheese evenly over the onions and steak, then pour the egg mixture into the pan. The eggs should just cover everything else in the pan. Place the skillet in the oven and cook for 8 minutes.

4. Turn the broiler on and cook for another 3 minutes, until the top of the frittata is brown. Remove from the oven and serve.

INGREDIENTS:

2 TABLESPOONS OLIVE OIL

1 LB. PEARL ONIONS

12 LARGE EGGS

½ CUP HEAVY CREAM OR HALF-AND-HALF

SALT AND PEPPER, TO TASTE

1 (7 TO 8 OZ.) STRIP STEAK, MINCED

4 TABLESPOONS UNSALTED BUTTER

2 TABLESPOONS CHOPPED FRESH PARSLEY

2 CUPS SHREDDED PARMESAN OR ASIAGO CHEESE

TAMAGOYAKI

YIELD: 2 SERVINGS / ACTIVE TIME: 15 MINUTES / TOTAL TIME: 15 MINUTES

This is a sweet-and-savory Japanese omelette that is traditionally made in a small rectangular pan. It takes a bit of practice to get just right, but once you master it, you'll find yourself making it all the time. It's equally good warm, cold, or in a sushi roll.

1. Place the eggs, salt, soy sauce, and mirin in a bowl and whisk to combine.

2. Place the vegetable oil in a rectangular cast-iron pan and warm over medium-high heat.

3. Pour a thin layer of the egg mixture into the pan, tilting and swirling to make sure the egg completely coats the bottom. When the bottom of the egg is just set and there is still liquid on top, use a chopstick to gently roll the egg up into a log. If you allow the egg to cook too much, it won't stick as you roll it.

4. When the first roll is at one end of the pan, pour another thin layer of egg mixture into the pan. When the bottom of this layer is set, roll the log back onto it. Roll the layer up to the other end of the pan. Repeat until all of the egg mixture has been used up.

5. Remove the omelette from the pan and let it set for a few minutes before trimming the ends and slicing into even pieces.

INGREDIENTS:

4	LARGE EGGS
¼	TEASPOON KOSHER SALT
1	TEASPOON SOY SAUCE
1	TABLESPOON MIRIN
1	TABLESPOON VEGETABLE OIL

BACON & ZUCCHINI QUICHE

YIELD: 6 TO 8 SERVINGS / ACTIVE TIME: 45 MINUTES / TOTAL TIME: 1 HOUR AND 30 MINUTES

Crisp, salty bacon is the perfect complement to zucchini in this summery quiche. The addition of garlic-herb goat cheese further highlights these ingredients.

1. Preheat the oven to 350°F.

2. In a 10-inch cast-iron skillet, sauté the bacon until just crispy, about 10 minutes. Use a slotted spoon to gather the pieces and put them on a plate lined with a paper towel to drain.

3. Add the zucchini, mushrooms, and garlic to the bacon fat, reduce the heat, and stir. Cook until zucchini is just soft, about 10 minutes.

4. Place the crust in a lightly greased 10-inch cast-iron skillet Sprinkle the bacon pieces on the bottom of the crust, and use a slotted spoon to layer the zucchini over them. Dot the mixture with the garlic-herb goat cheese.

5. In a medium bowl, whisk the eggs until thoroughly combined. Add the half-and-half, salt, and pepper, and whisk to combine.

6. Pour the egg mixture over the other ingredients, shaking the pan gently to distribute evenly.

7. Put the skillet in the oven and bake for 35 to 40 minutes, or until the quiche is puffy and golden brown and the eggs are set. Remove from the oven.

8. Allow to sit for 10 minutes before slicing and serving.

INGREDIENTS:

- ¾ LB. THICK-CUT BACON, CHOPPED
- 1 SMALL ZUCCHINI, CUT INTO THIN ROUNDS
- ½ CUP SLICED MUSHROOMS
- 1 GARLIC CLOVE, MINCED
- 1 BAKED CRUST (SEE PAGE 579)
- 3-5 OZ. GARLIC-HERB GOAT CHEESE
- 4 EGGS
- 1½ CUPS HALF-AND-HALF
- ½ TEASPOON SALT
- ½ TEASPOON FRESHLY GROUND PEPPER

BEET & GOAT CHEESE QUICHE

YIELD: 6 TO 8 SERVINGS / **ACTIVE TIME:** 45 MINUTES / **TOTAL TIME:** 2 HOURS

Beets are beautiful and good for you, and they taste great. All good reasons to cook them up and put them in a quiche, where their color, texture, and flavor all work beautifully. Add fresh goat cheese and a hint of thyme, and you have an elegant, easy, and fabulous meal.

1. Preheat the oven to 400°F and place the piecrust in a greased 10-inch cast-iron skillet.

2. Put the beet slices and onion in a pouch of heavy-duty aluminum foil. Drizzle with olive oil and close up securely. Put the pouch in the oven and roast the beets and onions for about 20 minutes, until soft, checking after 10 to 15 minutes. Remove pouch from oven and let sit while you prep the other ingredients.

3. In a large bowl, whisk the eggs until thoroughly combined. Add the milk, thyme, and garlic, and whisk to combine.

4. Carefully open the pouch of beets and onions and distribute over the piecrust. Pour the egg mixture over this, and dot with pieces of the goat cheese.

5. Cover the skillet with foil and bake for 40 minutes. Remove foil from skillet and continue to bake another 10 to 15 minutes, or until the quiche is golden brown and the eggs are set. A knife inserted in the center should come out clean.

6. Allow to sit for about 30 minutes before slicing and serving.

INGREDIENTS:

1 **FLAKY PASTRY CRUST (SEE PAGE 580)**

4-5 **RED OR GOLDEN BEETS (OR A COMBINATION), PEELED AND SLICED THIN**

2 **TABLESPOONS MINCED YELLOW ONION**

1 **TEASPOON OLIVE OIL**

6 **EGGS**

1½ **CUPS WHOLE MILK**

2 **TEASPOONS DRIED THYME**

2 **GARLIC CLOVES, PRESSED**

½ **CUP FRESH GOAT CHEESE**

SMOKED SALMON & DILL QUICHE

YIELD: 6 TO 8 SERVINGS / ACTIVE TIME: 30 MINUTES / TOTAL TIME: 1 HOUR AND 30 MINUTES

Any good deli in New York City will serve smoked salmon for breakfast—typically on a bagel with a schmear of cream cheese, a few capers, and a sprig of dill. Putting smoked salmon and dill in a quiche makes for a breakfast dish that is still fantastic for fans of the fish, but is mellower and therefore more palatable for those who might not be.

1. Preheat the oven to 350°F.

2. Working with the crust in a lightly greased 10-inch cast-iron skillet, brush the mustard over the bottom of the dough. Place the salmon pieces in the pie.

3. In a large bowl, whisk the eggs until thoroughly scrambled. Add the half-and-half, salt, and pepper, and whisk to combine. Add the dill and mix well.

4. Pour the egg mixture over the salmon pieces, shaking the pan gently to distribute evenly. Sprinkle the cubes of cream cheese evenly on top.

5. Put the skillet in the oven and bake for 35 to 40 minutes, or until the quiche is puffy and golden brown and the eggs are set.

6. Remove from the oven and allow to sit for 10 minutes before slicing and serving.

INGREDIENTS:

1 **FLAKY PASTRY CRUST (SEE PAGE 580)**

1 **TEASPOON DIJON MUSTARD**

1 **LB. SMOKED SALMON, CUT OR TORN INTO NICKEL-SIZED PIECES**

4 **EGGS**

1 **CUP HALF-AND-HALF**

1 **TEASPOON SALT**

½ **TEASPOON GROUND BLACK PEPPER**

1 **TABLESPOON DILL, FINELY MINCED**

1 **(3 OZ.) PACKAGE OF CREAM CHEESE, CUT INTO SMALL CUBES**

SPINACH, HAM & CHEESE STRATA

YIELD: 4 TO 6 SERVINGS / ACTIVE TIME: 20 MINUTES / TOTAL TIME: 1 HOUR

A nourishing nibble that makes for a filling breakfast, brunch, or lunch. As long as the base includes eggs, milk, bread, and cheese, the remainder can be tailored to personal taste. It's the ideal way to use up leftovers or, in this case, showcase the flawless combination of ham and Swiss cheese.

1. Place the eggs and milk in a large mixing bowl and stir to combine. Add the cheese and nutmeg and stir to incorporate. Add the bread cubes, transfer the mixture to the refrigerator, and chill for 30 minutes.

2. Preheat the oven to 400°F.

3. Add the ham or bacon, onion, and spinach to the egg-and-bread mixture and stir until evenly distributed. Season with salt and pepper.

4. Coat a 10-inch cast-iron skillet with the olive oil. Pour in the strata, place the skillet in the oven, and bake for 25 minutes.

5. Remove from the oven and let cool for 10 minutes before cutting into wedges and serving.

INGREDIENTS:

- 7 EGGS, BEATEN
- 2 CUPS WHOLE MILK
- 4 OZ. SWISS CHEESE, SHREDDED
- LARGE PINCH OF GROUND NUTMEG
- 3 CUPS BREAD CUBES
- 4 OZ. HAM OR BACON, DICED
- 1 YELLOW ONION, MINCED
- 3 OZ. SPINACH, COARSELY CHOPPED
- SALT AND PEPPER, TO TASTE
- 2 TEASPOONS OLIVE OIL

CHICKEN SAUSAGE HASH

YIELD: 4 TO 6 SERVINGS / **ACTIVE TIME:** 15 MINUTES / **TOTAL TIME:** 30 MINUTES

You can follow this recipe step-by-step and have breakfast on the table in a half hour. Or you can cook the sausage and potatoes the night before, start with Step 3, and have it ready in a flash. Serve this with hot sauce, salsa, or maple syrup.

1. Warm a 12-inch cast-iron skillet over medium-high heat and then add 2 tablespoons of the oil. When the oil is shimmering, add the chicken sausage and cook until browned all over, about 8 minutes. Remove the sausage from the pan and set aside. When cool enough to handle, chop the sausage into bite-sized pieces.

2. Add the remaining oil to the pan. When the oil is shimmering, add the potatoes, season with salt and pepper, and cook until browned. Cover the pan and let steam for 5 minutes.

3. Remove the lid, add the onion, and cook, while stirring occasionally, until the onion is browned, about 5 minutes.

4. Gently fold in the chopped sausage and continue to cook until the potatoes are fork-tender, about 10 minutes.

5. Using a large spoon, press down on the hash and then make six indentations. Crack an egg into each indentation. Cover the pan and cook until the egg whites are firm, about 5 minutes. Serve immediately.

INGREDIENTS:

¼ CUP OLIVE OIL

2 LARGE LINKS OF SPICY CHICKEN SAUSAGE

2 YUKON GOLD POTATOES, DICED INTO ½-INCH CUBES

SALT AND PEPPER, TO TASTE

1 YELLOW ONION, DICED

6 EGGS

CORNED BEEF HASH

YIELD: 4 SERVINGS / ACTIVE TIME: 15 MINUTES / TOTAL TIME: 35 MINUTES

Start your day out right with this hearty breakfast hash. The recipe originated in the 1950s and the name comes from the French word *hacher*, which means "to chop." If roast beef is easier to come by than corned beef, feel free to use that.

1. Place 3 tablespoons of the vegetable oil in a 12-inch cast-iron skillet and warm over medium-high heat. When the oil is shimmering, add the potatoes and cook, while stirring occasionally, until they are golden brown, about 10 minutes.

2. Reduce the heat to medium and add the onion and bell pepper. Cook, while stirring occasionally, for 2 minutes. Add the corned beef and cook until browned, about 8 minutes. Pour in the tomato sauce, tomato paste, and hot sauce, stir to coat, and allow the hash to simmer, while stirring occasionally, for 15 minutes.

3. While the hash is simmering, place the remaining vegetable oil in another cast-iron skillet and warm over medium heat. When the oil is shimmering, crack the eggs into the skillet and cook until the whites are cooked through. To cut down on dishes, you can also make four indentations in the hash, crack the eggs into them, and cook until the whites are set.

4. To serve, spoon the hash onto plates and top each portion with a fried egg. Sprinkle the chives on top and serve immediately.

INGREDIENTS:

- 5 TABLESPOONS VEGETABLE OIL
- 2 YUKON GOLD POTATOES, DICED INTO ¼-INCH CUBES
- 1 YELLOW ONION, SLICED INTO THIN HALF-MOONS
- 1 RED OR GREEN BELL PEPPER, SEEDED AND SLICED THIN
- 1½ LBS. COOKED CORNED BEEF, DICED
- 1 CUP TOMATO SAUCE
- 2 TABLESPOONS TOMATO PASTE
- 1 TEASPOON HOT SAUCE
- 4 LARGE EGGS
- CHIVES, CHOPPED, FOR GARNISH

LAMB & SWEET POTATO HASH

YIELD: 4 TO 6 SERVINGS / ACTIVE TIME: 20 MINUTES / TOTAL TIME: 13 TO 17 HOURS

This meal is the perfect way to use up that leftover leg of lamb from Easter dinner. The sweet, savory, and spicy combination of the lamb and sweet potato puts traditional breakfast hash to shame, and there's nothing wrong with drizzling a little maple sugar over the top to satisfy your midmorning sweet tooth.

1. To prepare the marinade, combine all of the ingredients in a small bowl and transfer to a 1-gallon resealable bag. Place the lamb in the bag, squeeze all of the air out of the bag, and place in the refrigerator for 12 to 16 hours.

2. To prepare the lamb, preheat the oven to 350°F. Place a cast-iron Dutch oven over medium-high heat and add the beef tallow or clarified butter. Remove the lamb from the bag, place in the pot, and sear for 5 minutes on each side.

3. Add the water to the pot, place it in the oven, and cook for 20 minutes, or until the center of the lamb reaches 140°F on an instant-read thermometer. Remove the pot from the oven, set the lamb aside, and drain the liquid from the pot. Let the lamb sit for 15 minutes, then mince.

4. To prepare the sweet potato hash, fill the pot with water and bring to a boil. Add the sweet potatoes and cook until they are just tender, about 5 minutes. Be careful not to over-cook them, as you don't want to end up with mashed potatoes. Drain potatoes and set aside.

5. Add the beef tallow or clarified butter, the poblano peppers, onions, garlic, and cumin to the pot and cook over medium heat until all of the vegetables are soft, about 10 minutes.

6. Return the potatoes and the lamb to the pot. Add the salt and cook for another 15 minutes. Add the oregano, season with salt and black pepper, and serve.

INGREDIENTS:

FOR THE MARINADE
- 4 GARLIC CLOVES, PUREED
- LEAVES FROM 3 SPRIGS OF OREGANO, MINCED
- ¼ CUP DIJON MUSTARD
- ¼ CUP CABERNET SAUVIGNON
- 1 TABLESPOON KOSHER SALT
- 1 TABLESPOON CRACKED BLACK PEPPER

FOR THE LAMB
- 1½ LBS. LEG OF LAMB, BUTTERFLIED
- 2 TABLESPOONS BEEF TALLOW OR CLARIFIED BUTTER
- 2 CUPS WATER

FOR THE SWEET POTATO HASH
- 2 SWEET POTATOES, PEELED AND MINCED
- 2 TABLESPOONS BEEF TALLOW OR CLARIFIED BUTTER
- 2 POBLANO PEPPERS, DICED (FOR MORE HEAT, SUBSTITUTE 1 LARGE JALAPEÑO PEPPER FOR ONE OF THE POBLANOS)
- 2 YELLOW ONIONS, MINCED
- 2-3 GARLIC CLOVES, MINCED
- 1 TABLESPOON CUMIN
- 1 TABLESPOON KOSHER SALT, PLUS MORE TO TASTE
- 1 TABLESPOON CHOPPED FRESH OREGANO
- FRESHLY GROUND BLACK PEPPER, TO TASTE

CHICKEN CONGEE

YIELD: 4 SERVINGS / ACTIVE TIME: 10 MINUTES / TOTAL TIME: 45 MINUTES

This, of course, is the beloved and creamy breakfast porridge from China. Since it's so simple, you really must make sure to use the freshest, highest-quality ingredients available. I add a little turmeric for color here, but it isn't traditional. You can also serve this with steamed bok choy, hard-boiled eggs, fried shallots, sliced green onions, mushrooms, or whatever sounds good—maybe even a thick slice of fried Spam.

1. Place the chicken, stock or salted water, and turmeric, if using, in a large cast-iron Dutch oven and bring to a simmer over medium heat. Simmer until the chicken is cooked through, about 15 minutes. Using a slotted spoon, remove the chicken, set it aside, and allow the stock to continue simmering. When the chicken is cool enough to handle, remove from the bones, shred into bite-sized pieces, and discard the bones.

2. Place the vegetable oil in a cast-iron wok or skillet and warm over medium heat. Add the garlic and cook until it is fragrant and golden brown. Add the rice, stir to coat, and cook until the rice is golden brown, about 4 minutes.

3. Add the rice to the stock and season with salt and pepper. Cook, while stirring occasionally, until the rice is tender, about 20 minutes.

4. Stir the shredded chicken into the pot and cook until warmed through. Ladle into warmed bowls and garnish with cilantro.

CHICKEN STOCK

1. Preheat the oven to 350°F. Lay the chicken carcasses and/or stewing pieces on a flat baking tray, place in the oven, and cook until they are golden brown, 30 to 45 minutes. Remove and set aside.

2. Meanwhile, in a large stockpot, add the vegetable oil and warm over low heat. Add the vegetables and cook until the moisture has evaporated. This allows the flavor of the vegetables to become concentrated.

3. Add the water and the salt to the stockpot. Add the chicken carcasses and/or stewing pieces and the aromatics, raise heat to high, and bring to a boil.

4. Reduce the heat and simmer for a minimum of 2 hours. Skim

INGREDIENTS:

4	**CHICKEN LEGS, SKIN REMOVED**
4	**CUPS CHICKEN STOCK (SEE RECIPE) OR SALTED WATER**
1	**TEASPOON TURMERIC (OPTIONAL)**
2	**TABLESPOONS VEGETABLE OIL**
1	**GARLIC CLOVE, MINCED**
1½	**CUPS LONG-GRAIN RICE**
	SALT AND PEPPER, TO TASTE
	CILANTRO, CHOPPED, FOR GARNISH

CHICKEN STOCK

10	**LBS. CHICKEN CARCASSES AND/OR STEWING CHICKEN PIECES**
½	**CUP VEGETABLE OIL**
1	**LEEK, TRIMMED, CAREFULLY WASHED, AND CUT INTO 1-INCH PIECES**
1	**LARGE YELLOW ONION, UNPEELED, ROOT CLEANED, CUT INTO 1-INCH PIECES**
2	**LARGE CARROTS, CUT INTO 1-INCH PIECES**
1	**CELERY STALK WITH LEAVES, CUT INTO 1-INCH PIECES**
10	**QUARTS WATER**
1	**TEASPOON SALT**
8	**SPRIGS OF PARSLEY**
5	**SPRIGS OF THYME**
2	**BAY LEAVES**
1	**TEASPOON PEPPERCORNS**

fat and impurities from the top as the stock cooks. Let the flavor be your guide as for when to stop cooking the stock. A stock will typically be ready after cooking for 4 to 5 hours.

5. When the stock is finished cooking, strain through a fine sieve or cheesecloth. Place stock in refrigerator to chill. Once cool, skim the fat layer from the top and discard. Use immediately, refrigerate, or freeze.

CHEESY HASH BROWNS

YIELD: 4 TO 6 SERVINGS / **ACTIVE TIME:** 20 MINUTES / **TOTAL TIME:** 1 HOUR

I f you want gooey goodness, this recipe is for you. Be careful not to overcook it or you'll go from gooey to overly chewy. The best cheeses to use in this recipe are those that melt well, like cheddar, Swiss, American, mozzarella, Monterey Jack, or Provolone.

1. Preheat the oven to 375°F.

2. Add the butter to a 10-inch cast-iron skillet and cook over medium-high heat. When the butter starts to foam, add the potatoes and season with the salt and pepper. Press the potatoes into the bottom of the pan. Cook for about 5 minutes.

3. In a mixing bowl, whisk the eggs and milk together. Pour the eggs over the potatoes, shaking the pan to help them penetrate to the bottom. Sprinkle liberally with the cheese.

4. Transfer the skillet to the oven and cook until just set, about 10 minutes. Serve immediately.

INGREDIENTS:

4	TABLESPOONS UNSALTED BUTTER
4	LARGE RUSSET POTATOES, SHREDDED WITH A CHEESE GRATER AND SQUEEZED DRY
1	TEASPOON SALT
½	TEASPOON PEPPER, OR TO TASTE
6	EGGS
½	CUP WHOLE MILK
1	CUP SHREDDED CHEESE

HANGTOWN FRY

YIELD: 4 SERVINGS / ACTIVE TIME: 25 MINUTES / TOTAL TIME: 40 MINUTES

While not the most beloved among the Bay Area's numerous contributions to the culinary world, this is certainly one of the most enduring. The unique combination of oysters, eggs, and bacon was created at the Cary House Hotel in Placerville (aka "Hangtown"), where it was the ultimate sign of conspicuous consumption among the gold miners who invaded the area in the 1800s. Once you get a taste, you just may be inspired to strike out for the West yourself.

1. Preheat the oven to 400°F.

2. Place the potatoes and 2 tablespoons of the olive oil in a mixing bowl. Season with salt, stir to combine, and then place the potatoes on a parchment-lined baking sheet. Place the potatoes in the oven and roast for 20 minutes. Remove from the oven, set aside, and leave the oven at 400°F.

3. Place the bacon in a cast-iron skillet and cook over medium heat until it is crispy, about 8 minutes. Transfer to a paper towel–lined plate to drain. When cool enough to handle, crumble into bite-sized pieces.

4. Pat the oysters dry. Combine the flour, cornmeal, onion powder, salt, and white pepper in a mixing bowl. Dip the oysters into the mixture until coated. Place the coated oysters on a plate and set aside.

5. Add olive oil to a 12-inch cast-iron skillet until it is ¾-inch deep and warm over medium heat. Working in batches, add the oysters and fry until they are golden brown all over, about 6 minutes. Transfer to a paper towel–lined plate to drain.

6. Drain the oil and add the potatoes and bacon to the skillet. Pour in the beaten eggs and cook until set, about 2 minutes. Arrange the fried oysters around the pan and place the skillet in the oven. Cook until cooked through and golden brown on top. Serve with hot sauce.

INGREDIENTS:

3-4	RED POTATOES, QUARTERED
2	TABLESPOONS OLIVE OIL, PLUS MORE FOR FRYING
12	SLICES OF THICK-CUT BACON
24	SMALL OYSTERS, FRESHLY SHUCKED
1	CUP ALL-PURPOSE FLOUR
1	CUP YELLOW CORNMEAL
1	TABLESPOON ONION POWDER
	SALT AND WHITE PEPPER, TO TASTE
6	EGGS, BEATEN
	HOT SAUCE, FOR SERVING

BREADS & FLATBREADS

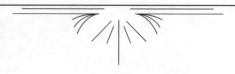

By now, you're probably wondering: Is there anything you can't make in cast iron? The answer is yes, but that's not the focus here.

When it comes to breads, the answer is pretty much no. (Well, again, the real answer is yes, but let's try to stay positive.) From mouthwatering Beer & Cheese Bread (see page 141) to simply perfect Paratha (see page 174), cast iron is for sure your bread-making pal, able to elicit those beautiful blisters, a perfectly crispy crust, a golden edge, and so much more. It was man's first choice for making tortillas (also not true, that was a hot stone, but isn't a griddle a nice step up?), and that's a nearly perfect food.

If you've never been a flatbread person, these are the recipes that will change your mind forever. (Disclaimer: We can't really guarantee that, it's mostly just based on years of watching a lot of wide eyes, big smiles, and changed lives result from a solid recipe.)

ROASTED GARLIC BREAD

YIELD: 1 SMALL LOAF / ACTIVE TIME: 25 MINUTES / TOTAL TIME: 3 HOURS

Be forewarned: If you love garlic (as I suspect you do if you want to make this recipe), the smell of this bread baking will make you drool. Once you can slice into it, eat it as is, toast it, top with a thin schmear of pesto, or serve it as a wonderful stand-in for traditional garlic bread.

1. Preheat the oven to 375°F.

2. Take as much of the paper skin off the head of garlic as possible without separating the cloves. With a sharp knife, cut off only as much of the top of the head as necessary to expose the cloves in their sleeves. Put the garlic cut side up on a piece of heavy-duty aluminum foil or in a garlic roaster. Pour the olive oil over the top of the garlic. Fold the aluminum foil up and over the garlic to cover it, crimping any edges together, or put the lid on the garlic roaster. Roast in the oven for 50 to 60 minutes.

3. Open the foil or roaster and allow the garlic to cool slightly. Extract the roasted cloves from their sleeves by squeezing the bottom so the cloves pop out. Put them on a plate or in a shallow bowl. Reserve the cooking oil.

4. Put the yeast and sugar in a measuring cup and drizzle in about ½ cup warm water. Hot water will kill the yeast, so it's important that the water be warm without being hot. Cover the measuring cup with plastic wrap and set it aside for about 15 minutes. If the yeast doesn't foam, it is not alive and you'll need to start over.

5. When the yeast is proofed, pour it into a large bowl and add the remaining cup of warm water. Stir gently to combine. Add the salt to the flour, and then add the flour to the yeast mixture. Stir with a wooden spoon until combined. The dough will be wet and sticky.

6. Put a dusting of flour on a flat surface and lift out the dough. With flour on your hands and more at the ready, begin kneading the dough so that it loses its stickiness. Don't overdo it, and don't use too much flour; just enough that it becomes more cohesive, about 5 minutes. Incorporate the roasted garlic cloves while you're kneading the dough.

7. Lightly grease a large bowl with some of the garlic-infused olive oil and place the dough in it. Cover the bowl with plastic wrap and allow to rise untouched until it has roughly doubled in size, at least 1 hour and up to several hours. Gently punch it down, score the

INGREDIENTS:

1	HEAD OF GARLIC
¼	CUP OLIVE OIL
¼	TEASPOON INSTANT YEAST
¼	TEASPOON SUGAR
1½	CUPS WATER (110 TO 115°F)
1	TEASPOON KOSHER SALT
3	CUPS ALL-PURPOSE FLOUR, PLUS MORE FOR DUSTING

Continued . . .

top with a sharp knife, re-cover with the plastic, and allow to rise again for another 30 minutes or so. Brush the surface with the remaining garlic-infused oil.

8. While the dough is on its final rise, preheat the oven to 450°F. Put a piece of parchment paper on the bottom of a cast-iron Dutch oven and put it in the oven with the lid on so it gets hot. When the oven is ready and the dough has risen, carefully remove the lid and gently scoop the dough from the bowl into the pot, scored side up. Cover and bake for 15 minutes. Remove the lid and continue to bake for another 15 to 20 minutes, until the top is golden and it sounds hollow when tapped.

9. Remove the pot from the oven and use kitchen towels to carefully remove the bread. Allow to cool before slicing.

TIP: Add ¼ cup fresh rosemary during the kneading process for additional flavor.

APPLESAUCE & OATMEAL BREAD

YIELD: 1 SMALL LOAF / **ACTIVE TIME:** 30 MINUTES / **TOTAL TIME:** 1 HOUR AND 30 MINUTES

This is an easy bread to make for a delicious midday snack. It's practically cake, but with far less sugar. Adding flaxseeds bumps up the nutritional goodness without compromising the flavor or texture of the bread.

1. Preheat the oven to 350°F. Put a 10-inch cast-iron skillet in the oven while it preheats.

2. In a large bowl, mix together the sugar, eggs, oil, and vanilla. In a separate bowl, combine the flours, baking powder, baking soda, cinnamon, nutmeg, and salt. Add the dry ingredients to the bowl of wet ingredients. Stir until thoroughly combined. Next, add the oats, applesauce, flaxseeds, and nuts, if desired. Stir to combine.

3. Using pot holders or oven mitts, carefully remove the skillet from the oven. Pour the batter in and dust the top with additional oats and some brown sugar, if desired. Bake until the bread sounds hollow when tapped on the top and a toothpick or knife inserted in the middle comes out clean, about 45 minutes.

4. Remove from the oven and let rest for about 5 to 10 minutes. Gently invert onto a plate. Allow to cool before cutting into wedges and serving.

INGREDIENTS:

- ¾ CUP SUGAR
- 2 LARGE EGGS
- ½ CUP VEGETABLE OIL
- 1 TEASPOON VANILLA EXTRACT
- ½ CUP WHOLE WHEAT FLOUR
- 1 CUP ALL-PURPOSE FLOUR
- ¼ TEASPOON BAKING POWDER
- ½ TEASPOON BAKING SODA
- 1 TEASPOON CINNAMON
- ¼ TEASPOON NUTMEG
- ½ TEASPOON SALT
- ½ CUP ROLLED OATS
- ¾ CUP CHUNKY APPLESAUCE
- ¼ CUP FLAXSEEDS
- ½ CUP CHOPPED WALNUTS OR SLIVERED ALMONDS (OPTIONAL)

WHOLE WHEAT CRANBERRY & PECAN BREAD

YIELD: 1 SMALL LOAF / **ACTIVE TIME:** 25 MINUTES / **TOTAL TIME:** 3 HOURS

This is a delicious, dense bread that is especially good toasted and served with fresh butter or cream cheese. It also makes a great complement to soft cheeses when cut into small pieces and served in place of crackers.

1. Put the yeast and sugar in a measuring cup and drizzle in about ½ cup warm water. Hot water will kill the yeast, so it's important that the water be warm without being hot. Cover the measuring cup with plastic wrap and set it aside for about 15 minutes. If the yeast doesn't foam, it is not alive and you'll need to start over.

2. When the yeast is proofed, pour it into a large bowl and add the remaining cup of warm water. Stir gently to combine. Combine the whole wheat flour and the all-purpose flour in a bowl. Add the salt to the flours, and then add the flour mixture to the yeast mixture. Stir with a wooden spoon until combined. The dough will be wet and sticky.

3. Put a dusting of all-purpose flour on a flat surface and lift out the dough. With flour on your hands and more at the ready, begin kneading the dough so that it loses its stickiness. As you're kneading, add in the cranberries and pecans so that they're distributed evenly in the dough. Don't overdo it, and don't use too much flour, just enough that the dough becomes more cohesive, about 5 minutes.

4. Place the dough in a large bowl, cover the bowl with plastic wrap, and allow to rise untouched until it has roughly doubled in size, at least 1 hour and up to several hours. Gently punch it down, score the top with a sharp knife, re-cover with the plastic, and allow to rise again for another 30 minutes or so.

5. While the dough is on its final rise, preheat the oven to 450°F. Put a piece of parchment paper on the bottom of a cast-iron Dutch oven and put it in the oven with the lid on so it gets hot. When the oven is ready and the dough has risen, carefully remove the lid and gently scoop the dough from the bowl into the pot, scored side up. Cover and bake for 15 minutes. Remove the lid and continue to bake for another 15 to 20 minutes, until the top is golden and it sounds hollow when tapped.

6. Remove the pot from the oven and use kitchen towels to carefully remove the bread. Allow to cool before slicing.

INGREDIENTS:

- ¼ TEASPOON INSTANT YEAST
- ¼ TEASPOON SUGAR
- 1½ CUPS WATER (110 TO 115°F)
- 1 TEASPOON KOSHER SALT
- 2 CUPS WHOLE WHEAT FLOUR
- 1 CUP ALL-PURPOSE FLOUR, PLUS MORE FOR DUSTING
- 1 CUP DRIED CRANBERRIES
- 1 CUP PECANS, CHOPPED

BISCUITS

YIELD: 4 TO 6 SERVINGS / ACTIVE TIME: 20 MINUTES / TOTAL TIME: 40 MINUTES

For fluffy buttermilk biscuits, you need to work with a very hot skillet. The golden crust on the bottom is as much of a delight as the airy, warm dough.

1. Preheat oven to 450°F.

2. In a large bowl, combine the flour, sugar, salt, and baking powder.

3. Using a fork or pastry knife, blend in 6 tablespoons of the butter to form a crumbly dough. Form a well in the middle and add ½ cup of the buttermilk. Stir to combine and form a stiff dough. Using your fingers works best! If it seems too dry, add 1 tablespoon more of the buttermilk, going to 2 tablespoons if necessary.

4. Put the remaining butter in a 12-inch cast-iron skillet and put the skillet in the oven.

5. Put the dough on a lightly floured surface and press out to a thickness of about 1 inch. Cut out biscuits using an inverted water glass. Place the biscuits in the skillet and bake for about 10 minutes, until golden on the bottom.

VARIATIONS: Biscuits can be served with savory or sweet additions. You can make miniature ham sandwiches by splitting the biscuits, putting some mayonnaise and grainy mustard on them, and putting in a slice of fresh-baked ham. You can fill them with scrambled eggs and bacon bits. You can slather them with butter and your favorite jam or honey. Or just eat them as is.

INGREDIENTS:

- 2 CUPS ALL-PURPOSE FLOUR, PLUS MORE FOR DUSTING
- 1 TEASPOON SUGAR
- 1 TEASPOON SALT
- 1 TABLESPOON BAKING POWDER
- 1 STICK OF UNSALTED BUTTER, CUT INTO PIECES
- ½ CUP BUTTERMILK, PLUS 2 TABLESPOONS

GLUTEN-FREE BISCUITS

YIELD: 4 TO 6 SERVINGS / **ACTIVE TIME:** 20 MINUTES / **TOTAL TIME:** 40 MINUTES

It is possible to make delicious gluten-free biscuits, though they'll be a bit more crumbly than those made with all-purpose flour.

1. Preheat oven to 450°F.

2. In a large bowl, combine the flours, potato starch, baking powder, maple sugar or syrup, cream of tartar, salt, and xanthan gum. Using a fork or pastry knife, blend in 5 tablespoons of the butter to form a crumbly dough.

3. Form a well in the middle and add ½ cup buttermilk. Stir to combine and form a stiff dough. Using your fingers works best! If it seems too dry, add 1 tablespoon more of the buttermilk, going to 2 tablespoons if necessary.

4. Put the remaining butter in a 12-inch cast-iron skillet and put the skillet in the oven.

5. Put the dough on a lightly floured surface and press out to a thickness of about 1 inch. Cut out biscuits using an inverted water glass. Place the biscuits in the skillet and bake for about 10 minutes, until golden on the bottom.

INGREDIENTS:

- 1½ CUPS RICE FLOUR, PLUS MORE FOR DUSTING
- 3 TABLESPOONS TAPIOCA FLOUR
- ⅓ CUP POTATO STARCH
- 1 TABLESPOON BAKING POWDER
- 1 TABLESPOON MAPLE SUGAR OR MAPLE SYRUP
- 2 TEASPOONS CREAM OF TARTAR
- ¼ TEASPOON SALT
- 1 TEASPOON XANTHAN GUM
- 7 TABLESPOONS UNSALTED BUTTER
- ½ CUP BUTTERMILK, PLUS 2 TABLESPOONS

RUSTIC WHOLE WHEAT BREAD

YIELD: 1 LOAF / ACTIVE TIME: 30 MINUTES / TOTAL TIME: 21 HOURS

Bread making is a delicate art, as the wrong measurements can lead to a flat loaf and a disappointed baker. That being said, this whole wheat masterpiece will leave no one disappointed, especially when it's served while still warm with plenty of farm-fresh butter.

1. Place the flours and water in a large mixing bowl and use your hands to combine the mixture into a dough. Cover the bowl with a kitchen towel and let the mixture set for 45 minutes to 1 hour.

2. Sprinkle the yeast and salt over the dough and fold until they have been incorporated. Cover the bowl with the kitchen towel and let stand for 30 minutes. Remove the towel, fold a corner of the dough into the center, and cover. Repeat every 30 minutes until all of the corners have been folded in.

3. After the last fold, cover the dough with the kitchen towel and let it sit for 12 to 14 hours.

4. Dust a work surface lightly with flour and place the dough on it. Fold each corner of the dough into the center, flip the dough over, and roll it into a smooth ball. Dust your hands with flour as needed. Be careful not to roll or press the dough too hard, as this will prevent the dough from expanding properly. Dust a bowl with flour and place the dough, seam side down, in the bowl. Let stand until it has roughly doubled in size, about 1 hour and 15 minutes.

5. Cut a round piece of parchment paper that is 1" larger than the circumference of your cast-iron Dutch oven. When the dough has approximately 1 hour left in its rise (this is also known as "proofing"), preheat the oven to 475°F and place the covered Dutch oven in the oven as it warms.

6. When the dough has roughly doubled in size, invert it onto a lightly floured work surface. Use a very sharp knife to score one side of the loaf. Using oven mitts, remove the Dutch oven from the oven. Use a bench scraper to transfer the dough onto the piece of parchment, scored side up. Hold the sides of the parchment and carefully lower the dough into the Dutch oven. Cover the Dutch oven and place it in the oven for 20 minutes.

7. Remove the lid and bake the loaf for an additional 20 minutes. Remove from the oven and let cool on a wire rack for at least 2 hours before slicing.

INGREDIENTS:

- 3¼ CUPS ALL-PURPOSE FLOUR, PLUS MORE FOR DUSTING
- 1¼ CUPS WHOLE WHEAT FLOUR
- 1½ CUPS WATER (90°F)
- JUST UNDER ¼ TEASPOON ACTIVE DRY YEAST
- 2¼ TEASPOONS SALT

RUSTIC WHITE BREAD

YIELD: 1 LOAF / ACTIVE TIME: 30 MINUTES / TOTAL TIME: 21 HOURS

Don't be thrown by the "white" in the name. Letting the dough rest overnight allows an incredible amount of flavor to develop, resulting in a loaf that is anything but bland.

1. Place the flour and water in a large mixing bowl and use your hands to combine the mixture into a dough. Cover the bowl with a kitchen towel and let the mixture set for 45 minutes to 1 hour.

2. Sprinkle the yeast and salt over the dough and fold until they have been incorporated. Cover the bowl with the kitchen towel and let stand for 30 minutes. Remove the towel, fold a corner of the dough into the center, and cover. Repeat every 30 minutes until all of the corners have been folded in.

3. After the last fold, cover the dough with the kitchen towel and let it sit for 12 to 14 hours.

4. Dust a work surface lightly with flour and place the dough on it. Fold each corner of the dough to the center, flip the dough over, and roll it into a smooth ball. Dust your hands with flour as needed. Be careful not to roll or press the dough too hard, as this will prevent the dough from expanding properly. Dust a bowl with flour and place the dough, seam side down, in the bowl. Let stand until it has roughly doubled in size, about 1 hour and 15 minutes.

5. Cut a round piece of parchment paper that is 1" larger than the circumference of your cast-iron Dutch oven. When the dough has approximately 1 hour left in its rise (this is also known as "proofing"), preheat the oven to 475°F and place the covered Dutch oven in the oven as it warms.

6. When the dough has roughly doubled in size, invert it onto a lightly floured work surface. Use a very sharp knife to score one side of the loaf. Using oven mitts, remove the Dutch oven from the oven. Use a bench scraper to transfer the dough onto the piece of parchment, scored side up. Hold the sides of the parchment and carefully lower the dough into the Dutch oven. Cover the Dutch oven and place it in the oven for 20 minutes.

7. Remove the lid and bake the loaf for an additional 20 minutes. Remove from the oven and let cool on a wire rack for at least 2 hours before slicing.

INGREDIENTS:

- 4½ CUPS ALL-PURPOSE FLOUR, PLUS MORE FOR DUSTING
- 1½ CUPS WATER (90°F)
- JUST UNDER ¼ TEASPOON ACTIVE DRY YEAST
- 2¼ TEASPOONS SALT

SOURDOUGH BREAD

YIELD: 1 LARGE LOAF / ACTIVE TIME: 20 MINUTES / TOTAL TIME: 30 HOURS

Sourdough is just four ingredients—water, starter, salt, and flour—but it has a complexity that is unmatched. If you have not made real artisan bread before, here is your chance to learn. Be warned: once you try a slice of this bread, you'll never go back to the pre-sliced stuff again.

1. Combine the 1⅔ cups water and the flour in a bowl and stir until no dry clumps remain and the dough has come together slightly. Cover with plastic wrap and let rest for 30 minutes.

2. Add the Sourdough Starter, salt, and the additional teaspoon of water to the dough. Knead for 10 minutes, until the dough is smooth and elastic. Place the dough in a bowl, cover with plastic wrap, and store in a naturally warm place for 4 hours.

3. Place the dough on a flour-dusted work surface and fold the left side of the dough to the right, fold the right side of the dough to the left, and fold the bottom toward the top. Form into a rough ball, return to the bowl, cover with plastic wrap, and let rest for 30 minutes.

4. After 30 minutes, place the ball of dough on a floured surface and repeat the folds made in Step 3. Form the dough into a ball, dust it with flour, and place it in a bowl with the seam facing up. Dust a clean kitchen towel with flour, cover the bowl with it, and place the bowl in the refrigerator overnight.

5. Approximately 2 hours before you are ready to bake the bread, remove it from the refrigerator and allow it to come to room temperature.

6. Preheat oven to 500°F. Place a covered cast-iron Dutch oven in the oven as it warms.

7. When the dough is at room temperature and the oven is ready, remove the Dutch oven from the oven and carefully place the ball of dough into the Dutch oven. Score the top of the dough with a very sharp knife or razor blade, making a long cut across the middle. Cover the Dutch oven, place it in the oven, and bake for 25 minutes.

8. Remove the Dutch oven, lower the oven temperature to 480°F, remove the lid, and bake the bread for another 25 minutes. Remove from the oven and let cool on a wire rack for 2 hours before slicing.

INGREDIENTS:

- 1⅔ CUPS FILTERED WATER (78°F), PLUS 1 TEASPOON
- 5 CUPS BREAD FLOUR, PLUS MORE FOR DUSTING
- ¾ CUP SOURDOUGH STARTER (SEE PAGE 129)
- 1½ TEASPOONS SALT

COUNTRY SOURDOUGH BREAD

YIELD: 1 LARGE LOAF / ACTIVE TIME: 20 MINUTES / TOTAL TIME: 2 DAYS

This sourdough uses a few different flours to give the bread a rustic, wheaty taste. Keep in mind that the hydration level in your levain needs to increase when you bake with whole wheat flour to balance out the additional density.

1. Place the 2¾ cups of the water and the flours in a bowl and mix until incorporated. Cover with plastic wrap and let stand for 1 hour.

2. Add the salt, the levain, and the remaining teaspoon of water to the dough. Transfer the dough to a flour-dusted work surface and knead until the dough is smooth and elastic, about 10 minutes.

3. Place the kneaded dough in a bowl and cover with plastic wrap. Place the bowl in a naturally warm spot and let stand for 4 hours.

4. Transfer the dough to a flour-dusted work surface. Fold the left side of the dough to the right, fold the right side of the dough to the left, and fold the bottom toward the top. Form into a rough ball, return to the bowl, cover with plastic wrap, and let rest for 30 minutes.

5. After 30 minutes, place the ball of dough on a floured surface and repeat the folds made in Step 4. Form the dough into a ball, dust it with flour, and place it in a bowl with the seam facing up. Dust a clean kitchen towel with flour, cover the bowl with it, and place the bowl in the refrigerator overnight.

6. Remove the dough from the refrigerator 2 hours before baking and allow it to come to room temperature.

7. Preheat the oven to 500°F. Place a covered cast-iron Dutch oven in the oven as it warms.

8. When the oven is ready, remove the Dutch oven and carefully place the dough into it. Score the top with a very sharp knife or razor blade, making one long cut across the middle. Cover the Dutch oven and place the bread in the oven.

9. Cook for 25 minutes, remove the Dutch oven, and lower the oven's temperature to 480°F. Remove the Dutch oven's cover, return the bread to the oven, and bake for another 25 minutes, until it sounds hollow when tapped.

10. Remove the bread from the oven, transfer to a wire rack, and allow to cool for 2 hours before slicing.

INGREDIENTS:

- 2¾ CUPS FILTERED WATER (78°F), PLUS 1 TEASPOON
- 4 CUPS BREAD FLOUR, PLUS MORE FOR DUSTING
- 1 CUP WHOLE WHEAT FLOUR
- ½ CUP ORGANIC RYE FLOUR
- 2 TEASPOONS SALT
- 1 CUP COUNTRY SOURDOUGH LEVAIN (SEE RECIPE)

COUNTRY SOURDOUGH LEVAIN

- ½ CUP BREAD FLOUR
- ¼ CUP WHOLE WHEAT FLOUR
- 3⅓ TABLESPOONS ORGANIC RYE FLOUR
- 3 TABLESPOONS SOURDOUGH STARTER (SEE PAGE 129)
- ⅓ CUP FILTERED WATER (85 TO 90°F)

COUNTRY SOURDOUGH LEVAIN

Place the ingredients in a mixing bowl and stir until thoroughly combined. Cover the bowl and let stand at room temperature for 8 hours.

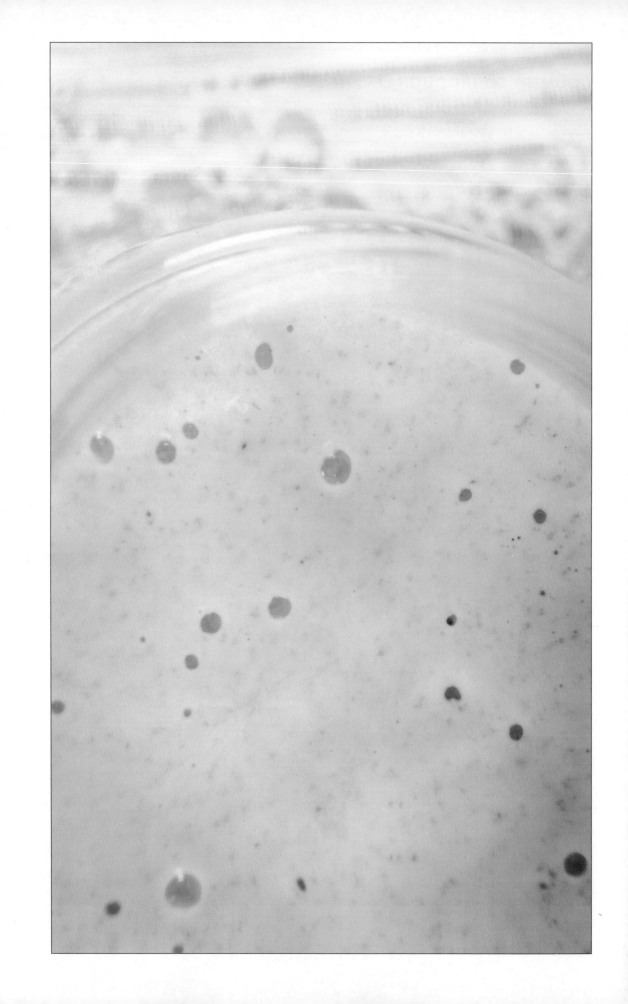

SOURDOUGH STARTER

YIELD: APPROXIMATELY ½ CUP / **ACTIVE TIME:** 1 HOUR / **TOTAL TIME:** 1 WEEK

The success of any sourdough loaf lies in the quality of the starter. While that's a lot of pressure, all you need to handle it is time—the longer the starter has to develop, the more flavor it will impart to the bread.

1. Combine the rye flour and 1 cup of the water in a large mason jar or bowl and stir until thoroughly combined. Put in a dark, naturally warm place and let stand for 24 hours.

2. The next day, discard three-quarters of the mixture. Add 1 cup of the water and 1 cup of the bread flour and stir until thoroughly combined. Let stand for 24 hours.

3. Repeat Step 2 for another 5 days. On the fourth or fifth day, the mixture should start to bubble.

4. After 1 week, you will have a viable sourdough starter. Store the starter in the refrigerator. If you will not be baking bread during a particular week, discard three-quarters of the starter and feed what remains with 1 cup water and 1 cup bread flour. When you are ready to make bread, start bulking up the starter 24 hours ahead of time, adding equal parts bread flour and water every 8 hours.

INGREDIENTS:

1   **CUP ORGANIC RYE FLOUR**

7   **CUPS WATER**

6   **CUPS BREAD FLOUR**

NO-KNEAD BREAD

YIELD: 1 SMALL LOAF / **ACTIVE TIME:** 20 MINUTES / **TOTAL TIME:** 24 HOURS

Use a 7-quart cast-iron Dutch oven for this recipe. This delicious bread is a great way to upgrade a pimento cheese sandwich—there is really nothing easier. Just remember that it takes up to two days to make, so plan ahead!

1. In a large bowl, add the yeast and sugar and top with the warm water. Stir to dissolve the yeast. Cover the measuring cup with plastic wrap and set it aside for about 15 minutes. If the yeast doesn't foam, it is not alive and you'll need to start over.

2. When the yeast is proofed, add the salt and flour. Stir until just blended with the yeast, sugar, and water. The dough will be sticky.

3. Cover the bowl with plastic wrap and set aside for at least 15 hours and up to 18 hours, preferably in a place that's 65 to 70°F.

4. The dough will be bubbly when you go to work with it. Lightly dust a work surface with flour and scoop the dough out onto it. Dust your fingers with flour so they don't stick to the dough. Fold it gently once or twice.

5. Transfer the dough to a clean, room-temperature bowl and cover with a kitchen towel. Let stand until doubled in size, another 1 to 2 hours.

6. While the dough is on its final rise, preheat the oven to 450°F, placing a cast-iron Dutch oven inside with the lid on so it gets hot. When the oven is ready and the dough has risen, carefully remove the lid and gently scoop the dough from the bowl into the Dutch oven. Cover and bake for 20 minutes. Remove the lid and continue to bake for another 25 minutes, until the top is golden and it sounds hollow when tapped.

7. Remove the Dutch oven from the oven and use kitchen towels to carefully transfer bread to a rack or cutting board. Allow to cool at least 20 minutes before serving.

INGREDIENTS:

- ½   **TABLESPOON ACTIVE DRY YEAST**
- ¼   **TEASPOON SUGAR**
- 1½   **CUPS WATER (110 TO 115°F)**
- 1½   **TEASPOONS KOSHER SALT**
- 3   **CUPS ALL-PURPOSE FLOUR, PLUS MORE FOR DUSTING**

GLUTEN-FREE BREAD

YIELD: 1 SMALL LOAF / ACTIVE TIME: 25 MINUTES / TOTAL TIME: 3 HOURS

We are fortunate to live in a time when gluten-free options are numerous. If you love bread and can't or don't want to eat gluten, make this recipe and dig in! You'll be amazed at the result—an equally crusty and fluffy loaf that tastes great.

1. Put the yeast and sugar in a measuring cup and drizzle in about ½ cup warm water. Hot water will kill the yeast, so it's important that the water be warm without being hot. Cover the measuring cup with plastic wrap and set it aside for about 15 minutes. If the yeast doesn't foam, it is not alive and you'll need to start over.

2. When the yeast is proofed, pour it into a large bowl and add remaining warm water. Stir gently to combine. Combine the salt and xanthan gum with the flours, and add the dry mixture to the yeast mixture. Stir with a wooden spoon until combined. Add up to an additional cup of warm water to accommodate the rice flour, which is tackier than regular flour. The dough should be wet and sticky.

3. Put a dusting of flour on a flat surface and lift out the dough. With flour on your hands and more at the ready, begin kneading the dough so that it loses its stickiness. Don't overdo it, and don't use too much flour, just enough that the dough starts to become more cohesive.

4. Place the dough in a large bowl, cover the bowl with plastic wrap, and allow to rise untouched for at least 1 hour and up to several hours. Gently punch it down, re-cover with the plastic, and allow to rise again for another 30 minutes or so.

5. While the dough is on its final rise, preheat the oven to 450°F. Put a piece of parchment paper on the bottom of a cast-iron Dutch oven and put it in the oven with the lid on so it gets hot. When the oven is ready and dough has risen, carefully remove the lid and gently scoop the dough from the bowl into the pot. Cover and bake for 15 minutes. Remove the lid and continue to bake for another 15 to 20 minutes, until the top is golden and it sounds hollow when tapped.

6. Remove the pot from the oven and use kitchen towels to carefully remove the bread. Allow to cool before slicing.

INGREDIENTS:

- ½ TEASPOON INSTANT YEAST
- ¼ TEASPOON SUGAR
- 1½ CUPS WATER (110 TO 115° F), PLUS MORE AS NEEDED
- 1 TEASPOON KOSHER SALT
- 1½ TEASPOONS XANTHAN GUM
- 3 CUPS BOB'S RED MILL GLUTEN-FREE FLOUR, PLUS MORE FOR DUSTING
- ⅓ CUP BOB'S RED MILL SWEET WHITE RICE FLOUR

SIMPLY SENSATIONAL IRISH SODA BREAD

YIELD: 1 LOAF / **ACTIVE TIME:** 30 MINUTES / **TOTAL TIME:** 1 HOUR AND 30 MINUTES

It wouldn't be St. Patrick's Day without Irish soda bread. According to the Culinary Institute of America, "With a history spanning more than two centuries, soda bread is a traditional Irish specialty. The first loaf, consisting of little more than flour, baking soda, salt, and sour milk, made its debut in the mid-1800s when baking soda found its way into Irish kitchens." Make this on a weekend morning when you have some extra time, then have slices of it later in the day with a cup of coffee or tea.

1. Preheat the oven to 450°F.

2. Combine the flour, sugar, salt, baking powder, baking soda, and caraway seeds in a large mixing bowl. Add the beaten eggs and stir to combine. Gradually add the buttermilk until the dough is sticky and messy. Stir in the raisins.

3. Generously butter a 10-inch cast-iron skillet. Scoop and spread the dough in it.

4. Place the skillet in the oven and bake for about 1 hour, until the top is crusty and brown and the bread sounds hollow when tapped. Insert a toothpick in the center to be sure the dough is cooked through; the toothpick should come out clean.

5. Remove from the oven, let cool slightly, and serve with fresh butter and orange marmalade.

INGREDIENTS:

4   CUPS ALL-PURPOSE FLOUR

½   CUP SUGAR

⅛   TEASPOON SALT

3¼   TEASPOONS BAKING POWDER

½   TEASPOON BAKING SODA

2   TABLESPOONS CARAWAY SEEDS

2   LARGE EGGS, LIGHTLY BEATEN

1½   CUPS BUTTERMILK

½   LB. RAISINS

       UNSALTED BUTTER FOR THE SKILLET, PLUS MORE FOR SERVING

       ORANGE MARMALADE, FOR SERVING

CHEESY SODA BREAD *with* CHIVES

YIELD: 1 LOAF / **ACTIVE TIME:** 40 MINUTES / **TOTAL TIME:** 1 HOUR AND 30 MINUTES

If you're looking for a savory version of a simple soda bread to serve with soup or stew, this is a great recipe.

1. Preheat the oven to 350°F.

2. In a large bowl, combine the flours, oats, sugar, baking powder, salt, and baking soda. Whisk to combine thoroughly. In another bowl, combine the butter, buttermilk, and egg.

3. Add the buttermilk mixture to the flour mixture and stir vigorously to blend. The dough will be sticky. Stir in the chives and 1 cup of the grated cheese.

4. Liberally grease a 12-inch cast-iron skillet with butter. Scoop and spread the dough into the skillet. Sprinkle the black pepper over the top, then sprinkle the remaining cheese over it. Using a sharp knife, make an *x* in the center of the dough, about ½-inch deep, to settle the cheese farther into the dough as it cooks.

5. Bake in the oven for about 1 hour and 15 minutes, until golden on top and a toothpick inserted in the center comes out clean. Allow to sit in the skillet for a few minutes before serving.

INGREDIENTS:

3   CUPS ALL-PURPOSE FLOUR

2   CUPS SPELT FLOUR

¾   CUP ROLLED OATS (NOT INSTANT)

2   TABLESPOONS SUGAR

1   TABLESPOON BAKING POWDER

1   TEASPOON SALT

1   TEASPOON BAKING SODA

1   STICK OF BUTTER, MELTED AND COOLED, PLUS MORE FOR THE SKILLET

2½   CUPS BUTTERMILK

1   LARGE EGG, LIGHTLY BEATEN

¼   CUP CHOPPED CHIVES

1¼   CUPS GRATED SHARP WHITE CHEDDAR CHEESE

FRESHLY GROUND BLACK PEPPER, TO TASTE

OLIVE LOAF

YIELD: 1 SMALL LOAF / **ACTIVE TIME:** 25 MINUTES / **TOTAL TIME:** 3 HOURS

The earthy-salty flavor of dark olives like Kalamatas is delicious in bread, too. If you don't want to take the time to slice a lot of Kalamata olives, use a top-shelf tapenade spread, which is easy to distribute in the dough.

1. Put the yeast and sugar in a measuring cup and drizzle in about ½ cup warm water. Hot water will kill the yeast, so it's important that the water be warm without being hot. Cover the measuring cup with plastic wrap and set it aside for about 15 minutes. If the yeast doesn't foam, it is not alive and you'll need to start over.

2. When the yeast is proofed, pour it into a large bowl and add the remaining cup of warm water. Stir gently to combine. Add the salt to the flour and add the dry mixture to the yeast mixture. Stir with a wooden spoon until combined. The dough will be wet and sticky.

3. Put a dusting of flour on a flat surface and lift out the dough. With flour on your hands and more at the ready, begin kneading the dough so that it loses its stickiness. Don't overdo it, and don't use too much flour, just enough that it becomes more cohesive, about 5 minutes. Incorporate the tapenade or olive pieces while you're kneading.

4. Place the dough in a large bowl, cover the bowl with plastic wrap, and allow to rise untouched for at least 1 hour and up to several hours, until doubled in size. Gently punch it down, re-cover with the plastic, and allow to rise again for another 30 minutes or so. Brush with the olive oil.

5. While the dough is on its final rise, preheat the oven to 450°F. Put a piece of parchment paper on the bottom of a cast-iron Dutch oven and put it in the oven with the lid on so it gets hot. When the oven is ready and the dough has risen, carefully remove the lid and gently scoop the dough from the bowl into the pot. Cover and bake for 15 minutes. Remove the lid and continue to bake for another 15 to 20 minutes, until the top is golden and it sounds hollow when tapped.

6. Remove the pot from the oven and use kitchen towels to carefully remove the bread from the Dutch oven. Let the loaf cool completely before slicing.

INGREDIENTS:

¼	TEASPOON INSTANT YEAST
¼	TEASPOON SUGAR
1½	CUPS WATER (110 TO 115°F)
1	TEASPOON KOSHER SALT
3	CUPS ALL-PURPOSE FLOUR, PLUS MORE FOR DUSTING
½	CUP TAPENADE OR KALAMATA OLIVES
1	TABLESPOON OLIVE OIL

BEER & CHEESE BREAD

YIELD: 1 LOAF / **ACTIVE TIME:** 15 MINUTES / **TOTAL TIME:** 1 HOUR AND 15 MINUTES

When you bake in cast-iron cookware, you end up with a beautiful golden crust. This quick, earthy bread should be slathered in honey and butter.

1. Preheat the oven to 400°F and lightly grease a 10-inch cast-iron skillet with the melted butter.

2. Place the flour, green onions, sugar, baking powder, salt, and dried parsley in a large bowl and stir to combine. Add the cheese and stir to incorporate, making sure it is coated with flour and not clumped together.

3. Add the beer and stir until just combined, taking care to not overmix.

4. Pour the dough into the greased skillet and smooth the top with a rubber spatula. Place in the oven and bake for 30 minutes, while rotating the pan once or twice.

5. Remove from the oven and let cool for 30 minutes before slicing.

INGREDIENTS:

1	TABLESPOON UNSALTED BUTTER, MELTED
3	CUPS ALL-PURPOSE FLOUR
1	CUP CHOPPED GREEN ONIONS
3	TABLESPOONS SUGAR
4	TEASPOONS BAKING POWDER
1½	TEASPOONS SALT
1	TABLESPOON DRIED PARSLEY
2	CUPS GRATED CHEDDAR CHEESE
1½	CUPS LAGER OR LIGHTER ALE

DINNER ROLLS

YIELD: 12 ROLLS / ACTIVE TIME: 1 HOUR / TOTAL TIME: 3 HOURS

These classic dinner rolls are light, flaky, buttery perfection. It's important to proof the yeast before adding it to your recipe to ensure that it is fresh and active. If it is, it reacts with the sugar and liquid and creates tiny bubbles. It also releases a smell that is described (appropriately enough) as "yeasty"—the aroma of fresh-baked bread. Yeast consumes sugar and releases carbon dioxide and, eventually, alcohol. This is the basis of making beer and wine, too. But in baking, the fermentation process stops when the live cells are cooked in the oven.

1. In a small bowl, combine ½ cup warm milk and the sugar. Sprinkle the yeast over it, stir, and set aside so the yeast can proof (about 10 minutes).

2. While the yeast is proofing, melt the butter in a 12-inch cast-iron skillet over medium-low heat, and remove from heat when melted.

3. When the yeast mix is frothy, stir in 3 tablespoons of the melted butter, the remaining milk, the salt, and the eggs. Then stir in the flour, mixing until all ingredients are incorporated. Transfer to a lightly floured surface and knead the dough for 5 to 10 minutes, until it is soft, springy, and elastic.

4. Coat the bottom and sides of a large mixing bowl (ceramic is best) with butter. Place the ball of dough in the bowl, cover loosely with plastic wrap, put it in a naturally warm, draft-free location, and let it rise until doubled in size, about 45 minutes to 1 hour.

5. Prepare a lightly floured surface to work on. Punch down the dough in the bowl and transfer it to the floured surface. Warm the skillet containing the butter so that it is melted again.

6. Break off pieces of the dough and shape them into 2-inch balls with your hands. Roll the balls in the butter in the skillet, and leave them in the skillet.

7. Cover the skillet loosely with a clean kitchen towel, put it in the warm, draft-free spot, and let the rolls rise until doubled in size, about 30 minutes. While they're rising, preheat the oven to 350°F.

8. When the rolls have risen and the oven is ready, cover the skillet with aluminum foil and bake in the oven for 20 minutes. Remove the foil and finish cooking, another 15 minutes or so, until the rolls are golden on top and light and springy. Serve warm.

INGREDIENTS:

- 1¼ CUPS WHOLE MILK, HEATED TO 110°F
- 3 TABLESPOONS SUGAR
- 1 TABLESPOON ACTIVE DRY YEAST
- 1 STICK OF UNSALTED BUTTER
- ¾ TEASPOON SALT
- 2 EGGS, AT ROOM TEMPERATURE AND LIGHTLY BEATEN
- 3½ CUPS CAKE OR BREAD FLOUR (NOT ALL-PURPOSE FLOUR), PLUS MORE FOR DUSTING

GARLIC KNOTS

YIELD: ABOUT 36 KNOTS / ACTIVE TIME: 45 MINUTES / TOTAL TIME: 1 HOUR AND 30 MINUTES

The knots will get that great cast-iron crust when they bake, then they can be bathed in garlic-parsley butter and put on a plate. Don't expect them to hang around for long, which is why this is a double batch of dough.

1. To prepare the sauce, melt the butter in a saucepan over medium heat. Add the garlic and reduce heat to medium-low. Allow to cook, stirring occasionally, for about 3 minutes. This takes some of the pungency out of the garlic and also infuses the butter with the flavor. Stir in the parsley and salt.

2. To prepare the knots, place the warm water and yeast in a large bowl and gently stir. When the mixture starts to foam, stir in the flour and salt and mix until the dough is just combined. It will be sticky.

3. Turn the dough out on a floured surface and start kneading until the flour is incorporated, adding more if necessary to make the dough malleable and smooth but not overdone.

4. Lightly grease a bowl and put the dough in it. Allow to rise until doubled in size, about an hour. Preheat the oven to 450°F.

5. Transfer to a lightly floured surface and push and stretch the dough into a large rectangle. If it resists, let it rest before stretching it further. Cut the rectangle into strips, and tie the strips into knots. Spread the olive oil over the bottom of a 12-inch cast-iron skillet. Tuck the knots into the skillet so they are slightly separated. Bake for about 15 minutes, until golden brown.

6. When the garlic knots come out of the oven, place a kitchen towel over your hand to pull them off the skillet into a large mixing bowl. Scoop a large spoonful of the garlic-parsley sauce over the knots and toss to coat, adding a bit more if necessary. Use another spoon to transfer the coated knots to a plate.

7. Continue to work in batches in the skillet until the dough is used up, or save the remaining dough in the refrigerator for up to 3 days. The sauce can also be refrigerated for several days and reheated. If desired, sprinkle grated Parmesan on top before serving.

INGREDIENTS:

FOR THE SAUCE

- 1 STICK OF UNSALTED BUTTER
- 8 GARLIC CLOVES, MINCED
- ⅓ CUP MINCED PARSLEY LEAVES
- 2 TEASPOONS SALT

FOR THE KNOTS

- 1½ CUPS WATER (110 TO 115°F)
- 2 TEASPOONS ACTIVE DRY YEAST
- 4 CUPS ALL-PURPOSE FLOUR, PLUS MORE FOR DUSTING
- 2 TEASPOONS SALT
- 1 TABLESPOON OLIVE OIL

  PARMESAN CHEESE, GRATED, FOR GARNISH (OPTIONAL)

YORKSHIRE PUDDING

YIELD: 4 TO 6 SERVINGS / **ACTIVE TIME:** 30 MINUTES / **TOTAL TIME:** 1 HOUR

This incredible treat is like a savory popover. It's traditionally served with roast beef and is in fact made with the juices from the meat. Begin your preparation about an hour before the roast beef will be ready, as the batter needs to sit for a while. If you want to make this delicious side dish but you're not having roast beef, you can substitute ½ cup melted butter for the drippings. Butter's smoking point is lower than the drippings, so keep an eye on the skillet as it heats up in the oven. The butter will be sizzling before long.

1. Preheat the oven to 400°F or increase the temperature when you take your roast beef out of the oven.

2. In a large bowl, mix the flour and salt together with a whisk. Make a well in the center of the flour, add the milk, and whisk until blended. Next, beat the eggs into the batter until thoroughly combined. Add the water, stir this in thoroughly, and set the batter aside for about 1 hour.

3. When your roast beef comes out of the oven, pour off ½ cup of drippings and put them in a 12-inch cast-iron skillet. Put the skillet in the oven and let the drippings get very hot so that they sizzle. Stir the batter while you're waiting so it's blended. Remove the skillet from the oven, pour the batter in, and return the skillet to the oven immediately.

4. Bake for about 30 minutes, or until the sides have risen and are gently browned.

5. Bring to the table where the roast beef awaits and serve with extra juices on the side.

INGREDIENTS:

1½ CUPS ALL-PURPOSE FLOUR

¾ TEASPOON SALT

¾ CUP WHOLE MILK, AT ROOM TEMPERATURE

3 LARGE EGGS, AT ROOM TEMPERATURE

¾ CUP WATER, AT ROOM TEMPERATURE

½ CUP BEEF TALLOW OR LARD

MUSHROOM, SPINACH & LEEK GALETTE

YIELD: 4 TO 6 SERVINGS / **ACTIVE TIME:** 30 MINUTES / **TOTAL TIME:** 1 HOUR AND 30 MINUTES

Caramelized leeks are even sweeter than onions and make a great complement to the earthy mushrooms and bright spinach that top this galette.

1. Preheat the oven to 375°F.

2. In a 10-inch cast-iron skillet, melt 2 tablespoons of the butter over medium heat and add the leeks. Cook, while stirring, until the leeks soften, about 2 minutes. Add the remaining 2 tablespoons of butter and the mushrooms, and stir to combine. Allow to cook over low heat, stirring occasionally, until the mushrooms are soft and the leeks are caramelized, about 10 minutes.

3. Raise heat to medium and add the baby spinach, stirring as the leaves wilt. When wilted, remove the skillet from heat. Transfer the vegetables to a bowl but leave the melted butter in the skillet.

4. On a lightly floured surface, roll out the crust so that it is about 1 inch larger than the bottom of the pan and lay the pastry crust in the pan.

5. Place the vegetable mixture in the center. Fold the extra crust over the filling. Sprinkle with Parmesan cheese and brush the crust with the half-and-half.

6. Put the skillet in the oven and bake for 20 to 30 minutes, until the crust is golden and puffy.

INGREDIENTS:

- 4   TABLESPOONS UNSALTED BUTTER
- 2   LEEKS, WHITE AND LIGHT GREEN PARTS ONLY, SLICED THIN AND RINSED WELL
- 1½   CUPS MUSHROOMS, SLICED
- 4   CUPS BABY SPINACH LEAVES
- 1   FLAKY PASTRY CRUST (SEE PAGE 580)
-   ALL-PURPOSE FLOUR, FOR DUSTING
- ½   CUP GRATED PARMESAN CHEESE
- 1   TABLESPOON HALF-AND-HALF

BEET & RICOTTA TART

YIELD: 4 TO 6 SERVINGS / **ACTIVE TIME:** 45 MINUTES / **TOTAL TIME:** 1 HOUR AND 30 MINUTES

I f you want to impress some lunch guests—or yourself, for that matter—make this beautiful tart. The flavors combine beautifully, and the deep red color is nice to look at.

1. Preheat the oven to 400°F.

2. Put the beet pieces in a large piece of aluminum foil. Drizzle with 1 tablespoon of olive oil. Bake for 30 to 40 minutes, until the beets are soft. Carefully remove from the oven, open the foil packet so that the beets cool, and reduce the temperature in the oven to 350°F.

3. In a skillet other than the cast-iron, heat the remaining tablespoon of the olive oil over medium heat, add the leeks, and cook, while stirring, until the leeks are soft and slightly caramelized, about 5 minutes. Set half of the leeks aside and add almost all the spinach, arugula, or radicchio to the pan, reserving some for the top. Cook over low heat, while stirring occasionally, for about 8 minutes. Drizzle the balsamic vinegar over the mixture about halfway through.

4. In a bowl, combine the ricotta, Parmesan, and egg, mixing well. Stir in the beets and the leek mixture, and season with salt and pepper.

5. On a lightly floured surface, roll out the crust so that it fits in a 12-inch cast-iron skillet. Melt the butter in the skillet, remove from heat, and lay the pastry crust in the pan. If desired, crimp the edge of the crust.

6. Place the ricotta-and-vegetable mixture in the center, leaving about an inch of crust along the outside. Brush the crust with half-and-half.

7. Put the skillet in the oven and bake for 25 to 30 minutes, until the crust is just golden.

8. Remove, top with the reserved spinach, arugula, or radicchio, and continue to bake for another 10 to 15 minutes, until the greens have wilted.

INGREDIENTS:

1   LARGE BEET, PEELED AND CHOPPED

2   TABLESPOONS OLIVE OIL

2   LEEKS, WHITE AND LIGHT GREEN PARTS ONLY, SLICED THIN AND RINSED WELL

3   CUPS SPINACH, ARUGULA, OR CHOPPED RADICCHIO

1   TABLESPOON BALSAMIC VINEGAR

1   CUP WHOLE MILK RICOTTA CHEESE

¼   CUP GRATED PARMESAN CHEESE

1   EGG

      SALT AND PEPPER, TO TASTE

1   FLAKY PASTRY CRUST (SEE PAGE 580)

1   TABLESPOON UNSALTED BUTTER

1   TABLESPOON HALF-AND-HALF

TOMATO, GOAT CHEESE & BASIL TART

YIELD: 4 TO 6 SERVINGS / **ACTIVE TIME:** 30 MINUTES / **TOTAL TIME:** 1 HOUR AND 30 MINUTES

If you want to throw together an elegant and easy-to-prepare tart that celebrates summer, this is it. Use a variety of tomatoes to add color and visual appeal, as the slice sizes will be different, too.

1. Preheat the oven to 350°F.

2. Put the tomato slices on a paper towel–lined plate, and sprinkle with the salt. Let the salt sit on the tomatoes for about 15 minutes, and then turn the slices over.

3. In a 12-inch cast-iron skillet, heat the olive oil over medium heat and add the onion. Cook, while stirring, until the onion is lightly browned, about 3 minutes. Season with salt and pepper. Transfer the onion to a bowl, but keep the oil in the skillet.

4. On a lightly floured surface, roll out the crust so that it is just larger than the bottom of the skillet and lay the pastry crust in the pan. If desired, crimp the edges.

5. Spread the onion over the bottom of the crust and dot with the goat cheese. Arrange the tomato slices so that they cover the bottom. Sprinkle with the crumbled feta or Parmesan-Romano blend. Drizzle lightly with olive oil.

6. Put the skillet in the oven and bake for 20 minutes. Increase the heat to 400°F and bake for an additional 10 minutes, until the top of the tart is toasted.

7. While tart is still warm, sprinkle the shredded basil leaves over the top.

INGREDIENTS:

- 1½ LBS. TOMATOES, SEEDED AND SLICED ¼-INCH THICK
- 1 TABLESPOON KOSHER SALT
- 2 TABLESPOONS OLIVE OIL, PLUS MORE FOR DRIZZLING
- 1 VIDALIA ONION, SLICED THIN
- SALT AND FRESHLY GROUND BLACK PEPPER, TO TASTE
- 1 FLAKY PASTRY CRUST (SEE PAGE 580)
- 1 CUP GOAT CHEESE
- ½ CUP CRUMBLED FETA CHEESE OR A BLEND OF GRATED PARMESAN & ROMANO
- 10 BASIL LEAVES, SHREDDED

FIG, PROSCIUTTO & CAMEMBERT TART

YIELD: 4 TO 6 SERVINGS / **ACTIVE TIME:** 45 MINUTES / **TOTAL TIME:** 1 HOUR AND 30 MINUTES

It's important to remain alert once you pop this tart into the oven, as the delicate figs will lose their flavor if overcooked.

1. Preheat the oven to 400°F.

2. Place a skillet other than the cast-iron over medium heat, heat the olive oil, and add the onion. Cook and stir until the onion is lightly browned, about 3 minutes. Add the prosciutto slices to the skillet and cook, while stirring, for an additional minute. Remove the skillet from heat.

3. Working on a flour-dusted surface, roll out the crust so it is just just slightly larger than the bottom of a 10-inch cast-iron skillet. Place the crust in the skillet, spread the Dijon mustard evenly over the bottom of the crust, and top with the onion-and-prosciutto mix.

4. Cut the Camembert into ¼-inch-thick wedges and distribute them evenly over the onion mix. Next place the fig halves over the cheese. Make sure you don't overcrowd.

5. In a small bowl, whisk together the balsamic vinegar and honey. Drizzle the sauce over the tart.

6. Put the skillet in the oven and bake for 20 to 25 minutes, until the cheese is melted and the figs have softened. Remove from the oven and let cool. Top with the arugula, garnish with the crumbled goat cheese, and serve.

INGREDIENTS:

2   TABLESPOONS OLIVE OIL

½   ONION, SLICED THIN

½   LB. PROSCIUTTO, CUT INTO 1-INCH SLICES

     ALL-PURPOSE FLOUR, FOR DUSTING

1   FLAKY PASTRY CRUST (SEE PAGE 580)

1   TABLESPOON DIJON MUSTARD

1   ROUND OF CAMEMBERT, AT ROOM TEMPERATURE

6-8   FRESH FIGS, STEMMED AND HALVED

3   TABLESPOONS AGED BALSAMIC VINEGAR

1   TABLESPOON HONEY

¼   CUP ARUGULA

¼   CUP CRUMBLED GOAT CHEESE, FOR GARNISH

FOCACCIA

YIELD: 4 TO 6 SERVINGS / **ACTIVE TIME:** 1 HOUR AND 30 MINUTES / **TOTAL TIME:** 3 HOURS

This is essentially a raised flatbread—like a crustier pizza—to which all kinds of yummy things can be added. It's become synonymous with Italian cuisine, and it's certainly popular in Italy, but it's also made throughout the Mediterranean region. You can find it in grocery stores, but there's nothing like a fresh piece right out of the skillet, still warm, with the exact toppings you want. This one is simple, as it needs nothing more than salt and some Parmesan cheese.

1. Proof the yeast by mixing it with the warm water. Let sit for 10 minutes until foamy.

2. In a bowl, combine the flour, salt, and yeast mix. Stir to combine. Transfer to a lightly floured surface and knead the dough until it loses its stickiness, adding more flour as needed, about 10 minutes.

3. Coat the bottom and sides of a large mixing bowl (ceramic is best) with a tablespoon of the olive oil. Place the ball of dough in the bowl, cover loosely with plastic wrap, put it in a naturally warm, draft-free location, and let it rise until doubled in size, about 45 minutes to 1 hour.

4. Preheat the oven to 450°F.

5. When doubled in size, turn the dough out onto a lightly floured surface and divide it in half. Put a tablespoon of the olive oil in a 12-inch cast-iron skillet, and press one of the pieces of dough into it. Drizzle some olive oil over it and sprinkle with salt and pepper, then with Parmesan. Cover loosely with plastic wrap and let rise for about 20 minutes. With the other piece, press it out onto a piece of parchment paper, follow the same procedure to top it, and let it rise.

6. Put the skillet on the middle rack of the oven and bake for 25 to 30 minutes, until golden brown. Remove from oven and let rest for 5 minutes before removing from skillet to cool further. Wipe any crumbs off the skillet, coat with more olive oil, and transfer the other round to the skillet. Bake for about 25 minutes, remove from skillet, and let cool.

7. If desired, you can put the extra dough in a plastic bag and store it in the refrigerator for up to 3 days to use later.

INGREDIENTS:

1	PACKET OF ACTIVE DRY YEAST (2¼ TEASPOONS)
2	CUPS WATER (110 TO 115°F)
4-4½	CUPS ALL-PURPOSE FLOUR, PLUS MORE FOR DUSTING
2	TEASPOONS SALT
2	TABLESPOONS OLIVE OIL, PLUS MORE FOR DRIZZLING
	SEA SALT AND FRESHLY GROUND BLACK PEPPER, TO TASTE
	PARMESAN CHEESE, GRATED, FOR TOPPING

CARAMELIZED ONION & LEEK FOCACCIA

YIELD: 4 TO 6 SERVINGS / ACTIVE TIME: 2 HOURS / TOTAL TIME: 3 HOURS

Caramelized onions, when sautéed in butter and oil until soft and browned, lose their bite and are transformed into something almost sweet. The addition of leeks makes for a more subtle and slightly sweeter topping.

1. In a 12-inch cast-iron skillet, add the butter and 2 tablespoons of oil and warm over medium-low heat. When the butter is melted, add the onion and leek slices. Increase the heat to medium-high and cook, while stirring, until the onion and leek start to soften, about 5 minutes. Reduce heat to low and allow to cook, stirring occasionally, until cooked down and browned, about 10 to 15 minutes. Set aside.

2. Proof the yeast by mixing it with the warm water. Let sit for 10 minutes until foamy.

3. Combine the flour, kosher salt, and pepper, and stir into the yeast mixture. Stir to combine well. The dough will be sticky. Transfer to a floured surface and knead the dough until it loses its stickiness, adding more flour as needed, about 10 minutes.

4. Coat the bottom and sides of a large mixing bowl (ceramic is best) with a tablespoon of the olive oil. Place the ball of dough in the bowl, cover loosely with plastic wrap, put it in a naturally warm, draft-free location, and let it rise until doubled in size, about 45 minutes to 1 hour.

5. Preheat the oven to 450°F.

6. Put the remaining olive oil in the skillet, and press the dough into it. Top with the caramelized onion/leek mix. Season generously with sea salt and pepper, then with Parmesan cheese. Cover loosely with plastic wrap and let rise for about 20 minutes.

7. Remove the plastic wrap, put the skillet on the middle rack of the oven, and bake for 25 to 30 minutes, until golden brown. Remove from oven and let rest for 5 minutes before removing from skillet to cool further.

INGREDIENTS:

1	STICK OF UNSALTED BUTTER
¼	CUP OLIVE OIL
1	YELLOW ONION, SLICED THIN
1	LARGE LEEK, WHITE AND LIGHT GREEN PARTS ONLY, SLICED THIN, AND RINSED WELL
1	TEASPOON ACTIVE DRY YEAST
1	CUP WATER (110 TO 115°F)
2-2½	CUPS ALL-PURPOSE FLOUR, PLUS MORE FOR DUSTING
1	TEASPOON KOSHER SALT
1	TEASPOON FRESHLY GROUND BLACK PEPPER, PLUS MORE FOR TOPPING
	SEA SALT, FOR TOPPING
	PARMESAN CHEESE, GRATED, FOR TOPPING

SPINACH & RICOTTA CALZONE

YIELD: 4 TO 6 SERVINGS / ACTIVE TIME: 1 HOUR / TOTAL TIME: 2 HOURS

This pizza "pie" is gooey with cheese and plenty of lovely green spinach. If you want to spice this up, try some red pepper flakes, either in the calzone or on the side.

1. To make the filling, place the olive oil, garlic, and red pepper flakes, if using, in a 12-inch cast-iron skillet over medium-high heat. Add the frozen spinach. Cook, while stirring, until the spinach is completely thawed, about 5 minutes.

2. Reduce heat to medium-low and cover, stirring occasionally, until the spinach is cooked through, another 15 minutes. Season with salt and pepper. Set aside but do not refrigerate. In a bowl, mix together the ricotta, egg, and Parmesan cheese.

3. To make the dough, combine the warm water and yeast in a large bowl, stirring to dissolve the yeast. When the mixture starts to foam, stir in the flour and salt and mix until the dough is just combined. It will be sticky.

4. Turn the dough out on a floured surface and start kneading until the flour is incorporated, adding more if necessary to make the dough malleable and smooth but not overdone.

5. Lightly grease a bowl and put the dough in it. Allow to rise while you prepare the filling and preheat the oven, about 30 minutes.

6. Preheat the oven to 400°F.

7. On a lightly floured surface, turn out the dough and separate it into two equal pieces. Roll each piece into a 12-inch circle.

8. Place one circle in the skillet. The dough should extend about halfway up the side. Spread the cooked spinach mixture evenly over the dough, then dollop with the ricotta mixture. Use a spatula or the back of a large spoon to distribute the ricotta mixture. Place the other dough circle over the filling and crimp to seal the edges together with your fingers. Cut 4 slits in the top.

9. Bake for 25 minutes, until the crust is a lovely golden brown. Use pot holders or oven mitts to remove the skillet. Allow to cool for about 10 minutes before slicing and serving.

INGREDIENTS:

FOR THE FILLING

- 2 TABLESPOONS OLIVE OIL
- 3 GARLIC CLOVES, MINCED
- 1 TEASPOON RED PEPPER FLAKES (OPTIONAL)
- 1 LB. FROZEN CHOPPED SPINACH
- SALT AND PEPPER, TO TASTE
- 2 CUPS FRESH RICOTTA CHEESE
- 1 EGG, LIGHTLY BEATEN
- ½ CUP GRATED PARMESAN CHEESE

FOR THE DOUGH

- 1½ CUPS WATER (110 TO 115°F)
- 2 TEASPOONS ACTIVE DRY YEAST
- 4 CUPS ALL-PURPOSE FLOUR, PLUS MORE FOR DUSTING
- 2 TEASPOONS SALT

PEPPERONI BREAD

YIELD: 6 TO 8 SERVINGS / **ACTIVE TIME:** 1 HOUR / **TOTAL TIME:** 3 HOURS

This is a favorite during football season, since the game hasn't actually started until this makes an appearance in front of the TV. Start in the morning for an afternoon game, as the dough needs to rise several times.

1. Proof the yeast by mixing it with the water and sugar in a large bowl and then stirring. Let sit until foamy, about 10 minutes. Add the salt and about half the flour to form a sticky dough. Cover the bowl with plastic wrap or a clean kitchen towel and let rise in a warm, draft-free place until it has doubled in size, about 1 hour.

2. Punch down the dough and add the remaining flour. Transfer to a floured surface and knead the dough until it's smooth and elastic, 8 to 10 minutes. Transfer to a lightly greased bowl and let sit for about 15 minutes.

3. On the floured surface, roll the dough out into a rectangle about 14 x 16 inches. Sprinkle with salt and pepper, spread the pieces of pepperoni around the dough, then the cheese, and top with a sprinkling of hot pepper flakes, oregano, and garlic powder. Roll up so that the dough maintains its length and then slice the roll into 6 or 8 rounds.

4. Grease a 10-inch cast-iron skillet with the butter and place the rounds in it. Cover with a clean kitchen towel and let them rise for about 1 hour. Preheat the oven to 375°F.

5. Bake the pepperoni bread for about 30 minutes, until golden on top and bubbling in the center. Serve immediately.

VARIATION: It's easy to make this into a full-blown meat lover's bread. In addition to the pepperoni, add about ¼ to ½ cup of any or each of diced pancetta, diced smoked ham, crumbled cooked bacon, sautéed sausage, or diced cooked meatballs.

INGREDIENTS:

1½   TEASPOONS ACTIVE DRY YEAST

1¼   CUPS WATER (110 TO 115°F)

1   TABLESPOON SUGAR

1½   TEASPOONS SALT, PLUS MORE TO TASTE

3½   CUPS ALL-PURPOSE FLOUR, PLUS MORE FOR DUSTING

    PEPPER, TO TASTE

½   LB. PEPPERONI, SLIVERED

2   CUPS GRATED MOZZARELLA CHEESE

1   TEASPOON RED PEPPER FLAKES

1   TEASPOON DRIED OREGANO

1   TEASPOON GARLIC POWDER

1   TABLESPOON UNSALTED BUTTER, MELTED

PIZZA DOUGH

YIELD: 2 BALLS OF DOUGH / ACTIVE TIME: 30 MINUTES / TOTAL TIME: 1 HOUR

This is bread making at its simplest: flour, water, salt, and yeast. With this super-easy recipe, you can create amazing pizzas that can be personalized with almost anything you have in the refrigerator or pantry, from traditional cheese to "gourmet." And while the flavor will become more complex and the crust crispier if you allow the dough to rise for a couple of hours (or up to 3 days in the refrigerator), you can also roll it out and bake it within 15 minutes of making it.

1. If you'll be making pizza within the hour, preheat the oven to 450°F.

2. In a large bowl, add the warm water and yeast, stirring to dissolve the yeast. When the mixture starts to foam, stir in the flour and salt and mix until the dough is just combined. It will be sticky.

3. Turn out on a floured surface and start kneading until the flour is incorporated, adding more if necessary to make the dough malleable and smooth but not overdone.

4. If cooking immediately, allow the dough to rest for 15 minutes. While it's doing so, put a 10-inch cast-iron skillet in the oven. Prepare the toppings for the pizza. If preparing ahead of time, place dough in the refrigerator for up to 3 days.

5. After 15 minutes, or when ready, put a piece of parchment paper under the dough. Start rolling and pushing it out to form a 9-inch round that will fit in the skillet. If it bounces back, let it rest before pushing or rolling it out again.

6. When the round is formed, remove the skillet from the oven. Add the olive oil and brush to distribute over the bottom. Transfer the dough to the skillet and add the toppings.

7. Bake for 12 to 15 minutes, until the crust starts to brown and the toppings are hot and bubbling. Remove and allow to cool for 5 minutes before lifting or sliding the pizza out and serving.

INGREDIENTS:

¾ CUP WATER (110 TO 115°F)

1 TEASPOON ACTIVE DRY YEAST

2 CUPS ALL-PURPOSE FLOUR, PLUS MORE FOR DUSTING

1½ TEASPOONS SALT

1 TABLESPOON OLIVE OIL

CLASSIC CORN BREAD

YIELD: 4 TO 6 SERVINGS / **ACTIVE TIME:** 1 HOUR / **TOTAL TIME:** 3 TO 4 HOURS

If you're going to make bread in a cast-iron skillet, you have to make corn bread. In fact, many restaurants now serve corn bread right in a cast-iron pan.

1. In a large bowl, combine the cornmeal, sugar, salt, and boiling water. Stir to combine and let sit for several hours in a cool, dark place or overnight in the refrigerator. Stir occasionally while the batter is resting.

2. When ready to make, preheat oven to 450°F.

3. Add flour, the 1 tablespoon of melted butter, eggs, baking powder, baking soda, and milk to the batter. Stir to thoroughly combine.

4. Heat the skillet over medium-high heat and melt the teaspoon of butter in it. Add the batter.

5. Transfer the skillet to the oven and cook for 15 minutes.

6. Reduce the heat to 250°F and cook another 40 minutes, or until the bread is golden brown on top and set in the center.

INGREDIENTS:

4   CUPS FINELY GROUND YELLOW CORNMEAL

¾   CUP SUGAR

1   TABLESPOON SALT

4   CUPS BOILING WATER

1   CUP ALL-PURPOSE FLOUR

1   TABLESPOON UNSALTED BUTTER, MELTED, PLUS 1 TEASPOON

2   EGGS, LIGHTLY BEATEN

2   TEASPOONS BAKING POWDER

1   TEASPOON BAKING SODA

1   CUP WHOLE MILK

CORN TORTILLAS

YIELD: 20 TORTILLAS / **ACTIVE TIME:** 50 MINUTES / **TOTAL TIME:** 50 MINUTES

You really should be making your own corn tortillas, as a warm tortilla lifted straight from a cast-iron griddle or skillet is a thing of beauty. The main ingredient, masa harina, is a corn flour that is available in most grocery stores.

1. Place the masa harina and salt in a bowl and stir to combine. Slowly add the warm water and oil (or lard) and stir until they are incorporated and a soft dough forms. The dough should be quite soft and not at all sticky. If it is too dry, add more water. If the dough is too wet, add more masa harina.

2. Wrap the dough in plastic (or place it in a resealable bag) and let it rest at room temperature for 30 minutes. It can be stored in the refrigerator for up to 24 hours; just be careful not to let it dry out.

3. Cut a 16-inch piece of plastic wrap and lay half of it across the bottom plate of a tortilla press.

4. Place a large cast-iron griddle across two burners and warm over high heat.

5. Pinch off a small piece of the dough and roll it into a ball. Place in the center of the lined tortilla press, fold the plastic over the top of the dough, and press down the top plate to flatten the dough. Do not use too much force. If the tortilla is too thin, you will have a hard time getting it off of the plastic. Open the press and carefully peel off the disk of dough. Reset the plastic.

6. Place the disk on the hot, dry griddle and toast for 30 to 45 seconds. Flip over and cook for another minute. Remove from the griddle and set aside. Repeat the process with the remaining dough.

INGREDIENTS:

- 2 **CUPS MASA HARINA, PLUS MORE AS NEEDED**
- ½ **TEASPOON SALT**
- 1 **CUP WARM WATER (110°F), PLUS MORE AS NEEDED**
- 2 **TABLESPOONS VEGETABLE OIL OR MELTED LARD**

ETHIOPIAN INJERA

YIELD: 1 INJERA / ACTIVE TIME: 1 HOUR / TOTAL TIME: 3 DAYS

If you've ever eaten at an Ethiopian restaurant, you know that the centerpiece of the meal is a thick, spongy bread that's placed in the middle of the table. The dishes go around it, and you eat by ripping apart the bread and scooping up the other foods. You can use it as almost a polenta or spongy pizza crust, topping it with whatever leftovers you want. While the ingredients are minimal, you have to plan ahead for the day you want to serve the injera, as the "flour" needs to sit for several days to break down the grain.

1. Proof the yeast by mixing with the warm water. Let sit for about 10 minutes until foamy.

2. Put the ground teff in a bowl and add the yeast mixture. Mix thoroughly until a stiff dough forms. Put a kitchen towel over the bowl and stick it in a draft-free, fairly warm place in your kitchen. Let it sit for 2 to 3 days. It will bubble, turn brown, and smell sour.

3. When ready to make the injera, add salt to the mix until some of the sour "bite" has dissipated. The mixture should resemble pancake batter.

4. Place a 10-inch cast-iron skillet over medium heat and brush with vegetable oil. Pour enough batter on the pan to coat the bottom. You want it to be thinner than a pancake but thicker than a crepe. Tilt to spread the batter over the bottom of the skillet. Cook until holes form in the bread and the edges crisp up and lift away from the pan. The bread should not be flipped, so be sure to let it cook thoroughly.

5. When cooked, lift it out with a spatula and put it on a plate or platter to cool. Place plastic wrap between injeras if you cook a batch of them. Serve warm with bowls of things like sautéed vegetables, grilled pieces of meat, creamed spinach, or sautéed mushrooms.

INGREDIENTS:

- ½ **TEASPOON ACTIVE DRY YEAST**
- 2 **CUPS WARM WATER (110 TO 115°F)**
- 1½ **CUPS GROUND TEFF (PUT THE GRAINS IN A FOOD PROCESSOR OR BLENDER TO REDUCE TO "FLOUR")**
- **SALT, TO TASTE**
- **VEGETABLE OIL, FOR THE SKILLET**

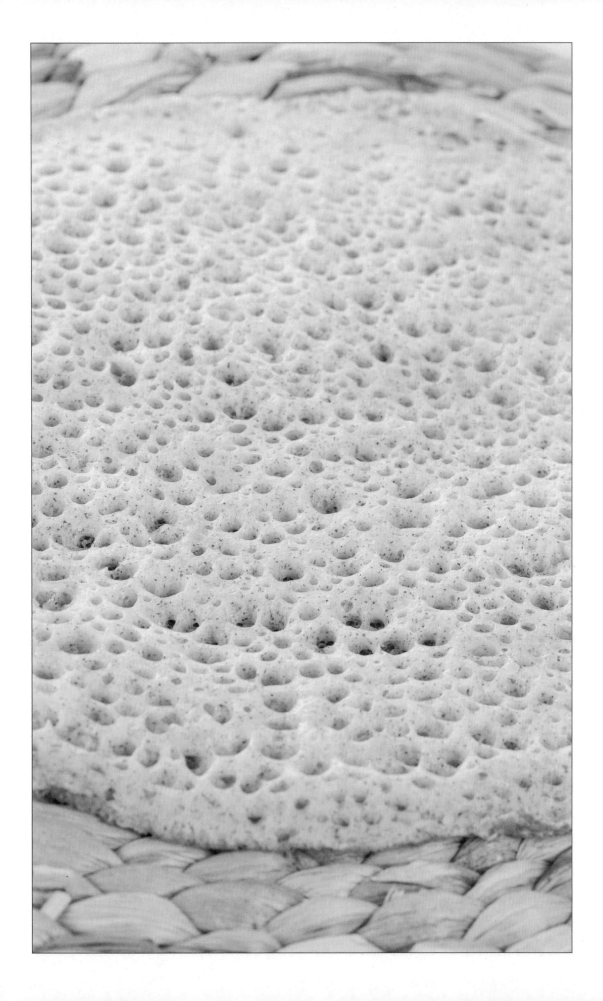

CHICKPEA CREPES

YIELD: 6 CREPES / **ACTIVE TIME:** 10 MINUTES / **TOTAL TIME:** 10 MINUTES

These gluten-free crepes—known as *besan pudla*—are perfect as a side, but they can be so much more. Use them as you would a tortilla and wrap around grilled carrots, dal, and rice for an Indian twist on a taco. The first few may not come out perfectly, but don't let that deter you. It's all about adjusting the heat and getting a feel for the timing.

1. Place the chickpea flour, water, turmeric, salt, and green onions (if using) in a bowl and stir to combine. Let the mixture rest for 15 minutes.

2. Place a cast-iron griddle over medium heat and coat it lightly with some of the ghee or olive oil.

3. Pour ¼ cup of the batter onto the griddle and cook until bubbles appear evenly across the surface. Flip the crepe over and cook until it is firm. Transfer the cooked crepes to a plate and tent with tinfoil to keep warm. Repeat with the remaining batter, adding more ghee (or olive oil) if the griddle starts to look dry.

INGREDIENTS:

2	CUPS CHICKPEA FLOUR
2	CUPS WATER
1	TEASPOON TURMERIC
½	TEASPOON SALT
3	GREEN ONIONS, SLICED THIN (OPTIONAL)
2	TABLESPOONS GHEE OR OLIVE OIL

PARATHA

YIELD: 8 SERVINGS / **ACTIVE TIME:** 25 MINUTES / **TOTAL TIME:** 30 MINUTES

There is something joyful in making flatbreads, don't you think? It harkens back to childhood. The soft dough. Gently rolling it into shape. It's like playing, but the results are edible, which is where the real joy comes in. We should all revel in a chance to play with our food.

1. Place the flours and salt in the bowl of a stand mixer. Turn on low and slowly add the warm water. Mix until incorporated and then slowly add the vegetable oil. When the oil has been incorporated, place the dough on a lightly floured work surface and knead until it is quite smooth, about 8 minutes.

2. Divide the dough into 8 small balls and dust them with flour.

3. Use your hands to roll out each ball into a long rope. Spiral each rope into a large disk.

4. Use a rolling pin to flatten the spiraled disks until they are no more than ¼-inch thick. Lightly brush each disk with a small amount of vegetable oil.

5. Place a cast-iron *tava*, cast-iron skillet, or griddle over very high heat for about 4 minutes. Brush the surface with some of the ghee or melted butter and place a disk of the dough on the surface. Cook until it is blistered and brown, about 1 minute. Turn over and cook the other side. Transfer the cooked paratha to a plate and repeat with the remaining disks. Serve warm or at room temperature.

NOTE: If you want to freeze any extras, make sure to place parchment paper between them to prevent them from melding together.

INGREDIENTS:

- 2 CUPS PASTRY FLOUR, PLUS MORE FOR DUSTING
- 1 CUP WHOLE WHEAT FLOUR
- ¼ TEASPOON SALT
- 1 CUP WARM WATER (110°F)
- 5 TABLESPOONS VEGETABLE OIL, PLUS MORE AS NEEDED
- 5 TABLESPOONS GHEE OR MELTED UNSALTED BUTTER

PITA BREAD

YIELD: 16 PITAS / **ACTIVE TIME:** 1 HOUR / **TOTAL TIME:** 2 HOURS

Pitas are delicious, somewhat chewy bread pockets that originated in the Mediterranean region. They can be filled with just about anything and are popular around the world, but are especially prevalent in Middle Eastern cuisine.

1. Proof the yeast by mixing with the warm water. Let sit for about 10 minutes until foamy.

2. In a large bowl, add the yeast mix into the all-purpose flour and stir until it forms a stiff dough. Cover and let the dough rise for about 1 hour.

3. Add the oil and salt to the dough and stir in the whole wheat flour in ½-cup increments. When finished, the dough should be soft. Turn onto a lightly floured surface and knead it until it is smooth and elastic, about 10 minutes.

4. Coat the bottom and sides of a large mixing bowl (ceramic is best) with butter. Place the ball of dough in the bowl, cover loosely with plastic wrap, put it in a naturally warm, draft-free location, and let it rise until doubled in size, about 45 minutes to 1 hour.

5. On a lightly floured surface, punch down the dough and cut into 16 pieces. Put the pieces on a baking sheet and cover with a kitchen towel while working with individual pieces.

6. Roll out the pieces with a rolling pin until they are approximately 7 inches across. Stack them between sheets of plastic wrap.

7. Warm a 10-inch cast-iron skillet over high heat and lightly oil the bottom. Cook the individual pitas for about 20 seconds on one side, then flip and cook for about a minute on the other side, until bubbles form. Turn again and continue to cook until the pita puffs up, another minute or so. Keep the skillet lightly oiled while cooking, and store the pitas on a plate under a clean kitchen towel until ready to serve.

INGREDIENTS:

1   PACKET OF ACTIVE DRY YEAST (2¼ TEASPOONS)

2½   CUPS WARM WATER (110 TO 115°F)

3   CUPS ALL-PURPOSE FLOUR, PLUS MORE FOR DUSTING

1   TABLESPOON OLIVE OIL, PLUS MORE FOR THE SKILLET

1   TABLESPOON SALT

3   CUPS WHOLE WHEAT FLOUR

    UNSALTED BUTTER, FOR GREASING THE BOWL

NAAN

YIELD: 8 PIECES / ACTIVE TIME: 1 HOUR / TOTAL TIME: 3 TO 4 HOURS

This is the bread that is traditionally served with Indian cuisine. It's usually cooked in a tandoor (clay oven) in India, but the cast-iron skillet works just fine.

1. Proof the yeast by mixing it with the sugar and ½ cup of the warm water. Let sit for 10 minutes until foamy.

2. In a bowl, add the remaining water, flour, salt, baking powder, and yeast mix. Stir to combine. Add the yogurt and 2 tablespoons of the butter and stir to form a soft dough.

3. Transfer to a lightly floured surface and knead the dough until it is springy and elastic, about 10 minutes.

4. Coat the bottom and sides of a large mixing bowl (ceramic is best) with butter. Place the ball of dough in the bowl, cover loosely with plastic wrap, put it in a naturally warm, draft-free location, and let it rise until doubled in size, about 1 to 2 hours.

5. Punch down the dough. Lightly flour a work surface again, take out the dough and, using a rolling pin, make a circle of it. Cut it into 8 slices (like a pie).

6. Heat the skillet over high heat until it is very hot, about 5 minutes. Working with individual pieces of dough, roll them out to soften the sharp edges and make the pieces look more like teardrops. Brush both sides with olive oil and, working one at a time, place the pieces in the skillet.

7. Cook for 1 minute, turn the dough with tongs, cover the skillet, and cook the other side for about a minute (no longer). Transfer cooked naan to a plate and cover with foil to keep warm while making the additional pieces. Serve warm.

TIP: You can add herbs or spices to the dough or the pan to make naan with different flavors, like adding ¼ cup chopped fresh parsley to the dough, or sprinkling the skillet lightly with cumin, coriander, or turmeric (or a combination) before cooking the pieces of naan. You can also use a seasoned olive oil to brush the pieces before cooking—one that has been infused with hot pepper flakes or roasted garlic.

INGREDIENTS:

- 1½ TEASPOONS ACTIVE DRY YEAST
- ½ TABLESPOON SUGAR
- 1 CUP WARM WATER (110 TO 115°F)
- 3 CUPS ALL-PURPOSE FLOUR OR 1½ CUPS ALL-PURPOSE AND 1½ CUPS WHOLE WHEAT PASTRY FLOUR, PLUS MORE FOR DUSTING
- ¼ TEASPOON SALT
- 1 TEASPOON BAKING POWDER
- ½ CUP PLAIN YOGURT
- 4 TABLESPOONS UNSALTED BUTTER, MELTED, PLUS MORE FOR GREASING THE BOWL
- ¼ CUP OLIVE OIL

STARCHES & SIDES

*W*hy, hello there, carbs. Have we told you lately that we love you? No, really, we do. You may be naughty, but you're also oh-so-very nice. Actually, you're not that bad, we're just giving you a hard time because we are in awe of your awesomeness. You're the Rihanna of foods.

The sides in this chapter show off your deliciousness and how well you play with others—and by others, we don't just mean as a side dish for protein, we mean cast iron. As you'll soon see, there's nothing better suited for a cast-iron skillet than Roasted Potatoes (see page 188). There's a side for every occasion, from Butternut Squash & Mash (see page 209) to the astonishingly perfect Black-Eyed Peas with Coconut (see page 213). As a matter of fact, we're so inspired we have to go make some right now. You would be wise to follow suit.

GLAZED SWEET POTATOES & CARROTS

YIELD: 4 SERVINGS / ACTIVE TIME: 20 MINUTES / TOTAL TIME: 40 MINUTES

Sugar brings out the best in already-sweet carrots and sweet potatoes, especially when it's part of a buttery sauce.

1. Peel and trim the carrots. Cut them in half and cut the halves in half lengthwise.

2. Peel and slice the sweet potatoes into spears (about the same size as the carrots).

3. Put the carrots and sweet potatoes in a 12-inch cast-iron skillet with the water, butter, sugar, and cayenne pepper, if desired. Bring to a boil over medium-high heat.

4. Once the mixture boils, reduce the heat to low and simmer for another 10 minutes, stirring occasionally.

5. When the carrots and sweet potatoes are tender and there is a buttery sauce in the skillet, sprinkle with salt. Garnish with the chopped parsley and serve.

INGREDIENTS:

¾ LB. CARROTS

¾ LB. SWEET POTATOES

¾ CUP WATER

4 TABLESPOONS UNSALTED BUTTER

2 TABLESPOONS SUGAR

CAYENNE PEPPER, TO TASTE (OPTIONAL)

SALT, TO TASTE

FRESH PARSLEY, CHOPPED, FOR GARNISH

CLASSIC SPANISH POTATO TORTILLA
with ROMESCO SAUCE

YIELD: 6 TO 8 SERVINGS / ACTIVE TIME: 30 MINUTES / TOTAL TIME: 2 HOURS

There is nothing more Spanish than a perfectly golden potato tortilla. You will find these tortillas sitting on the counter in homes all across Spain, ready to be sliced into thick pieces as a snack or light meal. Hearty, filling, and easy to master, it's as good on its own as it is with this flavor-packed sauce.

1. Place the potatoes, onion, vegetable oil, and olive oil in a large cast-iron Dutch oven. The potatoes should be submerged in the oil. If not, add more vegetable oil as needed. Bring to a gentle simmer over low heat and cook until the potatoes are tender, about 30 minutes. Remove from heat and let cool slightly.

2. Use a slotted spoon to remove the potatoes and onion from the oil. Reserve the oil.

3. Place the eggs and salt in a large bowl and whisk to combine. Add the potatoes and onion to the eggs.

4. Warm a 12-inch cast-iron skillet over high heat. Add ¼ cup of the reserved oil and swirl to coat the bottom and sides of the pan. Pour the egg mixture into the pan and stir vigorously to ensure that the mixture does not stick to the sides. Cook for 1 minute and remove from heat.

5. Place the pan over low heat, cover, and cook for 3 minutes.

6. Carefully invert the tortilla onto a large plate. Return it to the skillet, cook for 3 minutes, and then invert it onto the plate. Return to the skillet and cook for another 3 minutes.

7. Remove the tortilla from the pan and let rest at room temperature for 1 hour. Slice into wedges and top each with a dollop of Romesco Sauce.

INGREDIENTS:

5	LARGE BROWN POTATOES, PEELED AND CUT ⅛-INCH THICK
1	SPANISH ONION, PEELED AND SLICED
½	CUP VEGETABLE OIL, PLUS MORE AS NEEDED
½	CUP OLIVE OIL
10	EGGS, AT ROOM TEMPERATURE
	LARGE PINCH OF SALT
	ROMESCO SAUCE (SEE RECIPE), FOR SERVING

ROMESCO SAUCE

¼	CUP OLIVE OIL
2	RED BELL PEPPERS, SLICED THIN
¼	CUP SLIVERED ALMONDS
2	YELLOW ONIONS, SLICED
4	GARLIC CLOVES, MINCED
2	TOMATOES, DICED
2	TEASPOONS SHERRY VINEGAR
1	TEASPOON SMOKED PAPRIKA

ROMESCO SAUCE

1. Place the olive oil, peppers, and almonds in a 12-inch cast-iron skillet and sauté for 4 minutes.

2. Add the onions, garlic, and tomatoes and cook until soft. Add the sherry vinegar and paprika and stir to combine.

3. Transfer the mixture to a food processor and puree until smooth. Store in an airtight container in the refrigerator for up to 1 week.

GRILLED GOAT CHEESE APPETIZER

YIELD: 4 SERVINGS / ACTIVE TIME: 5 MINUTES / TOTAL TIME: 15 MINUTES

Without a doubt, the most famous chef in Argentina (and Uruguay) is Francis Mallmann. Renowned for his use of fire in cooking, he continually tries to return to and honor the most primal techniques while still elevating the ingredients. This recipe, which has been adapted to make indoors, remains a revelation. If you have the ability to make it over an open fire, try that as well. The additional smoke will be welcome.

1. Arrange the goat cheese slices on a plate and place them in the freezer.

2. Place a cast-iron griddle or skillet over very high heat for 10 minutes.

3. Place the ½ cup of olive oil, red wine vinegar, olives, walnuts, red pepper flakes, and oregano in a bowl and stir to combine.

4. Lightly oil the griddle or skillet with the remaining olive oil. Place the cheese in a single layer and cook until brown and crusty on the bottom, about 2 minutes.

5. Use a spatula to remove the cheese and arrange the rounds on the toasted baguette slices. Spoon the olive mixture on top of the cheese, season with salt and pepper, and serve.

INGREDIENTS:

1 (8 OZ.) LOG OF GOAT CHEESE, SLICED INTO 10 ROUNDS

½ CUP OLIVE OIL, PLUS 1 TEASPOON

1 TEASPOON RED WINE VINEGAR

1 CUP DRY SALT-CURED BLACK OLIVES, PITTED AND CHOPPED

¼ CUP CHOPPED WALNUTS

LARGE PINCH OF RED PEPPER FLAKES, OR TO TASTE

2 TEASPOONS MINCED FRESH OREGANO LEAVES

1 SOURDOUGH BAGUETTE, SLICED AND TOASTED

SALT AND PEPPER, TO TASTE

ROASTED POTATOES

YIELD: 4 TO 6 SERVINGS / ACTIVE TIME: 5 MINUTES / TOTAL TIME: 1 HOUR

A classic side dish, made even better thanks to a little browning and crisping in a cast-iron pan. If you'd like to spice this up a little bit, try adding a pinch of cayenne pepper during the last 5 minutes of cooking.

1. If using red potatoes, cut them in half.

2. Place a 12-inch cast-iron skillet over medium-low heat for 5 minutes.

3. Place the potatoes, olive oil, salt, and pepper in a bowl and toss to coat.

4. Arrange the potatoes in a single layer in the skillet and cook for 10 minutes, while stirring occasionally.

5. Cover the pan, reduce the heat, and cook until the potatoes are fork-tender, about 30 minutes.

INGREDIENTS:

2½ LBS. RED OR FINGERLING POTATOES

2 TABLESPOONS OLIVE OIL

1 TEASPOON KOSHER SALT

PEPPER, TO TASTE

POTATO PANCAKES

YIELD: 6 SERVINGS / ACTIVE TIME: 1 HOUR AND 30 MINUTES / TOTAL TIME: 2 HOURS

The key to great potato pancakes is getting as much liquid out of the grated potatoes as possible before adding them to the hot oil.

1. Squeeze as much liquid out of the potatoes as possible. Set aside half of the potatoes in a colander to drain. Take half of the potatoes, mix them with the onion, and process the mixture in a food processor or blender to create a rough puree. Don't overblend or chop, as the mix will get too starchy.

2. Put the puree in a separate colander to drain. Let both colanders drain for another 20 to 30 minutes. Push down on both to release more liquid and squeeze them again before continuing.

3. Combine the contents of the colanders in a large bowl. Add the eggs and bread crumbs. Stir to thoroughly combine. Season with salt and pepper.

4. Heat a 12-inch cast-iron skillet over medium-high heat and add the oil. Take spoonfuls of the potato mix and place them in the oil. Cook for about 3 minutes per side. The pancakes should be golden brown on the outside and cooked through on the inside. You may need to adjust the heat to get the right cooking temperature, especially if you have more than three pancakes in the skillet at once.

5. Using a slotted spoon, transfer the cooked pancakes to a paper towel–lined plate. Keep warm until ready to serve.

INGREDIENTS:

6	LARGE RUSSET POTATOES, WASHED, PEELED, AND GRATED OR SHREDDED
1	LARGE ONION, GRATED OR MINCED
3	EGGS, BEATEN
¼	CUP BREAD CRUMBS
	SALT AND PEPPER, TO TASTE
1	CUP VEGETABLE OIL

SWEET POTATO PANCAKES

YIELD: 6 TO 8 SERVINGS / **ACTIVE TIME:** 1 HOUR / **TOTAL TIME:** 1 HOUR AND 30 MINUTES

Sweet potatoes aren't as moist as russet potatoes, so you won't need as much draining time with them. You will need to chop them finer to make a dough, however. Experiment until you get the right consistency. These pancakes will probably not hold together as well as regular potato pancakes, but they are equally yummy and versatile. Serve with spinach and sour cream or refried beans, or put some on a baking sheet, top with grated cheddar, and broil for a couple of minutes to melt the cheese.

1. Place the sweet potatoes in a colander and squeeze as much liquid out of the sweet potatoes as possible.

2. Combine the potatoes and onion and process in a food processor or blender to turn the vegetables into a rough puree. Don't overblend or chop, as the mix will get too starchy.

3. Squeeze the puree through a fine sieve to remove excess liquid, then let the mix sit and drain on its own for about 20 to 30 minutes.

4. Put the puree into a large bowl and add the eggs, matzo meal, and sugar. Stir to combine and season with salt and pepper.

5. Place a 12-inch cast-iron skillet over medium-high heat and add the oil. Take spoonfuls of the sweet potato mixture and place them in the oil. Cook for about 3 minutes per side. The pancakes should be golden brown on the outside and cooked through on the inside. You may need to adjust the heat to get the right cooking temperature, especially if you have more than three pancakes in the skillet at one time.

6. Use a slotted spoon to transfer the cooked pancakes to a paper towel–lined plate. Keep warm until ready to serve.

INGREDIENTS:

6   LARGE SWEET POTATOES, WASHED, PEELED, AND MINCED

1   LARGE ONION, GRATED OR MINCED

3   EGGS, BEATEN

½   CUP MATZO MEAL

½   TEASPOON SUGAR

    SALT AND PEPPER, TO TASTE

1   CUP VEGETABLE OIL

FRENCH POTATO TART

YIELD: 4 TO 6 SERVINGS / **ACTIVE TIME:** 45 MINUTES / **TOTAL TIME:** 2 HOURS

The crème fraîche blankets very thin potato slices much like a traditional gratin.

1. Preheat the oven to 400°F.

2. In a bowl, add the crème fraîche, salt, pepper, nutmeg, garlic, and thyme. Stir to combine. Add the potato slices and ham, if using, and fold gently to cover with the crème.

3. On a lightly floured surface, roll out one crust so that it is just larger than the bottom of a 10-inch cast-iron skillet and lay it in the skillet.

4. Layer the potato slices in the crust, creating even, tight layers. Once all the potatoes are used up, use a rubber spatula to scrape the cream mixture into the skillet and distribute the mixture evenly.

5. On a lightly floured surface, roll out the top crust and crimp the edges with the bottom crust to seal. Blend the egg yolk with the half-and-half and brush the mixture over the top crust. Cut 4 to 5 slits in the middle.

6. Put the skillet in the oven and bake for 15 minutes. Reduce temperature to 350°F and continue to bake for 1 hour, or until potatoes are tender.

7. Serve hot or at room temperature.

INGREDIENTS:

1¼ CUPS CRÈME FRAÎCHE (SEE PAGE 566)

1 TABLESPOON KOSHER SALT

½ TEASPOON BLACK PEPPER

PINCH OF GRATED NUTMEG

2 GARLIC CLOVES, CRUSHED

2 TEASPOONS CHOPPED FRESH THYME

4 YUKON GOLD POTATOES, PEELED AND SLICED VERY THIN

1 CUP DICED HAM (OPTIONAL)

ALL-PURPOSE FLOUR, FOR DUSTING

2 FLAKY PASTRY CRUSTS (SEE PAGE 580)

1 EGG YOLK

1 TABLESPOON HALF-AND-HALF

PATATAS BRAVAS

YIELD: 4 SERVINGS / **ACTIVE TIME:** 45 MINUTES / **TOTAL TIME:** 1 HOUR AND 15 MINUTES

Native to Spain, this smoky potato dish can be found in tapas bars all across that country.

1. Place the potatoes, onion, and 1 tablespoon of the olive oil in a mixing bowl and toss to coat.

2. Line a large cast-iron wok with foil, making sure that the foil extends over the side. Add the soaked wood chips and place the wok over medium heat.

3. When the wood chips are smoking heavily, place a wire rack above the wood chips and add the potatoes, onion, and garlic. Cover the wok with a lid, fold the foil over the lid to seal the wok as best you can, and smoke for 20 minutes. After 20 minutes, remove from the burner and keep the wok covered for another 20 minutes.

4. Meanwhile, to make *salsa brava*, combine the tomatoes, paprika, vinegar, and remaining olive oil in a blender and puree. Set the mixture aside.

5. Remove the garlic and onion from the smoker. Peel and roughly chop. Add to the mixture in the blender and puree until smooth. Season the *salsa brava* with salt. Serve the potatoes with sour cream and the *salsa brava*.

INGREDIENTS:

- 4   MEDIUM POTATOES, CUT INTO THICK PIECES AND PARBOILED
- 1   ONION, WITH SKIN AND ROOT, HALVED
- 3   TABLESPOONS OLIVE OIL
- 2   CUPS WOOD CHIPS, SOAKED IN COLD WATER FOR 30 MINUTES
- 1   HEAD OF GARLIC, TOP ½ INCH REMOVED
- 1   (14 OZ.) CAN OF DICED TOMATOES, DRAINED
- 1   TABLESPOON SWEET PAPRIKA
- 1   TABLESPOON SHERRY VINEGAR

   SALT, TO TASTE

   SOUR CREAM, FOR SERVING

POTATO & TOMATO GRATIN

YIELD: 4 TO 6 SERVINGS / ACTIVE TIME: 15 MINUTES / TOTAL TIME: 45 MINUTES

A testament to the brilliance of French cuisine, this layered dish has all the flavor in the world and is as simple as can be to make. Try serving it with grilled chicken and sautéed kohlrabi.

1. Preheat your oven to 350°F.

2. Place the garlic, parsley, and thyme in a small bowl, stir to combine, and set it aside while you prepare the tomatoes.

3. Lightly oil a 12-inch cast-iron skillet or enameled cast-iron gratin dish and then add a layer of the tomato slices. Season with salt and pepper and add a layer of potatoes and a sprinkle of the garlic-and-parsley mixture. Drizzle with olive oil and continue the layering process until all of the tomatoes, potatoes, and garlic-and-parsley mixture have been used.

4. Cover with foil, place in the oven, and bake for 20 minutes. Remove from the oven and remove the foil. If tomatoes haven't released enough liquid to soften the potatoes, add a bit of the stock. Replace the foil and continue baking for 15 minutes.

5. Remove the foil, cook for an additional 5 minutes, and serve warm.

INGREDIENTS:

4   GARLIC CLOVES, MINCED

     LEAVES FROM 1 SMALL BUNCH OF PARSLEY, MINCED

2   TABLESPOONS MINCED FRESH THYME LEAVES

     OLIVE OIL, TO TASTE

2   LBS. TOMATOES, SLICED ¼-INCH THICK

     SALT AND PEPPER, TO TASTE

4   WAXY POTATOES, SLICED ¼-INCH THICK

     CHICKEN STOCK (SEE PAGES 102–3), AS NEEDED

POUTINE

YIELD: 4 TO 6 SERVINGS / ACTIVE TIME: 35 MINUTES / TOTAL TIME: 45 MINUTES

A stone-cold Canadian classic that the recent celebration of comfort food has ushered into the mainstream. The joyful squeak provided by biting into the cheese curds is just one of the many pleasures available in this dish.

1. Place the vegetable oil in a large cast-iron Dutch oven and heat to 275°F. Add the potatoes and fry for 5 minutes, while stirring occasionally. Use a slotted spoon to remove the potatoes, transfer to a paper towel–lined plate, and let them cool completely.

2. Heat the oil to 350°F. Add the cooled potatoes and fry until golden brown, about 5 minutes. Transfer to a paper towel–lined plate and sprinkle with salt.

3. Place the butter in a saucepan and warm over medium-high heat. When it is melted, add the flour and cook, while stirring, until the mixture is smooth, about 2 minutes.

4. Add the garlic and cook until soft, about 2 minutes. Stir in the stock, ketchup, vinegar, and Worcestershire sauce, season with salt and pepper, and bring to a boil. Cook, while stirring, until the gravy has thickened, about 6 minutes.

5. Remove from heat and pour gravy over each serving of fries. Top each with a handful of the cheese curds and serve immediately.

BEEF STOCK

1. Preheat oven to 350°F. Lay the bones on a flat baking tray, place in oven, and cook until they are golden brown, 30 to 45 minutes. Remove and set aside.

2. Meanwhile, in a large stockpot, add the vegetable oil and warm over low heat. Add the vegetables and cook until the moisture has evaporated. This allows the flavor of the vegetables to become concentrated.

3. Add the water, salt, bones, aromatics, and tomato paste to the stockpot, raise heat to high, and bring to a boil.

INGREDIENTS:

4	CUPS VEGETABLE OIL
2	RUSSET POTATOES, CUT INTO STRIPS
	SALT AND PEPPER, TO TASTE
4	TABLESPOONS UNSALTED BUTTER
¼	CUP ALL-PURPOSE FLOUR
1	GARLIC CLOVE, MINCED
4	CUPS BEEF STOCK (SEE RECIPE)
2	TABLESPOONS KETCHUP
1	TABLESPOON APPLE CIDER VINEGAR
½	TABLESPOON WORCESTERSHIRE SAUCE
2	CUPS CHEESE CURDS

BEEF STOCK

10	LBS. BEEF BONES
½	CUP VEGETABLE OIL
1	LEEK, TRIMMED, RINSED WELL, AND CUT INTO 1-INCH PIECES
1	LARGE YELLOW ONION, UNPEELED, ROOT CLEANED, CUT INTO 1-INCH PIECES
2	LARGE CARROTS, PEELED AND CUT INTO 1-INCH PIECES
1	CELERY STALK WITH LEAVES, CUT INTO 1-INCH PIECES
10	QUARTS WATER
1	TEASPOON SALT
8	SPRIGS OF PARSLEY
5	SPRIGS OF THYME
2	BAY LEAVES
1	TEASPOON PEPPERCORNS
1	CUP TOMATO PASTE

4. Reduce heat so that the stock simmers and cook for a minimum of 2 hours. Skim fat and impurities from the top as the stock cooks. As for when to stop cooking the stock, let the flavor be your guide.

5. When the stock is finished cooking, strain through a fine strainer or cheesecloth. Place stock in refrigerator to chill. Once cool, skim the fat layer from the top and discard. This will produce about 6 quarts and will keep in the freezer for about 6 months.

ZUCCHINI FRITTERS *with* SUMAC YOGURT

YIELD: 4 SERVINGS / ACTIVE TIME: 15 MINUTES / TOTAL TIME: 30 MINUTES

Zucchini has a number of wonderful uses, and turning it into fritters is one of the easiest ways to get people excited about this summer squash. Staghorn sumac is native to the eastern United States, but its citric quality is massively underutilized outside of Middle Eastern cuisine. That is, until you try this recipe.

1. Grate the zucchini into a large bowl. Line a colander with cheese-cloth and then place the grated zucchini in the colander, salt it, and let stand for 1 hour. Then press down to remove as much water from the zucchini as you can.

2. Place the zucchini, flour, Parmesan, and egg in a mixing bowl and stir to combine.

3. Use your hands to form handfuls of the mixture into balls and then gently press down on the balls to form them into patties.

4. Place the canola oil in a 12-inch cast-iron skillet and warm over medium-high heat.

5. Working in batches, place the patties into the oil, taking care not to crowd the skillet. Cook until golden brown, about 5 minutes. Flip them over and cook, until the fritters are also golden brown on that side, another 5 minutes. Remove from the skillet and drain on a paper towel–lined plate.

6. Place the yogurt, lemon juice, and sumac powder in a small bowl and stir to combine.

7. Season the fritters with salt and pepper and serve the yogurt mixture on the side.

INGREDIENTS:

1½ LBS. ZUCCHINI

SALT AND PEPPER, TO TASTE

¼ CUP ALL-PURPOSE FLOUR

¼ CUP GRATED PARMESAN CHEESE

1 EGG, BEATEN

3 TABLESPOONS CANOLA OIL

1 CUP YOGURT

2 TEASPOONS FRESH LEMON JUICE

2 TABLESPOONS SUMAC POWDER

ASPARAGUS *with* PANCETTA & GARLIC CREAM SAUCE

YIELD: 4 SERVINGS / ACTIVE TIME: 20 MINUTES / TOTAL TIME: 35 MINUTES

Asparagus has a unique, earthy flavor that teams with the richness of pancetta and the creamy garlic sauce to produce this well-rounded dish.

1. Bring a pot of salted water to a boil. While waiting for the water to boil, remove the woody, white parts of the asparagus and discard them.

2. When the water is boiling, add the asparagus and cook until tender, about 2 minutes. Drain and set aside.

3. Place the garlic, cream, and butter in a 10-inch cast-iron skillet and bring to a simmer over medium heat. Once simmering, add the cornstarch, stirring until the sauce coats the back of a spoon.

4. Place the pancetta in a 12-inch cast-iron skillet and cook over medium-high heat until it turns a light golden brown, about 8 minutes. Add the pancetta to the garlic-and-cream mixture and stir to combine. Season with salt and pepper, pour over the asparagus, and serve.

INGREDIENTS:

SALT AND PEPPER, TO TASTE

2   BUNCHES OF ASPARAGUS

3   GARLIC CLOVES, MINCED

2   CUPS HEAVY CREAM

3   TABLESPOONS UNSALTED BUTTER

1   TABLESPOON CORNSTARCH

1   CUP DICED PANCETTA

CHARRED BRASSICAS *with* PICKLED RAMPS & BUTTERMILK CAESAR DRESSING

YIELD: 4 TO 6 SERVINGS / ACTIVE TIME: 20 MINUTES / TOTAL TIME: 45 MINUTES

Broccoli, Brussels sprouts, and cauliflower are but a few of the fine members of the brassica family. Charring them brings out their sweet side, which pairs wonderfully with the creamy and slightly acidic buttermilk dressing.

1. Place the garlic, anchovies, mayonnaise, buttermilk, Parmesan, lemon zest, Worcestershire sauce, salt, and pepper in a food processor and puree until combined. Season to taste and set the dressing aside.

2. Bring a large pot of salted water to a boil. Add the cauliflower, cook for 1 minute, remove with a slotted spoon, and transfer to a paper towel–lined plate. Wait for the water to return to a boil, add the broccoli, and cook for 30 seconds. Use a slotted spoon to remove the broccoli and let the water drip off before transferring it to the paper towel–lined plate.

3. Place the canola oil and Brussels sprouts, cut side down, in a 12-inch cast-iron skillet. Add the broccoli and cauliflower, season with salt and pepper, and cook over high heat without moving the vegetables. Cook until charred, turn over, and cook until charred on that side. Remove and transfer to a bowl.

4. Add the Pickled Ramps and dressing to the bowl and toss to evenly coat. Garnish with additional Parmesan and red pepper flakes and serve.

PICKLED RAMPS

1. Place all of the ingredients, except for the ramps, in a small saucepan and bring to a boil over medium heat.

2. Add the ramps, reduce the heat, and simmer for 1 minute. Transfer to a mason jar, cover with plastic wrap, and let cool completely. Once cool, cover with a lid and store in the refrigerator for up to 1 week.

INGREDIENTS:

1	LARGE GARLIC CLOVE, MINCED
2	ANCHOVY FILLETS
⅔	CUP MAYONNAISE
¼	CUP BUTTERMILK
¼	CUP GRATED PARMESAN CHEESE, PLUS MORE FOR GARNISH
	ZEST OF 1 LEMON
1	TEASPOON WORCESTERSHIRE SAUCE
1	TEASPOON SALT, PLUS MORE TO TASTE
½	TEASPOON BLACK PEPPER, PLUS MORE TO TASTE
1	SMALL HEAD OF CAULIFLOWER, CUT INTO BITE-SIZED PIECES
1	HEAD OF BROCCOLI, CUT INTO FLORETS
¼	CUP CANOLA OIL
4	OZ. BRUSSELS SPROUTS, TRIMMED AND HALVED
10-12	PICKLED RAMPS (SEE RECIPE)
	RED PEPPER FLAKES, FOR GARNISH

PICKLED RAMPS

½	CUP CHAMPAGNE VINEGAR
½	CUP WATER
¼	CUP SUGAR
1½	TEASPOONS SALT
¼	TEASPOON FENNEL SEEDS
¼	TEASPOON CORIANDER SEEDS
⅛	TEASPOON RED PEPPER FLAKES
10	SMALL RAMP BULBS

BUTTERNUT SQUASH & MASH

YIELD: 6 TO 8 SERVINGS / ACTIVE TIME: 25 MINUTES / TOTAL TIME: 45 MINUTES

A great twist on basic mashed potatoes that is perfect for the fall, as the spices add a bit of warmth and the brown sugar brings everything together. This dish is perfect to carry with you to the table and serve right from the pot.

1. Place the butter in a large enameled cast-iron Dutch oven and melt over medium heat. Add the shallots, garlic, ginger, cinnamon, cardamom, and brown sugar and stir to distribute the spices. Cook, while stirring, until the sugar has just melted and the spices are fragrant.

2. Add the potatoes, squash, table salt, stock, and milk and bring to a simmer. Cook until the squash and potatoes are tender, about 20 minutes.

3. Drain the potatoes and squash and reserve 1 cup of the cooking liquid. Mash the potatoes and squash with a masher or a ricer, adding the cooking liquid if needed. Stir in the nutmeg, season with salt and white pepper, and serve.

INGREDIENTS:

1	STICK OF UNSALTED BUTTER
2	SHALLOTS, SLICED
4	GARLIC CLOVES, CHOPPED
1	TABLESPOON MINCED GINGER
2	TEASPOONS CINNAMON
1	TEASPOON GROUND CARDAMOM
¼	CUP BROWN SUGAR
4	YUKON GOLD POTATOES, PEELED AND QUARTERED
2	LBS. BUTTERNUT SQUASH, PEELED, SEEDED, AND CUBED
2	TEASPOONS TABLE SALT, PLUS MORE TO TASTE
1½	CUPS CHICKEN STOCK (SEE PAGES 102–3)
2	CUPS WHOLE MILK
⅛	TEASPOON NUTMEG
	WHITE PEPPER, TO TASTE

DAL

YIELD: 4 SERVINGS / **ACTIVE TIME:** 20 MINUTES / **TOTAL TIME:** 1 HOUR AND 40 MINUTES

This is an everyday staple in most parts of India, appearing in myriad guises. It's a simple stew of yellow peas, orange lentils, or mung beans that should be slightly soupy so that its deliciousness can seep down into the basmati rice.

1. Place the vegetable oil in a large cast-iron Dutch oven and warm over medium-high heat.

2. Add the onion, garlic, red pepper flakes, curry leaves (if using), and salt and sauté until the onion is slightly translucent, about 2 minutes.

3. Add the yellow split peas, water, and turmeric to a large cast-iron Dutch oven and bring to a simmer. Cover and gently simmer for 1 hour, removing the lid to stir the dal 2 or 3 times.

4. Remove the lid and simmer, while stirring occasionally, until the dal has thickened, about 30 minutes. When the dal has the consistency of porridge, stir in the peas, and cook until they are warmed through.

5. To serve, ladle the dal over the rice.

INGREDIENTS:

2	TABLESPOONS VEGETABLE OIL
1	YELLOW ONION, DICED
2	GARLIC CLOVES, MINCED
2	TEASPOONS RED PEPPER FLAKES, OR TO TASTE
2	CURRY LEAVES (OPTIONAL)
1	TEASPOON SALT
1½	CUPS YELLOW SPLIT PEAS, SORTED AND RINSED
4	CUPS WATER
1	TEASPOON TURMERIC
1	CUP FRESH PEAS
2	CUPS COOKED BASMATI RICE

BLACK-EYED PEAS *with* COCONUT

YIELD: 4 SERVINGS / ACTIVE TIME: 10 MINUTES / TOTAL TIME: 1 HOUR AND 15 MINUTES

Black-eyed peas have a wonderful starchiness and nutty taste that is utilized far too infrequently. You can use canned peas in this preparation, but dried ones will be better.

1. Drain the black-eyed peas, place them in a large enameled cast-iron Dutch oven, and cover with water. Bring the water to a simmer and cook until the black-eyed peas are tender, about 45 minutes. Drain and set them aside.

2. Place the coconut oil in the Dutch oven and warm over medium heat. When the oil starts to shimmer, add the yellow onion, green onions, tomatoes, habanero, and Berbere Spice and sauté for 2 minutes.

3. Add the coconut milk and stock and bring to a simmer. Reduce the heat to low and gently simmer until the liquid has slightly reduced, about 10 minutes.

4. Return the black-eyed peas to the pot and continue to simmer for 15 minutes.

5. Stir in the cilantro and serve immediately.

TIP: This can be served on its own or over quinoa, millet, or rice.

BERBERE SPICE

Use a mortar and pestle or spice grinder to combine all of the ingredients.

INGREDIENTS:

- 1 CUP DRIED BLACK-EYED PEAS, SOAKED IN COLD WATER FOR 8 HOURS
- ¼ CUP COCONUT OIL
- 1 YELLOW ONION, PEELED AND SLICED
- ½ CUP CHOPPED GREEN ONIONS
- 2 TOMATOES, CHOPPED
- 1 HABANERO PEPPER, STEMMED, SEEDED, AND CHOPPED
- 2 TEASPOONS BERBERE SPICE (SEE RECIPE)
- 1 CUP COCONUT MILK
- 1 CUP CHICKEN STOCK (SEE PAGES 102–3)
- 1 CUP CILANTRO LEAVES, CHOPPED

BERBERE SPICE

- 1 TEASPOON FENUGREEK SEEDS
- 1 TEASPOON RED PEPPER FLAKES
- 2 TABLESPOONS SWEET PAPRIKA
- ½ TEASPOON GROUND CARDAMOM
- 1 TEASPOON NUTMEG
- ⅛ TEASPOON GARLIC POWDER
- ⅛ TEASPOON GROUND CLOVES
- ⅛ TEASPOON CINNAMON
- ⅛ TEASPOON ALLSPICE

EGYPTIAN FAVA BEANS

YIELD: 4 SERVINGS / ACTIVE TIME: 10 MINUTES / TOTAL TIME: 20 MINUTES

*F*ul medames is a beloved breakfast dish in Egypt, and the recipe is so enduring that it is said to have been enjoyed by the pharaohs. Since then, it has become popular throughout the Middle East. This will keep well in the refrigerator or freezer, so don't hesitate to make a big batch. If you are using dried fava beans, soak them overnight and boil for an hour before using.

1. Place the beans and garlic in a cast-iron Dutch oven, cover by ½ inch with water, and bring to a boil. Reduce the heat and simmer for 10 minutes.

2. Drain and add the olive oil, lemon juice, salt, pepper, red pepper flakes, and cumin. Lightly mash the beans with a fork and stir to combine.

3. Drizzle with additional olive oil, transfer to a platter, and place the pieces of hard-boiled egg on top. Garnish with the parsley or mint and, if desired, serve with the feta cheese and black olives.

INGREDIENTS:

2   CUPS CANNED FAVA BEANS, DRAINED

4   GARLIC CLOVES, CHOPPED

¼   CUP OLIVE OIL, PLUS MORE TO TASTE

JUICE OF 2 LEMONS

SALT AND PEPPER, TO TASTE

LARGE PINCH OF RED PEPPER FLAKES

1   TEASPOON GROUND CUMIN

2   HARD-BOILED EGGS, EACH CUT INTO 6 WEDGES

2   TABLESPOONS MINCED PARSLEY OR MINT, FOR GARNISH

FETA CHEESE, CRUMBLED, FOR SERVING (OPTIONAL)

BLACK OLIVES, FOR SERVING (OPTIONAL)

HOME-STYLE BAKED BEANS

YIELD: 6 TO 8 SERVINGS / ACTIVE TIME: 30 MINUTES / TOTAL TIME: 1½ TO 2 HOURS

At times, cooking in a cast-iron skillet makes you picture cowboys cooking over an open fire while their horses hang out behind them, and nothing is more quintessential to cast-iron cooking than baked beans. Baked beans are delicious and filling on their own, but they are the perfect accompaniment to grilled sausages, hot dogs, hamburgers, pork chops, or barbecued chicken.

1. Preheat the oven to 325°F.

2. Heat a 12-inch cast-iron skillet over medium heat and cook half of the bacon slices until just soft, about 8 minutes. Transfer to a paper towel–lined plate to drain.

3. Add the remaining slices of bacon, increase heat, and cook, flipping often, until browned. Reduce the heat to medium. Add the onion and bell pepper and cook, stirring occasionally, until the vegetables soften, another 8 minutes or so.

4. Add the salt, beans, barbecue sauce, mustard, and brown sugar. Stir, season with additional salt and a generous grind of fresh pepper, and leave on the stove until the sauce just starts to simmer.

5. Lay the partially cooked pieces of bacon on top of the beans and transfer the skillet to the oven.

6. Bake for 1 hour and check. The bacon should be crisp and browned, and the sauce should be thick. The dish can cook for another 15 to 30 minutes if the consistency isn't right. Be careful not to overcook, as the beans will start to dry out. An hour and 15 to 20 minutes is about right.

7. Remove from the oven and allow to cool slightly before serving.

INGREDIENTS:

6   SLICES OF THICK-CUT BACON

½   ONION, DICED

½   CUP DICED BELL PEPPER

1   TEASPOON SALT, PLUS MORE TO TASTE

2   (14 OZ.) CANS OF PINTO BEANS, RINSED AND DRAINED

1   CUP BARBECUE SAUCE

1   TEASPOON DIJON MUSTARD

2   TABLESPOONS DARK BROWN SUGAR

FRESHLY GROUND PEPPER, TO TASTE

PUERTO RICAN RICE *&* PIGEON PEAS

YIELD: 4 SERVINGS / **ACTIVE TIME:** 30 MINUTES / **TOTAL TIME:** 1 HOUR AND 10 MINUTES

The crusty layer of rice that results when you make the rice in a *caldera* is known as *pegao*, and, like all delicacies, getting it right is an art. So don't be discouraged if you get it wrong the first time, and know that it is well worth doing right. Serve this alongside marinated chicken or roast pork.

1. Place the rice in a colander and rinse it three times to remove any starch. Set aside.

2. Place the bacon in a large, wide cast-iron *caldera* and cook it slowly over medium heat until it is very crispy, about 10 minutes. Transfer to a paper towel–lined plate. Leave the rendered fat in the pot. When the bacon is cool enough to handle, crumble it into bite-sized pieces.

3. Add the garlic powder, onion powder, cumin, oregano, achiote (or turmeric), and pepper to the pot and sauté for 20 seconds. Quickly add the Sofrito and onion, stir to combine, and cook for 3 minutes.

4. Add the rice and stir to combine. Cook for 3 minutes and then add the vegetable oil, tomato paste, capers, olives, and pigeon peas. Stir gently to combine and cook, without stirring, for 1 or 2 minutes to allow the bottom layer of rice to stick to the bottom of the pan. If you do not want the crispy layer of rice, skip this step.

5. Add the water and salt and bring to a boil. Turn off the heat and quickly drape a clean kitchen towel over the pot. Place the lid on top and wrap the towel around the lid, making sure it does not hang down over the sides, as it might catch fire. Turn the heat to high. Cook for 30 seconds and then reduce the heat to low. Simmer for 35 minutes.

6. Raise the heat to high and wait 1 minute. Turn off the heat and let the rice steam for 5 minutes. Fluff with a fork, garnish with the crumbled bacon, and serve.

SOFRITO

Place the ingredients in a blender and puree until smooth.

NOTE: If you can find them, add a bunch of culantro and a cubanelle pepper to the blender for a more authentic Sofrito.

INGREDIENTS:

4	CUPS LONG-GRAIN WHITE RICE
2	OZ. UNCURED BACON
1	TABLESPOON GARLIC POWDER
1	TABLESPOON ONION POWDER
1	TABLESPOON GROUND CUMIN
1	TEASPOON DRIED OREGANO
1	TABLESPOON GROUND ACHIOTE OR TURMERIC
½	TEASPOON GROUND BLACK PEPPER
1	CUP SOFRITO (SEE RECIPE)
½	CUP CHOPPED YELLOW ONION
1	TABLESPOON VEGETABLE OIL
2	TABLESPOONS TOMATO PASTE
1	TABLESPOON CAPERS
10	SPANISH OLIVES, CHOPPED
1	(14 OZ.) CAN OF PIGEON PEAS, DRAINED
5	CUPS WATER
2	TEASPOONS KOSHER SALT

SOFRITO

1	RED BELL PEPPER, ROASTED AND PEELED
½	YELLOW ONION, CHOPPED
6	GARLIC CLOVES
¼	CUP OLIVE OIL
	ZEST AND JUICE OF 1 LIME
	LEAVES FROM 1 LARGE BUNCH OF CILANTRO
1	TEASPOON DRIED OREGANO
	LARGE PINCH OF SALT

PERSIAN RICE *with* TAHDIG

YIELD: 4 SERVINGS / ACTIVE TIME: 10 MINUTES / TOTAL TIME: 50 MINUTES

In Iranian culture, the crispy layer of rice—known as *tahdig*—at the bottom of the pot is a coveted morsel. Once you get it down, you'll see why. Serve with Chicken Kebabs (see page 367) or roasted fish.

1. Place the salt, water, and rice in a saucepan and bring to a boil. Boil for 10 minutes.

2. While the rice is boiling, place the saffron (or turmeric) and warm water in a small bowl and let it steep.

3. Drain the rice and rinse under warm water.

4. Place the butter in a 12-inch cast-iron skillet and melt it over medium-high heat. When it starts to sizzle, carefully pour the infused water into the skillet and bring to a simmer.

5. Add the cooked rice, turn off the burner, and drape a clean kitchen towel over the pan. Place the lid on top and wrap the towel around the lid, making sure it does not drape down over the sides, as it might catch fire.

6. Turn the heat to low and let the rice cook until the bottom is browned and crispy, about 30 minutes. Remove from heat and let cool for 5 minutes.

7. To loosen the *tahdig*, place the skillet in a large dish containing 1 inch of cold water and let it sit for 5 minutes. Invert onto a large platter and serve.

INGREDIENTS:

2   TEASPOONS KOSHER SALT

3½   CUPS WATER, AT ROOM TEMPERATURE

2   CUPS BASMATI RICE, RINSED WELL

    LARGE PINCH OF SAFFRON OR 1 TEASPOON TURMERIC

¼   CUP WARM WATER (110°F)

4   TABLESPOONS UNSALTED BUTTER

QUINOA SKILLET CASSEROLE

YIELD: 6 SERVINGS / **ACTIVE TIME:** 30 MINUTES / **TOTAL TIME:** 1 HOUR

Quinoa looks and cooks like a grain, but it's actually a seed that has grown in the Andes Mountains of South America for millennia. It's high in protein and fiber and loaded with magnesium, iron, and vitamin B6. Quinoa has plenty of health benefits, but one of the drawbacks of this nutritious food is that it can become sticky, like oatmeal—a texture that isn't always appealing. With the cast-iron skillet, you can cook the quinoa so that it gets almost crackly-crunchy. Combined with the veggies and hot peppers, this is a delish dish.

1. In a small saucepan with a tight-fitting lid, add the quinoa and the broth. Bring to a boil, stir, cover, and reduce the heat to low, simmering for about 15 minutes or until the grains are translucent. Remove from heat and let sit, still covered, for at least 5 more minutes so the quinoa fully absorbs the broth.

2. Place a 12-inch cast-iron skillet over medium-high heat, add the olive oil, and then add the corn, red pepper, onion, and jalapeño. Stir, cooking, until the onion is soft and the peppers are starting to brown, about 5 to 8 minutes.

3. Stir in the quinoa, season with salt, and cook over medium-high heat to brown the quinoa slightly.

4. Cook for another 10 minutes, while stirring occasionally. Stir in the cheese, remove from heat, and serve.

INGREDIENTS:

1   CUP QUINOA

2   CUPS CHICKEN BROTH

1½ TABLESPOONS OLIVE OIL

    KERNELS FROM 1 EAR OF COOKED CORN

½   RED BELL PEPPER, SEEDED AND DICED

½   CUP CHOPPED YELLOW ONION

1   JALAPEÑO PEPPER, SEEDED AND SLICED

½   TEASPOON SALT

1   CUP GRATED CHEDDAR CHEESE

POLENTA CAKE *with* MUSHROOMS & ONIONS

YIELD: 4 TO 6 SERVINGS / ACTIVE TIME: 30 MINUTES / TOTAL TIME: 1 HOUR AND 15 MINUTES

Think vegetarian shepherd's pie with this recipe—the mushrooms and onions are the "meat" and the polenta bakes on top the way a layer of mashed potatoes would. A cast-iron skillet is a natural home for this hearty and rustic dish.

1. Preheat the oven to 400°F.

2. Melt 6 tablespoons of the butter in a 12-inch cast-iron skillet over medium heat. Add the onion slices and increase the heat to medium-high. Sauté the onions until just soft, about 3 minutes. Add the mushroom pieces and continue to cook over medium-high heat, while stirring frequently, until the mushrooms and onions are soft and reduced in volume, about 8 minutes. Stir in the Worcestershire sauce and season with salt and pepper. Remove the skillet from the heat.

3. In a heavy saucepan, whisk together the polenta and water. Heat over medium heat and bring to a boil, whisking to prevent lumps from forming. When bubbling, reduce the heat to low and simmer, uncovered, for a couple of minutes or until smooth. Season with salt and pepper.

4. Pour the polenta over the mushroom-and-onion mixture, smoothing the surface with the back of a spoon. Cut the remaining 2 tablespoons of butter into thin pieces and dot the surface of the polenta with them.

5. Put the skillet in the oven and bake for 30 minutes, until it is lightly golden and coming away from the edges of the pan (the filling should be bubbling hot). Allow to cool for 10 minutes before serving.

6. Cut into wedges and serve immediately.

INGREDIENTS:

1	STICK OF UNSALTED BUTTER
1-1½	CUPS THINLY SLICED ONIONS
2	LBS. MUSHROOMS, STEMMED AND CHOPPED
1	TEASPOON WORCESTERSHIRE SAUCE
	SALT AND PEPPER, TO TASTE
1	CUP POLENTA
3	CUPS WATER

SKILLET MAC & CHEESE

YIELD: 6 TO 8 SERVINGS / ACTIVE TIME: 30 MINUTES / TOTAL TIME: 1 HOUR

There's nothing like homemade macaroni and cheese, but it can get as messy when you have to use several pots and pans to make and serve it. Here comes your cast-iron skillet to the rescue!

1. Preheat the oven to 425°F.

2. Put the macaroni in a 12-inch cast-iron skillet and add cold water so that it reaches 1½ inches below the top. Stir in the salt, turn heat to high, and cook the macaroni for about 10 minutes. Test a piece after about 7 minutes. The pasta should be al dente—nearly cooked through but still a bit chewy. When it is cooked, drain it in a colander over a large mixing bowl so the water is retained.

3. Put your skillet back on the stove over medium heat and add the butter. When it's melted, stir in the flour, with a wooden spoon if possible, to prevent lumps from forming. When it is starting to bubble, start slowly adding the milk, whisking constantly as you add it. Add about ½ cup at a time, being sure to whisk it in thoroughly before continuing. When all the milk is stirred in, let the sauce simmer over low heat until thickened, about 10 minutes.

4. Reduce the heat to medium-low and stir in the sour cream. When the mix is warm again, add the cheeses, stirring gently as they melt. Season with the salt, pepper, and cayenne.

5. Finally, add the macaroni gently into the cheese sauce. If it seems too thick, add some of the reserved water. The consistency should be like a thick stew. When the noodles are hot, transfer the skillet to the oven.

6. Bake for about 15 minutes, then check. The dish should be bubbling and the cheese on top starting to brown. This takes somewhere between 15 and 25 minutes. Be careful not to let it burn. Let the macaroni cool slightly before serving.

INGREDIENTS:

- 1 LB. ELBOW MACARONI OR PREFERRED PASTA
- 1 TABLESPOON SALT
- 3 TABLESPOONS UNSALTED BUTTER, AT ROOM TEMPERATURE
- 3½ TABLESPOONS ALL-PURPOSE FLOUR
- 1½ CUPS WHOLE MILK, AT ROOM TEMPERATURE OR SLIGHTLY WARMED
- ¼ CUP SOUR CREAM
- ¾ LB. SHARP WHITE CHEDDAR CHEESE, GRATED
- ¼ LB. GRUYÈRE CHEESE, GRATED
- SALT AND PEPPER, TO TASTE
- DASH OF CAYENNE PEPPER

MAC & CHEESE *with* BROWN BUTTER BREAD CRUMBS

YIELD: 6 SERVINGS / **ACTIVE TIME:** 15 MINUTES / **TOTAL TIME:** 1 HOUR

The cheese in this dish will stick to your ribs. Reserve it for those nights when you're especially hungry and can afford to relax after the meal.

1. Preheat oven to 400°F.

2. Fill an enameled cast-iron Dutch oven with water and bring to a boil. Add some salt and then add the macaroni. Cook until slightly under al dente, about 6 to 7 minutes. Drain and set aside.

3. Place the pot over medium heat and add 3 tablespoons of the butter. Cook until the butter starts to give off a nutty smell and browns. Add the bread crumbs, stir, and cook until the bread crumbs start to look like wet sand, 4 to 5 minutes. Remove and set aside.

4. Wipe the Dutch oven out with a paper towel, place over medium-high heat, and add the onion and the remaining butter. Cook, while stirring, until the onion is translucent and soft, about 7 to 10 minutes. Add the flour and whisk until there are no lumps. Add the mustard, turmeric, granulated garlic, and white pepper and whisk until combined. Add the half-and-half or light cream and the milk and whisk until incorporated.

5. Reduce heat to medium and bring the mixture to a simmer. Once you start to see small bubbles forming around the outside of the mixture, add the cheeses one at a time, whisking to combine before adding the next one. When all the cheese has been added and the mixture is smooth, cook until the flour taste is gone, 10 to 15 minutes. Return the pasta to the pot, stir, and top with the bread crumbs.

6. Place in the oven and bake for 10 to 15 minutes. Remove the pot from the oven and serve.

TIP: If you can't find Boursin, whisk some cream cheese and a little softened butter together.

INGREDIENTS:

- SALT AND PEPPER, TO TASTE
- ½ LB. ELBOW MACARONI
- 7 TABLESPOONS UNSALTED BUTTER
- 2 CUPS BREAD CRUMBS (USE PANKO FOR AN EXTRA CRUNCHY TOP)
- ½ YELLOW ONION, MINCED
- 3 TABLESPOONS ALL-PURPOSE FLOUR
- 1 TABLESPOON YELLOW MUSTARD
- 1 TEASPOON TURMERIC
- 1 TEASPOON GRANULATED GARLIC
- 1 TEASPOON WHITE PEPPER
- 2 CUPS HALF-AND-HALF OR LIGHT CREAM
- 2 CUPS WHOLE MILK
- 1 LB. AMERICAN CHEESE, SLICED
- 10 OZ. BOURSIN CHEESE
- 1 LB. EXTRA SHARP CHEDDAR CHEESE, SLICED

NOODLES & CABBAGE

YIELD: 6 TO 8 SERVINGS / ACTIVE TIME: 30 MINUTES / TOTAL TIME: 2 HOURS AND 30 MINUTES

A deceptive dish: it only has five ingredients, and yet it is the ultimate in comfort cooking. If you're committed to making it, know that the longer you cook the cabbage, the sweeter it becomes.

1. Place half of the butter in a large enameled cast-iron Dutch oven and melt it over medium heat.

2. Add the cabbage. If it doesn't fit initially, push down what does fit in the pot and add more as that wilts. Cover with a lid and cook for 10 minutes.

3. Remove the lid and add the remaining butter. Cover and cook for an additional 30 minutes, while stirring occasionally.

4. Reduce the heat to low and cook until the cabbage is extremely soft and browned, about 1 hour. Season with white pepper to taste.

5. About 20 minutes before the cabbage will be finished cooking, bring a pot of salted water to a boil. Place the egg noodles in the boiling water and cook until they are al dente, about 8 minutes. Drain, transfer to a large bowl, add the cabbage, and toss to combine. Serve immediately.

INGREDIENTS:

1½   STICKS OF SALTED
     BUTTER, DIVIDED INTO
     TABLESPOONS

2   HEADS OF GREEN CABBAGE,
     CORED AND SLICED AS
     THIN AS POSSIBLE

     SALT AND WHITE PEPPER,
     TO TASTE

1   LB. WIDE EGG NOODLES

ONION BHAJI

YIELD: 4 SERVINGS (12 FRITTERS) / **ACTIVE TIME:** 20 MINUTES / **TOTAL TIME:** 20 MINUTES

These fritters, which are a popular snack in India, can be varied in dozens of ways. Try adding shredded carrot, chilies, a bit of coconut, or even threads of parsnip to get an idea of what else you might like to incorporate.

1. Place the eggs in a bowl and beat them. Add the onions, flour, coriander, cumin, serrano pepper, and salt and stir to combine.

2. Place the vegetable oil in an 10-inch cast-iron skillet and warm over medium heat. When it starts to shimmer, place a large spoonful of the onion batter and fry until golden brown, about 30 to 45 seconds.

3. Turn the fritter over and fry until it is crisp and golden brown all over, about 30 seconds. Transfer to a paper towel–lined plate to drain.

4. Repeat with the remaining batter, adding and heating more oil if it starts to run low. When all of the fritters have been cooked, serve immediately.

INGREDIENTS:

2	EGGS
3	LARGE RED ONIONS, SLICED INTO THIN HALF-MOONS
5	OZ. ALL-PURPOSE FLOUR
1	TEASPOON GROUND CORIANDER
1	TEASPOON CUMIN
1	SERRANO PEPPER, SEEDED AND MINCED
½	TEASPOON SALT
1	CUP VEGETABLE OIL, PLUS MORE AS NEEDED

POLENTA CAKE *with* GREENS

YIELD: 4 TO 6 SERVINGS / ACTIVE TIME: 30 MINUTES / TOTAL TIME: 1 HOUR

Polenta is cornmeal cooked into porridge and then baked or fried. It forms a lovely, bright yellow cake that is moist yet firm. It can be topped with all kinds of things, but in this recipe, it is the base for sautéed vegetables. Delicious!

1. Preheat the oven to 400°F.

2. Liberally oil a 12-inch cast-iron skillet and put it in the oven for a few minutes.

3. In a heavy saucepan, whisk together the polenta and water. Place over medium heat and bring to a boil, whisking to prevent lumps from forming. When bubbling, reduce the heat to low and simmer, uncovered, for a couple of minutes or until smooth. Season with salt and pepper.

4. Pour the polenta into the skillet. Put the skillet in the oven and bake for about 30 minutes, until the polenta is lightly golden and coming away from the edge of the pan.

5. While it's baking, make the greens. Bring a large pot of salted water to a boil, add the greens, and boil until very tender, 15 to 20 minutes. Drain in a colander and squeeze to remove excess moisture. Cut the greens into pieces. Heat the 3 tablespoons of olive oil in a pan, add the garlic, and cook, while stirring, until fragrant, about 2 minutes. Add the red pepper flakes, stir, and then add the greens. Cook until heated through. Season with salt and pepper. Keep warm until polenta is cooked.

6. Cut the polenta into wedges, top with greens, and sprinkle with Romano.

VARIATION: Substitute ½ lb. baby spinach leaves and ½ lb. kale (tough stems removed) for the 1 lb. of mixed greens.

INGREDIENTS:

- 3 TABLESPOONS OLIVE OIL, PLUS MORE FOR THE SKILLET
- 1 CUP POLENTA
- 3 CUPS WATER
- SALT AND PEPPER, TO TASTE
- 1 LB. BITTER GREENS (KALE, SWISS CHARD, ESCAROLE, OR DANDELION), STEMMED
- 3 GARLIC CLOVES, CHOPPED
- RED PEPPER FLAKES, TO TASTE
- ROMANO CHEESE, GRATED, FOR TOPPING

SPICY SHRIMP POLENTA

YIELD: 4 TO 6 SERVINGS / ACTIVE TIME: 30 MINUTES / TOTAL TIME: 1 HOUR

If you're looking for a recipe for a fun cocktail party finger food, this is it—essentially a take on fish tacos but much easier to eat while standing. Plus, it's naturally gluten-free.

1. Preheat the oven to 400°F.

2. Heat the canola oil in a 12-inch cast-iron skillet over medium-high heat. When hot but not smoking, add the shrimp. Stirring constantly and with a light touch, sauté the shrimp until just pink, about 3 to 5 minutes. Remove the pan from heat and use a slotted spoon to transfer the shrimp to a paper towel–lined plate. Keep the oil in the skillet.

3. In a heavy saucepan, whisk together the polenta and water. Heat over medium heat and bring to a boil, whisking to prevent lumps from forming. When bubbling, reduce the heat to low and simmer, uncovered, for a couple of minutes or until smooth. Remove saucepan from heat and stir in the horseradish and red pepper flakes. Season with salt and pepper. Taste the polenta to see if the horseradish is strong enough for you. If you think it could use more, add another ½ teaspoon, but be careful not to overdo it. Stir in the shrimp.

4. Pour the polenta into the skillet, smoothing the surface with the back of a spoon. Put the skillet in the oven and bake for about 30 minutes, until the polenta is lightly golden and coming away from the edge of the pan. Allow to cool for 5 to 10 minutes, then work quickly and carefully to invert the polenta cake onto a platter. Allow to cool to room temperature.

5. Cut the polenta into wedges and top each piece with a sprig of cilantro. Serve immediately.

INGREDIENTS:

3   TABLESPOONS CANOLA OIL

½   LB. SMALL SHRIMP, THAWED (IF FROZEN), PEELED, AND HALVED

1   CUP POLENTA

3   CUPS WATER

1   TEASPOON HORSERADISH, OR TO TASTE

1   TEASPOON RED PEPPER FLAKES

    SALT AND FRESHLY GROUND BLACK PEPPER, TO TASTE

    FRESH CILANTRO, FOR GARNISH

THANKSGIVING SIDES

Why do we always pick on Valentine's Day when discussing made-up holidays? The clear winner is Thanksgiving. And what a wonderfully delicious fabrication it is. The story and menu that circulates in grade schools across the country may not be entirely (or even remotely) accurate, but that shouldn't stop you from getting in the kitchen and whipping up a glorious feast.

On a day that is as much about side dishes as it is about family, we make sure you'll go in ready to put a smile on everyone's face.

BREAD DRESSING

YIELD: 10 SERVINGS / ACTIVE TIME: 15 MINUTES / TOTAL TIME: 1 HOUR AND 15 MINUTES

Everyone knows that stuffing goes inside the bird, but if you are making that same recipe alongside the turkey, it is known as dressing. Follow whatever route you want with this preparation—it's delicious either way.

1. Preheat the oven to 325°F.

2. Place the butter in a 10-inch cast-iron skillet and melt over medium heat. Pour out 2 tablespoons and reserve.

3. Add the onion and celery and cook, while stirring, until soft, about 6 minutes. Remove the pan from heat.

4. Place the bread cubes in a large bowl and stir in the cooked onion and celery. Add the thyme, season with salt and pepper, and stir to combine.

5. Add the broth and stir to incorporate. Let the mixture sit until the bread absorbs most of the broth.

6. Place the dressing in the cast-iron skillet and pour the reserved butter on top. Place in the oven and bake until browned, about 1 hour. Serve immediately.

INGREDIENTS:

1   STICK OF UNSALTED BUTTER

1   YELLOW ONION, CHOPPED

1   CUP CHOPPED CELERY

6   CUPS OF DAY-OLD BREAD CUBES

¾   TEASPOON DRIED THYME

SALT AND PEPPER, TO TASTE

3   CUPS CHICKEN BROTH

CRANBERRY SAUCE

YIELD: 6 TO 8 SERVINGS / ACTIVE TIME: 5 MINUTES / TOTAL TIME: 10 MINUTES

Take the can out of the equation with this bright, not-overly-sweet holiday classic that is ready in a flash.

1. Place all of the ingredients in a cast-iron Dutch oven and stir to combine.

2. Bring to a simmer over medium heat and cook, while stirring occasionally, for 8 minutes.

3. Taste and add more sugar if needed. Serve warm or chilled.

INGREDIENTS:

2   CUPS FRESH CRANBERRIES

1   CUP SUGAR, PLUS MORE TO TASTE

1   CUP WATER

1   TABLESPOON ORANGE ZEST

JALAPEÑO *&* CHEDDAR CORN BREAD

YIELD: 12 SERVINGS / ACTIVE TIME: 15 MINUTES / TOTAL TIME: 55 MINUTES

A simple batter with a burst of umami thanks to all that cheese. This will be somewhat spicy, so cut back on the jalapeños if you, or a loved one, prefer things mild.

1. Preheat the oven to 400°F.

2. Place the butter in a 10-inch cast-iron skillet and place the pan in the oven as it warms.

3. Place the flour, cornmeal, sugar, baking powder, baking soda, and kosher salt in a mixing bowl and stir to combine. Add the eggs and buttermilk and beat with a large spoon until you have a thick batter.

4. Add the jalapeños and the cheeses and stir to evenly distribute.

5. Remove the skillet from the oven and pour the melted butter into the batter. Stir to combine, then pour the batter back into the skillet.

6. Place in the oven and bake until puffy and golden brown, about 40 minutes. Let cool slightly before serving.

NOTE: This can also be made in a cornstick pan or muffin pan.

INGREDIENTS:

6	TABLESPOONS UNSALTED BUTTER
1	CUP ALL-PURPOSE FLOUR
1	CUP YELLOW CORNMEAL
½	CUP SUGAR
1¾	TEASPOONS BAKING POWDER
1½	TEASPOONS BAKING SODA
1	TEASPOON KOSHER SALT
2	LARGE EGGS, BEATEN
2	CUPS BUTTERMILK
3	GREEN JALAPEÑO PEPPERS, SEEDED AND SLICED
½	CUP GRATED CHEDDAR CHEESE
½	CUP GRATED MONTEREY JACK CHEESE

SALAD *with* CHARRED LEMON DRESSING

YIELD: 4 TO 6 SERVINGS / ACTIVE TIME: 20 MINUTES / TOTAL TIME: 30 MINUTES

Charring the lemons adds an intriguing bit of smoke to this terrific twist on a simple vinaigrette.

1. Place a 12-inch cast-iron skillet over high heat for 5 minutes.

2. Add the lemons to the skillet and let them char.

3. Transfer the lemons to a large strainer set over a bowl. Use a large spoon to crush the lemons and let the juice fall into the bowl. Discard the lemon peels and seeds.

4. Stir in the olive oil, salt, and pepper. Taste and season accordingly.

5. Place the remaining ingredients in a salad bowl and toss to combine. Add half of the dressing, toss to coat, and serve with the remaining dressing on the side.

INGREDIENTS:

3	LARGE LEMONS, QUARTERED
1	CUP OLIVE OIL
	SALT AND PEPPER, TO TASTE
4	CUPS BUTTER LETTUCE
6	RADISHES, SLICED THIN
2	TABLESPOONS MINCED CHIVES
¼	CUP GRATED PARMESAN CHEESE

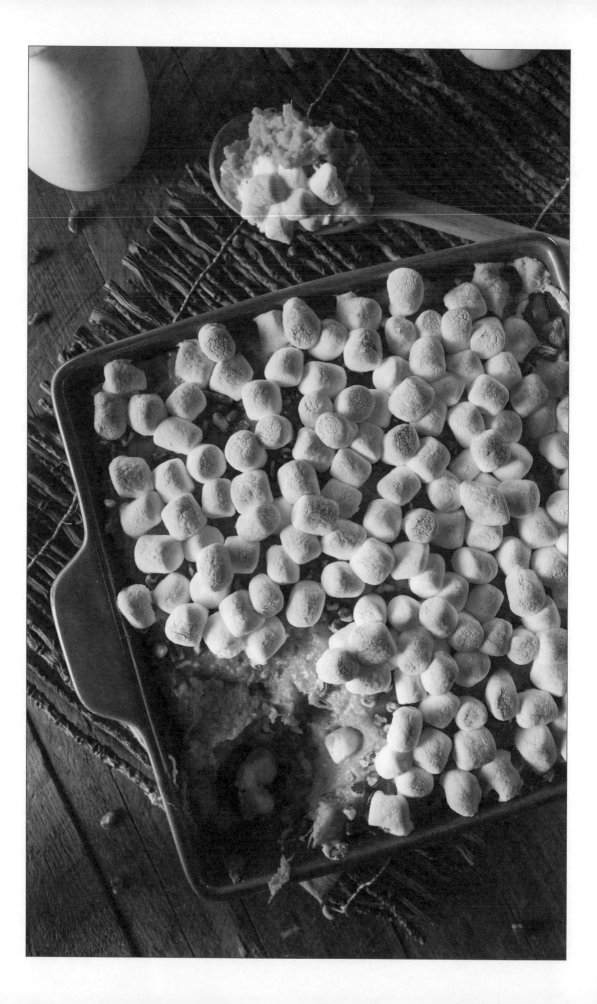

SWEET POTATOES *with* MARSHMALLOWS

YIELD: 4 TO 6 SERVINGS / **ACTIVE TIME:** 10 MINUTES / **TOTAL TIME:** 1 HOUR AND 30 MINUTES

Beautiful to look at and heavenly to tuck into, this sweet treat is one of those decadent dishes that everyone loves and no one misses until the next Thanksgiving comes around.

1. Preheat your oven to 375°F.

2. Pierce the skin of the sweet potatoes with a fork a few times. Place on a foil-lined baking sheet and let roast for 50 minutes, or until extremely soft. When the sweet potatoes have cooled, slice in half and scoop out the flesh.

3. Reserve 1 teaspoon of the melted butter. Place the rest in a large bowl with the sweet potatoes, bourbon or rum, brown sugar, vanilla, salt, and pepper and mash until combined.

4. Lightly coat a 10-inch cast-iron skillet or enameled cast-iron casserole dish with the reserved butter. Fill the pan with the sweet potato mixture and arrange the marshmallows on top.

5. Place the skillet or casserole dish on a baking sheet in case of overflow. Place in the oven and bake until the marshmallows start to brown, about 30 minutes. Serve warm or at room temperature.

INGREDIENTS:

5   LARGE SWEET POTATOES

1   STICK OF UNSALTED BUTTER, MELTED

¼   CUP BOURBON OR DARK RUM

½   CUP LIGHT BROWN SUGAR

1   TEASPOON VANILLA EXTRACT

1   TEASPOON KOSHER SALT

1   TEASPOON FINELY GROUND BLACK PEPPER

4   CUPS MINIATURE MARSHMALLOWS

MEAT

(Beef, Veal, Lamb, Pork & Rabbit)

*H*aving pretty much everything available at the push of a button is one of the ultimate indicators of how fortunate we are to live in these times.

That convenience isn't just nice when you need a new pair of shoes—it's also handy in the kitchen, opening every home to a number of previously out-of-reach preparations, such as the Rabbit Ragù on page 350. Now, there are no excuses for not trying new recipes.

Particularly when you consider what cast iron is able to bring to the table. That celebrated ability to distribute and hold heat truly shines when charged with a meat-based preparation, effortlessly providing the crispy, seared exterior and juicy interior we all crave. Whether it's the mouthwatering Carne Asada (see the facing page), the fragrant Thai Crying Tiger Beef (see page 275), or classic French bistro fare like the Steak au Poivre (see page 255), there's something every carnivore will be dying to sink their teeth into.

CARNE ASADA

YIELD: 4 TO 6 SERVINGS / ACTIVE TIME: 30 MINUTES / TOTAL TIME: 3 HOURS

This succulent classic provides a lot of flavor considering how little heavy lifting there is. This is the traditional version, but it can easily be tweaked according to taste. Most people would make this on the grill, but even flame cannot touch cast iron here. Serve with warm corn tortillas (see page 169 for homemade), rice, and a piquant salsa.

1. Place all of the ingredients, except for the steak, in a shallow dish or large resealable plastic bag and stir to combine. Add the steak, place it in the refrigerator, and let marinate for at least 2, and up to 24, hours.

2. Approximately 30 minutes before you are going to cook the steak, remove it from the marinade, pat it dry, and let it come to room temperature.

3. Place a cast-iron grill pan over high heat and add enough vegetable oil to sear the steak. When the oil starts to smoke, add the steak and cook on each side for 6 minutes for medium-rare.

4. While the steak is cooking, pour the marinade into a saucepan, bring to a boil, and let boil for 5 minutes.

5. Remove the steaks and let them rest for 5 minutes before slicing into thin strips, making sure to cut against the grain. Drizzle the warmed marinade over the top and serve.

INGREDIENTS:

1   JALAPEÑO PEPPER, SEEDED AND MINCED

3   GARLIC CLOVES, MINCED

½   CUP CHOPPED CILANTRO

¼   CUP VEGETABLE OIL, PLUS MORE AS NEEDED

    JUICE OF 1 SMALL ORANGE

2   TABLESPOONS APPLE CIDER VINEGAR

2   TEASPOONS CAYENNE PEPPER

1   TEASPOON ANCHO CHILI POWDER

1   TEASPOON GARLIC POWDER

1   TEASPOON PAPRIKA

1   TEASPOON KOSHER SALT

1   TEASPOON CUMIN

1   TEASPOON DRIED OREGANO

¼   TEASPOON FRESHLY GROUND BLACK PEPPER

2   LBS. FLANK OR SKIRT STEAK, TRIMMED

STRIP STEAK *with* MUSHROOMS *and* FINGERLING POTATOES

YIELD: 6 SERVINGS / **ACTIVE TIME:** 30 MINUTES / **TOTAL TIME:** 1 HOUR

Once you get this recipe down, there's no reason to ever visit that fancy local steak house again. For an added jolt of flavor, take whatever butter you have left over and mix it with some chopped thyme leaves. Place this on the steaks before serving and enjoy.

1. Preheat oven to 375°F.

2. Place the salt and red pepper flakes in a bowl. Use a spice grinder or a mortar and pestle to grind the peppercorns, fennel seeds, mustard seeds, and coriander seeds into a powder. Place the powder in the bowl with the salt and red pepper flakes and stir to combine.

3. Place steaks on a plate and season liberally with the seasoning blend. Set the steaks aside and let stand at room temperature for 1 hour.

4. Place the potatoes in a 12-inch cast-iron skillet and cover with water. Cook over high heat until the potatoes are tender but not mushy. Drain and set aside.

5. Wipe the skillet with a paper towel, add the olive oil, and warm over medium-high heat. Add the steaks to the pan, making sure you don't overcrowd. Cook steaks for 2 minutes, turn them over, and add 1 chunk of butter and 1 sprig of thyme for each steak. Cook steaks for 2 minutes, while spooning the butter over the steaks. Remove steaks and set aside. Remove thyme sprigs and discard.

6. Add the shallot and the remaining chunk of butter to the pan. Cook for 1 minute and add the cremini mushrooms. Cook for 5 minutes and then add the shiitake and oyster mushrooms. Cook for 3 more minutes and add the Cabernet Sauvignon. After 30 seconds, add the potatoes, Worcestershire sauce, tamari or soy sauce, and fish sauce. Stir until the mushrooms are evenly coated.

7. Return the steaks and their juices to the skillet. Place the skillet in the oven and cook until the steaks are warmed through, about 3 minutes.

8. Remove the skillet from the oven and slice the steaks at a 45° angle every 2 inches. Scoop the potatoes and vegetables onto a plate, top with the sliced steak, sprinkle with the fresh thyme leaves, and serve.

INGREDIENTS:

- 2 TABLESPOONS KOSHER SALT OR COARSE SEA SALT
- ½ TEASPOON RED PEPPER FLAKES
- ½ TEASPOON WHOLE BLACK PEPPERCORNS
- ½ TEASPOON FENNEL SEEDS
- ½ TEASPOON MUSTARD SEEDS
- ½ TEASPOON CORIANDER SEEDS
- 6 (7 OZ.) STRIP STEAKS
- 2 LBS. FINGERLING POTATOES, HALVED LENGTHWISE
- 2 TABLESPOONS OLIVE OIL
- 1½ STICKS OF UNSALTED BUTTER, AT ROOM TEMPERATURE AND DIVIDED INTO 7 CHUNKS
- 6 SPRIGS OF THYME, PLUS 2 TABLESPOONS OF LEAVES FOR GARNISH
- 1 LARGE SHALLOT, MINCED
- 2 LBS. CREMINI MUSHROOMS, CLEANED AND QUARTERED
- 1 LB. SHIITAKE MUSHROOMS, STEMMED AND SLICED THIN
- 1 LB. OYSTER MUSHROOMS, SLICED THIN
- ½ CUP CABERNET SAUVIGNON
- ¼ CUP WORCESTERSHIRE SAUCE
- 2 TABLESPOONS LIGHT TAMARI OR LIGHT SOY SAUCE
- 2 TABLESPOONS FISH SAUCE

CHIMICHURRI STRIP STEAK
with OREGANO POTATOES & ONIONS

YIELD: 4 SERVINGS / ACTIVE TIME: 20 MINUTES / TOTAL TIME: 24 HOURS

If you are feeling adventurous and want the authentic taste for this dish, you can ask your local butcher where to purchase some beef tallow. Serve this Argentinian dish with a simple salad of tomatoes, cucumbers, greens, and onions—you'll quickly fall in love with it.

1. To prepare the chimichurri sauce, place all of the ingredients in a blender and puree until smooth.

2. Transfer half of the sauce and the steaks to a container and let them marinate in the refrigerator overnight. Refrigerate the other half of the sauce in a separate container.

3. Preheat oven to 375°F.

4. Remove the steaks from the marinade and season both sides with salt. Set aside and let come to room temperature as you cook the potatoes and onions.

5. Place the white sweet potatoes, the Yukon Gold potatoes, and 1 tablespoon of salt in a 12-inch cast-iron skillet. Cover with water, bring to a boil, and cook until the potatoes are tender. Drain and set aside.

6. Wipe the pan with a paper towel, add the olive oil and beef tallow, and warm over medium-high heat. Add the steaks and cook for 2 minutes on each side. Remove the steaks from the pan and set aside.

7. Place the potatoes, onion, 3 tablespoons of chimichurri sauce, salt, and pepper in the pan and cook, while stirring, until the onion is cooked through, about 10 minutes. Add the vinegar, wine, and oregano and cook until the vinegar and wine have nearly evaporated, 5 minutes.

8. Return the steaks to the pan and place the skillet in the oven for 5 minutes.

9. Remove the pan from the oven, divide between serving plates, top with the remaining chimichurri sauce, and serve with a small salad.

INGREDIENTS:

FOR THE CHIMICHURRI SAUCE

2	TABLESPOONS CHOPPED FRESH OREGANO
¼	CUP OLIVE OIL
2	CUPS CHOPPED FRESH PARSLEY
1½	CUPS CHOPPED CILANTRO LEAVES
1	SMALL WHITE OR YELLOW ONION, CHOPPED
2	SCALLIONS
1	JALAPEÑO PEPPER, SEEDED TO TASTE
¼	TABLESPOON SALT
¼	TABLESPOON PEPPER
¼	TABLESPOON ONION POWDER
¼	TABLESPOON GARLIC POWDER
1	TABLESPOON SUGAR
⅓	CUP WATER

FOR THE STEAK, POTATOES & ONIONS

4	(5 TO 6 OZ.) NEW YORK STRIP STEAKS
	SALT AND PEPPER, TO TASTE
2	WHITE SWEET POTATOES, PEELED AND DICED
2	YUKON GOLD POTATOES, PEELED AND DICED
1	TABLESPOON OLIVE OIL
2	TABLESPOONS BEEF TALLOW
1	LARGE WHITE ONION, SLICED THIN
¼	CUP WHITE VINEGAR OR RED WINE VINEGAR
⅓	CUP DRY RED WINE (CABERNET SAUVIGNON, TEMPRANILLO, OR RIOJA)
1	TABLESPOON CHOPPED FRESH OREGANO

TIP: Beef tallow is the rendered fat of beef, and it makes a great substitute for butter. If you can't find beef tallow at your local butcher, you can always ask him for some beef fat, grind it in a food processor until fine, and cook it in a slow cooker for 6 to 8 hours. Then strain the fat through a coffee filter and store the liquid in the refrigerator until ready to use. To get 1 cup of tallow you'll need 1 lb. of beef fat.

STEAK AU POIVRE

YIELD: 2 SERVINGS / ACTIVE TIME: 40 MINUTES / TOTAL TIME: 2 HOURS

When making this French classic, keep in mind that you'll get the best results from the best ingredients. Go farm-fresh for the meat, shallots, chives, and cream, if at all possible. Bon appétit!

1. Preheat oven to 200°F.

2. Pat the steaks dry and season both sides with kosher salt.

3. Put the peppercorns in a sealed plastic bag and, working on a hard, flat surface, pound them with a meat tenderizer or mallet to crush them. Pour them onto a plate and press both sides of the steaks into them, distributing peppercorns evenly over the meat.

4. Place a 12-inch cast-iron skillet over medium-high heat for 5 minutes. Add the oil and swirl to coat the bottom of the pan. Put the steaks in the pan and sear on both sides, cooking for about 3 minutes a side for medium-rare.

5. Transfer steaks to a platter in the oven and keep warm as you make the sauce.

6. With the skillet over medium heat, add a tablespoon of the butter, let it melt, and add the shallots. As they sauté, stir up the bits stuck to the bottom of the pan. Cook until shallots are browned, about 3 minutes. Turn off the heat, pour the Cognac in the pan, swirl it around, and using a long-handled lighter, ignite it. The flame will subside in a minute or so. Turn the heat back on and cook the sauce until it is nearly boiling, while stirring constantly.

7. Add the cream and any juices from the platter the steaks are on. Reduce the heat and cook the sauce until somewhat reduced, about 5 minutes. Stir in the remaining tablespoon of butter.

8. Put the steaks on a plate and pour the sauce over them. Garnish with rosemary, if desired.

INGREDIENTS:

- 2 (8 OZ.) BONELESS STRIP STEAKS
- KOSHER SALT, TO TASTE
- 1 TABLESPOON WHOLE BLACK PEPPERCORNS
- 1 TEASPOON VEGETABLE OIL
- 2 TABLESPOONS UNSALTED BUTTER, CUT INTO PIECES
- 2 SMALL SHALLOTS, MINCED
- ⅓ CUP COGNAC OR OTHER BRANDY
- ½ CUP HEAVY CREAM
- SPRIGS OF ROSEMARY, FOR GARNISH (OPTIONAL)

COUNTRY FRIED STEAKS *and* GRAVY

YIELD: 2 SERVINGS / **ACTIVE TIME:** 40 MINUTES / **TOTAL TIME:** 2 HOURS

Try your hand at one of the most iconic Southern inventions—the Country Fried Steak! Be advised: high-quality ingredients will go a long way in this dish.

1. Preheat oven to 200°F and place an ovenproof serving dish in it.

2. Prep steaks by patting them dry then seasoning both sides with kosher salt.

3. Add the cup of flour and ½ teaspoon of pepper to a shallow dish or bowl and dredge the steaks in it. Make sure they are evenly coated.

4. Place a 12-inch cast-iron skillet over medium-high heat for 5 minutes. Add the oil and the butter, coating the bottom of the pan. Put the steaks in the pan and fry on both sides, cooking for about 5 minutes a side.

5. Transfer steaks to the serving dish in the oven and keep warm as you make the gravy.

6. For the gravy, reduce the heat and pour out all but 2 tablespoons of the leftover pan drippings. Mix in the 2 tablespoons of flour, creating a roux. Continue to stir while turning the heat back up to medium.

7. Once the roux is smooth, slowly add the milk, stirring constantly until incorporated. If the gravy is too thick, add more milk. If too thin, continue to cook it until it reduces. Season with a sprinkle of salt and plenty of black pepper. Cover the steaks with the gravy and serve.

INGREDIENTS:

- 2 (4 OZ.) ROUND STEAKS OR CUBE STEAKS
- KOSHER SALT, TO TASTE
- 1 CUP ALL-PURPOSE FLOUR, PLUS 2 TABLESPOONS
- ½ TEASPOON FRESHLY GROUND BLACK PEPPER, PLUS MORE TO TASTE
- 1 CUP PEANUT, VEGETABLE, OR CANOLA OIL
- 2 TABLESPOONS UNSALTED BUTTER, CUT INTO PIECES
- ¾ CUP WHOLE MILK, PLUS MORE AS NEEDED

STEAK WITH PEPPERS & ONIONS

YIELD: 4 SERVINGS / ACTIVE TIME: 20 MINUTES / TOTAL TIME: 2 TO 24 HOURS

Steak, peppers, and onions—you can only survive such simplicity when the mix of flavors is this flawless. If you somehow end up with leftovers, be sure to slice the meat further and put everything on a crusty French roll with some arugula.

1. Place 7 tablespoons of the vegetable oil in a large bowl. Add the garlic, Worcestershire sauce, red wine vinegar, and mustard powder and stir to combine. Add the beef and stir until it is coated. Cover and refrigerate for at least 2, and up to 24, hours. Stir the beef once or twice while it marinates.

2. Remove the meat from the marinade and allow it to come to room temperature. Reserve the marinade.

3. Place a 12-inch cast-iron skillet over medium-high heat and add the remaining vegetable oil. When it starts to shimmer, add the meat and cook until it is browned all over, about 8 minutes. Remove from the pan and set aside.

4. Place the reserved marinade in a small saucepan and bring to a boil. Boil for 5 minutes, remove from heat, and set aside.

5. Reduce the heat to medium, add the onions and peppers, and cook, without stirring, until they are browned, about 3 minutes. Add the marinade and bring it to a simmer. Place the beef back in the pan and cook for an additional 2 minutes. Season with salt and pepper and serve.

INGREDIENTS:

- ½   CUP VEGETABLE OIL
- 1   GARLIC CLOVE, MINCED
- 2   TEASPOONS WORCESTERSHIRE SAUCE
- 2   TEASPOONS RED WINE VINEGAR
- 1   TABLESPOON MUSTARD POWDER
- 2   LBS. SIRLOIN TIPS, CUT INTO BITE-SIZED PIECES
- 2   YELLOW ONIONS, SLICED
- 2   RED BELL PEPPERS, SEEDED AND SLICED

     SALT AND PEPPER, TO TASTE

OVER-ROASTED NEW YORK STRIP STEAK *with* WHIPPED POTATOES *and* SWISS CHARD

YIELD: 2 SERVINGS / **ACTIVE TIME:** 45 MINUTES / **TOTAL TIME:** 1 HOUR AND 30 MINUTES

As fall temperatures go from brisk to chilly, standing out by the grill doesn't seem quite as appealing. But that doesn't mean you have to say goodbye to the enchanting flavor of a quality steak.

1. Place the steak on a plate and let stand at room temperature for 20 to 30 minutes, as this will ensure that it cooks evenly. Preheat the oven to 475°F.

2. Place the potatoes in a saucepan, cover with cold water, and add the salt. Bring to a boil, reduce heat so that the potatoes simmer, and cook until tender, about 12 minutes. Strain and set aside.

3. Combine the cream and 6 tablespoons of the butter in a saucepan and heat until the butter is melted. Remove from heat, place the potatoes in the bowl of a stand mixer fitted with the whisk attachment, and add half of the cream-and-butter mixture. Whisk until the potatoes are smooth, adding more of the mixture as needed to achieve the desired consistency. Set aside.

4. Place a 12-inch cast-iron skillet over high heat and add the canola oil. Season the steak liberally with salt and cracked black pepper. When the oil begins to smoke, carefully place the steak in the skillet and cook for 2 minutes on each side.

5. When both sides of the steak have been seared, use kitchen tongs to turn the steak onto the edge where the fat is. Hold the steak in place until the fat has rendered, about 2 minutes. Lay the steak flat in the pan and add the remaining butter, thyme, crushed garlic cloves, and shallot. Using a large spoon, baste the steak with the juices in the pan and cook for another minute. Remove from heat and place the steak on a wire rack resting in a baking sheet.

6. Place the steak in the oven and cook for 3 minutes. Remove and let stand for 8 to 10 minutes before slicing. The steak should be medium-rare, with an internal temperature of 145°F.

7. While the steak is resting, place the olive oil in a 12-inch cast-iron skillet and warm over medium-high heat. When the oil starts to smoke, add the Swiss chard and minced garlic and cook until the chard is wilted. Season with salt and pepper.

8. To serve, cut the steak into desired portions and plate alongside the potatoes and Swiss chard.

INGREDIENTS:

1-LB. NEW YORK STRIP STEAK

3 IDAHO POTATOES, PEELED AND CUT INTO 1-INCH PIECES

1 TABLESPOON SALT, PLUS MORE TO TASTE

1 CUP HEAVY CREAM

1 STICK OF UNSALTED BUTTER

2 TABLESPOONS CANOLA OIL

CRACKED BLACK PEPPER, TO TASTE

3 SPRIGS OF THYME

3 GARLIC CLOVES, CRUSHED, PLUS 1 TABLESPOON MINCED GARLIC

1 SHALLOT, HALVED

2 TABLESPOONS OLIVE OIL

½ BUNCH OF SWISS CHARD, STEMMED AND CHOPPED

YANKEE SHORT RIBS
with ROASTED POTATOES *&* CARROTS

YIELD: 4 SERVINGS / ACTIVE TIME: 30 MINUTES / TOTAL TIME: 3 HOURS AND 30 MINUTES

This recipe is a twist on the New England classic—the Yankee pot roast. Short rib is an amazing cut from the brisket that benefits from cooking at low temperatures for a long time, which makes it the perfect candidate for low and slow cooking in a Dutch oven.

1. Preheat the oven to 300°F.

2. Place the canola oil in a large skillet and warm it over medium-high heat. Pat the short ribs dry and season generously with salt.

3. Place the short ribs in the skillet and cook, while turning, until they are browned all over.

4. Transfer the browned short ribs to a Dutch oven with the onions, carrots, potatoes, stock, and bay leaves. Cover, place the Dutch oven in the oven, and cook until the short ribs are fork-tender and the meat easily comes away from the bone, about 3 to 4 hours.

5. Remove from the oven, strain through a fine sieve, and reserve the cooking liquid. Set the short ribs and vegetables aside.

6. Place the reserved liquid in a pan with the rosemary, thyme, and red wine. Cook over high heat until the sauce has reduced and started to thicken.

7. Season with salt and pepper. Divide the short ribs and vegetables between the serving plates and spoon 2 to 3 tablespoons of the sauce over each portion.

INGREDIENTS:

2	TABLESPOONS CANOLA OIL
4	LBS. BONE-IN SHORT RIBS
	SALT AND PEPPER, TO TASTE
2	LARGE ONIONS, SLICED
4	CARROTS, DICED
4	LARGE POTATOES, DICED
8	CUPS BEEF STOCK (SEE PAGES 200–201)
4	BAY LEAVES
2	SPRIGS OF ROSEMARY
2	SPRIGS OF THYME
½	CUP RED WINE

SPAGHETTI *and* MEATBALLS

YIELD: 4 TO 6 SERVINGS / **ACTIVE TIME:** 30 MINUTES / **TOTAL TIME:** 1 HOUR

You can't miss with these meatballs, whether you put them over pasta, in a sub, or on their own with a little sauce and cheese.

1. Fill a cast-iron Dutch oven with water. Add a tablespoon of salt and bring to a boil. Add the pasta and cook for 7 to 10 minutes or until al dente. Drain and transfer the pasta to a bowl. Add 2 tablespoons of the olive oil, toss to coat, and set aside.

2. Place the Dutch oven over high heat and add the remaining olive oil.

3. Add the garlic, onion, and parsley and cook for 7 to 10 minutes, or until the onion starts to caramelize. Remove the mixture from the pot and let cool.

4. When the onion-and-garlic mixture has cooled, place it in a bowl with all of the meats, the cream, bread pieces, eggs, Parmesan, and basil. Season with salt and pepper and gently stir to combine. Make sure not to overwork the mixture or the meatballs could get a little tough. Place a small piece of the mixture in the Dutch oven and cook until it is cooked through. Taste and adjust seasoning if necessary. Then form the remaining mixture into meatballs.

5. Place half of the meatballs in the Dutch oven and cook over medium-high heat for 3 minutes. Gently flip with a flexible spatula and cook for 3 minutes. Repeat with the remaining meatballs. Once all the meatballs are seared, remove and set on a paper towel–lined plate to drain. Drain any grease from the Dutch oven and wipe clean.

6. Place the marinara sauce in the Dutch oven and warm over medium-low heat. Add the meatballs, cover the pot, and cook until the meatballs are cooked through, about 15 minutes.

7. When the meatballs are nearly done cooking, add the pasta to the Dutch oven and stir until heated through. Serve with garlic bread on the side.

INGREDIENTS:

- 1   TABLESPOON SALT, PLUS MORE TO TASTE
- 1   LB. SPAGHETTI OR LINGUINE
- ¼   CUP OLIVE OIL
- 2   GARLIC CLOVES, MINCED
- 1   WHITE ONION, MINCED
- 2   TABLESPOONS CHOPPED FLAT-LEAF PARSLEY
- 1   LB. GROUND BEEF (85% LEAN)
- 1   LB. GROUND PORK
- 1   LB. GROUND VEAL
- 1   CUP LIGHT CREAM
-      5-INCH SECTION OF ITALIAN BREAD, CRUST REMOVED, MINCED
- 2   EGGS
- ¾   CUP GRATED PARMESAN CHEESE
- 1   TABLESPOON MINCED BASIL
-      BLACK PEPPER, TO TASTE
- 6   CUPS MARINARA SAUCE
- 1   LOAF OF GARLIC BREAD, SLICED

BEST. BURGERS. EVER.

YIELD: 3 TO 4 BURGERS / ACTIVE TIME: 30 MINUTES / TOTAL TIME: 30 MINUTES

A burger hot off the grill is a delicious thing. It's a staple of American dining. But if you want the Best. Burger. Ever., you won't produce it on the grill. You'll make it in a cast-iron skillet. Why? Because the fat in the meat creates its own sauce, helping to brown and flavor the meat as it cooks. All of this drips off the grill. The cast iron holds the heat steady and hot, too, turning the surface of the burger the perfect, crispy dark brown from side to side. If your mouth is watering now, wait until you make these at home.

1. Refrigerate the ground beef until ready to use.

2. When it's time to make the burgers, brush a 12-inch cast-iron skillet with a thin sheen of oil, and heat it over medium-high heat. Don't overhandle the meat, simply take a handful of it (about 3 oz.) and form into a patty. Make 3 or 4, depending on how many will fit in the skillet.

3. Put the patties in the skillet and don't touch them. Let them start to cook over medium-high heat. Sprinkle some salt and pepper over them. Let them cook on one side for about 3 minutes.

4. When you flip the burgers, if you want cheese on one or all of them, put it on now.

5. Leave the burgers to cook on this side for 3 or 4 minutes. Scoop the burgers off the skillet with the spatula, slide each one onto a bun, top with whatever you like, and enjoy.

TIP: The kind of meat you use matters. The meat-to-fat ratio should be about 80–20. Most ground beef found in the grocery store is 85–15 or 90–10. If you have to go with one of these, choose the fattier proportion. The best thing to do, though, is ask the meat department to grind the meat for you. You want a chuck cut with a good amount of fat in it. The fat should show up as almost chunky in the meat, not pulverized.

INGREDIENTS:

1   LB. GROUND BEEF

VEGETABLE OIL, FOR THE SKILLET

SALT AND PEPPER, TO TASTE

HAMBURGER BUNS, FOR SERVING

SLICES OF CHEESE (OPTIONAL), FOR SERVING

LETTUCE, TOMATO, ONION (OPTIONAL), FOR SERVING

KETCHUP, MUSTARD, PICKLES, MAYONNAISE (OPTIONAL), FOR SERVING

BEEF STROGANOFF

YIELD: 4 TO 6 SERVINGS / **ACTIVE TIME:** 40 MINUTES / **TOTAL TIME:** 1 HOUR AND 30 MINUTES

This dish is originally Russian and is made with pieces of beef served in a rich sauce that includes sour cream (*smetana*). It reportedly became popular in the mid-1800s. This is amazing on a cold winter day paired with a side of whole wheat bread and a cold cider.

1. Heat the olive oil in a 12-inch cast-iron skillet over medium-high heat. Add the beef strips so they fit in the skillet (or work in batches). Fry them in the skillet, while turning so that all sides get browned, about 3 minutes. Transfer the beef pieces to a plate and cover with foil to keep warm.

2. Add a bit more oil if necessary, and sauté the onion, garlic, and mushrooms until soft, about 5 minutes. In the skillet, add the beef broth, Sherry, and Worcestershire sauce. Bring to a boil, scraping the browned bits of meat and vegetables off the bottom of the pan. Put the flour in a bowl and add some of the heated sauce, using a whisk to form a paste. Add a bit more sauce to the bowl, and when the flour is fully incorporated, transfer all of it into the skillet and stir until incorporated. Continue to cook until the sauce thickens.

3. Reduce the heat and add the sour cream. Add the beef back to the skillet. When everything is hot, season with salt and pepper, and serve over the egg noodles.

INGREDIENTS:

- 1 TABLESPOON OLIVE OIL, PLUS MORE AS NEEDED
- 1 LB. STEW BEEF, CUT INTO STRIPS
- 1 SMALL ONION, MINCED
- 2 GARLIC CLOVES, PRESSED
- ½ CUP SLICED MUSHROOM CAPS
- 1½ CUPS BEEF BROTH
- ¼ CUP DRY SHERRY
- 1 TABLESPOON WORCESTERSHIRE SAUCE
- ¼ CUP ALL-PURPOSE FLOUR
- ½ CUP SOUR CREAM
- SALT AND PEPPER, TO TASTE
- ½ LB. EGG NOODLES, COOKED, FOR SERVING

SUKIYAKI

YIELD: 2 TO 4 SERVINGS / ACTIVE TIME: 5 MINUTES / TOTAL TIME: 15 MINUTES

A modest Japanese preparation that will become a family favorite. Cook it on an induction burner in the center of your table for an authentic experience, or just make it on the stovetop and ladle into individual bowls.

1. Bring a large pot of salted water to a boil. Add the noodles to the boiling water and cook for 2 minutes. Drain, rinse with cold water, and set the noodles aside.

2. Place the vegetable oil in a cast-iron Dutch oven and warm over medium-high heat. When the oil starts to shimmer, add the sugar and steak and cook until the steak is browned all over, about 2 minutes.

3. Add the mirin, sake, soy sauce, and Dashi Broth (or water) and stir to combine.

4. Carefully arrange the noodles, green onions, cabbage, mushrooms, spinach, and tofu in the broth. Cover and steam until the cabbage is wilted. Ladle into warmed bowls.

DASHI BROTH

1. In a medium saucepan, add the water and the kombu. Soak for 20 minutes, remove the kombu, and score gently with a knife.

2. Return the kombu to the saucepan and bring to a boil. Remove the kombu as soon as the water boils, so that the stock doesn't become bitter.

3. Add the bonito flakes and return to a boil. Turn off the heat and let the stock stand.

4. Strain through a fine sieve and chill the stock in the refrigerator. You will have approximately 6 cups.

INGREDIENTS:

SALT, TO TASTE

¾ LB. UDON NOODLES OR SHIRATAKI NOODLES

1 TABLESPOON VEGETABLE OIL

3 TABLESPOONS BROWN SUGAR

1 LB. RIB EYE, SLICED VERY THIN

½ CUP MIRIN

½ CUP SAKE

⅓ CUP SOY SAUCE

1 CUP DASHI BROTH (SEE RECIPE) OR WATER

1 BUNCH OF GREEN ONIONS, SLICED INTO 2-INCH PIECES

2 CUPS CHOPPED NAPA CABBAGE

1 BUNCH OF ENOKI MUSHROOMS

6 LARGE SHIITAKE MUSHROOMS

1 CUP FRESH SPINACH

½ LB. TOFU, DRAINED AND CUT INTO ¼-INCH CUBES

DASHI BROTH

8 CUPS COLD WATER

2 OZ. KOMBU

1 CUP BONITO FLAKES

BEEF SHAWARMA

YIELD: 4 TO 6 SERVINGS / **ACTIVE TIME:** 10 MINUTES / **TOTAL TIME:** 2 HOURS

The secret to this dish is sumac, a popular spice in Middle Eastern cuisine that adds a beguiling sourness to dishes. This is typically served in a sandwich to be eaten on the go but is just as nice out on the patio with friends, a side of lemon rice, and a light cucumber salad.

1. Place the meat in the freezer for 30 minutes so that it will be easier to slice. After 30 minutes, use an extremely sharp knife to slice it as thin as possible.

2. Place the sliced meat in a large mixing bowl. Add the olive oil, vinegar, lemon juice, cinnamon, coriander, pepper, cardamom, cloves, mace, nutmeg, and garlic powder and stir to combine. Place the meat in the refrigerator and let it marinate for 1 hour. If you have time, let the meat marinate overnight for even more flavor.

3. Place the sliced onions in a baking dish and cover with water. Add a pinch of salt and several ice cubes. Place in the refrigerator for at least 30 minutes and up to 4 hours.

4. Remove the meat from the refrigerator and let it come to room temperature. Drain the onions, squeeze them to remove any excess water, and place them in a bowl. Add the sumac powder and toss to coat. Set aside.

5. Warm a cast-iron grill pan over high heat. When it is warm, add the meat in batches and cook until it is browned all over.

6. To serve, place a dollop of yogurt on a pita and top with some of the meat, onions, cucumbers, tomatoes, and mint or parsley leaves.

INGREDIENTS:

3 LBS. SIRLOIN

6 TABLESPOONS OLIVE OIL

3 TABLESPOONS RED WINE VINEGAR

JUICE OF 2 LEMONS

2 TEASPOONS CINNAMON

2 TABLESPOONS CORIANDER

1 TABLESPOON BLACK PEPPER

1 TEASPOON CARDAMOM

1 TEASPOON GROUND CLOVES

½ TEASPOON MACE

⅛ TEASPOON GROUND NUTMEG

1 TABLESPOON GARLIC POWDER

2 YELLOW ONIONS, SLICED INTO THIN HALF-MOONS

SALT, TO TASTE

1 TEASPOON SUMAC POWDER

1 CUP PLAIN GREEK YOGURT, FOR SERVING

PITA BREAD (SEE PAGE 177), FOR SERVING

2 PERSIAN CUCUMBERS, DICED, FOR SERVING

2 ROMA TOMATOES, DICED, FOR SERVING

½ CUP FRESH MINT OR PARSLEY LEAVES, TORN, FOR SERVING

THAI CRYING TIGER BEEF

YIELD: 4 SERVINGS / **ACTIVE TIME:** 15 MINUTES / **TOTAL TIME:** 30 MINUTES

A lot of theories abound as to why this dish is called Crying (or Weeping) Tiger, but all of them agree that it is delicious. You may also end up with tears in your eyes, overwhelmed by the good fortune of happening upon this dish.

1. Pat the steak dry. Place it in a bowl and add the soy sauce, oyster sauce, and the 1 tablespoon of brown sugar. Stir to combine and then let the steak marinate for 10 minutes.

2. Place a cast-iron grill pan over high heat and spray it with non-stick cooking spray. Add the steak and cook on each side for 5 minutes for medium. Transfer to a plate, cover with foil, and let rest for 5 minutes before slicing into thin strips, making sure to cut across the grain.

3. To make the dipping sauce, place the tomato, lime juice, fish sauce (if using), remaining brown sugar, cilantro, Toasted Rice Powder, and red pepper flakes in a bowl and stir to combine. The powder won't dissolve, but it will lightly bind the rest of the ingredients together.

4. Divide the dipping sauce between the serving bowls. Top with the slices of beef, garnish with the soft herb leaf mix, and serve alongside the white rice.

TOASTED RICE POWDER

1. Heat a cast-iron skillet over medium-high heat. Add the rice and toast until browned.

2. Remove and grind into a fine powder with a mortar and pestle.

INGREDIENTS:

- 2 LBS. FLANK STEAK
- 2 TABLESPOONS SOY SAUCE
- 1 TABLESPOON OYSTER SAUCE
- 1 TABLESPOON BROWN SUGAR, PLUS 1 TEASPOON
- 1 LARGE TOMATO, SEEDED AND DICED
- ⅓ CUP LIME JUICE
- ¼ CUP FISH SAUCE (OPTIONAL)
- 2 TABLESPOONS MINCED CILANTRO LEAVES
- 1½ TABLESPOONS TOASTED RICE POWDER (SEE RECIPE)
- 1 TABLESPOON RED PEPPER FLAKES
- 1 CUP SOFT HERB LEAF MIX (MINT, THAI HOLY BASIL, AND CILANTRO), FOR GARNISH
- 1½ CUPS COOKED WHITE RICE, FOR SERVING

TOASTED RICE POWDER
- ½ CUP JASMINE RICE

BRAZILIAN POT ROAST

YIELD: 4 TO 6 SERVINGS / **ACTIVE TIME:** 30 MINUTES / **TOTAL TIME:** 2 HOURS AND 30 MINUTES

This hearty and warming stew hails from northern Brazil. It's seasoned with annatto, a popular ingredient that is used to flavor and color meat. If you can't find annatto, you can either omit it or use turmeric, which will lend the dish a different deliciousness. If you want to be extra authentic, stir in 12 to 16 whole pods of okra for the last 15 minutes of cooking and serve with rice and black beans.

1. Preheat your oven to 325°F.

2. Pat the chuck roast dry and season it lightly all over with salt, annatto (if using), and cumin.

3. Place the vegetable oil in a large cast-iron Dutch oven and warm over medium heat. When the oil starts to smoke, add the chuck roast and cook until it is brown on all sides, 10 to 15 minutes. Remove the roast and set it aside.

4. Add the carrots, onion, potatoes, and garlic and cook until they are lightly browned, about 10 minutes. Return the roast to the pan and add the broth. It should not cover the meat.

5. Cover the Dutch oven and place it in the oven. Cook until the roast is tender, about 2 hours. Remove the roast from the pot, let it cool slightly, and then cut it into bite-sized pieces. Place the pieces back in the pot, stir to incorporate, and then ladle into warmed bowls.

INGREDIENTS:

   4-LB. CHUCK ROAST

   SALT AND PEPPER, TO TASTE

1 TABLESPOON ANNATTO POWDER (OPTIONAL)

1 TABLESPOON GROUND CUMIN

2 TABLESPOONS VEGETABLE OIL

2 LARGE CARROTS, PEELED AND CHOPPED

1 LARGE YELLOW ONION, CHOPPED

2 LARGE POTATOES, PEELED AND CHOPPED

5 GARLIC CLOVES, MINCED

2 CUPS BEEF BROTH

HUNGARIAN GOULASH

YIELD: 6 TO 8 SERVINGS / ACTIVE TIME: 30 MINUTES / TOTAL TIME: 2 HOURS AND 30 MINUTES

A rich and hearty dish that will be even better the next day. Redolent with the flavors of Eastern Europe—sweet paprika, earthy caraway, garlic, and sour cream—it is the comfort food you never knew you needed. Take your time making this; you will be rewarded.

1. Place the oil in a large cast-iron Dutch oven and warm over medium heat. When the oil starts to smoke, add the meat in batches and cook until it is browned all over, taking care not to crowd the pot. Remove the browned meat and set aside.

2. Reduce the heat to medium-low. Wait 2 minutes and then add the onions, carrots, and peppers. Stir to coat with the pan drippings and sauté until the vegetables are golden brown, about 10 minutes. Add the caraway seeds, stir to incorporate, and cook until the seeds are fragrant, about 1 minute.

3. Add the flour, paprika, tomato paste, garlic, sugar, salt, and pepper and stir to incorporate. Add the broth and use a wooden spoon to scrape up any browned bits from the bottom of the pan.

4. Bring the goulash to a boil, reduce the heat, and let it simmer until it thickens slightly, about 10 minutes. Add the meat back to the Dutch oven, cover, and simmer over low heat until the meat is very tender, about 2 hours.

5. Approximately 20 minutes before the goulash will be done, bring water to a boil in a large pot. Add the egg noodles to the boiling water and cook until al dente. Drain and set aside.

6. To serve, stir in the sour cream and ladle the goulash over the cooked egg noodles.

INGREDIENTS:

- 2 TABLESPOONS VEGETABLE OIL
- 3 LBS. BEEF CHUCK, TRIMMED
- 3 YELLOW ONIONS, CHOPPED
- 2 CARROTS, PEELED AND CHOPPED
- 2 BELL PEPPERS, SEEDED AND CHOPPED
- 1 TEASPOON CARAWAY SEEDS
- ¼ CUP ALL-PURPOSE FLOUR
- 3 TABLESPOONS SWEET HUNGARIAN PAPRIKA
- 3 TABLESPOONS TOMATO PASTE
- 2 GARLIC CLOVES, MINCED
- 1 TEASPOON SUGAR
- SALT AND PEPPER, TO TASTE
- 2 CUPS BEEF BROTH
- 1 LB. WIDE EGG NOODLES
- 1 CUP SOUR CREAM

SHEPHERD'S PIE

YIELD: 4 TO 6 SERVINGS / ACTIVE TIME: 45 MINUTES / TOTAL TIME: 1 HOUR AND 30 MINUTES

This "pie" doesn't have a crust. Instead, it has a top layer of mashed potatoes, which blankets the beef mixture and helps keep it juicy. In that sense, it works like a pie. Semantics aside, it's one of the best comfort foods you can make.

1. Preheat the oven to 350°F.

2. Put the potato pieces in a large saucepan or pot and cover with cold water. Add the salt. Bring the water to a boil, reduce to a simmer, and cook the potatoes until soft, about 20 minutes. When they can be easily pierced with a sharp knife, they're cooked.

3. Drain the potato pieces and put them in a large bowl. Add 6 tablespoons of the butter and the milk and use a potato masher to make the mashed potatoes. If the mashed potatoes are too soupy, add yogurt in 1-tablespoon increments until they are creamy. Season with salt and pepper and set aside.

4. Place a 12-inch cast-iron skillet over medium heat, add the olive oil and onion, and cook until the onion is just soft, about 2 minutes. Add the ground beef and stir to break apart while it browns. When there is just a little pink left in the meat, drain the fat from the skillet. Stir in the peas and, if desired, the corn. Season with salt and pepper.

5. Spread the mashed potatoes over the meat and vegetables, distributing the potatoes evenly and smoothing the top. Cut the remaining 2 tablespoons of butter into slivers and dot the potatoes with them.

6. Cover with foil and bake for 30 minutes. Remove the foil and cook another 10 minutes until the potatoes are just browned.

7. Allow to cool for 5 minutes before serving.

INGREDIENTS:

6   RUSSET POTATOES, PEELED AND CUBED

½   TEASPOON SALT, PLUS MORE TO TASTE

1   STICK OF BUTTER, DIVIDED INTO TABLESPOONS

½   CUP WHOLE MILK

  PLAIN YOGURT, AS NEEDED

  PEPPER, TO TASTE

1   TABLESPOON OLIVE OIL

½   YELLOW ONION, MINCED

1   LB. GROUND BEEF

1   (14 OZ.) CAN OF PETIT POIS (PEAS), DRAINED, OR 2 CUPS HIGH-QUALITY FROZEN PEAS

½   (14 OZ.) CAN OF CORN, DRAINED (OPTIONAL)

BEEF BOURGUIGNON SHEPHERD'S PIE

YIELD: 4 TO 6 SERVINGS / **ACTIVE TIME:** 1 HOUR / **TOTAL TIME:** 4 HOURS AND 30 MINUTES

This is a decadent shepherd's pie with loads of butter and cream. Celebrate its richness and don't skimp when purchasing the ingredients.

1. Preheat the oven to 325°F.

2. Put the potato pieces in a large saucepan or pot and cover with cold water. Add the salt. Bring the water to a boil, reduce to a simmer, and cook the potatoes until soft, about 20 minutes.

3. Drain the potato pieces and put them in a large bowl. Add 6 tablespoons of the butter and the half-and-half, and use a potato masher to make the mashed potatoes. Stir in the shredded cheese. The mixture should be creamy. If it is too thick, add more half-and-half in 1-tablespoon increments until it has the right consistency. Season with salt and pepper and set aside.

4. In a 12-inch cast-iron skillet, sauté the bacon in the oil until it starts to lightly brown, about 3 minutes. Remove with a slotted spoon and place on a paper towel–lined plate.

5. Next, cook the beef in the oil and bacon fat, turning to brown on all sides. Use the slotted spoon to put the beef with the bacon. Put the carrot, onion, and mushrooms in the skillet and cook, while stirring, until just softened, about 3 minutes. Put the beef and bacon into the skillet with the vegetables. Add the flour and continue to cook, while stirring, for another 5 minutes.

6. Stir in the wine and the broth, then the tomato paste, garlic, thyme, and bay leaf. The liquid should barely cover the meat and vegetables. Bring to a low boil over medium heat. Season with salt and pepper, cover tightly with foil, and place in the oven for 3 hours, until the meat is very tender.

7. Return the skillet to the stove, remove the foil, and simmer over low heat for 5 to 10 minutes to reduce the sauce. Skim off any fat and remove the bay leaf. Increase the oven temperature to 350°F.

8. Spread the mashed potatoes over the beef and vegetables, distributing the potatoes evenly and smoothing the top. Cut the remaining 2 tablespoons of butter into slivers and dot the potatoes with them.

9. Cover with foil and bake for 20 minutes. Remove the foil and cook another 10 minutes, until the potatoes are just browned.

INGREDIENTS:

- 6   RUSSET POTATOES, PEELED AND CUBED
- ½   TEASPOON SALT, PLUS MORE TO TASTE
- 1   STICK OF UNSALTED BUTTER
- ½   CUP HALF-AND-HALF, PLUS MORE AS NEEDED
- ½   CUP SHREDDED WHITE CHEDDAR CHEESE
-   PEPPER, TO TASTE
- 3   SLICES OF BACON, CUT INTO ½-INCH PIECES
- 1   TABLESPOON OLIVE OIL
- 1½   LBS. STEW BEEF, CUT INTO CHUNKS
- 1   CARROT, PEELED AND SLICED
- ½   YELLOW ONION, DICED
- ½   CUP SLICED WHITE MUSHROOMS
- 1   TABLESPOON ALL-PURPOSE FLOUR
- 1½   CUPS DRY RED WINE
- 1   CUP BEEF BROTH
- 1   TABLESPOON TOMATO PASTE
- 1   GARLIC CLOVE, SMASHED
- ¼   TEASPOON DRIED THYME
- 1   BAY LEAF

SKILLET MEATLOAF *with* BACON

YIELD: 4 TO 6 SERVINGS / ACTIVE TIME: 10 MINUTES / TOTAL TIME: 1 HOUR

What kind of cookbook would this be without a take on this all-American darling? It's a standard in most homes because it's good enough to eat every single day.

1. Preheat the oven to 375°F.

2. Place the beef, pork, onion, garlic powder, bread crumbs, milk, eggs, tomato paste, and Worcestershire sauce in a bowl and use a large spoon or your hands to combine.

3. Coat a 10-inch cast-iron skillet with vegetable oil. Place the meat mixture in the pan and form it into a dome. Place 4 slices of bacon over the top and place the other 4 on top in the opposite direction, weaving them together.

4. Place the skillet in the oven and bake for 45 minutes. Remove and let cool for 10 minutes before slicing into wedges.

INGREDIENTS:

1½   LBS. GROUND BEEF

½   CUP GROUND PORK

1   YELLOW ONION, MINCED

2   TEASPOONS GARLIC POWDER

1   CUP BREAD CRUMBS

¼   CUP WHOLE MILK

2   EGGS, CRACKED AND LIGHTLY BEATEN

2   TABLESPOONS TOMATO PASTE

2   TABLESPOONS WORCESTERSHIRE SAUCE

2   TEASPOONS VEGETABLE OIL

8   SLICES OF BACON

BEEF & CORN CASSEROLE
with ENSALADA CHILEANA

YIELD: 8 TO 10 SERVINGS / ACTIVE TIME: 30 MINUTES / TOTAL TIME: 1 HOUR AND 30 MINUTES

This homey layered pie is beloved in Chile, primarily because of the *pino* that forms the bottom layer: a liberally seasoned mixture of beef, olives, raisins, and hard-boiled eggs. If you can track down *choclo*—an heirloom variety of corn—your dish will become noticeably stronger for it. If you can't find it, no worries: fresh or frozen corn kernels will still get the job done.

1. Preheat your oven to 350°F.

2. Place the oil in a 12-inch cast-iron skillet and warm over medium-high heat. When the oil starts to smoke, add the onions and sauté until translucent. Add the beef, cumin, paprika, half of the salt, and the pepper and cook, while stirring constantly, until all of the liquid has evaporated and the beef has started to brown.

3. Add the raisins and olives, stir to incorporate, and remove the skillet from heat.

4. Place the corn, sugar, milk, cream, melted butter, and the remaining salt in a food processor and puree until combined but still slightly chunky. Pour the puree into a bowl and stir in the basil.

5. Layer the sliced eggs on top of the beef mixture and press down on the mixture slightly. Top with the corn-and-basil mixture, place the skillet in the oven, and bake until the top is golden brown, about 1 hour. If the top is not brown enough, place it under the broiler for approximately 1 minute.

6. Remove from the oven and serve with the Ensalada Chileana.

ENSALADA CHILEANA

1. Place the onion in a bowl of salted ice water and soak for 30 minutes.

2. Drain, squeeze to remove any excess liquid, and place in a bowl. Add the tomatoes and toss to combine. Season with salt, add the olive oil, and toss to coat.

INGREDIENTS:

3   TABLESPOONS VEGETABLE OIL

4   YELLOW ONIONS, CHOPPED

1½   LBS. GROUND BEEF

1½   TABLESPOONS CUMIN

2   TEASPOONS SWEET PAPRIKA

2   TEASPOONS SALT

½   TEASPOON GROUND BLACK PEPPER

¾   CUP GOLDEN RAISINS

1   CUP BLACK OLIVES, PITTED AND CHOPPED

3   CUPS CORN KERNELS

1   TABLESPOON SUGAR

½   CUP WHOLE MILK

½   CUP HEAVY CREAM

⅓   CUP UNSALTED BUTTER, MELTED AND SLIGHTLY COOLED

1   CUP CHOPPED BASIL LEAVES

3   HARD-BOILED EGGS, SLICED

    ENSALADA CHILEANA (SEE RECIPE), FOR SERVING

ENSALADA CHILEANA

1   LARGE ONION, SLICED

    SALT, TO TASTE

2   LARGE TOMATOES, CUT INTO WEDGES

1   TEASPOON OLIVE OIL

BEEF & PORK BURGERS
with CARAMELIZED ONION MAYONNAISE

YIELD: 6 SERVINGS / ACTIVE TIME: 40 MINUTES / TOTAL TIME: 3 HOURS AND 30 MINUTES

A good burger is hard to beat. This particular preparation is an homage to Miles Smith Farm in Loudon, New Hampshire, where they raise exquisite Scottish Highlander beef cattle.

1. Place the beef and pork in a mixing bowl and season with salt and pepper. Stir to combine, cover, and place in the refrigerator.

2. Place the butter in a 10-inch cast-iron skillet and melt over medium-low heat.

3. Add the onions and a pinch of salt and cook, while stirring frequently, until the onions develop a deep brown color, about 20 to 30 minutes. Remove from heat and let cool completely.

4. Transfer the cooled onions to a blender and puree until smooth. Place the puree and mayonnaise in a mixing bowl, season with salt and pepper, and stir to combine. Place the mixture in the refrigerator for at least 2 hours.

5. When ready to serve, place a cast-iron skillet over medium-high heat. Form the beef-and-pork mixture into 6 balls and gently press down until they are patties.

6. Place the burgers in the skillet and cook for 8 to 10 minutes. Flip the burgers over and cook until cooked through, about 5 to 8 minutes. If you're worried that they will dry out, don't fret. The pork fat will keep them moist and flavorful.

7. Spread the mayonnaise on one half of a bun. Place a burger on the other half of the bun, top each with a slice of cheese, and assemble.

INGREDIENTS:

1	LB. GROUND BEEF
1	LB. GROUND PORK
	SALT AND PEPPER, TO TASTE
2	TABLESPOONS UNSALTED BUTTER
2	SWEET ONIONS, SLICED THIN
½	CUP MAYONNAISE
6	BRIOCHE BUNS, TOASTED
6	SLICES OF PREFERRED CHEESE

KEFTA *with* WARM CHICKPEAS *and* SALAD

YIELD: 4 TO 6 SERVINGS / ACTIVE TIME: 30 TO 35 MINUTES / TOTAL TIME: 2 HOURS AND 10 MINUTES

Think of kefta as a Moroccan meatball, with the lemon zest lending a welcome brightness to these typically earthy elements.

1. To prepare the kefta, place all of the ingredients, except for the skewers and olive oil, in a bowl and stir until well combined. Cook a small bit of the mixture and taste. Adjust seasoning as necessary and then form the mixture into 18 ovals.

2. Place three meatballs on each skewer. Add the olive oil to a cast-iron Dutch oven and warm over medium-high heat. Working in batches, add three skewers to the pot and sear the kefta for 2 minutes on each side. Remove the skewers and set aside.

3. To prepare the chickpeas, place all of the ingredients in the Dutch oven and reduce the heat to medium. Cover and cook for 1 hour.

4. Remove lid, check the beans for doneness, and raise heat to medium-high. Cook for an additional 30 minutes or until approximately 85 percent of the liquid has evaporated

5. Add the kefta skewers to the pot, cover, and remove it from heat. Let stand for 10 minutes so the kefta get cooked through.

6. To prepare the salad, place all of the ingredients in a small mixing bowl and stir until combined.

7. When the kefta are cooked through, remove the skewers and set aside. Place the chickpeas and salad on a plate, top with the kefta, and serve.

INGREDIENTS:

FOR THE KEFTA

1	LB. GROUND BEEF (MINIMUM 85% LEAN RECOMMENDED)
1	LB. GROUND LAMB
½	CUP MINCED WHITE ONION
2	GARLIC CLOVES, ROASTED AND MASHED
	ZEST OF 1 LEMON
1	CUP MINCED PARSLEY
2	TABLESPOONS MINT LEAVES
1	TEASPOON CINNAMON
2	TABLESPOONS CUMIN
1	TABLESPOON PAPRIKA
1	TEASPOON GROUND CORIANDER
	SALT AND PEPPER, TO TASTE
6	WOODEN SKEWERS
¼	CUP OLIVE OIL

FOR THE CHICKPEAS

½	CUP DRIED CHICKPEAS, SOAKED OVERNIGHT AND DRAINED
4	CUPS CHICKEN STOCK (SEE PAGES 102–3)
½	ONION, DICED
½	CUP MINCED CILANTRO STEMS
2	TABLESPOONS OLIVE OIL
	JUICE OF 1 LEMON
¼	TEASPOON SAFFRON
1	TABLESPOON CUMIN
1	TEASPOON CINNAMON

½ TEASPOON RED PEPPER
 FLAKES

SALT AND PEPPER, TO TASTE

FOR THE SALAD

1 LARGE TOMATO, CUT INTO
 ½-INCH-THICK SLICES

1 ENGLISH CUCUMBER,
 SEEDED AND CUT INTO
 ½-INCH-THICK SLICES

½ CUP CHOPPED PARSLEY

JUICE OF ½ LEMON

DOLLOP OF SOUR CREAM
 OR GREEK YOGURT

SALT AND PEPPER, TO TASTE

2-3 TABLESPOONS PRESERVED
 LEMON RIND, MINCED
 (OPTIONAL)

SWEDISH MEATBALLS

YIELD: 4 TO 6 SERVINGS / ACTIVE TIME: 1 HOUR / TOTAL TIME: 1 HOUR AND 20 MINUTES

This is excellent with a side of buttered noodles or boiled and buttered new potatoes seasoned with dill, basil, or parsley. You can also serve it as an appetizer at an intimate gathering, paired with lingonberry jam or red currant jelly.

1. Tear the slices of bread into strips and place them in a bowl with the milk. Let the bread soak.

2. Place the meats, eggs, salt, nutmeg, allspice, and white pepper in a large bowl and use a wooden spoon or your hands to combine.

3. Remove the bread from the milk and squeeze to remove any excess liquid. Tear the bread into small pieces and stir into the meat mixture.

4. Place 2 tablespoons of the butter in a large cast-iron Dutch oven and melt over medium heat. Add the onion and sauté until it is translucent. Add the onion to the meat mixture and stir to combine.

5. Form the meat mixture into balls that are each about the size of a golf ball.

6. Place the remaining butter in a 12-inch cast-iron skillet and melt over medium heat. Working in batches, add the meatballs to the skillet and cook, while turning frequently, until they are browned all over. Use a slotted spoon to remove the browned meatballs and set them aside.

7. Sprinkle the flour into the skillet and stir to incorporate. Add the stock 2 tablespoons at a time, while stirring, until it is emulsified. You should have a thick gravy in the skillet when all of the stock has been incorporated.

8. Return the meatballs to the skillet, gently stir to coat with the sauce, and reduce the heat to low. Cover the pan and simmer for 10 minutes.

9. Stir in the sour cream or Crème Fraîche and serve with lingonberry jam or red currant jelly.

INGREDIENTS:

5 SLICES OF WHITE SANDWICH BREAD, CRUSTS REMOVED

¾ CUP WHOLE MILK

1½ LBS. GROUND BEEF

¾ LB. GROUND PORK

¼ LB. GROUND VEAL (OPTIONAL)

2 LARGE EGGS

2 TEASPOONS KOSHER SALT, PLUS MORE TO TASTE

1 TEASPOON NUTMEG

1 TEASPOON ALLSPICE

1 TEASPOON WHITE PEPPER

1 STICK OF UNSALTED BUTTER

1 SMALL YELLOW ONION, MINCED

¼ CUP ALL-PURPOSE FLOUR

4 CUPS BEEF STOCK (SEE PAGES 200–201), AT ROOM TEMPERATURE

½ CUP SOUR CREAM OR CRÈME FRAÎCHE (SEE PAGE 566)

LINGONBERRY JAM OR RED CURRANT JELLY, FOR SERVING

VEAL SCALLOPINI

YIELD: 4 SERVINGS / ACTIVE TIME: 15 MINUTES / TOTAL TIME: 20 MINUTES

This is an unexpected Italian preparation. The veal will get slightly crispy, exactly what you want alongside the meaty olives and the vibrant lemon juice. If you don't eat veal, try this with chicken.

1. Warm a 12-inch cast-iron skillet over medium heat for 5 minutes.

2. Place the flour, nutmeg, salt, and pepper on a large plate and stir to combine.

3. Place the butter in the pan. When it is sizzling, dredge the veal in the seasoned flour until the scallops are coated lightly on both sides. Working in batches, place the veal in the skillet and cook for about 1 minute on each side, until it is browned and the juices run clear. Set the cooked veal aside.

4. Deglaze the pan with the stock. Add the olives, lemon zest, and lemon juice, stir to combine, and cook until heated through.

5. To serve, plate the veal and pour the pan sauce over each cutlet.

INGREDIENTS:

½ CUP ALL-PURPOSE FLOUR

½ TEASPOON NUTMEG

   SALT AND PEPPER, TO TASTE

2 TABLESPOONS UNSALTED BUTTER

1 LB. VEAL CUTLETS (ABOUT 4), POUNDED THIN

½ CUP VEAL STOCK OR BEEF STOCK (SEE PAGES 200–201)

¼ CUP GREEN OLIVES, SLICED

   ZEST AND JUICE OF 1 LEMON

KIBBEH BIL SANIEH

YIELD: 4 SERVINGS / ACTIVE TIME: 20 MINUTES / TOTAL TIME: 1 HOUR AND 20 MINUTES

If you're unfamiliar, kibbeh is a deeply flavorful Levantine dish consisting of ground meat, bulgur, and onions. This version leans heavily on the smoky depth of Aleppo pepper, but if you can't track it down, red pepper flakes will do.

1. Preheat the oven to 350°F.

2. Place half of the oil in a 12-inch cast-iron skillet and warm over medium heat. When it is smoking, add half of the onion and sauté until translucent, about 3 minutes. Add two-thirds of the ground beef and cook, while stirring, until lightly browned, about 8 minutes. Transfer the meat-and-onion mixture to a bowl, add the pine nuts and half of the allspice, and stir to combine. Set the mixture aside.

3. Place the remaining beef, onion, and allspice in a food processor with the bulgur, tomato paste, Aleppo pepper, and tablespoon of salt. Pulse until it is a paste.

4. Grease the cast-iron skillet and cover the bottom of the pan with the meat-and-bulgur paste. Press down to create an even layer. Top with the mixture of meat, onion, and pine nuts and score it in a diamond pattern. Drizzle the remaining oil over the top, season with salt, and place the skillet in the oven. Bake for 1 hour, until the bulgur is tender. Serve with the lemon wedges.

INGREDIENTS:

2   TABLESPOONS VEGETABLE OIL

1   LARGE YELLOW ONION, MINCED

1½   LBS. GROUND BEEF

½   CUP PINE NUTS

2   TEASPOONS ALLSPICE

2   CUPS BULGUR WHEAT, RINSED

1   TABLESPOON TOMATO PASTE

1   TABLESPOON ALEPPO PEPPER

1   TABLESPOON KOSHER SALT, PLUS MORE TO TASTE

LEMON WEDGES, FOR SERVING

LIVER *and* ONIONS

YIELD: 4 TO 6 SERVINGS / ACTIVE TIME: 40 MINUTES / TOTAL TIME: 7 HOURS

If you're not sure about liver, give this pungent, buttery recipe a try. You may change your mind. Serve this with homemade mashed potatoes, which are the perfect food to soak up the oil and butter from the liver and onions. If you want to be completely decadent, serve it with some creamed spinach, too.

1. To prep the liver, put it in a glass bowl and cover with the milk. Cover the bowl with plastic wrap and refrigerate the meat for 5 to 6 hours.

2. Heat a 12-inch cast-iron skillet over medium heat. Add 3 table-spoons of butter. When the butter is melted, add the onion slices. Stir to separate and coat with the butter. Cook over medium heat just until the onions begin to soften, about 6 minutes. Reduce heat to low and cook, while stirring occasionally, for 30 to 40 minutes.

3. While the onions are cooking, remove the liver from the milk. Cut into 2 pieces and pat dry with paper towels. Put the flour on a plate and season with salt and pepper. Gently press the liver pieces into the flour to coat them. Shake off excess.

4. Heat another cast-iron skillet over medium heat. Add the remaining butter. When hot but not browned, add the liver pieces. Sauté the pieces for about 2 to 3 minutes a side so that they are browned on the outside but slightly pink inside. Be careful not to overcook them.

5. When done, transfer the liver to a plate and pile on the caramelized onions. Sprinkle the parsley over the top and serve.

INGREDIENTS:

1	LB. CALF'S LIVER (NOT BEEF LIVER, WHICH IS NOT AS TENDER)
1½	CUPS WHOLE MILK
5	TABLESPOONS UNSALTED BUTTER
2	ONIONS, SLICED THIN
½	CUP ALL-PURPOSE FLOUR
	SALT AND FRESHLY GROUND PEPPER, TO TASTE
	FRESH PARSLEY, CHOPPED, FOR GARNISH

SALT-CRUSTED LAMB *with* LEMON-HERB DRESSING

YIELD: 4 TO 6 SERVINGS / ACTIVE TIME: 20 MINUTES / TOTAL TIME: 45 MINUTES

An extremely dramatic dish that is very straightforward to prepare—just brown the meat and pack it in salt. As the meat bakes, the salt becomes hard and seals in the juices. When you're ready to serve it, bring a small mallet with you to the table and crack it open for a show-stopping presentation.

1. Preheat the oven to 350°F.

2. Warm a 12-inch cast-iron skillet over high heat for 5 minutes. You want the pan to be extremely hot.

3. Rub the lamb with the grapeseed oil and season with pepper. Place the lamb in the hot skillet and cook until the racks are browned on both sides, about 6 minutes. Remove from the pan and let cool.

4. Place the salt and water in a mixing bowl and work the mixture with your hands to combine. Add the egg whites in small increments until the salt resembles damp sand. It should clump when you ball it in one of your hands.

5. When the lamb is cool, spread a thin layer of the salt mixture on the bottom of a rectangular baking dish. Place the lamb on top and pack the rest of the salt on top, making sure the meat is completely covered. Place in the oven and bake until an instant-read thermometer reads 130°F, about 20 minutes.

6. Use a mallet to break the lamb out of the crust. Let the meat rest for 5 minutes before serving alongside the Lemon-Herb Dressing.

TIP: This is also a great way to cook a whole salmon, if you have the room in your oven, or a roast beef.

INGREDIENTS:

4	RACKS OF LAMB, TRIMMED
2	TABLESPOONS GRAPESEED OIL
	BLACK PEPPER, TO TASTE
8	CUPS KOSHER SALT
¼	CUP WATER
8	EGG WHITES
	LEMON-HERB DRESSING (SEE RECIPE), FOR SERVING

LEMON-HERB DRESSING

	ZEST OF 3 LEMONS
2	TABLESPOONS MINCED FRESH ROSEMARY
1	TABLESPOON FENNEL SEEDS
1	GARLIC CLOVE, MINCED
½	CUP OLIVE OIL
	SALT AND PEPPER, TO TASTE

LEMON-HERB DRESSING

1. Place the lemon zest, rosemary, fennel seeds, and garlic in a bowl and stir to combine.

2. Add the olive oil in a slow stream and whisk to incorporate. Season with salt and pepper before serving.

BRAISED LAMB SHOULDER *with* MINTY PEAS

YIELD: 4 TO 6 SERVINGS / ACTIVE TIME: 30 MINUTES / TOTAL TIME: 4 HOURS

Lamb has a great fat-to-protein ratio, and is all but made to pair with mint. Cooking this dish in a Dutch oven allows the fat to render and the meat to reach falling-off-the-bone tenderness for a mouthwatering meal that you'll never have leftovers of.

1. Preheat the oven to 300°F. Add the canola oil to a 12-inch cast-iron skillet and warm it over medium-high heat. Season all sides of the lamb shoulder liberally with salt. When the oil starts to glisten, place the lamb in the pan and cook, while turning occasionally, until it is brown on all sides.

2. Place the onion, carrots, bay leaves, peppercorns, water, and rosemary in a cast-iron Dutch oven or baking dish. When the lamb shoulder is browned all over, place it in the Dutch oven or baking dish, cover, and cook in the oven until the lamb is fork-tender, approximately 3½ hours.

3. When the lamb shoulder is close to ready, place the sprigs of mint and peas in a saucepan and cover with water. Cook over medium heat until the peas are tender, approximately 4 minutes for fresh peas and 7 minutes if using frozen. Drain, discard the sprigs of mint, and serve alongside the lamb shoulder.

INGREDIENTS:

2   TABLESPOONS CANOLA OIL

    5-LB., BONE-IN LAMB
    SHOULDER

    SALT, TO TASTE

1   SMALL ONION, DICED

2   CARROTS, PEELED AND
    DICED

3   BAY LEAVES

2   TABLESPOONS BLACK
    PEPPERCORNS

2   CUPS WATER

2   SPRIGS OF ROSEMARY

3   SPRIGS OF MINT

3   CUPS PEAS

COTTAGE PIE

YIELD: 4 TO 6 SERVINGS / ACTIVE TIME: 20 MINUTES / TOTAL TIME: 1 HOUR AND 30 MINUTES

Most people are familiar with shepherd's pie. This riff uses lamb and peas to ramp up the flavor, and it is perfect for those spring days when the chill of winter creeps back in and you need a hearty dish to keep your spirits up.

1. Preheat the oven to 350°F. Place the canola oil and butter in a 12-inch cast-iron skillet and warm over medium-high heat. Add the onion and sauté until lightly brown, about 4 minutes.

2. Add the lamb and thyme and cook, while stirring, until the lamb is browned.

3. Add the stock, reduce the heat to medium-low, and let the mixture gently simmer until the stock has nearly evaporated, about 20 minutes.

4. Add the peas to the skillet, stir to combine, and cook until warmed through.

5. Transfer the mixture from the skillet to a baking dish. Season the mashed potatoes with salt and pepper and then cover the lamb-and-peas mixture with the potatoes. Smooth the top with a rubber spatula and bake in the oven until the top is golden brown, about 40 minutes. Remove from the oven and serve.

INGREDIENTS:

1 TABLESPOON CANOLA OIL

1 TABLESPOON UNSALTED BUTTER

1 SPRING ONION, DICED

1 LB. GROUND LAMB

1 TABLESPOON FRESH MINCED THYME LEAVES

1 CUP BEEF STOCK (SEE PAGES 200–201)

1 CUP PEAS

5 POTATOES, PEELED, COOKED, AND MASHED

SALT AND PEPPER, TO TASTE

ROGAN JOSH

YIELD: 4 SERVINGS / **ACTIVE TIME:** 20 MINUTES / **TOTAL TIME:** 1 HOUR AND 20 MINUTES

A traditional dish from the Kashmir Valley in India. If you want a slightly more substantial meal, serve it over basmati rice and with a warm flatbread such as Naan (see page 178) or Paratha (see page 174). It's also a fantastic make-ahead dish that tastes just as good—if not better—the next day.

1. Place the canola oil in a large cast-iron Dutch oven, wok, or skillet and warm over high heat. Season the lamb with salt. When the oil starts to smoke, add the lamb and cook, while turning occasionally, until it is lightly browned all over, about 12 minutes. Remove with a slotted spoon and set aside.

2. Add the onions, ginger, garlic, curry, turmeric, cayenne, and garam masala and sauté for 2 minutes.

3. Add the tomatoes, yogurt, and water and bring to a gentle boil. Return the lamb to the pot or pan, lower the heat, cover, and simmer until the lamb is very tender, about 1 hour. Remove the cover occasionally to stir and make sure the dish is not burning.

4. Ladle into warmed bowls, garnish with the cilantro and red onion, and serve with the basmati rice.

INGREDIENTS:

¼ CUP CANOLA OIL

2 LBS. BONELESS LAMB SHOULDER, CUT INTO 1-INCH PIECES

KOSHER SALT, TO TASTE

2 LARGE YELLOW ONIONS, SLICED THIN

2 TABLESPOONS MINCED GINGER

2 GARLIC CLOVES, MINCED

1 TABLESPOON CURRY POWDER, PLUS 1 TEASPOON

1 TEASPOON TURMERIC

1 TEASPOON CAYENNE PEPPER, OR TO TASTE

1 TEASPOON GARAM MASALA

1 (14 OZ.) CAN OF CRUSHED TOMATOES

1 CUP PLAIN YOGURT

2 CUPS WATER

CILANTRO LEAVES, CHOPPED, FOR GARNISH

RED ONION, DICED, FOR GARNISH

1½ CUPS COOKED BASMATI RICE, FOR SERVING

SZECHUAN CUMIN LAMB

YIELD: 4 SERVINGS / **ACTIVE TIME:** 10 MINUTES / **TOTAL TIME:** 20 MINUTES TO 2 HOURS

This extremely fragrant recipe possesses equally heady flavors thanks to the considerable heat and the unique buzz that the Szechuan peppercorn supplies. If you aren't a fan of lamb, you can easily substitute beef.

1. Place the cumin seeds and Szechuan peppercorns in a dry cast-iron skillet and toast over medium heat until they are fragrant, about 1 minute. Do not let the spices burn. Remove and grind to a fine powder with a mortar and pestle.

2. Place the salt, 2 tablespoons of the canola oil, the dried chilies, red pepper flakes, and the toasted spice mixture into a large bowl and stir to combine. Add the lamb pieces and toss until they are coated. Let stand for at least 10 minutes and up to 2 hours.

3. Heat a 12-inch cast-iron skillet over high heat until the pan is extremely hot, about 10 minutes. Add the remaining oil, swirl to coat, and then add the lamb and onion. Cook, while stirring occasionally, until the lamb is browned all over, about 10 minutes.

4. Garnish with the scallions and cilantro and serve alongside the white rice.

INGREDIENTS:

- 3 TABLESPOONS CUMIN SEEDS
- 2 TEASPOONS SZECHUAN PEPPERCORNS
- 1 TEASPOON KOSHER SALT
- 3 TABLESPOONS CANOLA OIL
- 4 WHOLE DRIED RED CHILIES
- 2 TEASPOONS RED PEPPER FLAKES
- 1½ LBS. BONELESS LAMB, SLICED THIN
- 1 YELLOW ONION, SLICED
- 2 SCALLIONS, SLICED THIN, FOR GARNISH
- ½ CUP CHOPPED CILANTRO LEAVES, FOR GARNISH
- 1½ CUPS COOKED WHITE RICE, FOR SERVING

IRISH LAMB STEW

YIELD: 4 SERVINGS / ACTIVE TIME: 30 MINUTES / TOTAL TIME: 2 HOURS AND 30 MINUTES

No food in this world can warm your soul more than this hearty, Old World–style stew containing tender lamb and root vegetables. Toast some thick slices of sourdough bread to serve alongside, and you've got the ideal antidote for a winter day.

1. Place the lamb and bay leaves in a large cast-iron Dutch oven and cover with cold water. Bring to a boil over high heat and cook for 5 minutes. Remove the lamb with a slotted spoon and set aside. Transfer the broth and bay leaves to a separate container.

2. Place half of the potatoes in a layer at the bottom of the Dutch oven. Top with a layer of half of the onions and another layer consisting of half of the rutabagas. Add the lamb, season with salt and pepper, and top with layers of the remaining potatoes, onions, and rutabagas. Add the broth and bay leaves and bring to a boil. Reduce heat so that the stew simmers, cover, and cook for 1 hour.

3. Remove the lid, add the parsley and carrots, and simmer for another hour.

4. Remove the parsley and bay leaves and ladle the stew into warmed bowls.

INGREDIENTS:

2   LBS. BONELESS LAMB SHOULDER, CUT INTO BITE-SIZED CUBES

2   BAY LEAVES

6   YUKON GOLD POTATOES, SLICED ¼-INCH THICK

3   YELLOW ONIONS, SLICED

2   LARGE RUTABAGAS, PEELED AND SLICED ¼-INCH THICK

    SALT AND PEPPER, TO TASTE

4   SPRIGS OF PARSLEY

2   LARGE CARROTS, PEELED AND SLICED ½-INCH THICK

POTJIEKOS

YIELD: 6 TO 8 SERVINGS / ACTIVE TIME: 40 MINUTES / TOTAL TIME: 3 HOURS

A South African stew that is traditionally made in a three-legged *potjie* over an open fire. This hearty dish is adapted from a recipe given to me by Johannesburg native and current LA resident Ruth Steinberg, who implores you to serve it with a warm smile.

1. Place the olive oil in a large *potjie* or cast-iron Dutch oven and warm over medium-high heat. When the oil starts to smoke, add the onions and sauté until lightly browned.

2. Add the curry powder, orange zest, chilies, curry leaves, bay leaves, and the lamb and cook until the lamb is browned all over, about 10 minutes.

3. Add the orange juice and enough water to cover the contents of the pot. Lower the heat and layer the yam, sweet potato, potatoes, carrots, and garlic on top. Reduce the heat, cover, and let the stew simmer for 2 hours.

4. Season to taste, ladle into warmed bowls, and serve alongside the rice and Atjar Chutney.

ATJAR CHUTNEY

1. Place all of the ingredients in a saucepan and simmer until the mixture has a jam-like consistency.

2. Remove from the heat, let cool, and store in the refrigerator in an airtight container for up to 6 months.

INGREDIENTS:

¼ CUP OLIVE OIL

4 LARGE YELLOW ONIONS, CHOPPED

4 TEASPOONS CURRY POWDER

ZEST AND JUICE OF 1 SATSUMA ORANGE

2 RED CHILIES, STEMMED, SEEDED, AND CHOPPED

4 CURRY LEAVES

4 BAY LEAVES

2 LBS. LAMB SHANK

1 LARGE WHITE YAM, PEELED AND CHOPPED

1 LARGE SWEET POTATO, PEELED AND CHOPPED

2 LARGE POTATOES, PEELED AND QUARTERED

4 LARGE CARROTS, PEELED AND CHOPPED

4 LARGE GARLIC CLOVES

2 CUPS FRESH SPINACH, STEMMED

SALT, TO TASTE

1½ CUPS COOKED LONG-GRAIN RICE, FOR SERVING

ATJAR CHUTNEY (SEE RECIPE), FOR SERVING

ATJAR CHUTNEY

2 LARGE GREEN MANGOES, PEELED, PITTED, AND DICED

1 CUP WHITE VINEGAR

¾ CUP SUGAR

½ CUP BLANCHED AND CHOPPED ALMONDS

1 LARGE RED ONION, CHOPPED

2 TABLESPOONS MINCED GINGER

1 TEASPOON CAYENNE PEPPER

1 TEASPOON MUSTARD SEEDS

2 GARLIC CLOVES, CHOPPED

1 TEASPOON SALT

CURRY BURGERS

YIELD: 4 TO 6 SERVINGS / ACTIVE TIME: 15 MINUTES / TOTAL TIME: 30 MINUTES

Switch up your burger game with this spicy Indian-influenced twist. Place them alongside some cardamom-flavored basmati rice and the creamy Raita, and you've got a signature dish for a backyard barbecue. If it's more of a casual affair than a sit-down dinner, you can also form them into meatballs and serve the lamb-and-beef mixture as an appetizer.

1. Place all of the ingredients, except for those designated for serving, in a large bowl and stir gently until just combined. Divide into 4 thick or 6 thin patties and let rest for 10 minutes at room temperature.

2. Heat a cast-iron skillet over medium-high heat. Add the burgers and cook until they are cooked through, 6 minutes per side. Remove from heat and let them rest for 5 minutes.

3. Serve on the hamburger buns with the additional cilantro, sliced tomato, Tomato Chutney, and Raita.

INGREDIENTS:

1   LB. GROUND LAMB

½   LB. GROUND BEEF

2   TABLESPOONS CURRY POWDER

1   TEASPOON CAYENNE PEPPER, OR TO TASTE

½   TEASPOON GROUND MUSTARD POWDER

½   RED ONION, MINCED

2   TEASPOONS MINCED GINGER

3   GARLIC CLOVES, MINCED

½   CUP CHOPPED CILANTRO LEAVES, PLUS MORE FOR SERVING

1   LARGE EGG

    SALT AND FRESHLY GROUND BLACK PEPPER, TO TASTE

4   WHOLE WHEAT HAMBURGER BUNS, FOR SERVING

1   LARGE RED TOMATO, SLICED, FOR SERVING

    TOMATO CHUTNEY (SEE RECIPE), FOR SERVING

    RAITA (SEE RECIPE), FOR SERVING

TOMATO CHUTNEY

1. Place the vegetable oil in a saucepan and warm over medium-high heat. When the oil starts to smoke, add the onion and sauté until translucent, about 3 to 4 minutes. Add the curry powder, cumin, and ginger and cook for another 2 minutes.

2. Add the tomatoes, vinegar, sugar, and salt, raise the heat to high, and bring to a boil. Reduce the heat and let the mixture simmer until it has reduced by about two-thirds, about 15 minutes.

3. Transfer the mixture to a food processor and pulse until it is blended but still slightly chunky. Store in an airtight container in the refrigerator for up to 2 weeks.

RAITA

Place all of the ingredients in a mixing bowl and stir to combine.

TOMATO CHUTNEY

- 1   TABLESPOON VEGETABLE OIL
- ½   CUP MINCED ONION
- ½   TEASPOON CURRY POWDER
- ½   TEASPOON CUMIN
- ½   TEASPOON GRATED GINGER
- 2   LARGE RED TOMATOES, SEEDED AND DICED
- ½   CUP APPLE CIDER VINEGAR
- ¼   CUP SUGAR
- ½   TEASPOON SALT

RAITA

- 1   CUP PLAIN YOGURT
- 2   TEASPOONS MINCED RED ONION
- ½   CUP CHOPPED AND SEEDED PERSIAN CUCUMBER
- 2   TABLESPOONS MINCED CILANTRO

MOUSSAKA

YIELD: 4 TO 6 SERVINGS / **ACTIVE TIME:** 1 HOUR AND 30 MINUTES / **TOTAL TIME:** 2 HOURS

This Greek dish is an incredible blend of lamb, eggplant, and spices. Topped with a cheesy crust, this is a great alternative to shepherd's pie.

1. Preheat the oven to 350°F.

2. Place the salt and cold water in a bowl. When dissolved, add the eggplant cubes and stir. Cover the bowl with plastic wrap and let the cubes soak for about 20 minutes. After soaking, drain in a colander and rinse the eggplant with cold water. Squeeze the cubes to remove excess water, place them on a pile of paper towels, and blot them as dry as possible. Set aside.

3. While the eggplant is soaking, heat a 10-inch cast-iron skillet over medium-high heat. Add a tablespoon of the olive oil to coat the bottom. Brown the lamb in the skillet until cooked, about 4 minutes. Use a slotted spoon to transfer the cooked meat to a bowl. Set aside.

4. Cook the prepared eggplant. Heat the skillet over medium-high heat again. Add ¼ cup of the olive oil and the eggplant, stirring frequently, until the cubes start to soften, about 5 minutes. Use the slotted spoon to add the cooked eggplant to the bowl with the lamb in it.

5. Put the skillet back on the heat and add the rest of the oil. Cook the onion and garlic together, while stirring constantly, until the onion is translucent, about 3 minutes. Add the lamb and eggplant and stir to combine. Add the wine, tomato sauce, parsley, oregano, and cinnamon. Stir to combine, reduce the heat to low, and simmer for about 15 minutes, stirring occasionally. Season with salt and pepper.

6. While the filling is simmering, make the crust. In a large bowl, beat the eggs lightly. Place a saucepan over medium heat, melt the butter, lower the heat slightly, and add the flour, stirring to form a paste. Slowly add the milk while stirring with a whisk. When the mixture reaches a boil, remove the saucepan from heat. Add about half of the mixture in the saucepan to the bowl containing the beaten eggs and stir briskly. Stir the tempered eggs into the mixture in the saucepan, add the cheese and dill or parsley, and then stir until thoroughly combined.

7. Even out the top of the lamb-and-eggplant mixture, then top with the crust. Put the skillet in the oven. Bake for 35 to 45 minutes, until the crust is set and golden brown.

8. Allow to rest for about 5 minutes before serving.

INGREDIENTS:

FOR THE FILLING

¼	CUP SALT
4	CUPS COLD WATER
1	LARGE EGGPLANT, ENDS TRIMMED AND CUT INTO CUBES
½	CUP OLIVE OIL
1	LB. GROUND LAMB
1	ONION, DICED
3	GARLIC CLOVES, MINCED
½	CUP DRY RED WINE
1	CUP TOMATO SAUCE
2	TABLESPOONS CHOPPED FRESH PARSLEY
1	TEASPOON DRIED OREGANO
½	TEASPOON CINNAMON
	SALT AND PEPPER, TO TASTE

FOR THE CRUST

5	EGGS
6	TABLESPOONS UNSALTED BUTTER
⅓	CUP ALL-PURPOSE FLOUR
2½	CUPS WHOLE MILK
⅔	CUP GRATED PARMESAN CHEESE
⅓	CUP CHOPPED FRESH DILL OR PARSLEY

PORK LOIN *with* DRIED CRANBERRY SAUCE

YIELD: 4 SERVINGS / ACTIVE TIME: 20 MINUTES / TOTAL TIME: 30 MINUTES

The beautiful, jewel-toned cranberries in this recipe are the ideal ornament for the rich flavor of the pork. Make sure to have your calibrated instant-read thermometer on hand so that your pork comes out juicy rather than overdone. Try serving this with baked sweet potatoes and roasted Brussels sprouts.

1. Pat the pork tenderloins dry and set aside.

2. Warm a 12-inch cast-iron skillet over medium heat. When it is warm, add the coconut oil and the pork and cook until the pork is browned all over.

3. Reduce the heat to low and cook until the pork registers 145°F on an instant-read thermometer, about 10 minutes. Remove the pork from the skillet and set aside.

4. Place all of the remaining ingredients, except for the butter, in the skillet, stir to combine, and bring to a simmer. Cook until the cranberries are tender, about 5 minutes. Stir in the butter and remove the skillet from heat.

5. To serve, slice the tenderloins into medallions and spoon the cranberry sauce over them.

TIP: If cranberries are a bit tart for your taste, substitute cherries.

INGREDIENTS:

2	PORK TENDERLOINS
2	TABLESPOONS COCONUT OIL
¾	CUP PORT WINE
2	TEASPOONS RED WINE VINEGAR
1	CUP DRIED CRANBERRIES
¼	CUP SUGAR
1	TEASPOON MINCED FRESH ROSEMARY (OPTIONAL)
½	TEASPOON BLACK PEPPER
3	TABLESPOONS UNSALTED BUTTER

STUFFED PORK CHOPS

YIELD: 4 SERVINGS / **ACTIVE TIME:** 1 HOUR / **TOTAL TIME:** 1 HOUR AND 30 MINUTES

When cool temperatures have you thinking about ways to roast meats with dried fruits and nuts, this recipe will appeal to everything you're craving.

1. Preheat the oven to 400°F.

2. Rinse the pork chops and pat them dry with a paper towel. Using a long, sharp knife, cut an incision into one edge of each pork chop to form a pocket. Season the chops with salt and pepper.

3. Place a 12-inch cast-iron skillet over medium-high heat. Add the olive oil and onion and cook, while stirring, until onion is soft, about 3 minutes. Reduce the heat to medium and add the bread cubes, dates, walnuts, port wine, and sage, stirring gently to combine. Cook for a couple of minutes until well blended. Remove pan from heat.

4. Fill the chops with the stuffing. Brush the skillet with oil, put it over medium-high heat, and add the chops, searing on each side for about 3 minutes. Add the chicken broth and white wine. Put the skillet in the oven and roast for about 20 minutes or until pork is cooked through. Baste with the pan juices halfway through. Let the chops rest for about 5 minutes before serving.

INGREDIENTS:

4   **BONELESS PORK CHOPS**

    SALT AND PEPPER, TO TASTE

2   **TABLESPOONS OLIVE OIL, PLUS MORE FOR THE SKILLET**

½   **ONION, MINCED**

1   **CUP CUBES OF THICK, CRUSTY BREAD (BAGUETTE OR SOURDOUGH)**

½   **CUP DATES, PITTED AND CHOPPED**

¼   **CUP CHOPPED WALNUTS**

2   **TABLESPOONS PORT WINE**

2   **TABLESPOONS CHOPPED FRESH SAGE**

2   **CUPS CHICKEN BROTH**

½   **CUP DRY WHITE WINE**

BRAISED PORK BELLY
with TOASTED FARRO, CORN *&* SNAP PEAS

YIELD: 4 TO 6 SERVINGS / **ACTIVE TIME:** 1 HOUR AND 30 MINUTES / **TOTAL TIME:** 24 HOURS

Whenever you mention pork belly, you get a group of people saying, "I don't like it, there's too much fat." While it is true that the belly does have a high fat content, it will render off if cooked properly, leaving a delicious, tender piece of meat.

1. The night before you're going to make the pork belly, preheat the oven to 350°F and place the farro on a baking sheet in an even layer. Place it in the oven and bake until it is a deep brown color. Remove from the oven, place it in a bowl, understanding that the grains will double in size, and cover with water. Soak overnight.

2. When you're ready to make the recipe, preheat the oven to 350°F. Place the ears of corn in the oven and cook until the kernels give slightly when squeezed, about 10 minutes. Remove from the oven and let cool. Lower the oven temperature to 250°F.

3. Place the pork belly skin side down and use a knife to score the flesh, slicing ⅛-inch deep in a diamond pattern. Season with salt and pepper and set aside.

4. Place the olive oil in a large cast-iron Dutch oven and warm over high heat. When the oil starts to smoke, carefully place the pork belly, skin side down, in the pot to begin rendering the fat. Sear until the skin is brown, turn over, and sear until brown on the other side. Remove the pork belly from the pot and set aside.

5. Add the onions, carrots, celery, and garlic to the Dutch oven and cook until brown. Add 4 sprigs of thyme and the tomato paste, stir to coat the vegetables, and then add the wine. Scrape up any browned bits from the bottom of the Dutch oven and cook until the liquid starts to thicken. Add the stock, bring to a boil, and return the pork belly to the pot. Cover the Dutch oven and transfer it to the oven. Cook until the pork belly is tender, 2 to 2½ hours.

6. When the pork belly is tender, strain and reserve the liquid, discard the vegetables, set the pork belly aside, and place the liquid in a saucepan. Cook over high heat until it is thick and syrupy. Set aside.

INGREDIENTS:

2	CUPS FARRO
3	EARS OF CORN, SHUCKED AND RINSED
	4-LB., SKIN-ON PORK BELLY
1	TABLESPOON SALT, PLUS MORE TO TASTE
	PEPPER, TO TASTE
2	TABLESPOONS OLIVE OIL
2	LARGE YELLOW ONIONS, CUT INTO 1-INCH PIECES
2	LARGE CARROTS, PEELED AND CUT INTO 1-INCH PIECES
4	CELERY STALKS, CUT INTO 1-INCH PIECES
6	GARLIC CLOVES, CRUSHED
6	SPRIGS OF THYME
3	TABLESPOONS TOMATO PASTE
2	CUPS WHITE WINE
8	CUPS CHICKEN STOCK (SEE PAGES 102–3)
6	CUPS WATER
1	SHALLOT, HALVED
1	BAY LEAF
4	OZ. SNAP PEAS, TRIMMED AND CHOPPED
4	TABLESPOONS UNSALTED BUTTER
¼	CUP SLICED CHIVES

Continued . . .

7. Drain the farro and place it in a large pot with the water, shallot, 1 tablespoon salt, remaining thyme, and bay leaf. Bring to a boil over medium-high heat and then reduce the heat so that the mixture simmers. Cook until the farro is al dente, about 20 minutes. Remove from heat, drain, discard the aromatics, and transfer to a bowl.

8. Remove the kernels from the roasted ears of corn. Bring a small pot of salted water to a boil, add the snap peas, and cook for 1 minute. Drain and add to the farro along with the corn, butter, and chives. Stir to combine, season with salt and pepper, and transfer to a serving dish.

9. Slice the pork belly and place on top of the farro-and-vegetable mixture. Spoon the reduced cooking liquid over the top and serve.

PORK *with* BLUE CHEESE POLENTA *and* DROPPED-PEACH HOT SAUCE

YIELD: 6 TO 8 SERVINGS / ACTIVE TIME: 40 MINUTES / TOTAL TIME: 6 HOURS

Peach season is a special time of year—just because a peach isn't at its peak doesn't mean you can't find some way to make the most of it. For this recipe, use overly ripe peaches (otherwise known as "dropped" or "Grade B" peaches) to create a hot sauce that is sweet, sour, and spicy.

1. Preheat the oven to 300°F. Season the pork shoulder generously with salt and pepper.

2. Place the pork shoulder in a 12-inch cast-iron skillet and cook over medium-high heat, turning until it is browned all over.

3. Transfer the pork shoulder to a cast-iron Dutch oven and add the onion, bay leaves, paprika, brown sugar, peppercorns, 4 cups of the stock, and mustard.

4. Cover the Dutch oven and place in the oven until the pork is fork-tender, about 4 hours. Remove from the oven, let cool slightly, and then shred with a fork.

5. Approximately 1 hour before the pulled pork will be finished cooking, place the cornmeal, the remaining 3 cups of stock, and the water in a large pot. Bring to a boil over medium-high heat, reduce heat so that the mixture simmers, and cook, while stirring frequently, until the mixture is thick, about 40 minutes to 1 hour.

6. Add half of the butter and stir to combine. Stir half of the blue cheese into the pot, season with salt and pepper, and remove from heat. Set aside.

7. Once you have removed the pork shoulder from the oven, raise the oven temperature to 400°F.

8. Arrange the peaches skin side down on a baking sheet or cast-iron skillet and place them in the oven. Cook until they begin to darken, about 10 minutes. You can also grill the peaches if you're after a slightly smokier sauce.

9. Remove the peaches from the oven and place in a medium sauce-pan. Add the vinegar, granulated sugar, garlic, peppers, and lemon juice and bring to a simmer over medium-low heat. Simmer for 10 minutes, transfer the mixture to a blender, and puree until smooth.

10. Stir the remaining butter into the polenta and spoon the polenta into warmed bowls. Lay some of the pulled pork over it, and then top with the hot sauce and remaining blue cheese.

INGREDIENTS:

6- TO 8-LB., BONE-IN PORK SHOULDER

SALT AND PEPPER, TO TASTE

1   LARGE ONION, DICED

3   BAY LEAVES

2   TEASPOONS PAPRIKA

¼   CUP BROWN SUGAR

2   TABLESPOONS WHOLE PEPPERCORNS

7   CUPS CHICKEN STOCK (SEE PAGES 102–3)

1   TABLESPOON MUSTARD

2   CUPS CORNMEAL

2   CUPS WATER

1   STICK OF UNSALTED BUTTER

1   CUP CRUMBLED BLUE CHEESE

8   OVERRIPE PEACHES, PITTED AND QUARTERED

2   CUPS APPLE CIDER VINEGAR

¾   CUP GRANULATED SUGAR

3   GARLIC CLOVES, CHOPPED

6   JALAPEÑO PEPPERS, SEEDED AND DICED

4   CAYENNE PEPPERS, SEEDED AND DICED

¼   CUP FRESH LEMON JUICE

PORK & APPLE CASSEROLE

YIELD: 4 SERVINGS / ACTIVE TIME: 30 MINUTES / TOTAL TIME: 1 HOUR

Thicker pork chops are key to making sure this casserole doesn't become too mushy. Once you have that ratio down, however, the combination of sweet apples and warm spices will be irresistible.

1. Preheat the oven to 325°F.

2. Place the apples, cinnamon, nutmeg, sugar, flour, and a pinch of salt in a mixing bowl and stir to combine. Transfer the mixture to a cast-iron Dutch oven and then add the apple cider.

3. Rub the pork tenderloin with the ground rosemary and thyme and a pinch of salt and pepper. Place the pork on top of the apple mixture, cover, and place in the oven. Cook until a meat thermometer inserted into the center of the tenderloin registers 145°F, about 40 minutes.

4. Remove the pork tenderloin from the oven and slice. Serve on beds of the apple mixture.

INGREDIENTS:

8   APPLES, SLICED

2   TEASPOONS CINNAMON

1   TEASPOON NUTMEG

¼   CUP SUGAR

¼   CUP ALL-PURPOSE FLOUR

    SALT AND PEPPER, TO TASTE

¼   CUP APPLE CIDER

    1½-LB. PORK TENDERLOIN

2   TABLESPOONS FRESHLY GROUND ROSEMARY LEAVES

2   TABLESPOONS FRESHLY GROUND THYME LEAVES

DWAEJI BULGOGI

YIELD: 4 SERVINGS / ACTIVE TIME: 5 MINUTES / TOTAL TIME: 45 MINUTES

In Korean, *bul* means "fire" and *gogi* translates to "meat." When you come across a dish that trumpets such simplicity, you can be sure you've got a winner. You can find gochujang online or in well-stocked grocery stores, and the subtle heat it adds makes it worth tracking down.

1. Place all of the ingredients, except for those designated for garnish or for serving, in a bowl and stir to combine. Let the meat marinate for at least 30 minutes and up to 1 hour.

2. Warm a 10-inch cast-iron skillet over high heat for 5 minutes. When it is extremely hot, add the marinated pork and sear until it is cooked through, about 5 minutes.

3. Garnish with the sesame seeds and chopped green onions and serve with the white rice, romaine lettuce leaves, and Musaengchae.

MUSAENGCHAE

1. Place all of the ingredients in a bowl and stir to combine.

2. Let marinate for at least 1 hour before serving.

INGREDIENTS:

2   LBS. PORK TENDERLOIN, SLICED THIN

4   GARLIC CLOVES, MINCED

1   TABLESPOON MINCED GINGER

½   CUP GOCHUJANG (KOREAN CHILI PASTE)

2   TABLESPOONS SOY SAUCE

3   TABLESPOONS SESAME OIL

    SESAME SEEDS, FOR GARNISH

2   GREEN ONIONS, CHOPPED, FOR GARNISH

1½ CUPS COOKED WHITE RICE, FOR SERVING

    ROMAINE LETTUCE LEAVES, FOR SERVING

    MUSAENGCHAE (SEE RECIPE), FOR SERVING

MUSAENGCHAE

3   CUPS SHREDDED DAIKON RADISH

1   TEASPOON KOREAN CHILI POWDER

2   TABLESPOONS RICE VINEGAR

1   TABLESPOON KOSHER SALT

1   TABLESPOON SUGAR

THICK-CUT PORK CHOPS
with STONE FRUIT *and* BULGUR WHEAT

YIELD: 4 SERVINGS / ACTIVE TIME: 15 TO 25 MINUTES / TOTAL TIME: 40 MINUTES

Pork is the perfect vehicle for stone fruit, as its slightly salty flavor allows the fruit's natural sweetness to shine.

1. Place the stock in a cast-iron Dutch oven and bring to a boil. Place the bulgur wheat, salt, lemon zest, pepper, and olive oil in a bowl and pour the warmed stock over it. Cover tightly with plastic wrap and set aside for 30 minutes.

2. Preheat the oven to 375°F. Wipe out the pot, place 2 tablespoons of the vegetable oil in it, and warm over medium heat. When the oil starts to glisten, place the stone fruit flesh side down in the Dutch oven and sear for about 3 minutes per side. Add the turnip and the cipollini onions and cook for about 2 minutes per side. Remove the mixture from the pot and set aside.

3. Season the pork chops with salt and pepper. Add the remaining vegetable oil and then place the pork chops in the Dutch oven. Cook for about 5 minutes on each side, until a crust starts to form and the centers of the chops are 140 to 145°F. Remove the pork chops and set aside.

4. Chop the onions. Add the turnip and the onions to the bulgur wheat. Fluff with a fork and place the mixture in the Dutch oven. Arrange the fruit around the edge of the pot and place it in the oven. Cook for 5 to 7 minutes, until warmed through. Remove, serve with the pork chops, and garnish with the thyme.

TIP: If you want to know if the oil is ready and aren't sure if it is glistening, flick a few drops of water into the oil. If the oil sizzles, it is ready.

INGREDIENTS:

2   CUPS CHICKEN STOCK (SEE PAGES 102–3)

1   CUP BULGUR WHEAT

1   TEASPOON SALT, PLUS MORE TO TASTE

    ZEST OF 1 LEMON

¼   TEASPOON CRACKED BLACK PEPPER, PLUS MORE TO TASTE

1   TABLESPOON OLIVE OIL

¼   CUP VEGETABLE OIL

4   PIECES OF PREFERRED STONE FRUIT, PITTED AND QUARTERED

1   TURNIP, PEELED AND MINCED

4-6 CIPOLLINI ONIONS, PEELED AND HALVED LENGTHWISE

4   (1-INCH THICK) PORK CHOPS

2   TABLESPOONS FRESH THYME LEAVES, FOR GARNISH

PORK CHOPS *with* CIDER *and* POTATOES

YIELD: 4 SERVINGS / ACTIVE TIME: 3 HOURS / TOTAL TIME: 4 HOURS

Apples and potatoes are the perfect accompaniments to pork, and the lovely sauce created in the skillet adds another element of deliciousness. Chops with the bones have more flavor, but boneless chops are fine, too.

1. Preheat the oven to 350°F.

2. Season the chops with salt and pepper. Place a 12-inch cast-iron skillet over medium-high heat. Add the olive oil and coat the bottom. Add the chops and sear on both sides, about 3 minutes a side. Transfer to a plate.

3. Add the shallots and garlic to the skillet and cook, while stirring, until shallots are translucent, about 3 minutes.

4. Reduce the heat to low and stir in the flour, cooking for about a minute. Slowly add the cider, using a whisk to combine it with the flour and shallots. When the cider has been incorporated, increase the heat to medium and stir occasionally as it comes to a boil. Let the mixture boil for a few minutes.

5. Stir in the parsley, sage, and thyme, then add the chops. When the sauce returns to a boil, remove the skillet from heat, cover it, and put the skillet in the oven. Bake for 1½ hours, until the chops are very tender.

6. When the chops have about 20 minutes of cooking time left, prepare the potatoes. Heat another cast-iron skillet over medium-high heat and add the butter. When it is melted, add the potatoes. Reduce the heat to low and cook, stirring occasionally, until they are fork-tender, about 20 minutes.

7. Serve the chops with the potatoes, drizzling some of the pan sauce over both.

INGREDIENTS:

4 (½-INCH THICK) BONE-IN OR BONELESS PORK CHOPS

 SALT AND PEPPER, TO TASTE

2 TABLESPOONS OLIVE OIL

2 SHALLOTS, SLICED THIN

3 GARLIC CLOVES, MINCED

3 TABLESPOONS ALL-PURPOSE FLOUR

1½ CUPS APPLE CIDER

2 TABLESPOONS CHOPPED FRESH PARSLEY

1 TEASPOON DRIED SAGE

1 TEASPOON FRESH THYME LEAVES

2 TABLESPOONS UNSALTED BUTTER

2 LBS. FINGERLING POTATOES, HALVED LENGTHWISE

HORSERADISH-CRUSTED PORK

YIELD: 4 SERVINGS / **ACTIVE TIME:** 30 MINUTES / **TOTAL TIME:** 30 MINUTES

For thousands of years, horseradish has been used as a pungent, spicy seasoning and as a cure for pretty much any ailment. While it may or may not have healing powers, it most certainly can clear out your sinuses, in the most pleasant way. In this super-flavorful, easy-to-make dish, it's paired with wasabi to amplify its effects.

1. Preheat the broiler on your oven.

2. Pat the cutlets dry and lightly coat each one with the wasabi paste.

3. In a bowl, combine 2 tablespoons of the olive oil, horseradish, parsley, chives, salt, and pepper. Add the bread crumbs and carefully stir to coat.

4. Place a 12-inch cast-iron skillet over medium heat and add the remaining olive oil. When the oil is shimmering, add the pork cutlets and cook until golden brown, about 5 minutes. Flip the cutlets over and cook until golden brown on this side.

5. Remove the pork from the skillet and dip each cutlet into the seasoned panko until completely coated. Return the coated cutlets to the skillet.

6. While keeping a close watch, place the pan under the broiler. Broil, while turning the cutlets over halfway through, until the crust is browned and crispy. Slice and serve with the lemon wedges and long-grain rice.

INGREDIENTS:

- 1½ LBS. PORK CUTLETS
- ¼ CUP WASABI PASTE
- ¼ CUP OLIVE OIL
- 2 TABLESPOONS HORSERADISH
- 1 TABLESPOON MINCED PARSLEY
- 2 TABLESPOONS MINCED CHIVES
- SALT AND PEPPER, TO TASTE
- 2 CUPS PANKO BREAD CRUMBS
- LEMON WEDGES, FOR SERVING
- 1½ CUPS COOKED LONG-GRAIN RICE

SUPER-EASY SPARERIBS

YIELD: 2 TO 4 SERVINGS / ACTIVE TIME: 20 MINUTES / TOTAL TIME: 2 HOURS

Oven-roasting in a skillet renders tender ribs with no hassle. Make these on a cold winter night, and you can almost pretend you're at a summertime picnic.

1. Preheat the oven to 350°F.

2. Season both sides of the pork spareribs with salt and pepper.

3. Place the ribs in a 12-inch cast-iron skillet, sprinkle with the lemon juice, and put the skillet in the oven. Bake for about 1½ hours, turning halfway through the cooking time.

4. For the second half of the cooking time, brush with barbecue sauce, if desired, and turn again for the last 15 minutes, putting barbecue sauce on the other side of the ribs. Serve immediately.

INGREDIENTS:

2 LBS. PORK SPARERIBS, CUT TO FIT THE SKILLET

SALT AND PEPPER, TO TASTE

JUICE OF ½ LEMON

1-2 CUPS BARBECUE SAUCE (OPTIONAL)

PORK PÂTÉ (*aka* GORTON)

YIELD: 10 TO 15 SERVINGS / **ACTIVE TIME:** 20 MINUTES / **TOTAL TIME:** 24 HOURS

This French Canadian delicacy is sure to be the centerpiece of any meal. Keep in mind that the added resting time is crucial to concentrating the flavors.

1. Preheat the oven to 300°F.

2. Place all of the ingredients in a cast-iron Dutch oven and stir to combine. Cover and cook over low heat until the pork falls apart at the touch of a fork, about 3 to 4 hours.

3. Remove from heat, discard the bay leaves, and transfer the pork shoulder to a plate. When the pork shoulder has cooled slightly, shred it with a fork.

4. Place the shredded pork and ½ cup of the juices from the pot in a blender. Puree until the mixture forms a paste, adding more of the juices as needed.

5. Season with salt and pepper, transfer the paste to a large jar, and then pour the remaining juices over it. Cover the jar and store it in the refrigerator overnight before serving.

INGREDIENTS:

- 3- TO 5-LB., BONE-IN PORK SHOULDER
- 3 ONIONS, SLICED
- 2 TEASPOONS GROUND CLOVES
- 1 TABLESPOON SALT, PLUS MORE TO TASTE
- 4 BAY LEAVES
- 2 TEASPOONS BLACK PEPPER, PLUS MORE TO TASTE
- 1 TEASPOON NUTMEG

DUTCH PEA SOUP

YIELD: 6 SERVINGS / ACTIVE TIME: 30 MINUTES / TOTAL TIME: 3 TO 4 HOURS

This thick soup is traditionally served around New Year's, and would typically feature rookworst. Since this sausage can be difficult to find outside of the Netherlands, this recipe uses kielbasa instead.

1. Place a cast-iron Dutch oven over medium-high heat and add the bacon fat or butter. Add the salt pork, carrot, celery, onion, leek, celeriac, potatoes, thyme, salt, and pepper and cook for 10 minutes or until the vegetables start to caramelize.

2. Add the chicken stock and the green split peas and reduce the heat to medium-low. Cook for 2 to 2½ hours or until the peas have broken down and your spoon can stand up in the pot. Make sure to stir the soup every 15 to 20 minutes to keep it from burning.

3. Top with the kielbasa, garnish with the additional thyme, and serve.

INGREDIENTS:

2 TABLESPOONS BACON FAT OR UNSALTED BUTTER

½ LB. SALT PORK, MINCED

1 LARGE CARROT, PEELED AND MINCED

1 CELERY STALK, MINCED

½ LARGE YELLOW ONION, MINCED

1 LEEK, WHITE PART ONLY, RINSED WELL AND SLICED THIN

1 BULB OF CELERIAC (CELERY ROOT), PEELED AND DICED (ABOUT 1½ CUPS)

2 SMALL POTATOES, PEELED AND DICED

3 TABLESPOONS CHOPPED FRESH THYME LEAVES, PLUS MORE FOR GARNISH

SALT AND PEPPER, TO TASTE

8 CUPS LOW-SODIUM CHICKEN STOCK

1½ CUPS DRIED GREEN SPLIT PEAS, RINSED

1 LB. KIELBASA, SLICED INTO 1-INCH-THICK ROUNDS

SPICY SAUSAGE STEW *with* SUMMER VEGETABLES

YIELD: 4 TO 6 SERVINGS / ACTIVE TIME: 35 MINUTES / TOTAL TIME: 1 HOUR

When everything looks so good at the farmers market in late summer, it's easy to end up with a lot of vegetables and no idea how to combine them. This dish, which features the perfect amount of spice, remedies that issue.

1. Heat a 12-inch cast-iron skillet over medium-high heat. Add the butter. When it is melted, add the onion and garlic and cook, while stirring, until translucent and slightly browned, about 5 minutes.

2. Add the sausage and cook, while turning, until it is browned all over, about 3 minutes. Stir in the spices. Top with the peppers, corn, zucchini, and tomato pieces. Stir and season with salt and pepper.

3. Cover the skillet, reduce the heat to medium, and cook for about 20 minutes, checking it occasionally to make sure there is enough liquid and that it's at a gentle simmer, not a rolling boil. Garnish with parsley, if desired. Serve immediately.

INGREDIENTS:

- 2 TABLESPOONS UNSALTED BUTTER
- 1 ONION, DICED
- 2 GARLIC CLOVES, MINCED
- 1 LB. ITALIAN SAUSAGE, SLICED
- 2 TEASPOONS CHILI POWDER
- ½ TEASPOON CAYENNE PEPPER
- 2 RED BELL PEPPERS, DICED
- 3 EARS OF CORN, SHUCKED AND CLEANED, KERNELS REMOVED
- 1 SMALL ZUCCHINI, CUT INTO THIN HALF-MOONS
- 4 TOMATOES, SEEDED AND CHOPPED
- SALT AND PEPPER, TO TASTE
- PARSLEY, FOR GARNISH (OPTIONAL)

POLENTA CONCIA

This ideal example of Italian cuisine was adapted from a recipe of the revered chef Antonio Carluccio—aka "the godfather of Italian gastronomy." His reverence for culinary history and appreciation for the finest ingredients resulted in 20 books that taught a generation of Europeans how to cook Italian cuisine. Make sure your cast iron is good and hot so the sausages take on a smoky flavor.

1. Place the porcini mushrooms in a bowl of lukewarm water and let them soak for about 30 minutes, until they are rehydrated and slightly more plump.

2. Warm a 12-inch cast-iron skillet over medium heat for 5 minutes. Place the sausage and olive oil in the skillet and cook, while turning occasionally, until the sausage is browned all over, about 10 minutes.

3. Add the garlic, onion, and rosemary and sauté for 5 minutes.

4. Drain the rehydrated mushrooms and squeeze them to remove any excess water. Chop the mushrooms, add them to the skillet, and sauté for 1 minute. Carefully add the wine to the pan and let it reduce for 1 minute.

5. Add the tomato sauce, stir to combine, and reduce the heat to low. Simmer for 20 minutes.

6. While the mixture in the skillet is simmering, place the water and salt in a saucepan and bring to a boil. Add the cornmeal and cook until tender, about 40 minutes. Serve alongside the sausage.

INGREDIENTS:

- 1 **CUP DRIED PORCINI MUSHROOMS**
- 1 **LB. SPICY ITALIAN SAUSAGE**
- ¼ **CUP OLIVE OIL**
- 2 **GARLIC CLOVES, MINCED**
- 1 **ONION, CHOPPED**
- 1 **SPRIG OF ROSEMARY**
- 3 **TABLESPOONS RED WINE**
- 2 **CUPS TOMATO SAUCE**
- 4 **CUPS WATER**
- **PINCH OF SALT**
- 1 **CUP COARSE CORNMEAL**

JAMBALAYA

YIELD: 4 TO 6 SERVINGS / ACTIVE TIME: 25 MINUTES / TOTAL TIME: 1 HOUR AND 15 MINUTES

Browning the sausages at the beginning of your preparation adds an indispensable element to this Cajun classic.

1. Place the sausage in a cast-iron Dutch oven and cook over medium-high heat. Cook for 2 minutes on each side, remove, and set aside.

2. Add the shrimp and cook for 1 minute on each side. Remove and set aside.

3. Add the oil, chicken, onion, bell pepper, and celery. Cook for 5 to 7 minutes or until the vegetables start to caramelize and the chicken is cooked through. Add the garlic and cook for another 2 minutes.

4. Add the tomatoes, the bay leaves, and all of the spices. Cook for 30 minutes, while stirring occasionally to prevent the contents of the Dutch oven from burning.

5. Add the rice, Worcestershire sauce, Tabasco™, and stock. Return the sausage to the pot, reduce heat to medium-low, cover, and cook for 25 minutes.

6. Return the shrimp to the pan, cover, and cook for 5 minutes. Ladle into bowls and garnish with scallions.

INGREDIENTS:

- ½ LB. ANDOUILLE SAUSAGE, CUT INTO ½-INCH-THICK ROUNDS
- ½ LB. SHRIMP (21/25), SHELLED AND DEVEINED
- ¼ CUP VEGETABLE OIL
- 4 BONELESS, SKINLESS CHICKEN THIGHS OR BREASTS, CUT INTO 2-INCH CUBES
- 1 LARGE YELLOW ONION, DICED
- 1 LARGE GREEN OR RED BELL PEPPER, DICED
- 2 CELERY STALKS, DICED (ABOUT 1 CUP)
- 3 GARLIC CLOVES, MINCED
- 2-3 PLUM TOMATOES, DICED
- 2 BAY LEAVES
- 2 TABLESPOONS PAPRIKA
- 2 TABLESPOONS DRIED THYME
- 1 TABLESPOON GRANULATED GARLIC
- 1 TABLESPOON GRANULATED ONION
- 1 TEASPOON CAYENNE PEPPER
- 1½ CUPS LONG-GRAIN RICE
- 2 TABLESPOONS WORCESTERSHIRE SAUCE
- TABASCO™, TO TASTE
- 3 CUPS CHICKEN STOCK (SEE PAGES 102–3)
- SALT AND PEPPER, TO TASTE
- SCALLIONS, CHOPPED, FOR GARNISH

PORK FRIED RICE

YIELD: 8 SERVINGS / ACTIVE TIME: 25 MINUTES / TOTAL TIME: 35 MINUTES

A comfort food classic. Using leftovers actually improves this dish. The next time you order Chinese food, add one or two sides of white rice, and you're halfway to another delicious meal.

1. Place the vegetable oil in a 12-inch cast-iron skillet and cook over medium-high heat until the oil just starts to shimmer. To ensure that you don't overheat the oil, add a small piece of the carrot to the pan. Once you see the carrot start to fry, the oil is ready.

2. Add the ginger and garlic and cook for about 2 minutes, or until they start to brown.

3. Raise the heat to high and add the pork. Cook for 5 minutes or until the pork starts to form a light crust.

4. Push the meat to one side of the pan and add the eggs. Scramble with a fork until the eggs are cooked through, roughly 2 minutes.

5. Add the carrots, rice, scallions, and peas and stir to incorporate. Add the soy sauce, rice vinegar, fish sauce, and sesame oil and cook, while stirring constantly, for 5 minutes. Serve immediately.

TIP: If you've been searching for that perfect umami flavor, fish sauce is akin to striking gold. Just be careful not to overdo it, as it can make the dish too pungent. A good rule of thumb is to add just enough fish sauce that you can vaguely smell it.

INGREDIENTS:

¼	CUP VEGETABLE OIL
1	TABLESPOON MINCED GINGER
3	GARLIC CLOVES, MINCED
1	LB. PORK TENDERLOIN, COOKED AND DICED
3-4	LARGE EGGS
2	CUPS MINCED CARROTS
4	CUPS COOKED WHITE RICE (DAY-OLD RICE PREFERRED)
4	SCALLIONS, CHOPPED
1	CUP FRESH OR FROZEN PEAS
2	TABLESPOONS LIGHT SOY SAUCE
1	TABLESPOON RICE VINEGAR
1	TABLESPOON FISH SAUCE
1	TABLESPOON SESAME OIL

RABBIT RAGÙ

YIELD: 4 SERVINGS / ACTIVE TIME: 30 MINUTES / TOTAL TIME: 2 HOURS

Rabbit is the ultimate sustainable protein. It's lean, it tastes great, and it's eco-friendly. Cooking the rabbit on the bone keeps it tender so that it can add even more flavor to an already complex and delicious sauce.

1. Place the olive oil in a large cast-iron Dutch oven and warm over medium heat. Season the pieces of rabbit with salt and pepper, dredge them in the flour, and shake to remove any excess. When the oil starts to smoke, add the rabbit and cook until the pieces are browned on both sides, about 6 minutes per side.

2. Use a slotted spoon to remove the rabbit and set it aside. Add the onion, celery, carrots, and garlic and sauté until browned. Add the tomato paste, stir to coat the vegetables, and cook for approximately 4 minutes.

3. Add the wine and let the mixture come to a boil. Lower the heat and cook until the wine has reduced by half, about 10 minutes.

4. Add the tomatoes, chicken broth, bay leaves, rosemary, and thyme and simmer for 2 minutes before adding the rabbit back to the pot. Simmer for 1½ hours.

5. Use a slotted spoon to remove the rabbit and set it aside. Remove the bay leaves, rosemary, and thyme. When the rabbit is cool enough to handle, pick the meat off the bones and shred it. Discard the bones and return the meat to the sauce.

6. To serve, spoon the ragù over the pappardelle or polenta and garnish with the Parmesan.

INGREDIENTS:

¼ CUP OLIVE OIL

2½- TO 3½-LB. RABBIT, CUT INTO 8 BONE-IN PIECES

KOSHER SALT AND GROUND BLACK PEPPER, TO TASTE

1 CUP ALL-PURPOSE FLOUR

1 YELLOW ONION, DICED

2 CELERY STALKS, DICED

2 CARROTS, PEELED AND DICED

1 GARLIC CLOVE, MINCED

2 TABLESPOONS TOMATO PASTE

½ CUP FULL-BODIED RED WINE

1 (28 OZ.) CAN OF CRUSHED TOMATOES

1 CUP CHICKEN BROTH

2 BAY LEAVES

2 SPRIGS OF ROSEMARY

4 SPRIGS OF THYME

2 CUPS WATER

2 TABLESPOONS UNSALTED BUTTER, CUT INTO SMALL PIECES

1 LB. COOKED PAPPARDELLE OR 4 CUPS COOKED POLENTA

PARMESAN CHEESE, GRATED, FOR GARNISH

POULTRY

Is chicken the most popular protein in the United States? Probably. Cheap, lean, and versatile, one can never have too many chicken-centered recipes in their repertoire. Those who are looking to spice up their evenings would be wise to try out the Chicken Vindaloo (see page 413) or the Yucatan Lime & Chicken Soup (see page 375).

But chicken is far from the only fowl on the block, and it's worth mixing things up with some turkey or duck. Rest assured, it all works wonderfully with cast iron, which provides the crispy skin and juicy inside that so often proves evasive when using other cookware. It's also wonderful for braising, which is how you get the delectable, falling-off-the-bone texture that makes dishes like the Five-Spice Turkey Breast (see page 429).

COCONUT CURRY CHICKEN *with* BASMATI RICE

YIELD: 4 TO 6 SERVINGS / **ACTIVE TIME:** 20 MINUTES / **TOTAL TIME:** 1 HOUR

This recipe proves that you don't need to order takeout in order to get good green curry at home. The creamy coconut milk tempers the spice in this just enough to ensure that your experience is pure pleasure.

1. Preheat the oven to 375°F. Rub 2 tablespoons of the green curry paste on the chicken and set aside for at least 30 minutes.

2. Place a 12-inch cast-iron skillet over medium-high heat and add the chicken thighs, skin side down. Cook until the skin is crispy, turn over, and cook for another 3 minutes. Remove the chicken from the pan and set aside.

3. Add the onions, peppers, ginger, and garlic and cook, while stirring, for 5 to 7 minutes. As the vegetables and aromatics cook, make sure you scrape the bottom of the pan to remove all of the browned bits from the bottom.

4. Add the remaining green curry paste and cook for an additional 3 minutes, until fragrant. Add the fish sauce, Madras curry powder, coconut milk, and Thai basil and stir until combined. Add the rice and water, stir, and then return the chicken to the pan. Cover and transfer the pan to the oven. Cook for 25 minutes, until the rice is tender and has absorbed all of the liquid. Serve with the lime wedges and garnish with the additional Thai basil and the cilantro.

TIP: To mash ginger and garlic, mince them first and then use a mortar and pestle. Make sure you reserve whatever juices are released and add them to the dish.

INGREDIENTS:

5   TABLESPOONS GREEN CURRY PASTE

4-6   BONELESS CHICKEN THIGHS

2   YELLOW ONIONS, CUT INTO ¼-INCH-THICK SLICES

2   RED BELL PEPPERS, SEEDED AND CUT INTO ¼-INCH-THICK SLICES

3   TABLESPOONS MASHED GINGER

1   GARLIC CLOVE, MASHED

3   TABLESPOONS FISH SAUCE

1   TABLESPOON MADRAS CURRY POWDER

1   (14 OZ.) CAN OF LITE COCONUT MILK

2   TABLESPOONS CHOPPED THAI BASIL, PLUS MORE FOR GARNISH

1   CUP BASMATI RICE, WASHED AND STRAINED

1   CUP WATER

LIME WEDGES, FOR SERVING

CILANTRO, CHOPPED, FOR GARNISH

SKILLET WINGS

YIELD: 4 TO 6 SERVINGS / *ACTIVE TIME:* 30 MINUTES / *TOTAL TIME:* 1 HOUR

These are a double whammy of sautéed goodness baked to perfection in a very hot oven. Invite over your wing-loving friends and see if they don't agree that these are the best ever. If you like fiery wings, swap out Frank's RedHot® sauce for your favorite heavy-duty hot sauce and add another pinch of cayenne pepper for good measure.

1. Preheat the oven to 500°F.

2. With a sharp knife, cut the wings at the joint so that you have three sections: the single-boned section, the double-boned section, and the tip. Discard the tips.

3. When the oven is almost to 500°F, place a 12-inch cast-iron skillet over medium-high heat and add the butter and oil. When this gets hot, add the wing sections and stir. Season with salt and pepper, sprinkle with cayenne, stir again, then coat the wings with a portion of the hot sauce (use just enough to coat the wings).

4. Put the skillet in the oven. Cook the wings for a couple of minutes, remove the skillet from the oven carefully, flip over each wing section, and coat with additional hot sauce. Put the skillet back in the oven and cook for another 2 minutes. Repeat this procedure for about 20 minutes, basting with the hot sauce in the skillet, until the wings are fully cooked and crispy all over.

5. Serve with the Blue Cheese Dressing, celery sticks, and carrot sticks.

INGREDIENTS:

6   WHOLE CHICKEN WINGS

1   TABLESPOON UNSALTED BUTTER

1   TABLESPOON VEGETABLE OIL

      SALT AND PEPPER, TO TASTE

⅛   TEASPOON CAYENNE PEPPER

7   OZ. FRANK'S REDHOT® SAUCE

      BLUE CHEESE DRESSING (SEE PAGE 359), FOR SERVING

      CELERY STICKS, FOR SERVING

      CARROT STICKS, FOR SERVING

BUFFALO CHICKEN WINGS

YIELD: 4 SERVINGS / ACTIVE TIME: 30 MINUTES / TOTAL TIME: 45 MINUTES

The classic we've all come know and love, now in the comfort of your home. This recipe can easily be altered, so don't hesitate to tinker and don't be bashful about tripling it if the gang is coming over.

1. Place the butter in a large saucepan and warm over medium heat. When it has melted, whisk in the vinegar, hot sauce, and cayenne (if using), making sure not to breathe in the spicy steam. Remove the pan from the stove and cover to keep warm while you cook the wings.

2. Place the vegetable oil in a large enameled cast-iron Dutch oven and slowly bring it to 375°F over medium heat. This can take up to 10 minutes.

3. While the oil is heating, pat the wings dry and, working in batches, toss them in the cornstarch.

4. Add the coated wings to the oil in batches and fry until they are crispy, about 10 minutes. Transfer the fried chicken wings to a wire rack and season with salt.

5. Add the cooked wings to the spicy sauce in the saucepan. Remove them with a slotted spoon, arrange them on a platter, and serve them with the Blue Cheese Dressing and celery sticks.

BLUE CHEESE DRESSING

1. Place the sour cream, mayonnaise, buttermilk, lemon juice, and pepper in a bowl and whisk to combine.

2. Add the blue cheese and stir to incorporate. The dressing will keep in the refrigerator for up to 1 week.

INGREDIENTS:

4	TABLESPOONS UNSALTED BUTTER
1	TABLESPOON WHITE VINEGAR
¾	CUP HOT SAUCE (TABASCO™ OR FRANK'S REDHOT® RECOMMENDED)
1	TEASPOON CAYENNE PEPPER (OPTIONAL)
6	CUPS VEGETABLE OIL
2	LBS. CHICKEN WINGS
1	CUP CORNSTARCH
	SALT, TO TASTE
	BLUE CHEESE DRESSING (SEE RECIPE), FOR SERVING
	CELERY STICKS, FOR SERVING

BLUE CHEESE DRESSING

¼	CUP SOUR CREAM
¼	CUP MAYONNAISE
¼	CUP BUTTERMILK
1	TABLESPOON FRESH LEMON JUICE
	PINCH OF BLACK PEPPER
1	CUP CRUMBLED BLUE CHEESE

FRIED CHICKEN

YIELD: 4 SERVINGS / ACTIVE TIME: 1 HOUR / TOTAL TIME: 1 HOUR AND 30 MINUTES

If you want the texture and flavor of deep-fried chicken without the mess, try this recipe. The cornflakes are essential!

1. Preheat the oven to 400°F. Place a 12-inch cast-iron skillet in the oven to get it hot.

2. Rinse and dry the chicken pieces.

3. In a shallow bowl or cake pan, whisk together the flour with some salt and pepper. Combine the milk and the vinegar and let the combination sit for 10 minutes to create buttermilk. When ready, place the buttermilk in a bowl with the beaten eggs. In another large bowl, combine the cornflakes, bread crumbs, paprika, and 2 tablespoons of the vegetable oil.

4. Coat the chicken pieces one at a time by dipping each in the flour, then the buttermilk mixture, then the crumb mixture, being sure to coat all sides. When coated, put the pieces on a plate, cover with plastic wrap, and refrigerate for about 15 minutes.

5. Wearing oven mitts, carefully take the skillet out of the oven and put the remaining oil in it. Warm on low until hot. Add the cold chicken pieces and turn in the hot oil until both sides are coated.

6. Put the skillet back in the oven and bake for about 30 minutes, turning the pieces after 15 minutes. The chicken is done when the juices run clear when pierced with a knife. Serve immediately.

INGREDIENTS:

3   CHICKEN LEGS, SEPARATED INTO DRUMSTICKS AND THIGHS

¼   CUP ALL-PURPOSE FLOUR

     SALT AND PEPPER, TO TASTE

1   CUP WHOLE MILK

1   TABLESPOON WHITE VINEGAR

2   EGGS, LIGHTLY BEATEN

1½   CUPS CORNFLAKES, FINELY CRUSHED

½   CUP PLAIN BREAD CRUMBS

1   TEASPOON PAPRIKA

1   CUP VEGETABLE OIL

GENERAL TSO CHICKEN

YIELD: 4 SERVINGS / **ACTIVE TIME:** 1 HOUR AND 30 MINUTES / **TOTAL TIME:** 2 HOURS

You'll never find yourself reaching for the takeout menu again after whipping up this Chinese food favorite in a cast-iron skillet. This recipe works wonders—and it includes one of our favorite sauces, sriracha.

1. Place the egg white in a mixing bowl. Add the sesame oil, 1 tablespoon of soy sauce, and ¼ cup cornstarch. Whisk to combine. Add the chicken pieces and marinate at room temperature for about 30 minutes.

2. In a small saucepan, heat the tablespoon of oil over medium-high heat. Add the ginger and garlic and stir for about a minute. Add in the broth, sriracha, sugar, remaining soy sauce, and tablespoon of cornstarch, and whisk to combine the ingredients. Continue to whisk until the sauce gets thick and glossy. Reduce the heat to low and cover to keep it warm.

3. Place a 10-inch cast-iron skillet over medium-high heat and add about ½ inch of vegetable oil. When hot, add the chicken one piece at a time so it doesn't splatter too much. Turn the pieces with a slotted spoon so that they brown on all sides. Cook until crispy, about 5 minutes. When the pieces are cooked, transfer them to a paper towel–lined plate to drain.

4. When all the pieces are cooked, stir them into the sauce with the scallions. Serve hot.

TIP: This dish is usually served with a bowl of white rice and a side of steamed broccoli. To coordinate the three parts, make the rice ahead of time and reheat on the stove over a low flame. The broccoli can be partially steamed ahead of time and then finished with additional steaming of about 10 minutes.

INGREDIENTS:

- 1   EGG WHITE
- 1½   TEASPOONS TOASTED SESAME OIL
- ¼   CUP LOW-SODIUM SOY SAUCE, PLUS 1 TABLESPOON
- ¼   CUP CORNSTARCH, PLUS 1 TABLESPOON
- 1   LB. SKINLESS, BONELESS CHICKEN THIGHS, CUT INTO BITE-SIZED PIECES
- 1   TABLESPOON VEGETABLE OIL, PLUS MORE FOR FRYING
- 2   TABLESPOONS MINCED GINGER
- 3   GARLIC CLOVES, MINCED
- 1   CUP CHICKEN BROTH
- 2   TEASPOONS SRIRACHA
- 3   TABLESPOONS SUGAR
- 3   SCALLIONS, SLICED THIN

CHICKEN GYOZA

YIELD: 4 TO 6 SERVINGS (30 GYOZA) / **ACTIVE TIME:** 25 MINUTES / **TOTAL TIME:** 40 MINUTES

Chef Ming Tsai made a name for himself at his restaurants in the Boston area, where his flair for combining exciting flavors and classic Asian techniques won him a huge following. While he added to his popularity by becoming a television personality, he never left his roots behind. This recipe is adapted from one of his standards.

1. Place the cabbage, salt, ground chicken, ginger, carrot, scallions, and garlic in a large bowl and stir until thoroughly combined.

2. Add the soy sauce, sesame oil, sesame seeds, red pepper flakes, and egg and stir to incorporate.

3. To assemble the gyoza, place one wrapper on a clean, dry surface. Spoon 2 teaspoons of the filling into the center and run a wet finger along the edge of half of the wrapper. Fold the wet edge of the wrapper over the filling and press it down on the dry edge. Use the tines of a fork to gently seal the wrapper closed. Repeat until all of the filling has been used.

4. Place a 10-inch cast-iron skillet over medium-high heat and add the vegetable oil. When the oil is hot but not smoking, remove the skillet from heat and arrange the gyoza in the pan so that they are touching one another. Place over medium heat and cook until the bottoms are a pale golden brown, 2 to 3 minutes.

5. Add the water to the skillet, cover it with a lid, and cook until the liquid has evaporated and the bottoms of the gyoza are browned, about 7 to 10 minutes. Add another 2 tablespoons of water if the skillet looks dry before the bottoms are browned. If there is still liquid in the pan after 10 minutes, remove the lid and cook for another 1 to 2 minutes.

6. Remove from the pan and serve immediately.

INGREDIENTS:

2   CUPS SHREDDED NAPA CABBAGE

1   TEASPOON KOSHER SALT

⅓   LB. GROUND CHICKEN

1   TABLESPOON MINCED FRESH GINGER

1   CARROT, PEELED AND COARSELY SHREDDED

2   SCALLIONS, CHOPPED

2   GARLIC CLOVES, MINCED

2   TABLESPOONS SOY SAUCE

2   TEASPOONS SESAME OIL

1   TABLESPOON SESAME SEEDS

    LARGE PINCH OF RED PEPPER FLAKES

½   EGG, LIGHTLY BEATEN

30   GYOZA WRAPPERS

¼   CUP VEGETABLE OIL

½   CUP WATER, PLUS MORE AS NEEDED

CHICKEN KEBABS

YIELD: 4 TO 6 SERVINGS / ACTIVE TIME: 20 MINUTES / TOTAL TIME: 2½ TO 24 HOURS

Once again, cast iron takes on a preparation that is universally associated with the grill and shows that it is more deserving of the job.

1. Place the paprika, turmeric, onion powder, garlic powder, oregano, olive oil, vinegar, yogurt, and salt in a large bowl and whisk to combine.

2. Add the chicken pieces and stir until they are coated. Cover the bowl and let them marinate for at least 2 hours. If you have time, you can also let the chicken marinate overnight.

3. Place a cast-iron grill pan over medium-high heat and warm for 10 minutes.

4. While the pan is heating up, thread the chicken onto skewers and season with salt and pepper.

5. Brush the grill pan with a light coating of olive oil and then add the chicken kebabs. Cook, while turning occasionally, until the chicken is golden brown and cooked through, approximately 10 minutes.

6. Serve warm or at room temperature with the lemon wedges.

INGREDIENTS:

- 2 TABLESPOONS PAPRIKA
- 1 TEASPOON TURMERIC
- 1 TEASPOON ONION POWDER
- 1 TEASPOON GARLIC POWDER
- 1 TABLESPOON DRIED OREGANO
- ¼ CUP OLIVE OIL, PLUS MORE AS NEEDED
- 2 TABLESPOONS WHITE WINE VINEGAR
- 1 CUP PLAIN GREEK YOGURT
- 1 TEASPOON KOSHER SALT, PLUS MORE TO TASTE
- 3 LBS. BONELESS, SKINLESS CHICKEN THIGHS, CUT INTO BITE-SIZED PIECES

  PEPPER, TO TASTE
- 2 LEMONS, CUT INTO WEDGES, FOR SERVING

CHICKEN TORTILLA SOUP

YIELD: 4 TO 6 SERVINGS / ACTIVE TIME: 30 MINUTES / TOTAL TIME: 1 HOUR AND 45 MINUTES

The secret weapon in this soup is the hint of adobo sauce. Make sure you use chicken thighs, as they are perfect for shredding and won't dry out.

1. Preheat the oven to 375°F. Cut six of the tortillas into small strips and set two aside.

2. Line a baking sheet with parchment paper and place the tortilla strips on the sheet. Brush the strips with 1 tablespoon of the oil and then sprinkle them with salt. Place the sheet in the oven and bake for 15 to 20 minutes or until they become crispy. Remove from the oven and set aside.

3. Place the remaining oil and the garlic in a cast-iron Dutch oven and cook over medium-high heat until the oil and garlic become fragrant, about 5 minutes.

4. Add the chicken to the pot and sear for 5 minutes on each side. Remove the chicken from the pan and set aside. The chicken will cook further in the soup so it's okay if it's not cooked through.

5. Place the onion, peppers, tomatoes, adobo sauce, cumin, and chilies in the pot and cook for 10 to 15 minutes, while stirring the mixture every couple of minutes.

6. Return the chicken to the pan. Add the 2 tablespoons of kosher salt, stock, and water and cook for 1 hour or until the chicken shreds when pressed against the side of the pot with a wooden spoon.

7. Add the reserved whole tortillas and continue cooking until they dissolve, about 10 minutes. Garnish with Cotija cheese, cilantro, and the crispy tortilla strips.

TIPS: If you don't want to turn on the oven, you can use your favorite kind of corn chips in place of the crispy tortillas.

INGREDIENTS:

8 CORN TORTILLAS (SEE PAGE 169)

3 TABLESPOONS VEGETABLE OIL

2 TABLESPOONS KOSHER SALT, PLUS MORE TO TASTE

3 GARLIC CLOVES, MINCED

6 BONELESS, SKINLESS CHICKEN THIGHS

½ LARGE YELLOW ONION, DICED

1 POBLANO PEPPER, SEEDED AND DICED

1 ANAHEIM PEPPER, SEEDED AND DICED

4 PLUM TOMATOES, DICED

2 TABLESPOONS ADOBO SAUCE FROM A CAN OF CHIPOTLES EN ADOBO

1 TABLESPOON CUMIN

2 DRIED CHILE DE ÁRBOL PEPPERS, SEEDED AND MINCED

4 CUPS CHICKEN STOCK (SEE PAGES 102–3)

1 CUP WATER

COTIJA CHEESE, FOR GARNISH

CILANTRO, CHOPPED, FOR GARNISH

TUSCAN CHICKEN *and* WHITE BEAN STEW

YIELD: 4 TO 6 SERVINGS / **ACTIVE TIME:** 45 MINUTES / **TOTAL TIME:** 1 HOUR AND 45 MINUTES

This stew is creamy, yet surprisingly light. This is due to the inclusion of pureed beans, which provide the same rich texture as cream without any of the heaviness.

1. Drain the cannellini beans and rinse them. Place in a cast-iron Dutch oven, cover with water, and cook over medium heat. Add the chicken bones, bay leaves, kosher salt, and rosemary. Cover and cook, while stirring occasionally, for about 1 hour, until the beans are soft and starting to fall apart.

2. While the beans are cooking, season the chicken with salt and pepper and set aside.

3. When the beans are done, pour them into a bowl. Remove the chicken bones, rosemary sprigs, and the bay leaves. Place the Dutch oven back on the stove and add the olive oil. Warm over medium heat and then add the chicken thighs. Cook for about 5 minutes on each side, until the chicken is cooked through. Remove from the pan and let cool. When cool, dice the chicken.

4. Place the onion, carrots, celery, peppers, garlic, red pepper flakes, tomatoes, and sage in the pot and cook for 20 minutes, until the vegetables are soft and have released their juices.

5. While the vegetables are cooking, transfer the beans to a blender and puree. Place the beans back in the pot and then stir in the Asiago and basil. Season with salt and pepper and cook for 7 to 10 minutes, until the cheese is melted. Return the diced chicken to the pot and cook until heated through. Drizzle with additional olive oil, garnish with the scallion, and serve.

TIPS: If you don't want to use a blender, you can mash the beans by hand until they are smooth.

INGREDIENTS:

- 1   LB. DRIED CANNELLINI BEANS, SOAKED OVERNIGHT
- 2   LBS. CHICKEN THIGHS, BONES AND SKINS REMOVED, BONES RESERVED
- 2   BAY LEAVES
- 1   TABLESPOON KOSHER SALT, PLUS MORE TO TASTE
- 2   SPRIGS OF ROSEMARY
-   PEPPER, TO TASTE
- 2   TABLESPOONS OLIVE OIL, PLUS MORE FOR DRIZZLING
- 1   YELLOW ONION, DICED
- 3   CARROTS, PEELED AND DICED
- 2   CELERY STALKS, DICED
- 1   YELLOW BELL PEPPER, SEEDED AND DICED
- 1   ORANGE BELL PEPPER, SEEDED AND DICED
- 3   GARLIC CLOVES, MINCED
- 1   TEASPOON RED PEPPER FLAKES
- 4   SMALL ROMA TOMATOES, DICED
- 2   TABLESPOONS CHOPPED FRESH SAGE
- 1½   OZ. ASIAGO CHEESE, GRATED
- ¼   CUP FRESH BASIL LEAVES, CHOPPED
-   ZEST AND JUICE OF ½ LEMON
-   SCALLIONS, CHOPPED, FOR GARNISH

WHITE CHICKEN CHILI

YIELD: 6 SERVINGS / ACTIVE TIME: 15 MINUTES / TOTAL TIME: 24 HOURS

You want the heat to be subtle in this chili to showcase the flavors of the green chilies and Sofrito. If you want to make this one special, use the recipe for Chicken Stock on pages 102–3.

1. Place the beans in a cast-iron Dutch oven and cover with water. Bring to a boil, reduce heat to medium-low, and cover the pot. Cook for 45 minutes to 1 hour, until the beans are tender. Drain and set the beans aside.

2. Place the pot back on the stove and warm the oil over medium-high heat. Add the chicken and cook for 5 minutes on each side. Remove the chicken and set aside.

3. Add the onion and garlic to the pot and cook until the onion is translucent, about 5 to 7 minutes.

4. Add the Sofrito and green chilies and cook, stirring occasionally, for 5 minutes.

5. Return the beans and the chicken to the Dutch oven. Add the remaining ingredients, reduce the heat to medium, cover, and cook for 1 hour.

6. Remove the cover, stir, and cook for an additional 30 minutes to 1 hour, until the chili has thickened and the chicken is falling apart.

TIP: If you want to roast your own green chilies, turn your broiler on. Place fresh green chilies on a baking sheet and coat them with vegetable oil. Place the sheet in the oven and cook until the skins of the chilies are charred, about 15 to 20 minutes. Remove the sheet from the oven and place the chilies in a bowl. Cover the bowl tightly with plastic wrap and set aside. After 30 minutes, use your fingers to remove the charred skins of the peppers. Dice the chilies and reserve until ready to use.

INGREDIENTS:

1   LB. WHITE BEANS, SOAKED OVERNIGHT AND DRAINED

¼   CUP VEGETABLE OIL

6   BONELESS, SKINLESS CHICKEN THIGHS

1   WHITE ONION, MINCED

3   GARLIC CLOVES, MINCED

1   CUP SOFRITO (SEE PAGE 218)

1   (7 OZ.) CAN OF DICED MILD GREEN CHILIES

6   CUPS CHICKEN STOCK

1   TABLESPOON WHITE PEPPER

3   TABLESPOONS DRIED OREGANO

1   TABLESPOON CUMIN

1   TABLESPOON ADOBO SEASONING

    SALT AND PEPPER, TO TASTE

YUCATAN LIME & CHICKEN SOUP

YIELD: 4 SERVINGS / **ACTIVE TIME:** 40 MINUTES / **TOTAL TIME:** 1 HOUR AND 30 MINUTES

This recipe was adapted from a preparation made famous by Patricia Quintana, the late, revered Mexican chef. Warm and soothing, vibrant and filling, it articulates everything that is at the heart of Mexican cuisine.

1. Place the tomatoes, unpeeled onion, and 16 of the garlic cloves in a large, dry cast-iron skillet and cook them over high heat, using tongs to occasionally turn them. Cook until they are blackened and tender. Remove the vegetables from the pan and let them cool slightly. Peel the onion and slice it in half. Core the tomatoes and then grate using the wide holes of a box grater, leaving the skins behind.

2. Place the chicken in a large cast-iron Dutch oven and pour in the stock (or water), making sure there is enough to cover. Add the lime halves, allspice berries, oregano, remaining garlic cloves, and a pinch of salt and bring to a boil over medium heat. Let the broth boil for 3 minutes.

3. Add the onion and charred garlic cloves, reduce the heat to low, and let the soup gently simmer for 30 to 45 minutes.

4. Using tongs, remove the chicken from the broth, place it in a large bowl, and let it cool. Let the broth gently simmer for another 10 minutes. Strain the broth and set it aside. Remove the chicken meat from the bones.

5. Place the vegetable oil in the Dutch oven and warm over medium heat. When it begins to shimmer, add the grated tomatoes and simmer until the fat starts to separate, about 5 minutes.

6. Add the strained broth and bring to a boil. Reduce the heat to low, simmer for 10 minutes, and then season with salt and pepper.

7. Add the chicken to the broth and cook until heated through. Ladle the soup into warmed bowls and garnish with the tortilla chips, scallions, and additional oregano. Serve with the minced jalapeño, chopped onion, and lime wedges.

INGREDIENTS:

4	ROMA TOMATOES
1	LARGE ONION, UNPEELED
21	GARLIC CLOVES, TRIMMED AND PEELED
3	BONE-IN, SKINLESS CHICKEN BREASTS (WITH RIB MEAT)
12	CUPS CHICKEN STOCK (SEE PAGES 102–3) OR WATER, PLUS MORE AS NEEDED
2	LIMES, HALVED
20	ALLSPICE BERRIES
1	TABLESPOON DRIED OREGANO, PLUS MORE FOR GARNISH
	SALT AND BLACK PEPPER, TO TASTE
1	CUP VEGETABLE OIL, PLUS 2 TABLESPOONS
2	CUPS TORTILLA CHIPS, CRUMBLED, FOR GARNISH
6	LARGE SCALLIONS, MINCED, FOR GARNISH
2	JALAPEÑO PEPPERS, SEEDED AND MINCED, FOR SERVING
	CHOPPED ONION, FOR SERVING
	LIME WEDGES, FOR SERVING

CHICKPEA & LEFTOVER TURKEY CHILI

YIELD: 6 TO 8 SERVINGS / ACTIVE TIME: 35 MINUTES / TOTAL TIME: 2 HOURS AND 35 MINUTES

While chili isn't always the first use for leftover turkey, this spicy combination is sure to make a lasting impression.

1. Place the olive oil in a cast-iron Dutch oven and warm over medium-high heat.

2. Add the onion, garlic, oregano, pepper, cumin, and chili powder. Cook for 5 minutes, stirring often.

3. Add the turkey stock, tomatoes, dried chilies, bell pepper, salt, chickpeas, and turkey.

4. Stir the mixture, cover, and reduce the heat to low. Cook for 2 hours, stirring occasionally.

5. Scoop chili into bowls and top with cheese and sour cream, if desired. Serve with the Rosemary Butter and Classic Corn Bread.

ROSEMARY BUTTER

1. Place the butter, salt, and rosemary in a bowl and beat until light and fluffy.

2. Place the whipped butter in a container and refrigerate until needed.

INGREDIENTS:

1	TABLESPOON OLIVE OIL
1	YELLOW ONION, DICED
5	GARLIC CLOVES, MINCED
1	TABLESPOON CHOPPED FRESH OREGANO
	PEPPER, TO TASTE
1	TABLESPOON CUMIN
2	TEASPOONS CHILI POWDER
2	CUPS TURKEY STOCK
½	LB. TOMATOES (CANNED OR FRESH)
3	DRIED RED NEW MEXICO CHILIES
1	RED BELL PEPPER, SEEDED AND DICED
	PINCH OF SALT
1	(14 OZ.) CAN OF CHICKPEAS
1	LB. LEFTOVER TURKEY
2	CUPS SHREDDED CHEDDAR CHEESE (OPTIONAL)
1	CUP SOUR CREAM (OPTIONAL)
	ROSEMARY BUTTER (SEE RECIPE), FOR SERVING
	CLASSIC CORN BREAD (SEE PAGE 166), FOR SERVING

ROSEMARY BUTTER

4	TABLESPOONS UNSALTED BUTTER, AT ROOM TEMPERATURE
	PINCH OF SALT
	LEAVES FROM 2 SPRIGS OF ROSEMARY, MINCED

CHICKEN *and* VEGETABLE STEW

YIELD: 6 SERVINGS / **ACTIVE TIME:** 15 TO 20 MINUTES / **TOTAL TIME:** 1 HOUR AND 45 MINUTES

A day's worth of protein, veggies, and flavor are packed into this stew—which requires minimal effort on your part.

1. Place the olive oil in a Dutch oven and warm over medium-high heat. Season the chicken thighs with salt and pepper and place them in the Dutch oven, skin side down. Cook for 5 minutes on each side. Remove and set aside.

2. Add the onion, celery, carrots, and parsnips to the pot and cook for 5 to 7 minutes, until the onion starts to get translucent. Season with a pinch of salt and pepper and then add the zucchini, squash, and garlic. Cook for 5 minutes, while stirring, until the garlic is fragrant.

3. Season with salt and pepper and add the chicken thighs, stock, and bay leaves. Reduce heat to medium, cover, and cook for 1½ hours or until the chicken is falling off the bone. Season with salt and pepper to taste. Discard the bay leaves and, if desired, garnish with fresh basil before serving.

INGREDIENTS:

2 TABLESPOONS OLIVE OIL

2 LBS. CHICKEN THIGHS

SALT AND PEPPER, TO TASTE

1 WHITE ONION, DICED

3 CELERY STALKS, DICED

2 CARROTS, DICED

2 PARSNIPS, DICED

1 ZUCCHINI, DICED

1 YELLOW SQUASH, DICED

3 GARLIC CLOVES, MINCED

8 CUPS CHICKEN STOCK (SEE PAGES 102–3)

2 BAY LEAVES

FRESH BASIL, CHOPPED, FOR GARNISH (OPTIONAL)

RICE & BEANS *with* CHICKEN THIGHS

YIELD: 6 SERVINGS / ACTIVE TIME: 15 MINUTES / TOTAL TIME: 1 HOUR AND 45 MINUTES

The Dutch oven is a truly amazing piece of cooking equipment that allows you to cook this recipe nice and slow to really bring out the delicate flavors of the spices and create a dish that is second to none.

1. Place the beans in a cast-iron Dutch oven and cover with water. Bring to a boil, reduce heat to medium-low, and cover the pot. Cook for 45 minutes to 1 hour, until the beans are tender. Drain and set the beans aside.

2. Place the pot back on the stove and add ¼ cup of the oil. Add the chicken and cook over medium-high heat for 5 minutes on each side. Remove the chicken from the Dutch oven, cut it into 12 pieces, and set aside.

3. Add the salt pork and the remaining oil to the pot and cook until some of the salt pork's fat has rendered, about 5 minutes. Add the Sofrito and the tomato sauce. Cook for 5 minutes, stirring constantly.

4. Add the rice to the pot, stir, and cook for 5 minutes. Add the remaining ingredients and return the chicken to the pot. Reduce heat to medium and cook for 10 minutes. Cover the Dutch oven and cook for another 20 to 30 minutes, or until the liquid has been absorbed and the rice is tender.

5. Uncover the pot and add the beans. Stir to combine and serve.

TIP: The rice at the bottom of the Dutch oven might get a little crunchy. That is actually preferred for this dish.

INGREDIENTS:

½   **LB. KIDNEY BEANS, SOAKED OVERNIGHT AND DRAINED**

½   **CUP VEGETABLE OIL**

4   **BONELESS, SKINLESS CHICKEN THIGHS**

2   **PIECES OF SALT PORK, MINCED (ABOUT ½ CUP)**

1   **CUP SOFRITO (SEE PAGE 218)**

1   **CUP OF SPANISH-STYLE TOMATO SAUCE, PUREED**

2   **CUPS WHITE RICE**

3   **CUPS CHICKEN STOCK (SEE PAGES 102–3)**

2   **PACKETS OF SAZÓN WITH ACHIOTE**

2   **TABLESPOONS DRIED OREGANO**

1   **CUP SPANISH OLIVES, WITH THE BRINE**

    ADOBO SEASONING, TO TASTE

CHICKEN POT PIE

YIELD: 4 TO 6 SERVINGS / ACTIVE TIME: 1 HOUR / TOTAL TIME: 2 HOURS

When you have leftover chicken, reach for this recipe. Simply prepare the chicken mixture in the skillet, top with a crust, and bake, and you'll have a delicious and satisfying meal.

1. Preheat the oven to 350°F.

2. In a small skillet other than the cast-iron skillet, heat the olive oil. Add the onion and garlic and cook, while stirring, for about 2 minutes. Add the carrot, reduce the heat to low, cover, and cook, while stirring occasionally, until the carrots start to soften and the onion caramelizes, about 5 minutes. Set aside.

3. Before starting to make the white sauce, be sure the milk is at room temperature. If it's not, microwave it so that it's just warm, about 15 to 20 seconds. Have the milk ready.

4. Place the butter in a 12-inch cast-iron skillet and melt over medium heat. Sprinkle the flour over it and stir quickly yet gently to blend. Reduce the heat slightly so the butter doesn't burn. Stir until the butter and flour form a soft paste.

5. Add just a little of the warm milk and stir constantly to blend it in. Add more milk in small increments, working after each addition to stir it into the flour-and-butter mixture smoothly. Work in this manner until all the milk has been incorporated. Continue to stir the sauce while cooking over low heat until it thickens, about 5 minutes.

6. Add the chicken pieces, green beans, and vegetable mixture from the other skillet. Season with salt and pepper. If you want a hint of heat, add the cayenne pepper.

7. On a flour-dusted work surface, roll out the crust so it will fit over the filling. Lay it gently on top, push down slightly to secure, and cut 3 or 4 slits in the middle. Brush the crust with the half-and-half.

8. Put the skillet in the oven and bake for 30 to 40 minutes, until the crust is browned and the filling is bubbly.

9. Remove from the oven and let cool slightly before serving.

INGREDIENTS:

2 TABLESPOONS OLIVE OIL

½ YELLOW ONION, DICED

1 GARLIC CLOVE, CHOPPED

1 CARROT, PEELED AND CHOPPED

1¼ CUPS WHOLE MILK, AT ROOM TEMPERATURE

2 TABLESPOONS UNSALTED BUTTER, CUT INTO SMALLER SLICES

2 TABLESPOONS ALL-PURPOSE FLOUR, PLUS MORE FOR DUSTING

1½ CUPS COOKED CHICKEN, CUT INTO BITE-SIZED PIECES

¾ CUP FROZEN GREEN BEANS, CHOPPED

SALT AND PEPPER, TO TASTE

½ TEASPOON CAYENNE PEPPER (OPTIONAL)

1 FLAKY PASTRY CRUST (SEE PAGE 580)

1 TABLESPOON HALF-AND-HALF

CHICKEN & ARTICHOKE HEART POT PIE

YIELD: 4 TO 6 SERVINGS / ACTIVE TIME: 45 MINUTES / TOTAL TIME: 1 HOUR AND 30 MINUTES

You could call this a pot pie Italian style, as the marinade from the artichoke hearts adds considerably to the flavor of the dish.

1. Preheat the oven to 350°F.

2. In a small skillet other than the cast-iron, heat the oil from the artichoke hearts. Add the onion and garlic and cook, while stirring, for about 2 minutes. Add the artichoke hearts, oregano, and, if desired, red pepper flakes. Reduce the heat to low, cover, and cook, while stirring occasionally, until the vegetables soften and caramelize, about 5 minutes. Set aside.

3. Before starting to make the white sauce, be sure the milk is at room temperature. If it's not, microwave it so that it's just warm, about 15 to 20 seconds. Have the milk ready.

4. In a 12-inch cast-iron skillet, melt the butter over medium heat. Sprinkle the flour over it and stir quickly yet gently to blend. Reduce the heat slightly so the butter doesn't burn. Stir until the butter and flour form a soft paste.

5. Add just a little of the warm milk and stir constantly to blend it in. Add more milk in small increments, working after each addition to stir it into the flour-and-butter mixture smoothly. Work in this manner until all the milk has been incorporated. Continue to stir the sauce while cooking over low heat until it thickens, about 5 minutes.

6. Add the chicken pieces, peas, and vegetable mixture from the other skillet. Season with salt and pepper.

7. On a flour-dusted work surface, roll out the crust so it will fit over the filling. Lay it gently on top, push down slightly to secure, and cut 3 or 4 slits in the middle. Brush the crust with the half-and-half.

8. Put the skillet in the oven and bake for 30 to 40 minutes, until the crust is browned and the filling is bubbly.

9. Remove from the oven and let cool slightly before serving.

INGREDIENTS:

- 2 TABLESPOONS OLIVE OIL FROM THE JAR OF ARTICHOKE HEARTS
- ½ YELLOW ONION, DICED
- 1 GARLIC CLOVE, CHOPPED
- 1 (6 OZ.) JAR OF QUARTERED, MARINATED ARTICHOKE HEARTS, DRAINED AND CHOPPED
- ½ TEASPOON DRIED OREGANO
- ½ TEASPOON RED PEPPER FLAKES (OPTIONAL)
- 1¼ CUPS WHOLE MILK, AT ROOM TEMPERATURE
- 2 TABLESPOONS UNSALTED BUTTER, CUT INTO SMALL PIECES
- 2 TABLESPOONS ALL-PURPOSE FLOUR, PLUS MORE FOR DUSTING
- 1½ CUPS COOKED CHICKEN, CUT INTO BITE-SIZED PIECES
- 1 CUP FROZEN PEAS
    SALT AND PEPPER, TO TASTE
- 1 FLAKY PASTRY CRUST (SEE PAGE 580)
- 1 TABLESPOON HALF-AND-HALF

MINI CHICKEN POT PIES

YIELD: 8 SERVINGS / **ACTIVE TIME:** 1 HOUR / **TOTAL TIME:** 2 HOURS AND 45 MINUTES

Here's the perfect landing spot for those vegetables you laid away in the freezer to counter your inevitable cravings. Each bite of peas and corn brings with it the sweetness of spring and summer, guaranteeing that this pot pie will brighten the darkest days.

1. Preheat the oven to 400°F.

2. Place the chicken breasts in a cast-iron skillet and drizzle with the olive oil. Place in the oven and bake until the internal temperature is 160°F, about 15 to 20 minutes. Remove and let cool. When cool enough to handle, cut the chicken into bite-sized cubes. Lower the oven temperature to 375°F.

3. Place the butter, carrots, celery, and onions in a large pot and cook over medium-high heat until the onions turn translucent, about 5 minutes. Place the stock in a separate saucepan and warm over medium-high heat.

4. Add the flour to the vegetable mixture and cook, while stirring constantly, until the mixture gives off a nutty aroma, about 2 minutes. Pour the warmed stock into the pan while stirring to prevent lumps from forming. When the stock has been incorporated and the mixture is smooth, add the chicken, corn, and peas. Cook for 2 minutes and then remove from heat.

5. Prepare the piecrusts. Place the flour, 2 teaspoons of the salt, pepper, parsley, and thyme in a large mixing bowl and stir to combine. Divide the butter into tablespoons and place the pieces in the freezer for 15 minutes.

6. Place the flour mixture and the butter in a food processor and pulse 4 to 5 times. Slowly pour the 1 cup of ice-cold water into the food processor and pulse until the mixture is just combined.

7. Transfer the dough to a lightly floured work surface and knead until it is smooth. Place the dough in the refrigerator for at least 20 minutes.

8. Remove the dough from the refrigerator and divide it into 16 pieces. Roll each piece to a thickness of ⅛ inch. Place one crust in eight miniature cast-iron skillets, making sure that the crust extends over the sides. Prick the crusts with a fork, cover each with a piece of parchment paper, and fill the crusts with uncooked rice. Place in the oven and bake for 15 minutes. Remove, discard the rice, and fill each crust with some of the chicken-and-vegetable mixture.

INGREDIENTS:

FOR THE FILLING

6   (4 OZ.) CHICKEN BREASTS

3   TABLESPOONS OLIVE OIL

1   STICK OF UNSALTED BUTTER

1   CUP DICED CARROTS

1   CUP DICED CELERY

2   CUPS DICED ONIONS

5   CUPS CHICKEN STOCK (SEE PAGES 102–3)

¾   CUP ALL-PURPOSE FLOUR

1   CUP FROZEN CORN

1   CUP FROZEN PEAS

FOR THE PIECRUSTS

5   CUPS ALL-PURPOSE FLOUR, PLUS MORE FOR DUSTING

2½   TEASPOONS SALT

1   TEASPOON PEPPER

2   TABLESPOONS CHOPPED PARSLEY LEAVES

1   TABLESPOON CHOPPED THYME LEAVES

4   STICKS OF UNSALTED BUTTER

1   CUP ICE-COLD WATER, PLUS 2 TEASPOONS

    UNCOOKED RICE, AS NEEDED

1   EGG YOLK

9. Lay another crust over the top of each skillet and crimp the edges. Place the 2 teaspoons of water, egg yolk, and remaining salt in a bowl and beat to combine. Cut a slit in each top crust and then brush it with the egg wash. Place the pies on a baking sheet, place in the oven, and bake until the top crusts are golden brown, 35 to 40 minutes. Remove from the oven and let cool slightly before serving.

CHICKEN FAJITAS

YIELD: 6 TO 8 SERVINGS / **ACTIVE TIME:** 30 MINUTES / **TOTAL TIME:** 5 HOURS

The trick is to bring this dish to the table while the meat and veggies are still sizzling, so you'll want to be sure you have any sides prepped ahead of time so you can go straight from stove to table with this. To start, you'll want tortillas, guacamole, salsa, sliced jalapeños, sliced black olives, and sour cream.

1. To prepare the chicken, place the orange juice, lime juice, garlic, jalapeño, cilantro, cumin, oregano, salt, and pepper in a bowl and stir. When thoroughly combined, add the olive oil. Put the chicken pieces in the mix, stir, cover with plastic wrap, and refrigerate for about 4 hours.

2. Place a 12-inch cast-iron skillet over medium-high heat. Remove the chicken from the marinade with a slotted spoon and put it in the skillet, stirring and turning the pieces so they brown on all sides. Cook thoroughly, about 8 to 10 minutes. Transfer the cooked chicken to a platter and cover loosely with foil.

3. To prepare the vegetables, reduce the heat to medium, add the oil, and then add the onion, peppers, and garlic. Cook, while stirring, until the vegetables soften, 3 to 5 minutes. Add the lime juice and cilantro and cook until the vegetables start to brown. Season with salt and pepper.

4. While the vegetables are still sizzling, push them to one side of the pan and put the chicken on the other side. Serve immediately.

VARIATION: You can use the same ingredients to make steak fajitas, but substitute 1 lb. of flank steak for the chicken and marinate it overnight. Don't slice the steak until it has been cooked.

INGREDIENTS:

FOR THE CHICKEN
½ CUP ORANGE JUICE
  JUICE OF 1 LIME
4 GARLIC CLOVES, MINCED
1 JALAPEÑO PEPPER, SEEDED AND DICED
2 TABLESPOONS CHOPPED FRESH CILANTRO
1 TEASPOON CUMIN
1 TEASPOON DRIED OREGANO
  SALT AND PEPPER, TO TASTE
3 TABLESPOONS OLIVE OIL
3-4 BONELESS, SKINLESS CHICKEN BREASTS, CUT INTO STRIPS

FOR THE VEGETABLES
2 TABLESPOONS OLIVE OIL
1 RED ONION, SLICED THIN
1 RED BELL PEPPER, SEEDED AND SLICED THIN
1 GREEN BELL PEPPER, SEEDED AND SLICED THIN
1 YELLOW BELL PEPPER, SEEDED AND SLICED THIN
2 JALAPEÑO OR SERRANO PEPPERS, SEEDED AND SLICED THIN
3 GARLIC CLOVES, MINCED
¼ CUP FRESH LIME JUICE
½ CUP CHOPPED FRESH CILANTRO
  SALT AND PEPPER, TO TASTE

CHICKEN *with* HERBS

YIELD: 4 SERVINGS / **ACTIVE TIME:** 10 MINUTES / **TOTAL TIME:** 40 MINUTES

When you want a dish that has lots of bright flavors but is still easy to make, this is the way to go. Serve it with mashed or roasted potatoes and a simply prepared vegetable, such as steamed green beans.

1. Place a 10-inch cast-iron skillet in the oven. Preheat the oven to 500°F.

2. Remove the skillet from the oven, add the oil, and then carefully place the chicken, skin side down, in the pan. Add the rosemary, return the skillet to the oven, and cook for 15 minutes.

3. Remove the pan from the oven and use a spatula to turn the chicken over. Return the skillet to the oven and cook for another 15 minutes.

4. Remove the skillet from the oven and transfer the chicken to a platter.

5. Place the skillet over medium heat, add the flour, and cook, while stirring, for 1 minute. Slowly whisk in the broth and wine and bring to a simmer. Add the dried oregano and basil and allow the mixture to simmer until it thickens slightly, about 5 minutes.

6. Add the butter and mustard, whisk to incorporate, and let the sauce simmer for another minute. Season with salt and pepper. Spoon the sauce over the chicken and serve with the potatoes and steamed green beans.

INGREDIENTS:

1   TABLESPOON VEGETABLE OIL

1   LB. CHICKEN PIECES (BREASTS, LEGS, OR A COMBINATION)

1   SPRIG OF ROSEMARY

¼   CUP ALL-PURPOSE FLOUR

1   CUP CHICKEN BROTH

¼   CUP DRY WHITE WINE

2   TABLESPOONS DRIED OREGANO

2   TEASPOONS DRIED BASIL

2   TABLESPOONS UNSALTED BUTTER

1   TEASPOON DIJON MUSTARD

    MASHED OR ROASTED POTATOES, FOR SERVING

    SALT AND PEPPER, TO TASTE

    STEAMED GREEN BEANS, FOR SERVING

CHICKEN LEGS *with* POTATOES *and* FENNEL

YIELD: 6 SERVINGS / **ACTIVE TIME:** 30 MINUTES / **TOTAL TIME:** 1 HOUR AND 10 MINUTES

There's something so classic about these flavors that it's hard to resist the potato-and-fennel combo. This is a great comfort food for a cold day, as it's likely to stick with you for a while.

1. Place a cast-iron Dutch oven over medium-high heat and add the ⅓ cup of the olive oil. While the oil heats up, rub the chicken legs with the remaining oil and season with the salt and pepper. When the oil is hot, add half of the chicken, skin side down, and cook until the skin is golden brown and crusted. Remove, set aside, and repeat with the remaining chicken legs.

2. Preheat the oven to 400°F. Add the shallots and garlic to the Dutch oven and use a wooden spoon to scrape all of the browned bits from the bottom. Cook until the shallots and garlic darken, about 3 minutes.

3. Turn the heat up to high and add the remaining ingredients, save the Chardonnay and the butter. Cook for about 15 minutes, while stirring every few minutes.

4. Add the wine and the butter, stir, and then return the chicken to the pan, skin-side up. Reduce the heat, cover, and cook until the potatoes are soft and the chicken is 155°F in the center, about 20 minutes. Remove the lid, transfer the Dutch oven to the oven, and cook until the chicken is 165°F in the center, about 10 minutes.

TIP: To check the temperature of the chicken, insert a kitchen thermometer at the fattest point. Digital thermometers are pretty cheap, about $10 to $15 for the basic model. To calibrate the thermometer, submerge the probe in a cup of ice water. It should read 32°F.

INGREDIENTS:

- ⅓ CUP OLIVE OIL, PLUS 2 TABLESPOONS
- 6 CHICKEN LEGS
- 1 TABLESPOON KOSHER SALT
- 1 TABLESPOON CRACKED BLACK PEPPER
- ½ CUP MINCED SHALLOTS
- 2 GARLIC CLOVES, MINCED
- 2 RED POTATOES, DICED
- 3-4 YELLOW POTATOES, DICED
- 3 FENNEL BULBS, DICED (RESERVE THE FRONDS FOR GARNISH)
- 1 TEASPOON CELERY SEEDS
- 1 TEASPOON FENNEL SEEDS
- ½ CUP SUN-DRIED TOMATOES
- 1 CUP CHARDONNAY
- 6 TABLESPOONS SALTED BUTTER

CORNISH GAME HENS *with* BABY BRUSSELS SPROUTS & CARAMELIZED ONIONS

YIELD: 4 SERVINGS / ACTIVE TIME: 20 TO 30 MINUTES / TOTAL TIME: 3 TO 9 HOURS

There is something so elegant about everyone getting their own bird. Brining will help the hens retain moisture, and keep them from getting dry if you overcook them, so it is well worth the additional time.

1. In a large stockpot, add the water, sugar, and salt and cook over medium-high heat until the sugar and salt dissolve. Add the remaining ingredients, remove from heat, and let cool to room temperature. Place the Cornish game hens in the brine, making sure they are completely covered, using a small bowl to weigh them down if necessary. Soak in the brine for 4 to 6 hours.

2. Preheat the oven to 375°F. Place the thyme, sage, rosemary, and minced garlic in a bowl and stir until combined.

3. Remove the Cornish game hens from the brine, pat dry, and rub with olive oil. Sprinkle with salt, pepper, and the herb-and-garlic mixture. Let the game hens stand at room temperature for approximately 30 minutes.

4. In a cast-iron Dutch oven, add 3 tablespoons of olive oil, the smashed garlic cloves, onion, and 1 tablespoon of salt. Cook over medium-high heat, reducing the heat if the onion starts to burn or dry out, until the onion is dark brown. Remove and set aside.

5. Place the Brussels sprouts, the remaining olive oil, and a pinch of salt in the Dutch oven. Stir until the brussels sprouts are evenly coated.

6. Spread the Brussels sprouts into a layer in the Dutch oven, cover with a layer of the garlic-and-onion mixture, and place the Cornish hens in the Dutch oven, breast side up. Put the ½ of a lemon in the center of the Dutch oven. Place the lemon quarters against the edge of the Dutch oven and between each hen. Place the Dutch oven in the oven and cook for 30 to 40 minutes.

7. Raise the heat to 400°F, remove the Dutch oven from the oven, and spin each hen 180°. Rub the top of each with the butter, return the Dutch oven to the oven, and cook for 20 minutes, or until the internal temperature of each hen is 165°F. Remove the Dutch oven from the oven and let stand for up to 30 minutes before serving.

TIPS: If you plan on removing and discarding the skin after the hens are cooked, try cooking them breast side down, as this will ensure that they are even juicier.

INGREDIENTS:

FOR THE BRINE (OPTIONAL)

5	CUPS WATER
1	CUP SUGAR
1	CUP SALT
2	BAY LEAVES
1	TABLESPOON CRACKED BLACK PEPPER
1	TABLESPOON CORIANDER SEEDS, GROUND
½	TABLESPOON FENNEL SEEDS, GROUND
½	TABLESPOON CELERY SEEDS, GROUND

FOR THE HENS

4	(3 LB.) CORNISH GAME HENS
1½	TABLESPOONS MINCED FRESH THYME
1½	TABLESPOONS MINCED FRESH SAGE
1½	TABLESPOONS MINCED FRESH ROSEMARY
11	GARLIC CLOVES, 3 MINCED, 8 SMASHED
5	TABLESPOONS OLIVE OIL, PLUS MORE FOR RUBBING
	SALT AND PEPPER, TO TASTE
1	LARGE WHITE ONION, SLICED
2	LBS. BABY BRUSSELS SPROUTS, HALVED
1	LEMON, QUARTERED, PLUS ½ OF A LEMON
4	TABLESPOONS UNSALTED BUTTER

ROASTED CHICKEN THIGHS *with* TABBOULEH

YIELD: 4 SERVINGS / ACTIVE TIME: 25 MINUTES / TOTAL TIME: 1 HOUR

Boneless, skinless chicken makes prep a lot easier for many dishes, but you need both to stick around in this preparation. Searing the skin renders the fat and adds a tremendous amount of flavor, and cooking it on the bone ensures that the meat remains moist and tender.

1. Preheat the oven to 450°F. Place the olive oil in a cast-iron skillet and warm over medium-high heat. Sprinkle salt, pepper, the paprika, cumin, and ground fennel on the chicken thighs. When the oil starts to smoke, place the thighs skin side down in the pan and sear until brown.

2. Turn the thighs over and place the pan in the oven. Cook until the internal temperature is 165°F, about 16 minutes. Halfway through the cooking time, add the tomatoes, garlic, and shallot to the pan.

3. When the chicken is fully cooked, remove from the oven and transfer to a plate. Leave the vegetables in the pan, add the white wine, and place over high heat. Cook for 1 minute, while shaking the pan. Transfer the contents of the pan to a blender, puree until smooth, and season to taste. Set aside.

4. Prepare the tabbouleh. Place the bulgur, water, shallot, thyme, and salt in a saucepan and bring to a boil. Remove from heat, cover the pan with foil, and let sit until the bulgur has absorbed all the liquid. Fluff with a fork, remove the shallot and thyme, and add the remaining ingredients. Stir to combine and season with salt and pepper.

5. To serve, place some of the tabbouleh on each plate. Top with a chicken thigh and spoon some of the puree over it.

INGREDIENTS:

FOR THE CHICKEN THIGHS

2	TABLESPOONS OLIVE OIL
	SALT AND PEPPER, TO TASTE
2	TEASPOONS PAPRIKA
2	TEASPOONS CUMIN
2	TEASPOONS GROUND FENNEL SEEDS
4	CHICKEN THIGHS
1	CUP CHERRY TOMATOES
2	GARLIC CLOVES, CRUSHED
1	SHALLOT, SLICED
½	CUP WHITE WINE

FOR THE TABBOULEH

1	CUP BULGUR WHEAT
2	CUPS WATER
1	SHALLOT, HALVED
2	SPRIGS OF THYME
1	TABLESPOON SALT, PLUS MORE TO TASTE
1	TABLESPOON CHOPPED CILANTRO
1	TABLESPOON CHOPPED PARSLEY
2	TABLESPOONS CHOPPED SCALLIONS
1½	TABLESPOONS FRESH LIME JUICE
½	CUP DICED TOMATO
½	CUP DICED CUCUMBER
½	TEASPOON MINCED GARLIC
3	TABLESPOONS OLIVE OIL
	PEPPER, TO TASTE

CHICKEN BOLOGNESE *with* PENNE

YIELD: 4 TO 6 SERVINGS / **ACTIVE TIME:** 45 MINUTES / **TOTAL TIME:** 2 HOURS

Bolognese is traditionally made with ground beef and pork. By substituting ground chicken, you end up with a lighter sauce that allows the other flavors in the dish to shine.

1. Place the canola oil and bacon in a cast-iron Dutch oven and cook over high heat until the bacon is crispy. Add the chicken, season with salt and pepper, and cook until it is browned and cooked through. Remove the bacon and the chicken and set aside.

2. Lower the heat to medium and add the carrots, celery, onions, and garlic. Season with salt and cook until the carrots are tender.

3. Return the bacon and chicken to the pan, add the thyme and Sherry, and cook until the wine is nearly evaporated. Add the tomato sauce and water, reduce the heat to low, and cook for approximately 45 minutes, while stirring often, until the sauce has thickened.

4. Add the cream and sage and cook for an additional 15 minutes.

5. Bring a large pot of salted water to a boil, add the penne, and cook until just before al dente. Reserve 1 cup of the pasta water, drain the penne, and then return it to the pot. Add the butter, bolognese, and reserved pasta water and stir to combine. Add the Parmesan and stir until melted. Garnish with additional Parmesan, the basil, and red pepper flakes, if desired.

INGREDIENTS:

2	TABLESPOONS CANOLA OIL
½	LB. BACON, CHOPPED
1½	LBS. GROUND CHICKEN
	SALT AND PEPPER, TO TASTE
1	CUP DICED CARROTS
1	CUP DICED CELERY
2	CUPS DICED ONIONS
3	GARLIC CLOVES, MINCED
1	TABLESPOON CHOPPED THYME LEAVES
2	CUPS SHERRY
8	CUPS TOMATO SAUCE
1	CUP WATER
1	CUP HEAVY CREAM
2	TABLESPOONS CHOPPED SAGE LEAVES
1	LB. PENNE
4	TABLESPOONS UNSALTED BUTTER
1	CUP GRATED PARMESAN CHEESE, PLUS MORE FOR GARNISH
1	TABLESPOON CHOPPED BASIL, FOR GARNISH
	RED PEPPER FLAKES, FOR GARNISH (OPTIONAL)

CHICKEN & QUINOA CASSEROLE

YIELD: 4 TO 6 SERVINGS / ACTIVE TIME: 45 MINUTES / TOTAL TIME: 1 HOUR AND 30 MINUTES

Quinoa is a so-called superfood that has been a part of the human diet for several thousand years. A seed that is prepared like a grain, it contains all nine amino acids and is rich in lysine, iron, magnesium, and riboflavin. Quinoa also has more fiber than grains. On its own, its flavor is somewhat nuttier than brown rice and its texture is grainier, making it a great base for this mélange of chicken and vegetables.

1. Heat a 12-inch cast-iron skillet over medium-high heat. Add the olive oil, onion, and garlic and cook for 2 minutes or until translucent.

2. Add the chicken pieces and frozen vegetables and continue to cook, while stirring, until the chicken pieces are browned, about 8 minutes. Stir in the turmeric and season with salt and pepper.

3. Add the tomatoes and water and bring to a boil. Stir in the quinoa, reduce the heat to medium, and cook for 15 to 20 minutes, until the quinoa is cooked and most of the liquid has evaporated. Stir in the parsley, sprinkle with the feta, and serve immediately.

INGREDIENTS:

- 1 TABLESPOON OLIVE OIL
- ½ ONION, DICED
- 2 GARLIC CLOVES, MINCED
- 1 LB. BONELESS, SKINLESS CHICKEN BREASTS, CUT INTO 1-INCH PIECES
- 1 CUP MIXED FROZEN VEGETABLES
- 1 TEASPOON TURMERIC
- SALT AND BLACK PEPPER, TO TASTE
- 1 (14 OZ.) CAN OF CRUSHED TOMATOES
- 1 CUP WATER
- 1 CUP QUINOA
- ¼ CUP CHOPPED PARSLEY
- ½ CUP FETA CHEESE, CRUMBLED

CAPRESE CHICKEN BAKE

YIELD: 6 SERVINGS / ACTIVE TIME: 15 MINUTES / TOTAL TIME: 45 MINUTES

By tossing a traditional caprese salad between layers of thinly sliced chicken breast, you transform what should be a ho-hum set of ingredients into a dazzling dinner.

1. Preheat oven to 375°F. Combine the garlic, oregano, granulated garlic, salt, and pepper in a bowl. Place 1 tablespoon of the olive oil and the sliced chicken breasts in a bowl and toss to coat. Dredge the chicken breasts in the garlic-and-spice mixture and set aside.

2. Place the remaining olive oil in a 12-inch cast-iron skillet and warm it over medium-high heat. Working in batches, sear the chicken breasts for 1 minute per side.

3. When all of the chicken has been seared, place half of the breasts in an even layer on the bottom of the skillet. Top with two-thirds of the tomatoes and mozzarella and half of the basil leaves. Place the remaining chicken breasts on top and cover with the remaining tomatoes, mozzarella, and basil.

4. Place the skillet in the oven and cook until the cheese is melted and bubbling, about 10 minutes. The temperature at the center of the chicken breasts should be 165°F. Remove the skillet from the oven and let rest for 10 minutes. Top with balsamic glaze, cut into 6 sections, and serve.

TIP: Balsamic glaze is a great product that can be found at most grocery stores. It can also be made at home by bringing balsamic vinegar to a boil in a small saucepan, reducing the heat, and letting it simmer for 10 to 15 minutes. It is ready when it is thick enough to coat the back of a spoon and has the consistency of melted chocolate. Remove from heat, let it cool, transfer to a jar or a squeeze bottle, and store in your refrigerator.

INGREDIENTS:

1 GARLIC CLOVE, MINCED

1 TEASPOON DRIED OREGANO

1 TEASPOON GRANULATED GARLIC

SALT AND PEPPER, TO TASTE

2 TABLESPOONS OLIVE OIL

2 LBS. BONELESS, SKINLESS CHICKEN BREASTS, HALVED ALONG THEIR EQUATOR

2 LBS. ROMA OR PLUM TOMATOES, SLICED INTO ¼-INCH-THICK ROUNDS

1 LB. FRESH MOZZARELLA CHEESE, SLICED INTO ¼-INCH-THICK PIECES

LEAVES FROM 1 BUNCH OF FRESH BASIL

BALSAMIC GLAZE, TO TASTE

CHICKEN & PANCETTA CASSOULET

YIELD: 6 SERVINGS / ACTIVE TIME: 30 TO 35 MINUTES / TOTAL TIME: 2½ TO 3½ HOURS

This French classic usually takes a few days to make and utilizes duck instead of chicken. This adaptation is quicker but doesn't sacrifice any of the dish's famous flavor.

1. Place the beans and the water in a cast-iron Dutch oven and cook until the beans are almost cooked through, about 50 minutes. Drain and set the beans aside.

2. Place the Dutch oven over medium-high heat and add the bacon fat and the pancetta. Cook for 5 minutes and then add the sausage. Cook the sausage for 7 to 10 minutes or until the fat has been rendered and the meat is slightly crispy.

3. Using a slotted spoon, remove the pancetta and sausage from the pan. Season the chicken thighs with salt and pepper, place them in the pan, and sear for 5 minutes per side. Remove the chicken from the pan and set aside.

4. Add the carrot, celery, and onion to the Dutch oven. Season with salt and pepper and cook, while stirring occasionally, until the vegetables start to caramelize, about 10 to 12 minutes.

5. Place the roasted garlic, tomatoes, thyme, parsley, cloves, and bay leaves in the pot. Stir and cook for 5 minutes. Deglaze the pan with the white wine and use a wooden spoon to scrape the browned bits from the bottom of the pan. Cook for 3 minutes.

6. Return the chicken, pancetta, sausage, and beans to the Dutch oven. Add the chicken stock, reduce the heat to medium-low or low, cover, and cook for 2 to 3 hours, checking every half-hour for doneness. The dish is done when almost all of the stock is gone.

7. Remove lid, discard the bay leaves, garnish with additional parsley, and serve.

TIP: If you want to roast garlic at home, all you need is 1 head of garlic. Remove the top (just enough to see the cloves inside their skins), preheat the oven to 375°F, and place the head of garlic in a square of aluminum foil. Drizzle the garlic with olive oil, place a pat of butter on top, and then close the foil over the garlic. Place in the oven and roast for 45 minutes to 1 hour. The garlic cloves should look slightly brown, be extremely fragrant, and be easy to squeeze from their skins.

INGREDIENTS:

- 1 **LB. DRIED CANNELLINI BEANS, SOAKED OVERNIGHT AND DRAINED**
- 8 **CUPS WATER**
- 2 **TABLESPOONS BACON FAT**
- ¼ **LB. PANCETTA, MINCED**
- ¾ **LB. SAUSAGE, DICED (GARLIC SAUSAGE PREFERRED; A MILD ITALIAN SAUSAGE WILL WORK)**
- 6-8 **BONELESS, SKINLESS CHICKEN THIGHS**
- **SALT AND PEPPER, TO TASTE**
- 1 **LARGE CARROT, PEELED AND MINCED**
- 3 **CELERY STALKS, MINCED**
- 1 **WHITE ONION, MINCED**
- 3-4 **LARGE GARLIC CLOVES, ROASTED**
- 3 **ROMA TOMATOES, DICED**
- **LEAVES FROM 6 TO 8 SPRIGS OF FRESH THYME**
- ¼ **CUP PARSLEY LEAVES, PLUS MORE FOR GARNISH**
- ½ **TABLESPOON WHOLE CLOVES**
- 3-4 **BAY LEAVES**
- ¼ **CUP DRY WHITE WINE**
- 4 **CUPS LOW-SODIUM CHICKEN STOCK**

CHICKEN LIVERS *with* MARSALA

YIELD: 4 SERVINGS / ACTIVE TIME: 10 MINUTES / TOTAL TIME: 10 MINUTES

Chicken livers: so rich, and yet so inexpensive. Here they're paired with a sweet fortified wine and the bright acid of mandarin oranges to produce a dish that is a dream come true on a chilly evening.

1. Place the olive oil and butter in a 12-inch cast-iron skillet and warm over medium heat.

2. When the butter is melted and sizzling, add the onion and sauté until it has softened, about 3 minutes.

3. Place the onion on one side of the skillet and place the chicken livers on the other. Cook the livers until they are slightly browned on both sides, about 2 minutes per side. Do not stir the onions.

4. Raise the heat to high and carefully add the wine. Let it boil for 1 minute so that the alcohol burns off.

5. Add the mandarin segments, stir to coat, and cook until they are ready to burst, about 1 minute. Serve immediately with the toast points.

TIP: If you have leftovers, finely chop everything and serve it chilled the next morning with some fluffy scrambled eggs.

INGREDIENTS:

- 1 TEASPOON OLIVE OIL
- 2 TABLESPOONS UNSALTED BUTTER
- 1 YELLOW ONION, SLICED INTO HALF-MOONS
- 1 LB. CHICKEN LIVERS, CLEANED
- ¼ CUP SWEET MARSALA WINE
- 1 MANDARIN ORANGE, SEGMENTED
- TOAST POINTS, FOR SERVING

SWEDISH CHICKEN *with* MUSHROOMS

YIELD: 4 SERVINGS / ACTIVE TIME: 10 MINUTES / TOTAL TIME: 30 MINUTES

Take your time browning the chicken legs here, as patience makes all the difference in this preparation. You can, of course, substitute bone-in chicken breasts for the legs, just keep in mind that you will need to increase the cooking time.

1. Place a cast-iron Dutch oven over medium-high heat and warm for 3 minutes.

2. Add the butter. When the butter is sizzling, arrange the chicken legs in the pot in a single layer. Brown for 4 minutes and then turn over. When the chicken is browned on both sides, transfer to a plate and set aside.

3. Place the mushrooms in the pot and sauté for 3 minutes without stirring. Stir and cook for another 2 minutes. Return the chicken to the pot and add the stock, potatoes, allspice, and white pepper.

4. Season with salt, cover the pot, and reduce the heat to medium. Simmer until the potatoes are fork-tender, about 10 minutes.

5. Stir in the cream and simmer for another 5 minutes. Garnish with the dill and serve with the Pickled Beets.

PICKLED BEETS

1. Place the water, vinegar, sugar, and salt in a saucepan and bring to a simmer over medium heat.

2. Add the beet and simmer for 2 minutes. Remove the pan from heat and let stand for 1 hour before serving.

INGREDIENTS:

- 1 TABLESPOON UNSALTED BUTTER
- 8 CHICKEN LEGS
- 2 CUPS BROWN MUSHROOMS, SLICED
- 1½ CUPS LOW-SODIUM CHICKEN STOCK
- 1 LB. NEW POTATOES, HALVED
- LARGE PINCH OF GROUND ALLSPICE
- ½ TEASPOON WHITE PEPPER
- SALT, TO TASTE
- ½ CUP HEAVY CREAM
- ½ CUP CHOPPED FRESH DILL, FOR GARNISH
- PICKLED BEETS (SEE RECIPE), FOR SERVING

PICKLED BEETS

- 1 CUP WATER
- ½ CUP WHITE VINEGAR
- 2 TEASPOONS SUGAR
- 2 TEASPOONS SALT
- 1 LARGE RED BEET, SLICED INTO MATCHSTICKS

CHICKEN & MUSHROOM CREPES

YIELD: 8 TO 10 SERVINGS (ABOUT 16 CREPES) / ACTIVE TIME: 1 HOUR / TOTAL TIME: 6 HOURS

Make this filling with leftover chicken and transform what might otherwise be a boring dinner into an elegant dining experience.

1. Heat a 12-inch cast-iron skillet over low heat and melt 2 tablespoons of the butter very slowly.

2. In a large mixing bowl, whisk the eggs until smooth. Add the salt and milk and whisk together until well blended. Whisk in the flour and, while whisking, add the melted butter. Keep whisking until the batter is smooth and there are no lumps. Cover the bowl with plastic wrap or a clean kitchen towel, put in a cool, dark place, and let rest for 3 or 4 hours before making the crepes.

3. While the crepe batter is settling, prepare the filling. Wipe your skillet and melt the butter over medium heat. Add the mushroom pieces and cook, stirring frequently, until softened and lightly browned, about 5 to 8 minutes. Add the chicken pieces, mushroom soup, Madeira or vermouth, and milk. Stir to combine and continue to cook until well blended, about 3 minutes. Stir in the chopped parsley. Add salt and pepper to taste. Put the mixture into a bowl, cover, and refrigerate until the crepes are cooked and ready to be filled.

4. When the crepe batter is ready, you'll need a spatula that won't scratch the surface of the skillet. Have that and a ladle for scooping out the batter ready by the stove.

5. Heat the skillet over medium-high heat and melt a slice of the remaining 2 tablespoons of butter in it. Stir the crepe batter to blend again. When the skillet is hot but not smoking (the butter should not brown), use the ladle to scoop about ¼ cup of batter into the skillet. When the batter hits the pan, tilt it gently to spread the batter evenly over the bottom. When the bottom is covered, cook for just over 1 minute and then flip the crepe over and cook the other side for about half the time. Tilt the skillet over a plate to slide the crepe out.

6. You should be able to make several crepes per slice of butter, but gauge how dry the pan is; if you think it needs butter, add some. If the pan gets too hot and the butter browns, wipe it out with a paper towel and start over.

INGREDIENTS:

FOR THE CREPES

- 4 TABLESPOONS UNSALTED BUTTER
- 3 EGGS
- ⅛ TEASPOON SALT
- 1 CUP WHOLE MILK, PLUS MORE AS NEEDED
- 14 TABLESPOONS ALL-PURPOSE FLOUR

FOR THE FILLING

- 4 TABLESPOONS UNSALTED BUTTER
- 1 LB. MUSHROOMS, STEMMED AND CHOPPED
- 1-2 CUPS COOKED CHICKEN, CUT INTO SMALL PIECES
- 1 (14 OZ.) CAN OF CREAM OF MUSHROOM SOUP
- 2 TABLESPOONS MADEIRA OR VERMOUTH
- ⅓ CUP WHOLE MILK
- 2 TABLESPOONS CHOPPED PARSLEY
- SALT AND PEPPER, TO TASTE

7. Continue making the crepes until all the batter is used up. As they cool on the plate, put pieces of waxed paper between them to keep them from sticking together.

8. Preheat the oven to 350°F. Take the chicken-and-mushroom mixture out of the refrigerator and bring to room temperature.

9. Lightly grease a 9 x 13–inch baking dish. Working with one crepe at a time, put a generous scoop of the filling in the middle and fold the crepe up around the filling. Place the crepe in the baking dish so that the folded part faces down. When the baking dish is filled with stuffed crepes, cover the dish with foil and bake for about 30 minutes until the filling is bubbling and hot.

10. Remove the foil and let cool for a few minutes before serving.

CHICKEN VINDALOO

YIELD: 4 TO 6 SERVINGS / **ACTIVE TIME:** 30 MINUTES / **TOTAL TIME:** 2½ TO 24 HOURS

As with many Indian—and to be more specific, Goan—recipes, there are a lot of ingredients in this dish, but it is ultimately simple to make and it comes together quickly. A word of advice: add as much cayenne pepper as you can handle, as this beloved preparation improves as it gets spicier.

1. Place the chicken pieces in a large bowl.

2. Place the garam masala, turmeric, paprika, mustard powder, sugar, cumin, cayenne pepper, vinegar, tomato paste, and 2 tablespoons of the vegetable oil in a separate bowl and stir to combine.

3. Coat the chicken pieces with the marinade, cover, and place in the refrigerator for at least 2 hours and overnight if time allows.

4. Place a large cast-iron Dutch oven over high heat and add the remaining vegetable oil. When the oil starts to shimmer, add the onion and cook until it is translucent. Reduce the heat to medium, add the garlic and ginger, and sauté for 1 minute.

5. Add the tomatoes, chicken, and the marinade and bring to a boil. Reduce the heat and simmer until the chicken is cooked through, about 18 minutes.

6. Garnish with the cilantro and serve.

INGREDIENTS:

  4-LB. CHICKEN, CUT INTO PIECES

1 TABLESPOON GARAM MASALA

1 TEASPOON TURMERIC

2 TEASPOONS SWEET PAPRIKA

1 TEASPOON DRY MUSTARD POWDER

2 TABLESPOONS SUGAR

1 TEASPOON GROUND CUMIN

½ TEASPOON CAYENNE PEPPER, OR TO TASTE

½ CUP RED WINE VINEGAR

¼ CUP TOMATO PASTE

5 TABLESPOONS VEGETABLE OIL

1 LARGE YELLOW ONION, SLICED

6 GARLIC CLOVES, MINCED

1 TABLESPOON MINCED GINGER

1 (14 OZ.) CAN OF DICED TOMATOES, DRAINED

  CILANTRO LEAVES, CHOPPED, FOR GARNISH

KOREAN CHICKEN THIGHS
with SWEET POTATO VERMICELLI

YIELD: 4 TO 6 SERVINGS / **ACTIVE TIME:** 45 MINUTES / **TOTAL TIME:** 3 HOURS AND 30 MINUTES

This is a Korean take on lo mein, the Chinese classic. The umami flavor of the sweet potato noodles, shiitake mushrooms, and cabbage is the perfect complement to the sweetness of the marinated chicken.

1. To prepare the marinade, place all of the ingredients in a blender and blend until smooth. Pour over the chicken thighs and let them marinate in the refrigerator for at least 2 hours.

2. Fill a large cast-iron Dutch oven with water and bring to a boil. Add the vermicelli and cook for about 6 minutes. Drain, rinse with cold water to keep them from sticking, and set aside.

3. Preheat the oven to 375°F. Remove the chicken from the refrigerator and place the pot back on the stove. Add the vegetable oil and warm over medium-high heat. Remove the chicken thighs from the marinade and place them skin side down in the Dutch oven. Reserve the marinade. Sear the chicken until a crust forms on the skin, about 5 to 7 minutes. Turn the chicken thighs over, add the reserved marinade, place the pot in the oven, and cook for about 15 to 20 minutes, until the centers of the chicken thighs reach 165°F.

4. Remove from the oven and set the chicken aside. Drain the Dutch oven and wipe it clean. Return it to the stove, add the cabbage, mushrooms, shallot, onion, garlic, scallion whites, and ginger, and cook for 8 minutes or until the cabbage is wilted.

5. Add the brown sugar, sesame oil, fish sauce, soy sauce, and rice vinegar to a small bowl and stir until combined. Add this sauce and the vermicelli to the pot, stir until the noodles are coated, and then return the chicken thighs to the Dutch oven. Top with the scallion greens and sesame seeds, return to the oven for 5 minutes, and serve.

INGREDIENTS:

FOR THE MARINADE

1	LEMONGRASS STALK, TENDER PART ONLY (THE BOTTOM HALF)
2	GARLIC CLOVES
1	TABLESPOON MINCED GINGER
1	SCALLION
¼	CUP BROWN SUGAR
2	TABLESPOONS CHILI PASTE
1	TABLESPOON SESAME OIL
1	TABLESPOON RICE VINEGAR
2	TABLESPOONS FISH SAUCE
1	TABLESPOON BLACK PEPPER

FOR THE CHICKEN THIGHS & VERMICELLI

10	OZ. SWEET POTATO VERMICELLI
2	TABLESPOONS VEGETABLE OIL
4-6	CHICKEN THIGHS
¼	HEAD OF NAPA CABBAGE, CHOPPED
4	OZ. SHIITAKE MUSHROOMS, SLICED THIN
1	SHALLOT, SLICED THIN
1	YELLOW ONION, SLICED THIN
2	GARLIC CLOVES, MINCED
2	SCALLIONS, CHOPPED, GREENS RESERVED
2	TABLESPOONS MINCED GINGER
¼	CUP BROWN SUGAR
2	TABLESPOONS SESAME OIL
2	TABLESPOONS FISH SAUCE
¼	CUP SOY SAUCE
¼	CUP RICE VINEGAR
¼	CUP SESAME SEEDS

THAI RED DUCK CURRY

YIELD: 4 SERVINGS / ACTIVE TIME: 15 MINUTES / TOTAL TIME: 30 MINUTES

Your local store will likely have precooked duck breasts available for purchase, but it's worth cooking your own just to have access to the rich rendered fat that results from searing in cast iron.

1. Use a very sharp knife to slash the skin on the duck breasts, while taking care not to cut all the way through to the meat.

2. Place a large cast-iron Dutch oven over medium-high heat. Place the duck breasts, skin side down, in the pot and sear until browned, about 4 minutes. This will render a lot of the fat.

3. Turn the duck breasts over and cook until browned on the other side, about 4 minutes. Remove the duck from the pot, let cool, and drain the rendered duck fat. Reserve the duck fat for another use.

4. When the duck breasts are cool enough to handle, remove the skin and discard. Cut each breast into 2-inch pieces.

5. Reduce the heat to medium, add the curry paste, and fry for 2 minutes. Add the coconut milk, bring to a boil, and cook for 5 minutes.

6. Reduce the heat, return the duck to the pot, and simmer for 8 minutes. Add the lime leaves, if using, the pineapple, fish sauce, brown sugar, and chilies, stir to incorporate, and simmer for 5 minutes. Skim to remove any fat from the top as the curry simmers.

7. Taste and add more fish sauce if needed. Stir in the cherry tomatoes and basil and serve alongside the rice.

INGREDIENTS:

- 4 BONELESS, SKIN-ON DUCK BREASTS
- ¼ CUP THAI RED CURRY PASTE
- 2½ CUPS COCONUT MILK
- 10 MAKRUT LIME LEAVES (OPTIONAL)
- 1 CUP DICED PINEAPPLE
- 1 TABLESPOON FISH SAUCE, PLUS MORE TO TASTE
- 1 TABLESPOON BROWN SUGAR
- 6 BIRD'S EYE CHILIES, STEMMED
- 20 CHERRY TOMATOES
- 1 CUP BASIL (THAI BASIL STRONGLY PREFERRED)
- 1½ CUPS COOKED JASMINE RICE, FOR SERVING

If you are looking for a spot to utilize the duck fat you reserved in this preparation, use it in place of oil the next time you roast potatoes. It will add a crisp exterior that gives way to a fluffy, flavorful inside.

PAD THAI

YIELD: 4 SERVINGS / ACTIVE TIME: 15 MINUTES / TOTAL TIME: 35 MINUTES

Y ou may be surprised that the most famous and popular Thai recipe is really very simple to make. The key is to balance the flavors properly so that you have a tangle of chewy noodles freighted with a delicious jumble of salty, sweet, sour, and spicy.

1. Place the noodles in a wide, shallow bowl and pour the boiling water over them. Stir and let rest until they have softened, about 15 minutes.

2. Place the oil in a large cast-iron wok or 12-inch cast-iron skillet and warm over medium-high heat.

3. When the oil starts to shimmer, add the chicken and sauté until cooked through, about 5 minutes. Remove the chicken from the pan and set aside.

4. Add the egg to the pan and stir. Add the noodles and return the chicken to the pan. Stir to incorporate and then add the tamarind paste, water, fish sauce, vinegar, brown sugar, scallions, bean sprouts, cayenne pepper, and peanuts. Stir to combine and serve immediately with the lime wedges.

INGREDIENTS:

- 6   OZ. THIN RICE NOODLES
- 2   CUPS BOILING WATER
- 3   TABLESPOONS VEGETABLE OIL
- 2   LARGE BONELESS, SKINLESS CHICKEN BREASTS, SLICED THIN
- 1   LARGE EGG
- ¼   CUP TAMARIND PASTE
- 2   TABLESPOONS WATER
- 1½   TABLESPOONS FISH SAUCE
- 2   TABLESPOONS RICE VINEGAR
- 1½   TABLESPOONS BROWN SUGAR
- 4   SCALLION GREENS, SLICED
- 1   CUP BEAN SPROUTS
- ½   TEASPOON CAYENNE PEPPER
- ¼   CUP PEANUTS, CRUSHED
- 2   LIMES, CUT INTO WEDGES, FOR SERVING

THAI BASIL CHICKEN

YIELD: 4 SERVINGS / **ACTIVE TIME:** 10 MINUTES / **TOTAL TIME:** 20 MINUTES

The key to making this dish is finding Thai holy basil, which has a light anise flavor that is able to hold up to the heat—meaning both temperature and spice. If you can't find Thai holy basil, you can substitute any other kind and the dish will be nice, but not quite the same.

1. Place the fish sauce, soy sauce, water, and sugar in a bowl and stir to combine. Set half of the mixture aside, add the chicken, and let the chicken marinate for 10 minutes.

2. Place the oil in a large cast-iron wok or skillet and warm over medium-high heat. When the oil starts to shimmer, add the shallots, bell peppers, chilies, and garlic and sauté for 2 minutes, until the onion and garlic start to brown.

3. Use a slotted spoon to remove the chicken from the marinade and add the chicken to the hot pan. Cook, while stirring, until it is almost cooked through, about 3 minutes.

4. Add the reserved mixture and cook for another minute.

5. Remove the pan from heat and stir in 1 cup of the basil. Serve immediately, and top with the remaining Thai basil leaves.

INGREDIENTS:

¼ CUP FISH SAUCE

¼ CUP SOY SAUCE

2 TABLESPOONS WATER

2 TABLESPOONS BROWN SUGAR

4 BONELESS, SKINLESS CHICKEN BREASTS, CHOPPED

2 TABLESPOONS VEGETABLE OIL

3 SHALLOTS, SLICED THIN

2 RED BELL PEPPERS, SEEDED AND SLICED

2 FRESH RED BIRD'S EYE CHILIES, SLICED THIN

3 GARLIC CLOVES, ROUGHLY CHOPPED

1½ CUPS THAI BASIL LEAVES

MOJO CHICKEN

YIELD: 4 SERVINGS / ACTIVE TIME: 30 MINUTES / TOTAL TIME: 2½ TO 8½ HOURS

This fiery, Cuban-inspired dish will wake up your taste buds every time. Ideally, it's made with sour orange juice—which is available at most Latin markets—but a combination of sweet orange and lemon juice works, too.

1. Place the onion, garlic, chilies, cilantro, thyme, cumin, allspice, orange juice, lemon juice, citric acid (if using), lime zest, lime juice, and olive oil in a food processor or blender and puree until smooth.

2. Pour the marinade into a resealable plastic bag and add the chicken. Let marinate for at least 2 hours and up to 8 hours, if time allows.

3. Preheat the oven to 350°F. Place a cast-iron grill pan over very high heat and warm.

4. Remove the chicken from the marinade and pat dry. Pour the marinade into a saucepan, bring to a boil over medium heat, and allow it to reduce as you cook the chicken.

5. When the pan is hot, add the chicken and cook until both sides are charred and the breasts are cooked through, about 4 minutes per side. The pan will start to smoke, so make sure an overhead fan is on or a window is open.

6. Season the sauce with salt and pepper and spoon it over the cooked chicken breasts.

INGREDIENTS:

1   YELLOW ONION, CHOPPED

10   GARLIC CLOVES, PEELED AND TRIMMED

2   SCOTCH BONNET PEPPERS, SEEDED AND CHOPPED

1   CUP CHOPPED CILANTRO LEAVES

1   TEASPOON DRIED THYME

1   TABLESPOON CUMIN

½   TEASPOON ALLSPICE

1   CUP ORANGE JUICE

½   CUP FRESH LEMON JUICE

½   TEASPOON CITRIC ACID (OPTIONAL)

    ZEST AND JUICE OF 1 LIME

¼   CUP OLIVE OIL

4   BONELESS, SKINLESS CHICKEN BREASTS

    SALT AND PEPPER, TO TASTE

PAELLA

YIELD: 4 TO 6 SERVINGS / ACTIVE TIME: 40 MINUTES / TOTAL TIME: 2 TO 3 HOURS

Sure, it's packed with chicken, sausage, and seafood, but saffron is the star of this meal, and its subtle, enigmatic flavor is certain to turn everyone's head right toward you.

1. Preheat the oven to 450°F. Place 2 tablespoons of the parsley, the olive oil, the lemon juice, salt, and pepper in a bowl and stir to combine. Add the chicken thighs to the bowl and marinate for 30 minutes to 1 hour.

2. Place a 12-inch cast-iron skillet over medium-high heat. Add the chicken to the pan and sear on each side for 3 to 5 minutes. Remove the chicken from the pan and set aside.

3. Place the shrimp in the pan and cook for 2 minutes on each side, until the shrimp are cooked approximately three-quarters of the way through. Remove shrimp and set aside.

4. Place the chorizo, pancetta, onion, bell pepper, and half of the garlic in the skillet and cook for 10 to 15 minutes, until the onion is slightly caramelized. Season with salt and pepper and add the tomatoes, rice, stock, the remaining garlic and parsley, the saffron, and the pimenton. Cook, while stirring often, for 10 minutes.

5. Reduce heat to medium-low and nestle the chicken down into the contents of the skillet. Cover the skillet with a lid or aluminum foil and cook for 10 minutes.

6. Uncover the skillet and add the mussels, shrimp, and peas. Cover the skillet, place it in the oven, and cook until the majority of the mussels have opened and the rice is tender. Discard any mussels that have not opened. If the rice is still a bit crunchy, remove the mussels and shrimp, set them aside, return the pan to the oven, and cook until the rice is tender.

INGREDIENTS:

½	CUP DICED PARSLEY
2	TABLESPOONS OLIVE OIL
1	LEMON, ONE HALF JUICED, ONE HALF CUT INTO WEDGES
	SALT AND PEPPER, TO TASTE
4-6	BONELESS, SKINLESS CHICKEN THIGHS
16-24	(16/20) SHRIMP, TAILS ON
½	LB. SPANISH CHORIZO
¼	CUP DICED PANCETTA
½	LARGE WHITE ONION, DICED
1	BELL PEPPER, SEEDED AND MINCED
4	GARLIC CLOVES, MINCED
1	CUP ROMA TOMATOES, DICED
3	CUPS SHORT-GRAIN RICE
6	CUPS CHICKEN STOCK (SEE PAGES 102–3)
1	TEASPOON SAFFRON
1	TABLESPOON PIMENTON (SPANISH PAPRIKA)
16-24	P.E.I. MUSSELS, SCRUBBED AND DEBEARDED
1	CUP FRESH PEAS

CHICKEN TSUKUNE

YIELD: 4 TO 6 SERVINGS / **ACTIVE TIME:** 10 MINUTES / **TOTAL TIME:** 20 MINUTES

Rich chicken thighs are essential here, as they ensure that the result is juicy and deeply flavorful. Make these ahead of time for a party or serve as part of a Japanese-themed dinner with miso soup and seaweed salad.

1. Place the ground chicken, egg, panko bread crumbs, miso, sake, mirin, and the pepper in a bowl and stir to combine. Cover the bowl and place it in the refrigerator while you make the Tare Sauce.

2. When the sauce has been prepared, remove the chicken mixture from the refrigerator and form it into compact pieces that are round or oblong.

3. Place a cast-iron grill pan over high heat and lightly coat with nonstick cooking spray.

4. When the pan is hot, add the meatballs and cook for 3 minutes. Turn over and cook until they are completely cooked through, about 4 minutes. Remove from the grill and lightly baste the cooked meatballs with the Tare Sauce.

5. Garnish the meatballs with the sesame seeds and scallions and serve alongside the remaining Tare Sauce.

NOTE: For a different presentation, thread the meatballs on skewers before adding them to the pan.

TARE SAUCE

1. Place the ingredients in a small saucepan and bring to a simmer over low heat. Simmer for 10 minutes, while stirring once or twice.

2. Remove from heat, let cool, and strain before using.

INGREDIENTS:

2   LBS. DARK CHICKEN MEAT, GROUND

1   LARGE EGG, LIGHTLY BEATEN

1   CUP PANKO BREAD CRUMBS

2   TEASPOONS MISO

2   TABLESPOONS SAKE

1½   TABLESPOONS MIRIN

½   TEASPOON FRESHLY GROUND BLACK PEPPER

    TARE SAUCE (SEE RECIPE)

1½   SCALLIONS, SLICED, FOR GARNISH

    SESAME SEEDS, FOR GARNISH

TARE SAUCE

½   CUP CHICKEN STOCK (SEE PAGES 102–3)

½   CUP SOY SAUCE

½   CUP MIRIN

¼   CUP SAKE

½   CUP BROWN SUGAR

2   GARLIC CLOVES, SMASHED

    1-INCH PIECE OF GINGER, SLICED

1½   SCALLIONS, SLICED

FIVE-SPICE TURKEY BREAST

YIELD: 4 SERVINGS / ACTIVE TIME: 30 MINUTES / TOTAL TIME: 2 HOURS

Proof that turkey isn't just for the holidays and doesn't need to be flanked by a number of rich sides. When searching for something to round out the plate, keep it simple: potatoes, rice, slippery noodles, or a salad.

1. Preheat your oven to 375°F.

2. Place the five-spice powder, cinnamon, brown sugar, and pepper in a small bowl and stir to combine.

3. Pat the turkey breast dry with paper towels and coat it liberally with the spice mixture.

4. Place the oil in a 12-inch cast-iron skillet and warm over medium heat. When the oil starts to shimmer, add the turkey, skin side down, and cook until it is browned, about 5 minutes.

5. Carefully turn the turkey over, cover the pan with foil, and place in the oven for 1½ hours.

6. Remove the pan from the oven and let the turkey rest for 15 minutes.

7. Place the turkey breast on a cutting board, remove the bone, slice, and serve.

TIP: You can also let the turkey cool down and make sandwiches on French bread with lots of shredded cabbage, carrots, and cilantro.

INGREDIENTS:

2　TABLESPOONS CHINESE FIVE-SPICE POWDER

1　TEASPOON CINNAMON

1　TABLESPOON BROWN SUGAR

1　TEASPOON FINELY GROUND BLACK PEPPER

1　BONE-IN, SKIN-ON WHOLE TURKEY BREAST

2　TABLESPOONS VEGETABLE OIL

JUICY TURKEY BURGERS

YIELD: 4 TO 6 SERVINGS / ACTIVE TIME: 20 MINUTES / TOTAL TIME: 1 HOUR

Ground turkey is a great way to reduce the fat in recipes where you'd normally use ground beef. Unfortunately, the taste is never the same, and it's for that very reason: less fat. It turns out that shredded zucchini can moisten—and flavor—ground turkey, making for a very satisfying (and low-fat) experience.

1. Place a 12-inch cast-iron skillet over medium-high heat and coat with about a teaspoon of olive oil. Add the onion and garlic and cook, while stirring, until the onion is translucent, about 3 minutes. Remove from heat and transfer the onion mix to a large bowl.

2. Add the bread crumbs, tamari or soy sauce, pepper, salt, sage, parsley, zucchini, and mozzarella. Stir until well combined. Add the turkey and stir to combine.

3. Form the meat into patties, wrap in plastic, and refrigerate for 30 minutes.

4. Heat the skillet over medium-high heat and add the remaining olive oil. Place the patties in the skillet and cook for about 4 minutes per side. Do not over-flip or flatten the patties while cooking.

5. To cook the patties completely, reduce the heat to medium and cover the skillet. Continue to cook for another 3 to 4 minutes. Press down gently on one of the patties to see if the juice is running clear. If it's still pink, continue to cook another minute or so.

6. Season with additional salt and pepper and serve on hamburger buns with toppings of your choice.

INGREDIENTS:

2   TEASPOONS OLIVE OIL

½   CUP MINCED ONION

2   GARLIC CLOVES, PRESSED

¾   CUP BREAD CRUMBS

1   TEASPOON TAMARI OR SOY SAUCE

½   TEASPOON FRESHLY GROUND PEPPER

1   TEASPOON SALT

¼   TEASPOON DRIED SAGE

1   TABLESPOON MINCED FRESH PARSLEY

½   CUP GRATED ZUCCHINI

¼   CUP GRATED MOZZARELLA CHEESE

1   LB. GROUND TURKEY

    HAMBURGER BUNS, FOR SERVING

    TOPPINGS OF CHOICE, FOR SERVING

SEAFOOD

L a mer. The sea. The big blue. Our oceans immediately draw out the poet in each of us, and just also happen to be the most abundant source of food on the planet.

Bursting with freshness, delectable brininess, and subtle sweetness, these plentiful fruits were made for the quick cooking and ample heat supplied by cast iron. It is the only material that can properly cook scallops, and its ability to crisp the skin of salmon adds another layer of loveliness to that rich fish. From the Cast-Iron Oysters with Butter and Juniper Cream (see page 438) to the unique flavor of Takoyaki (see page 441), this chapter dives deep to explore the incredible bounty provided by the ocean.

SALMON CAKES

YIELD: 6 TO 8 CAKES / ACTIVE TIME: 1 HOUR / TOTAL TIME: 1 HOUR AND 30 MINUTES

Canned salmon isn't as high-quality as fresh salmon, but it's still quite good. With the healthy add-ins, and the fact that the end product is a cake that will be topped with a dressing like tartar or cocktail sauce, the canned salmon is great for ease of use and presentation.

1. Drain the liquid from the cans of salmon and empty the fish into a bowl, flaking it apart with a fork. Add the eggs, bread crumbs, onion, hot sauce, and parsley and stir to combine. Season with salt and pepper.

2. Place a 12-inch cast-iron skillet over medium-high heat. Add 1 tablespoon of the oil. Add 3 or 4 individual heaping spoonfuls of fish mix to the skillet, pressing down on the tops of each to form a patty. Brown the cakes on each side for about 5 minutes. Try to turn the cakes over just once. If you're worried about them not getting cooked through, put a lid on the skillet for a minute or so after they've browned on each side.

3. Transfer the cakes to a plate and cover with foil to keep them warm while you cook the next batch. Serve on a platter with lemon wedges.

VARIATIONS: Salmon cakes can be served many ways, including: on a bun with lettuce, tomato, red onion, and, instead of ketchup or mustard, tartar or cocktail sauce; on top of a green salad with lemon-dill dressing on the side; or as miniature cakes, served as finger foods with toothpicks and dipping sauces.

INGREDIENTS:

- 4 **(6 OZ.) CANS OF SALMON (RED SALMON PREFERRED)**
- 2 **LARGE EGGS, LIGHTLY BEATEN**
- ¼ **CUP BREAD CRUMBS**
- ¼ **CUP MINCED ONION**
- 1 **TEASPOON FRANK'S REDHOT® SAUCE**
- 1 **TEASPOON DRIED PARSLEY**

  SALT AND FRESHLY GROUND PEPPER, TO TASTE
- 2 **TABLESPOONS PEANUT OR OLIVE OIL**

  LEMON WEDGES, FOR SERVING

BAKED CRAB DIP

YIELD: 4 TO 6 SERVINGS / **ACTIVE TIME:** 15 MINUTES / **TOTAL TIME:** 30 MINUTES

A rich and creamy dip that is able to support the sweet crab, the heat supplied by the cayenne pepper, and the pungency provided by the mustard powder.

1. Preheat the oven to 400°F.

2. Place an 8-inch cast-iron skillet over medium heat and add the olive oil. When the oil starts to shimmer, add the onion and bell pepper and sauté until the onion is translucent, about 5 minutes.

3. Add the mustard powder and cayenne, stir to coat, and transfer the mixture to a large bowl.

4. Squeeze the spinach to remove any excess water and add it to the bowl with the remaining ingredients. Stir to combine, return the mixture to the skillet, and smooth the top.

5. Place in the oven and bake until the dip is browned and bubbly, about 15 minutes. Remove and serve with the sliced baguette, potato chips, or rice crackers.

INGREDIENTS:

1   TABLESPOON OLIVE OIL

1   YELLOW ONION, MINCED

2   RED BELL PEPPER, SEEDED AND DICED

1   TEASPOON DRY MUSTARD POWDER

½   TEASPOON CAYENNE PEPPER, OR TO TASTE

3   CUPS FROZEN SPINACH, THAWED

1   TEASPOON KOSHER SALT

1   CUP CREAM CHEESE

½   CUP MAYONNAISE

2   TABLESPOONS MINCED SCALLION

¾   LB. COOKED CRABMEAT

1   BAGUETTE, SLICED, FOR SERVING (OPTIONAL)

THICK-CUT POTATO CHIPS, FOR SERVING (OPTIONAL)

RICE CRACKERS, FOR SERVING (OPTIONAL)

CAST-IRON OYSTERS
with BUTTER *and* JUNIPER CREAM

YIELD: 2 SERVINGS / **ACTIVE TIME:** 15 MINUTES / **TOTAL TIME:** 15 MINUTES

Grilling oysters brings out their beautiful briny flavor and gives you an excuse to break out your cast-iron oyster pan. If you don't have a cast-iron oyster pan, you can also make this recipe using a standard skillet. Just pour a thick layer of coarse salt in the bottom and nestle the oysters down into it.

1. Preheat your grill or broiler to high.

2. Place the butter, gin, and black pepper in a bowl and whisk to combine. Place in the refrigerator.

3. Place the cream, shallots (or onion), and juniper berries in a saucepan and warm over low heat for 2 minutes. Remove from heat and let the mixture steep.

4. Arrange the oysters in a cast-iron oyster pan. Top each with a spoonful of the chilled butter and a splash of the juniper cream. Make sure to leave the juniper berries in the pot. Place the pan on the grill or beneath the broiler and cook until the oysters are caramelized and the liquid is bubbling, about 3 minutes.

5. Garnish with chopped parsley or chervil and serve immediately.

INGREDIENTS:

3   **TABLESPOONS UNSALTED BUTTER, SOFTENED**

2   **OZ. GIN**

1   **TEASPOON GROUND BLACK PEPPER**

¼   **CUP HEAVY CREAM**

2   **SHALLOTS OR 1 SMALL YELLOW ONION, MINCED**

4   **WHOLE JUNIPER BERRIES**

12   **OYSTERS, SHUCKED**

    PARSLEY OR CHERVIL, CHOPPED, FOR GARNISH

TAKOYAKI

YIELD: 4 SERVINGS (20 FRITTERS) / **ACTIVE TIME:** 20 MINUTES / **TOTAL TIME:** 20 MINUTES

Growing up, this was my father's go-to dish for a party, and I have to say he was on point: these are unusual and delicious enough to impress and simple enough to partner with a nice, cold beer. Plus, since we lived across the street from the Pacific, the smell of them cooking mingling with the cool ocean air made these an utterly irresistible bite. These freeze well and can be reheated in a warm pan, so don't hesitate to make a larger batch.

1. Place 2 tablespoons of the water, the egg, and broth in a bowl and stir until combined.

2. Sprinkle the flour over the mixture and stir until all of the flour has been incorporated, adding water in 1-tablespoon increments as needed. The mixture should be a thick batter.

3. Lightly oil a cast-iron takoyaki pan and warm over medium heat. When the pan is hot, pour the batter into a measuring cup with a spout. Fill the wells of the pan halfway and add a pinch of octopus, scallion, and pickled ginger, plus a drizzle of the Yakisoba Sauce. Fill the wells the rest of the way with the batter, until they are almost overflowing.

4. Cook the fritters for approximately 2 minutes and use a chopstick to flip each one over. Turn the fritters as needed until they are golden brown on both sides and piping hot. Remove from the pan and set aside.

5. To serve, garnish the fritters liberally with a drizzle of takoyaki sauce, a bit of the mayonnaise, shredded seaweed, and bonito flakes.

YAKISOBA SAUCE

Place all of the ingredients in a mixing bowl and whisk until combined.

INGREDIENTS:

- 2 TABLESPOONS WATER, PLUS MORE AS NEEDED
- 1 LARGE EGG
- 1½ CUPS DASHI BROTH (SEE PAGE 271)
- ¾ CUP ALL-PURPOSE FLOUR
- 1 CUP MINCED COOKED OCTOPUS
- GREENS FROM 2 SCALLIONS, SLICED THIN
- ¼ CUP MINCED PICKLED GINGER
- ¼ CUP YAKISOBA SAUCE (SEE RECIPE)
- TAKOYAKI SAUCE, FOR GARNISH
- KEWPIE JAPANESE MAYONNAISE, FOR GARNISH
- SHREDDED NORI, FOR GARNISH
- BONITO FLAKES, FOR GARNISH

YAKISOBA SAUCE

- 2 TEASPOONS SAKE
- 2 TEASPOONS MIRIN
- 2 TEASPOONS SOY SAUCE
- 2 TEASPOONS OYSTER SAUCE
- 2 TEASPOONS WORCESTERSHIRE SAUCE
- 1 TABLESPOON SUGAR
- 1 TABLESPOON KETCHUP
- SALT AND WHITE PEPPER, TO TASTE

ESCARGOT À LA BOURGUIGNONNE

YIELD: 4 SERVINGS / **ACTIVE TIME:** 10 MINUTES / **TOTAL TIME:** 15 MINUTES

If you love garlic, French food, and picturesque presentation, this is the recipe for you. The satisfyingly chewy snails are slathered in a buttery sauce and baked in little shells that you can find online or in upscale shops. If you really want to get glamorous, keep an eye out for escargot tongs while you're perusing.

1. Preheat the oven to 400°F.

2. Place the garlic, butter, shallot, parsley, and wine in a food processor and pulse until combined.

3. Use a teaspoon to put a small knob of the garlic-and-butter mixture into each of the snail shells. Top with a snail and then a bit more of the garlic-and-butter mixture.

4. Place the stuffed snail shells in a cast-iron snail pan or on a thick bed of salt in a cast-iron skillet. Place the pan in the oven and roast until the butter starts to sizzle, about 5 minutes. Serve immediately with the toasted slices of baguette.

INGREDIENTS:

3   GARLIC CLOVES, MINCED

1   STICK OF BUTTER, AT ROOM TEMPERATURE

1   SMALL SHALLOT, MINCED

1   CUP MINCED PARSLEY LEAVES

¼   CUP WHITE WINE

24   SNAILS

24   SNAIL SHELLS (AVAILABLE ONLINE)

1   BAGUETTE, SLICED AND TOASTED, FOR SERVING

CAROLINA CRAB CAKES

YIELD: 6 CAKES / ACTIVE TIME: 1 HOUR / TOTAL TIME: 1 HOUR AND 30 MINUTES

With these cakes, if you want great flavor, you have to go for top-quality crabmeat. This is the kind that's in the refrigerated section of your store's fish department. Don't buy crabmeat that's canned like tuna. It has neither the flavor nor the consistency needed for these cakes.

1. To prepare the sauce, place all of the ingredients in a bowl and stir to combine. Cover and chill in the refrigerator.

2. To prepare the crab cakes, in a large bowl, combine the crabmeat, onion, bread crumbs, Worcestershire sauce, Old Bay seasoning, hot sauce, parsley, and mayonnaise. Mix the milk into the egg and add to the crab mix, blending gently but thoroughly. Season with salt and pepper. If the mixture seems dry, add more mayonnaise.

3. Place a 12-inch cast-iron skillet over medium-high heat. Add the oil. It should be about ¼-inch deep. When oil is hot, add 3 or 4 individual heaping spoonfuls of crab mix to the skillet, pressing down on the tops of each to form a patty. Brown the cakes on each side for about 3 minutes. Try to turn the cakes over just once. If you're worried about them not getting cooked through, put a lid on the skillet for a minute or so after they've browned on each side.

4. Transfer the cakes to a plate and cover with foil to keep them warm while you cook the next batch.

5. Serve on a platter with lemon wedges and remoulade sauce on the side.

INGREDIENTS:

FOR THE REMOULADE SAUCE

- 1 CUP MAYONNAISE
- 2 TABLESPOONS MUSTARD (CREOLE PREFERRED, OTHERWISE WHOLE GRAIN OR DIJON WILL DO)
- 1 TEASPOON CAJUN SEASONING
- 1 TABLESPOON SWEET PAPRIKA
- 1 TABLESPOON PICKLE JUICE OR FRESH LEMON JUICE
- 1 TABLESPOON LOUISIANA-STYLE HOT SAUCE, OR TO TASTE
- 1 GARLIC CLOVE, MINCED
- 2 TABLESPOONS MINCED FRESH PARSLEY (OPTIONAL)

  SALT AND FRESHLY GROUND BLACK PEPPER, TO TASTE

FOR THE CRAB CAKES

- 1 LB. LUMP CRABMEAT (BLUE CRAB PREFERRED)
- ¼ CUP MINCED ONION
- ½ CUP BREAD CRUMBS
- 1 TEASPOON WORCESTERSHIRE SAUCE
- 1 TEASPOON OLD BAY SEASONING
- 2 TABLESPOONS HOT SAUCE
- 1 TEASPOON DRIED PARSLEY
- 1 TABLESPOON MAYONNAISE
- 1 TABLESPOON WHOLE MILK
- 1 LARGE EGG, LIGHTLY BEATEN

  SALT AND FRESHLY GROUND PEPPER, TO TASTE
- ¼ CUP PEANUT OR OLIVE OIL

  LEMON WEDGES, FOR SERVING

LOBSTER CIOPPINO

YIELD: 6 SERVINGS / ACTIVE TIME: 30 TO 40 MINUTES / TOTAL TIME: 1 HOUR AND 30 MINUTES

This fisherman's stew originated in San Francisco, but this version pays homage to the true land of lobster: Maine.

1. Place 3 inches of water in a cast-iron Dutch oven and bring to a boil. Place the lobster in the pot, cover, and cook for 5 to 7 minutes, until the shell is a bright reddish orange. Remove the lobster from the pot and set aside. Drain the cooking liquid and return the Dutch oven to the stove.

2. Add the water and bring to a boil. Add the cleaned mussels and clams, cover the pot, and cook for 3 to 5 minutes, until the majority of the shells have opened. Drain, set aside the clams and mussels, and reserve the liquid. Discard any clams and mussels that do not open.

3. Place the Dutch oven over medium-high heat and add the olive oil. When the oil is warm, add the fennel and cook for 3 minutes, until the fennel is soft and slightly translucent.

4. Add the shallots and garlic. Stir and cook for 5 minutes.

5. Add the tomato paste and stir to incorporate. Add the red wine and cook until it is almost evaporated, about 5 minutes. Scrape the bottom with a wooden spoon to remove any bits that are stuck.

6. Add the tomatoes, white wine, stock, bay leaves, red pepper flakes, and a pinch of salt and pepper. Reduce heat to medium-low, cover, and cook for 30 minutes.

7. While the stew is cooking, use a lobster cracker or a heavy knife to crack the lobster open. Remove the tail first. Using a kitchen towel, grab the tail where it connects to the body and twist until it detaches. Do this over a bowl to catch any juices that get released. Use the cracker or knife to crack open the shell and remove the meat. If you are using a knife, press the tail flat on a cutting board, top side down, carefully cut down the length of the tail, and then remove the meat.

8. Next, move to the claws. If using a cracker, crack each claw at the joint and then crack the top part of the claw until the shell opens. Grab the bottom piece of the claw and twist it sideways. Once it is loose, pull straight back to remove the shell. The cartilage should also come out with it. Remove all of the meat and discard the shells. If you are using a knife, use the flat of the knife to crack the shells open. Set the lobster meat aside.

INGREDIENTS:

- 1¼-LB. LOBSTER
- 2 CUPS WATER
- 1 LB. P.E.I. MUSSELS, WASHED AND DEBEARDED
- 12 LITTLENECK CLAMS, WASHED AND SCRUBBED
- 2 TABLESPOONS OLIVE OIL
- ½ LARGE FENNEL BULB, SLICED THIN
- 2 SHALLOTS, MINCED
- 3 GARLIC CLOVES, MINCED
- 1 (6 OZ.) CAN OF TOMATO PASTE
- 1 CUP RED WINE (ZINFANDEL PREFERRED)
- 1 (28 OZ.) CAN OF WHOLE SAN MARZANO TOMATOES, LIGHTLY CRUSHED BY HAND
- 1 CUP WHITE WINE (CHARDONNAY PREFERRED)
- 2 CUPS FISH STOCK (SEE PAGE 454)
- 2 BAY LEAVES
- 1 TEASPOON RED PEPPER FLAKES
- SALT AND PEPPER, TO TASTE
- 1 LB. HALIBUT, SKINNED AND CUT INTO LARGE CUBES
- 1 LOAF OF SOURDOUGH OR CRUSTY ITALIAN BREAD, FOR SERVING

9. Remove the legs from the lobster and add the remaining carcass to the pot. Uncover the pot and cook for 20 minutes.

10. Add the halibut to the pot and cook for 5 minutes. Add the lobster meat, clams, mussels, and the reserved cooking liquid and cook for 2 minutes. Serve with a loaf of sourdough or crusty Italian bread.

TIP: If you can't get fresh lobster, use whatever fresh fish is available. You can also purchase lobster that has been pre-cleaned if you want to avoid doing the cracking and cleaning yourself.

FISH STEW

YIELD: 4 TO 6 SERVINGS / ACTIVE TIME: 20 MINUTES / TOTAL TIME: 1 HOUR

Muscatel lends sweetness as well as floral and nutty notes to this buttery stew. As a result, it tastes nowhere near as light as it actually is.

1. Place 2 tablespoons of the butter in a cast-iron Dutch oven and melt over medium-high heat. Add the carrots, onion, potatoes, and celery and cook for 5 to 7 minutes or until the vegetables start to caramelize.

2. Add the fennel, garlic, and thyme. Cook for another 3 to 5 minutes, until the fennel softens. Add the remaining butter and stir until it melts.

3. Sprinkle the flour over the vegetables and stir until they are evenly coated. Cook, while stirring occasionally, for 5 minutes.

4. Add the Muscatel and cook, while stirring, for 2 minutes. Make sure to scrape any bits from the bottom of the pan to add flavor to the dish.

5. Reduce heat to medium. Add the stock, stir, and cook for 20 minutes, until the flavor of the flour dissipates.

6. Add the fish and fava beans. Season with salt and pepper, cover, and cook until the beans are tender and the fish is flaky, about 12 minutes.

INGREDIENTS:

- 4 TABLESPOONS UNSALTED BUTTER
- 3 CARROTS, DICED
- 1 LARGE VIDALIA ONION, DICED
- 2 YUKON GOLD POTATOES, DICED
- 5 CELERY STALKS, DICED
- 2 FENNEL BULBS, SLICED THIN, FRONDS RESERVED FOR GARNISH
- 3 GARLIC CLOVES, MINCED
- ¼ CUP MINCED FRESH THYME
- ¼ CUP ALL-PURPOSE FLOUR
- 1½ CUPS MUSCATEL
- 4 CUPS FISH STOCK (SEE PAGE 454)
- 1 LB. HAKE, SKINNED
- 1 LB. COD, SKINNED
- 1½ CUPS SHELLED FAVA BEANS
- SALT AND PEPPER, TO TASTE

MEL'S NEW ENGLAND CLAM CHOWDER

YIELD: 6 SERVINGS / ACTIVE TIME: 30 MINUTES / TOTAL TIME: 1 HOUR AND 30 MINUTES

This take on traditional clam chowder is packed with cherrystone clams, bacon, and potatoes, and is too good to pass up.

1. Place the bacon in a cast-iron Dutch oven and cook, while stirring occasionally, over medium-high heat until the bacon is crispy. Drain the fat from the pan and add the thyme, celery, onions, butter, and garlic. Reduce the heat to medium and cook until the onions are translucent. Add the ⅓ cup of flour and mix until all the vegetables are coated. Cook for 10 minutes, while stirring frequently and scraping the bottom of the pan to keep anything from burning.

2. Add the potatoes and clam juice and cook until the potatoes are tender, about 20 minutes. Add the Worcestershire sauce and Tabasco™, stir, and then add the cream. Cook until the chowder is just thick enough to coat a spoon. Add the cherrystone clams and cook until heated through, about 10 minutes. Season with salt and pepper and ladle into warmed bowls.

INGREDIENTS:

- ½   LB. BACON, MINCED
- 2   TABLESPOONS MINCED FRESH THYME
- 4   CUPS MINCED CELERY
- 4   SPANISH ONIONS, MINCED
- 4   TABLESPOONS UNSALTED BUTTER
- 6   GARLIC CLOVES, MINCED
- ⅓   CUP ALL-PURPOSE FLOUR, PLUS 1 TABLESPOON
- 1½   LBS. CREAMER POTATOES, MINCED
- 2   CUPS PURE CLAM JUICE
- 2   TABLESPOONS WORCESTERSHIRE SAUCE
- 3   DASHES OF TABASCO™
- 2   CUPS HEAVY CREAM
- 6   (6½ OZ.) CANS OF BAR HARBOR WHOLE MAINE CHERRYSTONE CLAMS, WITH JUICE

  SALT AND PEPPER, TO TASTE

ROMESCO DE PEIX

YIELD: 6 TO 8 SERVINGS / ACTIVE TIME: 25 MINUTES / TOTAL TIME: 40 MINUTES

This fish stew is inspired by one of chef Jordi Artal's signature dishes. His perspective on Catalonian cuisine has placed him at the forefront of the Spanish culinary world, and this particular dish will transport you right to the seashore on a summer evening.

1. Place the almonds in a 12-inch cast-iron skillet and toast them over medium heat until they are just browned. Transfer them to a food processor and pulse until they are finely ground.

2. Place the saffron and boiling water in a bowl and let steep.

3. Place the olive oil in a large cast-iron Dutch oven and warm over medium heat. When it starts to shimmer, add the onion and bell peppers and cook, while stirring often, until the peppers are tender, about 15 minutes.

4. Add the sweet paprika, smoked paprika, bay leaf, and tomato paste and cook, while stirring constantly, for 1 minute. Add the Sherry and bring to a boil. Boil for 5 minutes and then add the stock, tomatoes, saffron, and the soaking liquid. Stir to combine, season with salt and pepper, and reduce heat so that the mixture simmers.

5. Add the ground almonds and cook until the mixture thickens slightly, about 8 minutes. Add the monkfish and mussels, stir gently to incorporate, and simmer until the fish is cooked through and a majority of the mussels have opened, about 5 minutes. Discard any mussels that do not open.

6. Divide the mixture between warmed bowls, garnish with the cilantro, and serve with the toasted crusty bread.

INGREDIENTS:

½ CUP SLIVERED ALMONDS

½ TEASPOON SAFFRON

¼ CUP BOILING WATER

½ CUP OLIVE OIL

1 LARGE YELLOW ONION, CHOPPED

2 LARGE RED BELL PEPPERS, SEEDED AND CHOPPED

2½ TEASPOONS SWEET PAPRIKA

1 TABLESPOON SMOKED PAPRIKA

1 BAY LEAF

2 TABLESPOONS TOMATO PASTE

½ CUP SHERRY

2 CUPS FISH STOCK (SEE PAGE 454)

1 (28 OZ.) CAN OF DICED TOMATOES

SALT AND PEPPER, TO TASTE

1½ LBS. MONKFISH FILLETS, CUT INTO LARGE PIECES

1 LB. MUSSELS, WASHED AND DEBEARDED

CILANTRO, CHOPPED, FOR GARNISH

CRUSTY BREAD, TOASTED, FOR SERVING

FISH STOCK

YIELD: 6 QUARTS / **ACTIVE TIME:** 20 MINUTES / **TOTAL TIME:** 3 HOURS AND 20 MINUTES

This stock is a quick and simple preparation, with the aromatics helping to round out the great flavor. Traditionally only white fish should be used, and the reasons for this are twofold: it is a good way to avoid incorporating extra oil into the stock, and fish like tuna and salmon add an overpowering flavor to stock. That said, if using this stock for a creamy or thick soup, don't hesitate to use a salmon carcass if you have one on hand. Fishmongers always have extra bones that they are happy to sell—or they might be game to just give them to you, one of many reasons to be friendly with the people from whom you buy ingredients.

1. In a large stockpot, add the vegetable oil and warm over low heat. Add the vegetables and cook until any additional moisture has evaporated. This will allow the flavor of the vegetables to become concentrated.

2. Add the whitefish bodies, the aromatics, the salt, and the water to the pot.

3. Raise heat to high and bring to a boil. Reduce heat so that the stock simmers and cook for a minimum of 2 hours. Skim fat and impurities from the top as the stock cooks. As for when to stop cooking the stock, let the flavor be the judge. I typically like to cook for 2 to 3 hours total.

4. When the stock is finished cooking, strain through a fine strainer or cheesecloth. Place stock in the refrigerator to chill.

5. Once cool, skim the fat layer from the top and discard. Use immediately, refrigerate, or freeze.

INGREDIENTS:

½ CUP VEGETABLE OIL

1 LEEK, TRIMMED AND CAREFULLY WASHED, CUT INTO 1-INCH PIECES

1 LARGE YELLOW ONION, UNPEELED, ROOT CLEANED, CUT INTO 1-INCH PIECES

2 LARGE CARROTS, CUT INTO 1-INCH PIECES

1 CELERY STALK WITH LEAVES, CUT INTO 1-INCH PIECES

10 LBS. WHITEFISH BODIES

8 PARSLEY SPRIGS

5 THYME SPRIGS

2 BAY LEAVES

1 TEASPOON WHOLE PEPPERCORNS

1 TEASPOON SALT

10 QUARTS WATER

SEARED SCALLOP & SWEET CORN CHOWDER

YIELD: 6 SERVINGS / ACTIVE TIME: 35 MINUTES / TOTAL TIME: 1 HOUR AND 15 MINUTES

It's hard not to feel blessed after tasting fresh corn and scallops and realizing that not everyone has them on their doorstep. This chowder is sweet, but setting that off with some smoked paprika and chili oil makes for a memorable bowl.

1. Place the butter in a 12-inch cast-iron skillet and cook over medium heat until it is melted. Add the onion and sauté until it starts to turn golden brown.

2. Add the bacon, celery, and garlic and cook, while stirring frequently, for 5 minutes.

3. Add the flour and stir to ensure that the mixture is well combined.

4. Add the corn, thyme, potatoes, cream, and milk, stir to combine, and bring to a simmer. Season with salt and pepper and cook until the potatoes are fork-tender, about 20 minutes.

5. Place the olive oil in another cast-iron skillet and warm over medium-high heat.

6. Pat the scallops dry and season with salt. When the oil is hot, place the scallops in and cook for about 2 to 3 minutes on each side, until golden brown.

7. Remove the sprigs of thyme from the soup and discard. Ladle the soup into warmed bowls and top each bowl with 1 scallop.

INGREDIENTS:

- 6 TABLESPOONS UNSALTED BUTTER
- 1 LARGE ONION, DICED
- 6 STRIPS OF BACON, COOKED AND DICED
- 2 CELERY STALKS, CHOPPED
- 2 GARLIC CLOVES, MINCED
- ¼ CUP ALL-PURPOSE FLOUR
- 3 CUPS FRESH CORN KERNELS (ABOUT 7 EARS OF CORN)
- 3 SPRIGS OF THYME
- 2 LARGE POTATOES, DICED
- ½ CUP HEAVY CREAM
- ½ CUP WHOLE MILK
- SALT AND PEPPER, TO TASTE
- 1 TABLESPOON OLIVE OIL
- 6 FRESH SCALLOPS

CRAB & OKRA SOUP

YIELD: 4 SERVINGS / ACTIVE TIME: 10 MINUTES / TOTAL TIME: 25 MINUTES

This recipe is steeped in the rich Afro-Caribbean culinary tradition. If you're not familiar, the combination of peanuts, coconut, and clams will be a revelation. And make sure you don't skip the lime wedges—that little touch of acid really ties the dish together.

1. Place the peanuts in a large, dry cast-iron skillet and toast over medium heat until they are browned. Remove them from the pan and set aside. Add the okra and cook, while stirring, until it is browned all over, about 5 minutes. Remove and set aside.

2. Place the coconut oil in a large enameled cast-iron Dutch oven and warm over medium heat. When it starts to shimmer, add the bell pepper, onion, habanero pepper, and potato and sauté until the onion is soft, about 5 minutes.

3. Add the stock (or water) and clam juice, bring to a simmer, and cook for 5 minutes. Add the coconut milk, return to a simmer, and season with salt.

4. Working in batches, transfer the soup to a blender and puree until smooth. Return the soup to the Dutch oven and simmer for another 5 minutes. Stir in the peanuts, okra, spinach, and crab and cook until the spinach has wilted.

5. Ladle the soup into warmed bowls and serve with lime wedges.

INGREDIENTS:

- 1   CUP PEANUTS, CHOPPED
- 10   OKRA PODS, SLICED INTO ½-INCH ROUNDS
- ½   CUP COCONUT OIL
- 1   RED BELL PEPPER, SEEDED AND DICED
- 1   YELLOW ONION, SLICED INTO HALF-MOONS
- 1   HABANERO PEPPER, STEMMED, SEEDED, AND CHOPPED
- 1   LARGE POTATO, PEELED AND DICED
- 4   CUPS VEGETABLE STOCK (SEE PAGE 562) OR WATER
- 1   CUP CLAM JUICE
- 1   CUP COCONUT MILK
     SALT, TO TASTE
- 4   CUPS FRESH SPINACH LEAVES
- 1   LB. LUMP CRABMEAT
     LIME WEDGES, FOR SERVING

SIMPLE SKILLET SALMON

YIELD: 4 TO 6 SERVINGS / ACTIVE TIME: 20 MINUTES / TOTAL TIME: 30 MINUTES

Start with super-fresh fish, and keep it simple—butter, lemon, salt, and pepper—and you can create a succulent dish that is ready in no time.

1. Rinse the fillets with cold water to ensure that any scales or bones are removed and pat them dry with paper towels. Rub the butter on both sides of the fillets, squeeze lemon over them, and season with salt and pepper.

2. Place a 12-inch cast-iron skillet over medium-high heat and add the tablespoon of olive oil. Add the fillets, flesh side down. Cook on one side for about 3 minutes, then flip them and cook for 2 minutes on the other side. Remove the pan from heat and let the fish rest in it for a minute before serving. The skin should peel right off.

INGREDIENTS:

3-4 LBS. SKIN-ON SALMON FILLETS

2 TABLESPOONS UNSALTED BUTTER, CUT INTO PIECES AND SOFTENED

1 LEMON, HALVED

SALT AND PEPPER, TO TASTE

1 TABLESPOON OLIVE OIL

HONEY-GLAZED SALMON

YIELD: 4 SERVINGS / ACTIVE TIME: 5 MINUTES / TOTAL TIME: 15 MINUTES

The rare recipe that is accessible for a beginner and still beloved by the most advanced chefs. The technique is straightforward and easy to master, and the results are nothing short of sublime. That it comes together in mere minutes is just another thing in its favor.

1. Pat the salmon fillets dry with a paper towel. Rub the olive oil into them and season with salt.

2. Place a 12-inch cast-iron skillet over medium-high heat and add the vegetable oil. When it starts to shimmer, place the salmon fillets, skin side down, in the pan and cook for 8 minutes.

3. Reduce the heat to medium and use a spatula to carefully flip the salmon fillets over. Cook for another 8 minutes.

4. While the salmon is cooking, place the honey, lemon zest, and lemon juice in a bowl and stir to combine.

5. When the salmon is cooked through, remove from the skillet, drizzle the honey glaze over the top, and serve.

INGREDIENTS:

4   SKIN-ON SALMON FILLETS

1   TABLESPOON OLIVE OIL

2   TABLESPOONS VEGETABLE OIL

    KOSHER SALT, TO TASTE

3   TABLESPOONS HONEY

    ZEST AND JUICE OF 1 LARGE LEMON

TEA-SMOKED SALMON

YIELD: 4 SERVINGS / **ACTIVE TIME:** 10 MINUTES / **TOTAL TIME:** 1 HOUR

Smoking food brings a whole different dimension of flavor that's totally worth exploring. A brief kiss can add a haunting flavor, while a good long time in the smoker brings something wild and unctuous to the table.

1. In a shallow dish, whisk together the oil, mirin, brown sugar, ginger, and orange zest. Add the salmon and let marinate for 30 minutes.

2. Line a large cast-iron wok with foil. You want the foil to extend over the sides of the wok. Add the rice, granulated sugar, tea, and orange peel and cook over high heat until the rice begins to smoke.

3. Place the salmon on a lightly oiled rack, set it above the smoking rice, and place the lid on top of wok. Fold the foil over the lid to seal the wok as best as you can.

4. Reduce heat to medium and cook for 10 minutes.

5. Remove from heat and let the wok cool completely, about 20 minutes. When done, the fish will be cooked to medium. Serve immediately.

INGREDIENTS:

½ CUP VEGETABLE OIL, PLUS MORE AS NEEDED

½ CUP MIRIN

1 TABLESPOON BROWN SUGAR

1 TABLESPOON MINCED GINGER

1 TEASPOON ORANGE ZEST

1 LB. SKINLESS, CENTER-CUT SALMON FILLETS

1 CUP WHITE RICE

½ CUP GRANULATED SUGAR

1 CUP GREEN TEA (GUNPOWDER PREFERRED)

1 ORANGE PEEL, DICED

TERIYAKI SALMON *with* CHINESE EGGPLANTS *and* BEAN SPROUTS

YIELD: 4 SERVINGS / ACTIVE TIME: 20 MINUTES / TOTAL TIME: 20 MINUTES

This recipe is perfect for people who are on the fence about seafood. Salmon is mild enough that it doesn't have an overpoweringly fishy taste and goes well with so many different preparations that it's a great way to ease a seafood nonbeliever into seeing the light. Plus, who can turn down homemade teriyaki sauce?

1. To prepare the teriyaki sauce, place all of the ingredients in a blender and puree until smooth. Transfer to a small saucepan and cook, while stirring, until the sauce starts to thicken. Remove from heat and set aside.

2. Preheat your oven to 375°F. Place the oil in a 12-inch cast-iron skillet and warm over medium-high heat. Add the eggplants, bell pepper, and scallion whites to the pan and cook for 5 minutes, while stirring occasionally. Add the bean sprouts and stir until all the vegetables are evenly coated by the oil.

3. Place your salmon on the vegetables, flesh side up. Season with salt, pepper, and teriyaki sauce and transfer the pan to the oven. Cook for 8 to 10 minutes, remove the pan from the oven, top with more teriyaki sauce, and serve.

INGREDIENTS:

FOR THE TERIYAKI SAUCE

1 TABLESPOON MINCED GINGER

2-3 GARLIC CLOVES, MINCED

1 TABLESPOON RICE OR WHITE VINEGAR

2 TABLESPOONS LIGHT BROWN SUGAR

¼ CUP LIGHT SOY SAUCE

1 TABLESPOON TAPIOCA STARCH OR CORNSTARCH

½ CUP WATER

FOR THE SALMON, CHINESE EGGPLANTS & BEAN SPROUTS

3 TABLESPOONS VEGETABLE OIL

4 CHINESE EGGPLANTS, CUT INTO ½-INCH-THICK SLICES ON A BIAS

1 RED BELL PEPPER, SEEDED AND JULIENNED

2 TABLESPOONS SCALLIONS, CHOPPED, GREENS RESERVED FOR GARNISH

1 CUP BEAN SPROUTS

1½ LBS. ATLANTIC SALMON FILLETS, SKIN REMOVED

SALT AND PEPPER, TO TASTE

BLACKENED TILAPIA

YIELD: 4 SERVINGS / **ACTIVE TIME:** 40 MINUTES / **TOTAL TIME:** 1 HOUR AND 30 MINUTES

The cast-iron skillet is perfect for blackening fish, which requires high heat and quick cooking. Tilapia is a wonderful fish for blackening, as it is a firm-fleshed fish that is fairly bland and thus benefits from generous seasoning. Although the result is delicious, the blackening process creates a lot of smoke, so be sure to turn the oven fan on or open the windows before you start cooking.

1. In a bowl, combine all the spices and set aside.

2. Place a 12-inch cast-iron skillet over high heat for about 10 minutes until very hot. While the skillet heats up, rinse the fillets and then pat dry with paper towels. Dip the fillets in the melted butter, covering both sides, and then press the seasoning mixture generously into both sides.

3. Put the fish in the skillet and cook for about 3 minutes per side, placing a bit of butter on top while the other side is cooking. Serve with lemon wedges.

INGREDIENTS:

2	TABLESPOONS PAPRIKA
1	TABLESPOON ONION POWDER
3	TABLESPOONS GARLIC POWDER
2	TABLESPOONS CAYENNE PEPPER
1½	TEASPOONS CELERY SALT
1½	TABLESPOONS FINELY GROUND BLACK PEPPER
1	TABLESPOON DRIED THYME
1	TABLESPOON DRIED OREGANO
1	TABLESPOON CHIPOTLE POWDER
4	(4 OZ.) BONELESS TILAPIA FILLETS
1	STICK OF BUTTER, MELTED
1	LEMON, CUT INTO 4 WEDGES, FOR SERVING

COCONUT-BRAISED VEGETABLES *with* HALIBUT

YIELD: 4 TO 6 SERVINGS / ACTIVE TIME: 30 MINUTES / TOTAL TIME: 1 HOUR

The kale is key to this one, providing a nice, soft bed for the halibut and ensuring that it remains moist and full of flavor.

1. Place the oil in a cast-iron Dutch oven and warm over medium-high heat. Add the bell peppers, habanero, sweet potatoes, and cabbage. Season with salt and pepper and cook, while stirring, for 5 to 7 minutes or until the sweet potatoes begin to caramelize.

2. Add the eggplant, ginger, and garlic and cook, while stirring often, for 10 minutes. Add the curry paste and stir to coat all of the vegetables. Cook for 2 minutes or until the contents of the pot are fragrant.

3. Add the bok choy, stock, paprika, cilantro, and coconut milk and cook for 15 to 25 minutes, until the liquid has been reduced by one-quarter.

4. Add the kale to the Dutch oven. Place the halibut fillets on top of the kale, reduce the heat to medium, cover, and cook for about 10 minutes or until the fish is cooked through.

5. Remove the cover and discard the habanero. Ladle the vegetables and the sauce into the bowls and top each one with a halibut fillet. Garnish with the scallions and serve.

INGREDIENTS:

- ¼ CUP OLIVE OIL
- 1 YELLOW BELL PEPPER, DICED
- 1 RED BELL PEPPER, DICED
- 1 HABANERO PEPPER, PIERCED
- 1 LARGE OR 2 SMALL WHITE SWEET POTATOES
- 1 CUP DICED RED CABBAGE
- SALT AND PEPPER, TO TASTE
- 3 GRAFFITI EGGPLANT, CUT INTO 2-INCH PIECES
- 2 TABLESPOONS MASHED GINGER
- 3-4 GARLIC CLOVES, MINCED
- 1-2 TABLESPOONS GREEN CURRY PASTE
- 2-3 BABY BOK CHOY, CHOPPED
- 4 CUPS FISH STOCK (SEE PAGE 454)
- 1-2 TABLESPOONS SWEET PAPRIKA
- 2 TABLESPOONS CHOPPED CILANTRO
- 3 (14 OZ.) CANS OF UNSWEETENED COCONUT MILK
- LEAVES FROM 2 BUNCHES OF TUSCAN KALE, TORN INTO LARGE PIECES
- 4-6 (4 OZ.) HALIBUT FILLETS
- SCALLIONS, CHOPPED, FOR GARNISH

RED SNAPPER *with* TOMATILLO SAUCE

YIELD: 4 SERVINGS / ACTIVE TIME: 10 MINUTES / TOTAL TIME: 10 MINUTES

This recipe comes together in under 15 minutes, but it's still as joyous and awe-inspiring as a fireworks show on the Fourth of July thanks to the charred vegetables.

1. Place a dry 12-inch cast-iron skillet over high heat and add the tomatillos, onion, garlic, and serrano pepper (if using). Cook until charred slightly and then transfer them to a blender. Add the bunch of cilantro and puree until smooth.

2. Place the oil in a 12-inch cast-iron skillet and warm over medium-high heat. When the oil starts to shimmer, add the red snapper fillets in a single layer, skin side down, and cook until they brown lightly. Do not turn them over.

3. Remove the pan from heat and allow it to cool for a few minutes. Carefully pour the tomatillo sauce over the fish. It will immediately start to simmer.

4. Place the skillet over medium heat and let it simmer until the fish is cooked through, about 4 minutes.

5. Garnish with the reserved cilantro and serve with the lime wedges and grilled vegetables.

INGREDIENTS:

1 LB. TOMATILLOS, HUSKED, RINSED, AND QUARTERED

½ WHITE ONION, CHOPPED

1 GARLIC CLOVE, CRUSHED

1 SERRANO PEPPER, STEMMED (OPTIONAL)

1 BUNCH OF FRESH CILANTRO, SOME LEAVES RESERVED FOR GARNISH

2 TABLESPOONS CORN OR VEGETABLE OIL

1½ LBS. SKINLESS RED SNAPPER FILLETS

LIME WEDGES, FOR SERVING

GRILLED VEGETABLES, FOR SERVING

PICKLED FRIED HERRING

YIELD: 4 SERVINGS / **ACTIVE TIME:** 20 MINUTES / **TOTAL TIME:** 12 HOURS AND 30 MINUTES

By combining flavors from the ocean and the forest, this dish is a wonderful ode to Scandinavian cuisine. If you have access to very tender, young pine needles, they will add a bright, evocative flavor to this rich, satisfying recipe.

1. Brush the herring fillets with the mustard.

2. Place a 12-inch cast-iron skillet over medium heat and add the butter. When it is sizzling, add the fillets and cook, while turning once, until both sides are lightly browned, 2 to 3 minutes. Remove the fillets with a thin spatula and transfer them to a baking dish.

3. Place the sugar and water in a saucepan and bring to a simmer over medium heat. Add the vinegar, salt, red onion, juniper berries, pine needles (if using), peppercorns, and bay leaves and let the mixture simmer for 2 minutes.

4. Pour the pickling liquid over the herring, sprinkle the dill over the fish, and let cool to room temperature. Cover the dish with plastic wrap and refrigerate for 12 hours or longer.

5. To serve, drain the fillets and serve with some of the pickling liquid and aromatics alongside the boiled new potatoes and toasted rye bread.

INGREDIENTS:

12   **WHOLE HERRING, BUTTERFLIED AND BONED**

½   **CUP DIJON MUSTARD**

1   **STICK OF UNSALTED BUTTER**

1   **CUP SUGAR**

1   **CUP WATER**

2   **CUPS WHITE VINEGAR**

2   **TABLESPOONS KOSHER SALT**

1   **RED ONION, SLICED THIN**

10   **JUNIPER BERRIES**

2   **SPRIGS OF FRESH, YOUNG PINE NEEDLES (OPTIONAL)**

6   **WHOLE BLACK PEPPERCORNS**

2   **BAY LEAVES**

½   **CUP CHOPPED FRESH DILL**

    BOILED NEW POTATOES, FOR SERVING

    DARK RYE BREAD, TOASTED, FOR SERVING

DUKKAH-SPICED SEA BASS

YIELD: 4 SERVINGS / ACTIVE TIME: 10 MINUTES / TOTAL TIME: 25 MINUTES

Dukkah is a Middle Eastern spice blend that's typically mixed with olive oil and served as a dip or used as a topping for hummus. But it can work in so many other recipes, including scrambled eggs, salad dressing, and this perfect weeknight preparation.

1. Pat the sea bass fillets dry with a paper towel. Place them on a plate and coat with a thick layer of the Dukkah. Let stand at room temperature for 15 minutes.

2. Place the olive oil, yogurt, and mint in a bowl and stir to combine. Set the mixture aside.

3. Place a 12-inch cast-iron skillet over medium heat and add the coconut oil. When the oil starts to shimmer, add the fillets and cook, while turning over once, until browned and cooked through, about 3 minutes per side.

4. Use a thin spatula to remove the fish from the pan and set it aside. Add the spinach and sauté until wilted, about 2 minutes.

5. Serve the fish with the spinach, a dollop of the mint-and-yogurt sauce, lemon wedges, and additional Dukkah.

DUKKAH

1. Place a 12-inch, dry cast-iron skillet over medium heat and add all of the ingredients other than the salt. Toast, while stirring continuously, until the seeds and nuts are lightly browned.

2. Remove from heat and use a mortar and pestle or a spice grinder to grind the mixture into a powder. Make sure to not grind the mixture too much, as you do not want it to be a paste.

3. Add the salt and stir to combine. The mixture will keep in an airtight container for a month.

INGREDIENTS:

4	(6 OZ.) SEA BASS FILLETS
2	TABLESPOONS DUKKAH (SEE RECIPE)
¼	CUP OLIVE OIL
1	CUP PLAIN GREEK YOGURT
	LARGE PINCH OF DRIED MINT
¼	CUP COCONUT OIL
6	CUPS FRESH SPINACH, RINSED
	LEMON WEDGES, FOR SERVING

DUKKAH

2	TABLESPOONS PUMPKIN SEEDS
2	TABLESPOONS HAZELNUTS OR PISTACHIOS
2	TABLESPOONS RAW PEANUTS
1	TEASPOON WHOLE BLACK PEPPERCORNS
1	TABLESPOON WHITE SESAME SEEDS
1	TEASPOON DRIED MINT
2	TABLESPOONS THYME LEAVES
1	TEASPOON CORIANDER SEEDS
1	TEASPOON CUMIN SEEDS
2	TEASPOONS KOSHER SALT

CORNMEAL-CRUSTED POLLOCK
with ROSEMARY CHIPS

YIELD: 2 TO 4 SERVINGS / ACTIVE TIME: 20 MINUTES / TOTAL TIME: 45 MINUTES

This New England twist on a British favorite is a must-try dish. Cook this up at the height of pollock season to really capture the essence of the fresh fish paired with the delicious cornmeal breading.

1. Place the canola oil in a cast-iron Dutch oven and bring to 350°F over medium-high heat.

2. When the oil is ready, place the sliced potatoes in the oil and cook until golden brown. Remove and set to drain on a paper towel–lined plate. Keep the oil at 350°F.

3. When drained to your liking, place the fried potatoes in a bowl with the rosemary and salt and toss to coat. Set aside.

4. Place the beaten eggs in a small bowl and the cornmeal in another. Dip the pollock fillets into the egg and then into the cornmeal, repeating until coated all over.

5. Place the battered pollock in the oil and cook until golden brown. Remove and set to drain on another paper towel–lined plate. Serve with the rosemary chips.

INGREDIENTS:

4	CUPS CANOLA OIL
5	POTATOES, SLICED INTO LONG, THIN STRIPS
3	TABLESPOONS MINCED FRESH ROSEMARY LEAVES
	SALT AND PEPPER, TO TASTE
2	EGGS, BEATEN
1	CUP CORNMEAL
1-1½	LBS. POLLOCK FILLETS

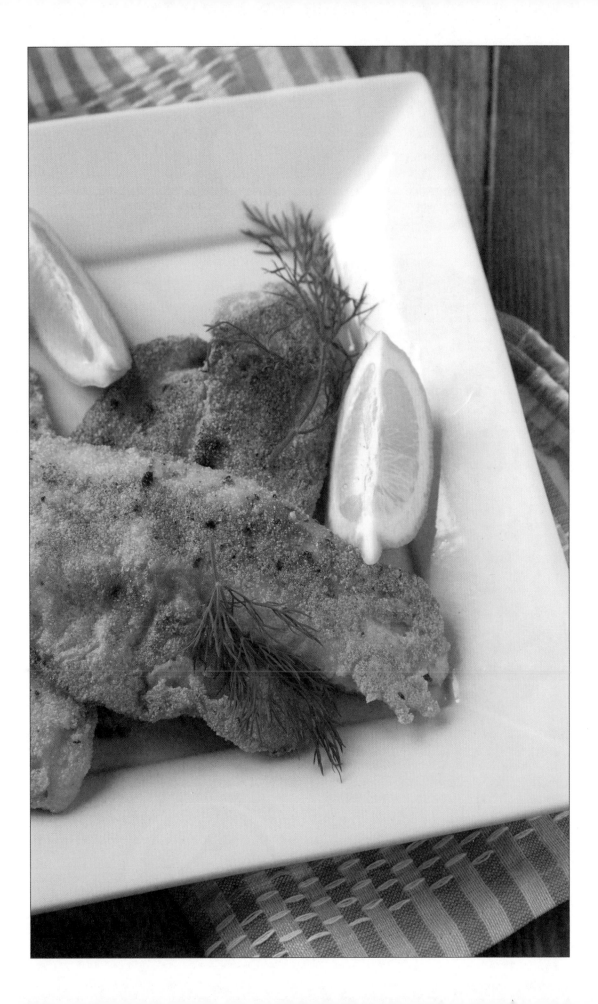

LINGUINE *with* CLAM SAUCE

YIELD: 4 TO 6 SERVINGS / **ACTIVE TIME:** 15 TO 20 MINUTES / **TOTAL TIME:** 30 TO 40 MINUTES

Easy, salty, and bursting with freshness. If you don't have much time but need to whip up something special, this dish won't let you down.

1. In a cast-iron Dutch oven, bring 4 quarts of water to a boil. Add the linguine and the sea salt. Cook for 7 minutes or until the pasta is just short of al dente. Drain, while reserving ½ cup of cooking water, and then set the linguine aside.

2. Place the Dutch oven over medium heat. Add half of the olive oil and all of the garlic to the pot and cook until the garlic starts to brown, about 2 minutes. Add the clams and wine, cover, and cook for 5 to 7 minutes or until the majority of the clams are open. Use a slotted spoon to transfer the clams to a colander. Discard any clams that do not open.

3. Add the clam juice, parsley, and pasta water to the Dutch oven. Cook until the sauce starts to thicken, about 10 minutes. Remove all the clams from their shells and mince one-quarter of them.

4. Return the linguine to the pot. Add the Parmesan, season with salt and pepper, and stir until the cheese begins to melt. Fold in the clams, drizzle with the remaining olive oil, and serve.

TIP: If you do not have access to fresh clams, you can use canned whole clams.

INGREDIENTS:

1	LB. LINGUINE
2	TABLESPOONS SEA SALT
½	CUP OLIVE OIL
3	GARLIC CLOVES, SLICED THIN
32	LITTLENECK CLAMS, SCRUBBED AND RINSED
1	CUP WHITE WINE
1	CUP CLAM JUICE
1	CUP CHOPPED ITALIAN PARSLEY
¼	CUP GRATED PARMESAN CHEESE
	SALT AND PEPPER, TO TASTE

CLAMS *with* CHORIZO

YIELD: 4 TO 6 SERVINGS / ACTIVE TIME: 15 MINUTES / TOTAL TIME: 15 MINUTES

Hailing from Spain's Basque country, this heady dish is as unique as the people who inhabit the region. Flavorful and light, it is perfect as part of a tapas-style meal.

1. Pick over the clams and discard any that are open, cracked, or damaged.

2. Place the olive oil in a 12-inch cast-iron skillet and warm over medium heat. When the oil starts to shimmer, add the onion and cook, without stirring, for 2 minutes. Add the garlic and tomatoes and cook, while stirring occasionally, until the tomatoes are browned and just beginning to burst, about 5 minutes. Add the chorizo, stir to incorporate, and cook for another 2 minutes.

3. Add the clams, cover the pot, and let them steam until the majority of the clams have opened, about 2 minutes.

4. Remove any clams that haven't opened and discard. Add the butter and stir until the butter has melted. Serve warm or at room temperature.

INGREDIENTS:

- 24 LITTLENECK CLAMS, SCRUBBED AND RINSED
- 1 TABLESPOON OLIVE OIL
- 1 YELLOW ONION, CHOPPED
- 3 GARLIC CLOVES, MINCED
- 2 CUPS CHERRY TOMATOES
- 2 OZ. SPANISH CHORIZO, MINCED
- 2 TABLESPOONS UNSALTED BUTTER, CUT INTO SMALL PIECES

MUSSELS *with* TOMATOES & ORZO

YIELD: 4 TO 6 SERVINGS / ACTIVE TIME: 30 MINUTES / TOTAL TIME: 45 MINUTES

The subtle sweetness of Prince Edward Island mussels lends this dish tons of flavor, and the mussels are perfectly sized when you take the rest of the dish's components into account. There's a lot of juice to sop up in this one, so serve with a warm loaf of bread and plenty of napkins.

1. Sort through the mussels and remove any open, cracked, or damaged ones. Next, use a thin kitchen towel and remove the "beards," which are the brown threads extending from where the two shells meet. Pull the threads toward the hinge until the beard separates from the mussel. Not every mussel will have a beard, so don't panic if you don't find one.

2. Preheat the oven to 350°F. Heat a 12-inch cast-iron skillet over medium-high heat and add the oil. When the oil is warm, add the garlic, shallot, and scallion whites and sauté for 3 minutes, while stirring constantly. Add the orzo and sun-dried tomatoes and stir to coat. Cook, while stirring occasionally, for about 10 minutes, until the orzo is slightly toasted.

3. Add the cherry tomatoes, stock, and white wine and transfer the skillet to the oven. Cook for about 10 minutes, until the orzo is cooked through and the tomatoes begin to split open.

4. Remove the skillet from the oven and place the hinge of each mussel into the orzo. Make sure the openings of the mussels are facing upward. Return to the oven and cook for 5 to 7 minutes, until the majority of the mussels are open. Remove from the oven and discard any unopened mussels. Drizzle with olive oil, season to taste, garnish with the basil and scallion greens, and serve with warm bread.

TIP: When you bring the mussels home from the market, put them in a bowl of fresh water until you begin to prepare the ingredients for the rest of the dish.

INGREDIENTS:

- 3 LBS. P.E.I. MUSSELS, WASHED
- 3 TABLESPOONS OLIVE OIL, PLUS MORE AS NEEDED
- 2 GARLIC CLOVES, SLICED THIN
- 1 LARGE SHALLOT, SLICED THIN
- 4 SCALLIONS, SLICED THIN, GREENS RESERVED FOR GARNISH
- 1 CUP ORZO
- ¼ CUP SUN-DRIED TOMATOES, SLICED THIN
- 2 PINTS OF CHERRY TOMATOES
- 1½ CUPS CHICKEN STOCK (SEE PAGES 102–3)
- ½ CUP WHITE WINE
- 2 TABLESPOONS UNSALTED BUTTER
- SALT AND PEPPER, TO TASTE
- ½ CUP CHOPPED BASIL LEAVES, FOR GARNISH
- 1 LOAF OF CRUSTY BREAD, WARMED AND SLICED

THAI MUSSELS

YIELD: 4 SERVINGS / ACTIVE TIME: 15 MINUTES / TOTAL TIME: 25 MINUTES

The combination of sweet, sour, and spicy that Thai cuisine is famous for is on full display in this delightful and flavorful dish. Tinker with the amount of lime juice until you get it just right, and don't be afraid to squeeze a little bit of lemon juice in there instead.

1. Wash the mussels thoroughly and discard any that aren't tightly closed.

2. Remove the cilantro leaves from the stems. Set the leaves aside and finely chop the stems.

3. Place the vegetable oil in a large cast-iron Dutch oven and warm until it is shimmering. Add the shallots, garlic, chopped cilantro stems, lemongrass, and the bird's eye chili and cook, while stirring, until the garlic is lightly browned, about 4 minutes.

4. Add the coconut milk and the fish sauce (if using) and bring to a boil. Add the mussels and immediately cover the pot.

5. Steam until the majority of the mussels are opened and the meat is still plump, about 5 minutes. Be careful not to overcook the mussels, as it will cause them to have a rubbery texture. Discard any unopened mussels.

6. Stir a few times to coat the mussels and add half of the lime juice. Taste and add more lime juice as needed. Ladle into warmed bowls, garnish with the reserved cilantro leaves, and serve with the rice noodles or white rice.

INGREDIENTS:

- 2 LBS. MUSSELS, WASHED AND DEBEARDED
- ½ CUP CILANTRO LEAVES AND STEMS
- 1 TABLESPOON VEGETABLE OIL
- 4 SHALLOTS, MINCED
- 2 GARLIC CLOVES, SLICED
- 1 LEMONGRASS STALK, CUT INTO 4 LARGE PIECES
- 1 BIRD'S EYE CHILI PEPPER, STEMMED AND SLICED
- 1 (14 OZ.) CAN OF COCONUT MILK
- 1 TABLESPOON FISH SAUCE (OPTIONAL)
- JUICE OF 1 LIME
- ½ LB. COOKED RICE NOODLES, FOR SERVING (OPTIONAL)
- 1 LB. COOKED WHITE RICE, FOR SERVING (OPTIONAL)

GARLIC SHRIMP

YIELD: 4 SERVINGS / ACTIVE TIME: 5 MINUTES / TOTAL TIME: 10 MINUTES

What's not to like here? Sweet, briny shrimp, loads of luscious butter, and a bit of mellowed garlic, all held together by the acidic kick of lemon. A culinary wonder that shines when made in cast iron.

1. Place a 10-inch cast-iron skillet over medium heat and add the butter.

2. When the butter has melted and is foaming, add the shrimp and cook, without stirring, for 2 minutes. Remove from the pan and set aside.

3. Reduce the heat to medium-low and add the garlic and lemon-pepper seasoning. Cook until the garlic has softened, about 2 minutes. Return the shrimp to the pan and cooked until warmed through, about 1 minute.

4. To serve, sprinkle with the lemon juice and garnish with the chives and chili pepper, if desired.

INGREDIENTS:

4   TABLESPOONS UNSALTED BUTTER, AT ROOM TEMPERATURE

1   LB. SHRIMP, PEELED AND DEVEINED

8   GARLIC CLOVES, MINCED

½   TEASPOON LEMON-PEPPER SEASONING

2   TEASPOONS FRESH LEMON JUICE

1   TEASPOON MINCED CHIVES OR PARSLEY, FOR GARNISH

1   RED CHILI PEPPER, SLICED THIN, FOR GARNISH (OPTIONAL)

GOANESE SHRIMP CURRY

YIELD: 4 SERVINGS / **ACTIVE TIME:** 10 MINUTES / **TOTAL TIME:** 20 MINUTES

Before stainless steel took over the market, two-handled cast-iron woks known as *balti* dishes were a staple in Indian kitchens. These beautiful pans, which are made for dishes like this one, go seamlessly from stove to table. While you should certainly snatch up one of these collector's items if it crosses your path, you can just as easily make this in a cast-iron skillet.

1. Place 4 of the shrimp, coconut, cumin seeds, chiles de árbol, tomatoes, and canola oil in a food processor and puree into a paste.

2. Place the cloves, cardamom pods, bay leaves, and cinnamon stick in a 12-inch cast-iron skillet and cook over medium heat until fragrant, about 1 minute. Stir in the onion, coriander, turmeric, black pepper, garlic, and ginger. Cook for 1 minute, add the shrimp paste, and stir to combine. Cook, while stirring often, for 4 minutes.

3. Add the coconut milk and water and bring to a boil. Add the jaggery (or brown sugar) and serrano peppers, stir to incorporate, and cook for another minute.

4. Reduce the heat, add the remaining shrimp and the cilantro, and simmer until the shrimp are pink and the sauce thickens slightly, 6 to 8 minutes.

5. Season with salt and ladle into warmed bowls.

NOTE: Jaggery is an unrefined sugar that typically comes from the sap of palm trees. It is frequently employed in Asian and Middle Eastern cuisines.

INGREDIENTS:

16   LARGE SHRIMP, PEELED AND DEVEINED

1   CUP GRATED UNSWEETENED COCONUT

1   TEASPOON CUMIN SEEDS

3   CHILES DE ÁRBOL, STEMMED

2   LARGE TOMATOES, CHOPPED

¼   CUP CANOLA OIL

5   WHOLE CLOVES

4   GREEN CARDAMOM PODS

2   BAY LEAVES

1   CINNAMON STICK

1   YELLOW ONION, CHOPPED

1   TABLESPOON GROUND CORIANDER

1   TEASPOON TURMERIC

1   TEASPOON GROUND BLACK PEPPER

2   GARLIC CLOVES, MASHED

1   TEASPOON MASHED GINGER

1   (14 OZ.) CAN OF COCONUT MILK

½   CUP WATER

2   TABLESPOONS JAGGERY OR BROWN SUGAR

2   SERRANO PEPPERS, SEEDED AND SLICED THIN

1   CUP CHOPPED CILANTRO

SALT, TO TASTE

LOBSTER SHEPHERD'S PIE

YIELD: 4 TO 6 SERVINGS / **ACTIVE TIME:** 45 MINUTES / **TOTAL TIME:** 1 HOUR AND 30 MINUTES

This recipe takes "fancy" food—lobster—and turns it into something down-to-earth yet elegant. It makes a wonderful dinner for a date night, and it also shines at a Sunday brunch with family and friends.

1. Preheat the oven to 350°F.

2. Put the potato pieces in a large saucepan or pot and cover with cold water. Add the salt. Bring the water to a boil, reduce to a simmer, and cook the potatoes until soft, about 20 minutes. When they can be easily pierced with a sharp knife, they're cooked.

3. Drain the potato pieces and put them in a large bowl. Add 6 tablespoons of the butter and the milk and use a potato masher to make the mashed potatoes. The mashed potatoes should be creamy. If they are too soupy, add the yogurt in 1-tablespoon increments until they have the right consistency. Season with salt and pepper and set aside.

4. In a 12-inch cast-iron skillet, melt 2 tablespoons of butter and cook the leeks over medium heat, while stirring, until they just soften, about 2 minutes. Reduce heat to low and cover. Cook an additional 5 to 8 minutes, stirring occasionally, until tender.

5. Stir in the flour and cook for 1 minute. Add the broth, raise the heat to medium-high, and bring to a boil. Reduce heat to low and let simmer, uncovered, for 2 minutes.

6. Stir in lobster, peas, corn, and Sherry and remove the skillet from heat.

7. Spread the mashed potatoes over the mixture, distributing the potatoes evenly and smoothing the top. Cut the remaining 2 tablespoons of butter into slivers and dot the potatoes with them.

8. Cover with foil and bake for 30 minutes. Remove the foil and cook another 10 minutes, until the potatoes are just browned.

9. Allow to cool slightly before serving.

INGREDIENTS:

- 6 RUSSET POTATOES, PEELED AND CUBED
- ½ TEASPOON SALT
- 10 TABLESPOONS UNSALTED BUTTER, DIVIDED INTO TABLESPOONS
- ½ CUP WHOLE MILK
- PLAIN YOGURT, AS NEEDED
- SALT AND PEPPER, TO TASTE
- 6 LARGE LEEKS, WHITE AND LIGHT GREEN PARTS ONLY, HALVED LENGTHWISE, CUT INTO ½-INCH PIECES, AND RINSED WELL
- 2 TABLESPOONS ALL-PURPOSE FLOUR
- 1 CUP CHICKEN OR VEGETABLE BROTH
- 3 CUPS COOKED LOBSTER MEAT
- ¾ CUP PEAS
- ½ CUP CORN
- 1 TABLESPOON DRY SHERRY

NEW ENGLAND LOBSTER ROLLS
with BROWNED BUTTER–MILK CRUMBS

YIELD: 2 TO 4 SERVINGS / **ACTIVE TIME:** 10 MINUTES / **TOTAL TIME:** 25 MINUTES

Summer means seafood in New England, and no transformation of the ocean's bounty is more iconic than the lobster roll. This classic traditionally comes in one of two styles—either with mayonnaise or browned butter—and this recipe provides the best of both worlds.

1. Place the butter in a small saucepan and melt it over low heat.

2. When the butter is melted, stir in the milk powder and cook until the mixture starts to turn golden brown.

3. Remove the pan from heat and strain through a fine sieve over a bowl. Store the crumbs in an airtight container and reserve the browned butter.

4. Place the buns in a cast-iron skillet with the reserved browned butter and cook for 1 minute on each side, until golden brown. Remove and set aside.

5. Place the lobster meat, mayonnaise, salt, and pepper in a mixing bowl and stir to combine.

6. Spoon the dressed lobster into the toasted buns, top with a generous amount of the browned butter–milk crumbs, and serve.

INGREDIENTS:

- 1   STICK OF UNSALTED BUTTER
- 1   CUP NONFAT MILK POWDER
- 2-4   HOT DOG OR HAMBURGER BUNS
-   MEAT FROM 2 TO 3 COOKED CHICKEN LOBSTERS
- 2   TABLESPOONS MAYONNAISE
-   SALT AND PEPPER, TO TASTE

LOBSTER TOSTADAS *with* CHARRED CORN SALSA *and* CILANTRO-LIME SOUR CREAM

YIELD: 4 SERVINGS / ACTIVE TIME: 20 MINUTES / TOTAL TIME: 1 HOUR AND 30 MINUTES

A tortilla is one of the most versatile tools in a chef's arsenal, able to bring together an astonishing amount of ingredients and still shine. Lobster and corn are natural partners, but charring the corn adds a bit of depth and mystery to this dish.

1. Preheat your gas or charcoal grill to 400°F.

2. Drizzle the corn with the olive oil, season with salt and pepper, and place them on the grill. Cook, while turning, until they are charred all over. Remove from the grill and let cool.

3. When the corn is cool enough to handle, remove the kernels and place them in a mixing bowl. Add the jalapeño, onion, garlic, lime juice, cilantro, and tomato and stir to combine.

4. Prepare the sour cream. Place all of the ingredients in a mixing bowl, stir to combine, and set aside.

5. Place the canola oil in a cast-iron Dutch oven and warm to 350°F over medium-high heat. Working with one tortilla at a time, place them into the oil and fry until golden brown. Remove from the oil, transfer to a paper towel–lined plate, and season with salt and paprika.

6. Spread some of the sour cream on each tortilla and top with the salsa and lobster meat. Garnish with jalapeño, cilantro, and red cabbage and serve with lime wedges.

INGREDIENTS:

FOR THE TOSTADAS & SALSA

2 EARS OF CORN, SHUCKED, AND RINSED

1 TABLESPOON OLIVE OIL

SALT AND PEPPER, TO TASTE

1 SMALL JALAPEÑO PEPPER, SEEDED AND DICED, PLUS MORE FOR GARNISH

¼ CUP DICED RED ONION

1 GARLIC CLOVE, MINCED

1½ TABLESPOONS FRESH LIME JUICE

¼ CUP CHOPPED CILANTRO, PLUS MORE FOR GARNISH

½ CUP DICED TOMATO

2 CUPS CANOLA OIL

8 CORN TORTILLAS (SEE PAGE 169)

PAPRIKA, TO TASTE

MEAT FROM 4 COOKED CHICKEN LOBSTERS

RED CABBAGE, DICED, FOR GARNISH

LIME WEDGES, FOR SERVING

FOR THE SOUR CREAM

½ CUP CHOPPED CILANTRO

¼ CUP FRESH LIME JUICE

1¼ CUPS SOUR CREAM

1½ TEASPOONS SALT

½ TEASPOON BLACK PEPPER

WALNUT & BROWN BUTTER SCALLOPS
with BUTTERNUT SQUASH

YIELD: 4 TO 6 SERVINGS / ACTIVE TIME: 40 MINUTES / TOTAL TIME: 1 HOUR AND 15 MINUTES

Here's another delicious and surprisingly simple recipe. If you are trying to impress someone, the combination of fresh, tender scallops and rich, nutty brown butter is a good start.

1. Place a 12-inch cast-iron skillet over medium-high heat. Remove the foot from each scallop and discard. Pat the scallops dry with a paper towel and lightly season both sides with salt and pepper.

2. Place 1 tablespoon of the butter and the olive oil in the pan. Add the scallops one at a time, softly pressing down as you place them in the skillet. Cook the scallops for approximately 3 minutes and then flip them over. The scallops should not stick to the pan when you go to flip them. If the scallops do stick, cook until a brown crust is visible. Once you have flipped the scallops, cook for 2 minutes, remove, and set aside.

3. Add the butternut squash, season with salt and pepper, and cook for 12 to 15 minutes or until tender and caramelized. Remove the squash and set aside.

4. Add the walnuts to the pan and cook, while stirring often, for 2 minutes or until the nuts are fragrant. Add the remaining butter to the pan and cook for 2 to 3 minutes, until it has browned.

5. Place the squash in the middle of a plate and then place the scallops around and on top of the squash. Spoon the walnuts and butter over the dish, garnish with the scallions, and serve.

TIPS: U10 is a unit of measurement that refers to the amount of scallops per pound, meaning that you will have 10 or fewer.

The foot of a scallop is a ½ × 1-inch milky white piece attached to the side. It can easily be peeled off.

INGREDIENTS:

- 24 JUMBO (U10) SCALLOPS
- SALT AND PEPPER, TO TASTE
- 1 STICK OF UNSALTED BUTTER
- 2 TABLESPOONS OLIVE OIL
- 3-4 BUTTERNUT SQUASH, PEELED, SEEDED, AND DICED
- 1 CUP RAW, SHELLED WALNUTS
- SCALLIONS, CHOPPED, FOR GARNISH

SEAFOOD PAELLA

YIELD: 4 TO 6 SERVINGS / **ACTIVE TIME:** 1 HOUR AND 30 MINUTES / **TOTAL TIME:** 2 HOURS

Paella is a rice dish that hails from Valencia, Spain. Its yellow hue comes from saffron threads, and it is chock-full of everything good: rice, meat, fish, and vegetables. This recipe is made with more seafood than meat, and it's for a smaller serving size than the traditional platter that can feed a party.

1. Preheat the oven to 425°F.

2. In a saucepan, bring the chicken broth to a simmer over medium heat.

3. Place a 12-inch cast-iron skillet over medium-high heat. Add the olive oil, onion, and garlic, and cook, stirring occasionally, until the onion is translucent, about 3 minutes. Add the paprika and saffron, and cook, while stirring, for another minute.

4. Add the rice, stirring to coat, then stir in the tomatoes and wine. Bring to a boil and cook until the liquid is reduced by half, about 2 minutes. Add the hot chicken broth and peas, stir, then bring to a boil and cook for 5 minutes. Season with salt and pepper.

5. Add the calamari and chorizo and stir to combine. Put the skillet in the oven and bake for about 30 minutes, until the calamari are soft. Scatter the shrimp and mussels over the top of the paella and return to the oven. Cook until the shrimp are opaque and the mussels have opened, 5 to 10 minutes, keeping an eye on the dish so the seafood on top doesn't overcook.

6. Remove from the oven, discard any mussels that didn't open, let rest for about 5 minutes, and serve.

INGREDIENTS:

4	CUPS CHICKEN BROTH
2	TABLESPOONS OLIVE OIL
1	YELLOW ONION, DICED
4	GARLIC CLOVES, MINCED
1	TEASPOON SMOKED PAPRIKA
½	TEASPOON SAFFRON, CRUSHED
2½	CUPS SHORT-GRAIN RICE
2	RIPE TOMATOES, SEEDED AND CHOPPED
1	CUP DRY WHITE WINE
1	TEASPOON SALT
	FRESHLY GROUND BLACK PEPPER, TO TASTE
1	CUP FROZEN PEAS
½	LB. CALAMARI, CUT INTO 1-INCH PIECES
½	LB. SPANISH CHORIZO, CUT INTO ¼-INCH ROUNDS
½	LB. SMALL SHRIMP, PEELED AND DEVEINED
16	MUSSELS, WASHED AND DEBEARDED

OYSTER SLIDERS *with* RED PEPPER MAYONNAISE

YIELD: 4 SERVINGS / ACTIVE TIME: 30 MINUTES / TOTAL TIME: 1 HOUR AND 15 MINUTES

The briny taste of the oysters and the sweetness of the King's Hawaiian Rolls pair together for the perfect summer meal. If you're not a fan of King's Hawaiian Rolls for some reason, you can always use potato buns or another sweet bread product to serve these on.

1. Preheat the oven to 400°F.

2. Place the red peppers on a baking sheet and bake, while turning occasionally, for 35 to 40 minutes, until they are blistered all over. Remove from the oven and let cool. When cool enough to handle, remove the skins and seeds and set the flesh aside.

3. Place the oil in an enameled cast-iron Dutch oven and bring it to 350°F over medium-high heat.

4. Place the cornmeal and salt in a bowl and stir to combine.

5. When the oil is ready, dip the oyster meat into the beaten eggs and the cornmeal-and-salt mixture. Repeat until evenly coated.

6. Place the oysters in the Dutch oven and fry until golden brown, about 3 to 5 minutes. Remove from the oil and set on a paper towel–lined plate to drain.

7. Place the butter in a skillet and melt over medium heat. Place the buns in the skillet and toast until lightly browned. Remove and set aside.

8. Place the roasted peppers and mayonnaise in a blender and puree until smooth. Spread the red pepper mayonnaise on the buns, add the fried oysters, and serve.

INGREDIENTS:

3	RED BELL PEPPERS
1	CUP CANOLA OIL
1	CUP CORNMEAL
	SALT, TO TASTE
½	LB. OYSTER MEAT
2	EGGS, BEATEN
1	TABLESPOON UNSALTED BUTTER
4	KING'S HAWAIIAN ROLLS
½	CUP MAYONNAISE

VEGETABLES

There was a time, not too long ago, when people shied away from a little char on their vegetables but gladly boiled them into a sad, defeated state. Thankfully, we've moved on from those days and learned to appreciate a crisp, verdant, or even raw vegetable. By embracing fresh flavor and learning how to enhance it with seasoning, we've come to show respect for the produce our farmers work so hard to harvest.

Using your cast-iron cookware, you can create truly masterful vegetable dishes that will appeal to vegetarians, vegans, and meat-eaters alike. Try a new-to-you vegetable—perhaps the Roasted Sunchokes (see page 553) or Honey Roasted Turnips with Hazelnuts (see page 520) pique your interest—or go with one of the twists on an old classic, such as the Winter Tomatoes with Thyme (see page 546) or Green Beans with Bacon on page 558 (which, in my opinion, is the ideal cast-iron skillet recipe). After a deep dive into this chapter, you'll realize mom was right after all: you should eat your vegetables.

MUSHROOM & CHARD SHEPHERD'S PIE

YIELD: 4 TO 6 SERVINGS / ACTIVE TIME: 45 MINUTES / TOTAL TIME: 1 HOUR AND 30 MINUTES

Here's a great recipe for a shepherd's pie that's filling and earthy but has no meat in it. It's topped with mashed potatoes, which makes it more of a meal. Serve with a big green salad for a special brunch or a light dinner.

1. Preheat the oven to 350°F.

2. After peeling and cubing the potatoes, give them a final rinse to get all the dirt off. Put the potato pieces in a large saucepan or pot and cover with cold water. Add the salt. Bring the water to a boil, reduce to a simmer, and cook the potatoes until soft, about 20 minutes. When they can be easily pierced with a sharp knife, they're cooked.

3. Drain the potato pieces and put them in a large bowl. Add 6 tablespoons of the butter and all of the milk and use a potato masher to make the mashed potatoes. The mashed potatoes should be creamy. If they are too soupy, add the yogurt in 1-tablespoon increments until they have the right consistency. Season with salt and pepper and set aside.

4. In a 12-inch cast-iron skillet, melt 3 tablespoons of the butter over medium heat. Add the onion and cook until just softened, about 3 minutes. Add the mushrooms, the chopped stems of the chard (not the leaves), and the Worcestershire sauce. Cook for about 3 minutes, while stirring frequently, then reduce the heat to low and continue to cook for another 5 minutes or so, until the mushrooms and chard stems are soft. If the mixture seems dry, add a tablespoon of olive oil.

5. Increase the heat to medium and add the chard leaves. Cook, while stirring constantly, until the leaves wilt, about 3 minutes. Remove the skillet from heat and season with salt and pepper.

6. Spread the mashed potatoes over the mixture, distributing the potatoes evenly and smoothing the top. Cut the remaining 2 tablespoons of butter into slivers and dot the potatoes with them.

7. Cover with foil and bake for 25 minutes. Remove the foil and cook another 10 minutes, until the topping is just browned and the filling is bubbly.

INGREDIENTS:

- 6 RUSSET POTATOES, PEELED AND CUBED
- ½ TEASPOON SALT, PLUS MORE TO TASTE
- 11 TABLESPOONS UNSALTED BUTTER, DIVIDED INTO INDIVIDUAL TABLESPOONS
- ½ CUP WHOLE MILK
  PLAIN YOGURT, AS NEEDED
  PEPPER, TO TASTE
- 1 SMALL ONION, MINCED
- 3 CUPS CHOPPED ASSORTED MUSHROOMS
- 1 BUNCH OF SWISS CHARD, STEMMED AND CHOPPED (OR 4 CUPS FRESH SPINACH LEAVES)
- 1 TABLESPOON WORCESTERSHIRE SAUCE
  OLIVE OIL, AS NEEDED

VEGGIE BURGERS

YIELD: 4 TO 6 SERVINGS / ACTIVE TIME: 30 MINUTES / TOTAL TIME: 1 HOUR

For those times when you want a break from meat but want the great taste and texture of a juicy hamburger, try making these vegetarian burgers. Be sure you have ripe tomatoes and avocadoes to put on them when serving.

1. In a food processor or blender, combine half the beans with the scallions and roasted red peppers. Pulse until you have a thick paste. Transfer to a large bowl.

2. Add the corn, bread crumbs, egg, cilantro, cumin, cayenne, pepper, and lime juice. Stir to blend. Add the remaining beans and stir vigorously to get all ingredients to stick together. Cover the bowl with plastic wrap and let sit at room temperature for about 30 minutes.

3. Heat a 12-inch cast-iron skillet over medium-high heat. Form mixture into 4 to 6 patties. Add the olive oil to the skillet and, when hot, add the patties. Cover the skillet and cook for about 5 minutes per side.

4. Serve immediately on hamburger buns with slices of tomato, avocado, and red onion.

INGREDIENTS:

- 1 (14 OZ.) CAN OF BLACK BEANS, DRAINED AND RINSED
- ⅓ CUP MINCED SCALLIONS
- ¼ CUP ROASTED RED PEPPERS, CHOPPED
- ¼ CUP COOKED CORN
- ¼ CUP PLAIN BREAD CRUMBS
- 1 EGG, LIGHTLY BEATEN
- 2 TABLESPOONS CHOPPED CILANTRO
- ½ TEASPOON CUMIN
- ½ TEASPOON CAYENNE PEPPER
- ½ TEASPOON FRESHLY GROUND BLACK PEPPER
- 1 TEASPOON FRESH LIME JUICE
- 1 TABLESPOON OLIVE OIL
  HAMBURGER BUNS, FOR SERVING
  TOMATO SLICES, FOR SERVING
  AVOCADO SLICES, FOR SERVING
  RED ONION, SLICED THIN, FOR SERVING

ROASTED CAULIFLOWER STEAKS

YIELD: 4 TO 6 SERVINGS / ACTIVE TIME: 30 MINUTES / TOTAL TIME: 1 HOUR

There's something about roasting cauliflower that accentuates its sweet, nutty flavor. Season it with warm, earthy spices like cumin and turmeric, and you have a delicious alternative to a starchy side, full of flavor and nutrition.

1. Preheat the oven to 425°F.

2. In a bowl, combine the oil, salt, pepper, and spices and whisk to mix thoroughly.

3. Cut the cauliflower cross-wise into ½-inch slices. Put the slices in the skillet and brush the tops liberally with the oil mixture. Turn the "steaks" over and brush the other side.

4. Put the steaks in a 12-inch cast-iron skillet, place the skillet in the oven, and roast for about 20 minutes, turning the pieces over after 10 minutes. A toothpick inserted in the flesh should go in easily to indicate that the cauliflower is cooked through.

5. Serve the slices hot, with a side of sour cream, if desired.

TIP: This recipe can be made with cauliflower florets, too. Instead of slicing the cauliflower into cross sections, just pick off the florets. Put them in the bowl of seasoned oil and toss to coat. Put the florets in the skillet and bake, shaking the pan halfway through to turn the pieces.

INGREDIENTS:

1½ TABLESPOONS OLIVE OIL

1 TEASPOON SALT

FRESHLY GROUND PEPPER, TO TASTE

½ TEASPOON CUMIN

½ TEASPOON CORIANDER

½ TEASPOON TURMERIC

¼ TEASPOON CAYENNE PEPPER

1 HEAD OF CAULIFLOWER, TRIMMED

SOUR CREAM, FOR SERVING (OPTIONAL)

VEGETABLE FRITTATA

YIELD: 4 SERVINGS / ACTIVE TIME: 20 MINUTES / TOTAL TIME: 40 MINUTES

Make this veggie-loaded egg dish as a hearty breakfast or a light dinner. It's a perfect thing to cook up with fresh ingredients bought at the local farmers market.

1. Preheat the broiler to low.

2. In a bowl, whisk the eggs until combined.

3. Heat a 10-inch cast-iron skillet over medium-high heat. Melt the butter in the skillet. Add the onion and garlic and cook, while stirring, until the onion is translucent, about 3 minutes.

4. Add the carrot and zucchini slices, lower the heat to medium, and cook, stirring occasionally, until softened, about 5 minutes. Add the red pepper and continue to cook, about 5 minutes. Add the parsley.

5. Pour the eggs over the vegetables. Shake the skillet to distribute evenly. Season with salt and pepper and sprinkle with red pepper flakes, if desired. Cover and cook until eggs are cooked through, about 10 minutes.

6. Put the skillet in the oven and cook for a few minutes to "toast" the top. Remove from the oven and let the frittata for a few minutes before serving.

TIP: Make this dish even heartier by adding sweet potatoes. Wash a large sweet potato and pierce it all over with a fork. Put it on a kitchen towel in the microwave and cook for 3 minutes. Using a dish towel, because it will be hot, turn the potato over and cook another 2 or 3 minutes. Allow to cool for a minute or so, and cut the potato into bite-sized pieces. Add it to the skillet after the red peppers.

INGREDIENTS:

6	EGGS
3	TABLESPOONS UNSALTED BUTTER
½	ONION, MINCED
2	GARLIC CLOVES, MINCED
2	CARROTS, PEELED AND SLICED THIN
½	SMALL ZUCCHINI, SLICED THIN
½	RED PEPPER, SEEDED AND SLICED THIN
⅓	CUP MINCED PARSLEY LEAVES
	SALT AND PEPPER, TO TASTE
1	TEASPOON RED PEPPER FLAKES (OPTIONAL)

BLISTERED SHISHITO PEPPERS

YIELD: 4 TO 6 SERVINGS / ACTIVE TIME: 5 MINUTES / TOTAL TIME: 10 MINUTES

Shishito peppers are slightly twisted, bright green, and utterly delicious. Eating them is a bit like putting your taste buds through a round of Russian roulette, since approximately one in every 10 is spicy, and there's no way to tell until you bite down. The rest are as mild as can be. If you can't find shishitos, you can easily substitute padrón peppers.

1. Add olive oil to a 12-inch cast-iron skillet until it is ¼-inch deep and warm over medium heat.

2. When the oil is shimmering, add the peppers and cook, while turning once or twice, until they are blistered and golden brown, about 2 minutes. Take care not to crowd the peppers in the pan, and work in batches if necessary.

3. Transfer the blistered peppers to a paper towel–lined plate. Season with salt and serve with lemon wedges.

INGREDIENTS:

OLIVE OIL, FOR FRYING

2 LBS. SHISHITO PEPPERS

MALDON SEA SALT, TO TASTE

1 LEMON, CUT INTO WEDGES, FOR SERVING

CRISPY & TENDER ASPARAGUS

YIELD: 4 SERVINGS / ACTIVE TIME: 20 MINUTES / TOTAL TIME: 30 MINUTES

Making asparagus in the skillet is almost like cooking it on the grill. The outside gets crisp while the inside becomes tender. The thinner the asparagus, the faster the stalks will cook, so if you are working with super-fresh, thin stalks, you may need to reduce the cooking times in the recipe.

1. Place a 12-inch cast-iron skillet over medium-high heat. When hot, add the oil and let that get hot. Add the asparagus. Using tongs, keep turning them so they cook evenly in the oil. Cook the asparagus until they are bright green and hot on the outside but tender on the inside.

2. Add the garlic, salt, and pepper, and shake the pan to distribute evenly. Cook for another 2 minutes. Transfer to a serving platter and serve with lemon wedges.

INGREDIENTS:

3   TABLESPOONS OLIVE OIL

1   BUNCH OF THIN ASPARAGUS, WOODY ENDS REMOVED

1   GARLIC CLOVE, MINCED

½   TEASPOON SALT

½   TEASPOON FRESHLY GROUND PEPPER

     LEMON WEDGES, FOR SERVING

ROASTED ROOT VEGETABLES

YIELD: 4 TO 6 SERVINGS / ACTIVE TIME: 20 MINUTES / TOTAL TIME: 1 HOUR

If you find yourself at home on a fall morning with bunches of root vegetables that looked so good at the farmers market but are now baffling you as a cook, this recipe is here to save the day.

1. Preheat the oven to 400°F.

2. In a large bowl, combine all the vegetables and pour the olive oil over them. Season with salt and pepper and toss to coat.

3. Put the vegetables in a 12-inch cast-iron skillet and sprinkle the rosemary over everything.

4. Put the skillet in the oven and bake for about 40 minutes, turning the vegetables over after the first 20 minutes. Serve warm.

VARIATION: Substitute Herbes de Provence for the rosemary. This is a French blend of rosemary, fennel, basil, thyme, marjoram, basil, tarragon, and lavender—all the goodness of a Provençal herb garden.

INGREDIENTS:

2   SMALL PARSNIPS, TRIMMED, SCRUBBED, AND CUT INTO BATONS

1   TURNIP, TRIMMED, SCRUBBED, AND CUT INTO BATONS

4   SMALL BEETS, TRIMMED, SCRUBBED, AND CUT INTO BATONS

4   CARROTS, TRIMMED, SCRUBBED, AND CUT INTO BATONS

½   ONION, SLICED

1   SMALL BULB FENNEL, TRIMMED AND CUT INTO MATCHSTICKS

¼   CUP OLIVE OIL

    SALT AND PEPPER, TO TASTE

2   TEASPOONS DRIED ROSEMARY

HONEY ROASTED TURNIPS *with* HAZELNUTS

YIELD: 4 TO 6 SERVINGS / ACTIVE TIME: 15 MINUTES / TOTAL TIME: 40 MINUTES

Turnips, elevated. Try to make this using the smallest turnips you can find, with Japanese turnips topping the list of desirable varieties. If you don't have any hazelnuts, or don't have enough, try using walnuts. The Crème Fraîche is not necessary, but we don't recommend going without it.

1. Preheat the oven to 350°F.

2. Place a 12-inch cast-iron skillet over medium-high heat for 5 minutes, until it is very hot.

3. Place the turnips, olive oil, and honey in a large bowl, season with salt and pepper, and toss to coat. Place the turnips in the skillet, cut side down, and transfer the skillet to the oven. Roast until tender, about 30 minutes.

4. While the turnips are roasting, place the Crème Fraîche, chives, lemon zest, and lemon juice in a bowl and whisk to combine. Season with salt and pepper and set aside.

5. To serve, sprinkle the hazelnuts over the turnips and drizzle the Crème Fraîche mixture over the top.

INGREDIENTS:

16 SMALL TURNIPS, TRIMMED AND QUARTERED

¼ CUP OLIVE OIL

½ CUP HONEY

SALT AND PEPPER, TO TASTE

¾ CUP CRÈME FRAÎCHE (SEE PAGE 566)

¼ CUP THINLY SLICED CHIVES

ZEST AND JUICE OF 1 LEMON

½ CUP HAZELNUTS, TOASTED AND CHOPPED

SCANDINAVIAN BEETS

YIELD: 4 TO 6 SERVINGS / **ACTIVE TIME:** 20 MINUTES / **TOTAL TIME:** 1 HOUR AND 15 MINUTES

In Scandinavia, beets are one of the most popular vegetables. And, when you top them with the traditional creamy sauce and fresh dill, you'll see why.

1. Preheat the oven to 400°F. Place a 12-inch cast-iron skillet in the oven and let it heat up while you prepare the beets.

2. Place the beets and vegetable oil in a bowl and toss to coat. Season with salt and toss to evenly distribute.

3. Using oven mitts or a pot holder, remove the skillet from the oven. Place the beets in the skillet in a single layer and add the water. Cover the skillet with aluminum foil, return it to the oven, and roast for 35 minutes. Remove the foil, return the skillet to the oven, and roast until the beets are tender, about 30 minutes. Remove and let the beets cool slightly.

4. When the beets are cool enough to handle, place a colander in the sink. With the water running, remove the skin from the beets and then slice them in half lengthwise. Place them in a bowl with the slices of apple.

5. Place the sour cream, mayonnaise, vinegar, and sugar in a bowl and whisk to combine.

6. To serve, place the beets and apples on a plate, top with a dollop of the sauce, and garnish with the dill.

INGREDIENTS:

10	SMALL BEETS, TOPS TRIMMED
2	TABLESPOONS VEGETABLE OIL
	SALT, TO TASTE
½	CUP WATER
1	LARGE TART APPLE, CORED AND SLICED INTO HALF-MOONS
½	CUP SOUR CREAM
2	TEASPOONS MAYONNAISE
1	TEASPOON WHITE WINE VINEGAR
1	TEASPOON SUGAR
½	CUP CHOPPED FRESH DILL, FOR GARNISH

CORN FRITTERS

YIELD: 4 SERVINGS / **ACTIVE TIME:** 20 MINUTES / **TOTAL TIME:** 40 MINUTES

Sweet yet substantive, fancy yet simple, corn fritters are a family chef's best friend because they work no matter the occasion.

1. In a large bowl, combine the egg, sugar, salt, butter, baking powder, flour, and milk and stir thoroughly. Add the corn and stir to incorporate.

2. Heat a 12-inch cast-iron skillet over medium-high heat and add the oil. Drop spoonfuls of batter into the skillet and gently press down on them. Brown on both sides, about 3 minutes per side. Remove with a spatula and put on a paper towel–lined plate to drain. Cover with foil to keep the cooked fritters warm. When all of the fritters are cooked, serve immediately.

TIP: The best corn to use for this is leftover cooked corn on the cob that's been in the refrigerator overnight. Otherwise, you can take frozen corn and thaw the kernels, drying them before putting them in the batter. If you use canned corn, be sure all water is drained from it, and choose a high-quality brand so the kernels are firm and sweet, not mushy.

INGREDIENTS:

1   EGG, BEATEN WELL

1   TEASPOON SUGAR

½   TEASPOON SALT

1   TABLESPOON UNSALTED BUTTER, MELTED

2   TEASPOONS BAKING POWDER

1   CUP ALL-PURPOSE FLOUR

⅔   CUP WHOLE MILK

2   CUPS COOKED CORN, AT ROOM TEMPERATURE

3   TABLESPOONS CANOLA OIL

CREAMED CORN

YIELD: 8 TO 10 SERVINGS / **ACTIVE TIME:** 30 MINUTES / **TOTAL TIME:** 1 HOUR

When you're tired of corn on the cob and in need of a little comfort, try this fresh spin on a canned classic.

1. Standing each ear of corn up in the middle of a large baking dish, use a sharp knife to cut down the sides and remove all the kernels. With the kernels off, take the blade of a dull knife and press it along each side of the ears to "milk" the cob of its liquid. Discard the milked cobs.

2. Place a 12-inch cast-iron skillet over medium heat and, when hot, lower the heat and add the butter so it melts slowly. When melted, add the corn kernels and milk from the cobs and stir to coat. Increase the heat to medium-high and add the water and half-and-half. Bring to a boil, while stirring constantly, and then reduce to low heat. Add the salt and pepper.

3. In a measuring cup, add the flour and warm water and mix until thoroughly combined. Drizzle the flour mixture into the corn, continuing to stir until the sauce thickens. If it gets too thick, add some more half-and-half. Serve hot.

INGREDIENTS:

12   EARS OF FRESH CORN, SHUCKED AND RINSED

3   TABLESPOONS UNSALTED BUTTER

1   CUP WATER, AT ROOM TEMPERATURE

1   CUP HALF-AND-HALF, PLUS MORE AS NEEDED

½   TEASPOON SALT

    FRESHLY GROUND BLACK PEPPER, TO TASTE

3   TABLESPOONS ALL-PURPOSE FLOUR

½   CUP WARM WATER (110°F)

SHERRIED MUSHROOMS *with* PINE NUTS

YIELD: 4 SERVINGS / ACTIVE TIME: 10 MINUTES / TOTAL TIME: 25 MINUTES

A simple roasted mushroom is a wonder to behold, but it is also a terrific foundation for a ton of great dishes. This dynamic mélange is one, featuring myriad tastes and textures.

1. Place a 12-inch cast-iron skillet over medium heat. When it is hot, add the pine nuts and toast until lightly browned. Remove from the pan and let cool. When they are cool enough to handle, mince and set aside.

2. Add 1 tablespoon of the olive oil, the salt, sugar, and shallot to the skillet and cook until the shallot is translucent. Add the Sherry and vinegar and cook for 5 minutes, until the liquid has reduced. Add the orange zest and then transfer the mixture to a bowl.

3. Add the remaining olive oil to the skillet and warm until it starts to smoke. Add the mushrooms and cook, without stirring, for 3 minutes. Add the butter, stir, and cook until the mushrooms are browned all over and wilted. Remove from the pan and add to the shallot-and-Sherry mixture. Toss to coat.

4. Garnish with the daikon radish, parsley, and toasted pine nuts and serve.

INGREDIENTS:

2   CUPS PINE NUTS

5   TABLESPOONS OLIVE OIL

    PINCH OF SALT

    PINCH OF SUGAR

1   LARGE SHALLOT, MINCED

1   CUP SHERRY

¼   CUP SHERRY VINEGAR

    ZEST OF 1 ORANGE

6   CUPS ASSORTED WILD MUSHROOMS (OYSTER, MAITAKE, SHIITAKE, ETC.)

4   TABLESPOONS UNSALTED BUTTER

1   CUP THINLY SLICED DAIKON RADISH, FOR GARNISH

    PARSLEY LEAVES, CHOPPED, FOR GARNISH

MARVELOUS MUSHROOMS

YIELD: 4 SERVINGS / ACTIVE TIME: 20 MINUTES / TOTAL TIME: 30 MINUTES

There are many kinds of mushrooms available, and you can mix and match them as you desire. Sautéing mushrooms in the skillet with lots of butter yields a rich, earthy stew that is delicious with steak and potatoes. Or simply serve these mushrooms as a topping for burgers or baked polenta with cheese.

1. Place a 12-inch cast-iron skillet over medium-high heat. Add the butter. When melted, add the mushrooms. Cook, while stirring, until the mushrooms begin to soften, about 5 minutes. Reduce the heat to low and let the mushrooms simmer, stirring occasionally, until they cook down, about 15 to 20 minutes.

2. Add the vermouth and stir, then season with salt and pepper. Simmer until the mushrooms are tender. Serve hot.

INGREDIENTS:

- 6 TABLESPOONS UNSALTED BUTTER, CUT INTO SMALL PIECES
- 1 LB. MUSHROOMS, SLICED
- 1 TEASPOON DRY VERMOUTH

  SALT AND PEPPER, TO TASTE

CREAMED PEARL ONIONS

YIELD: 8 SERVINGS / ACTIVE TIME: 35 MINUTES / TOTAL TIME: 35 MINUTES

A rich, comforting dish that is right at home beside a roasted chicken or turkey. Fresh pearl onions are ideal, but in the interest of saving time, I've elected to use frozen pearl onions. They come in red or white, and a mix of the two makes for a visually stunning presentation. If you're lucky to live in an area where shallots are abundant, don't hesitate to toss a few of those in, too.

1. Place 2 tablespoons of the butter in a 12-inch cast-iron skillet and melt over medium-low heat. Add the flour and cook, while stirring constantly, until it is golden brown, about 6 minutes. Gradually whisk in the stock and bring to a boil, whisking until the roux is smooth. Remove the skillet from heat and whisk in the cream.

2. Place the skillet over medium-high heat and cook, while stirring frequently, until the sauce thickens, about 8 minutes.

3. Add the wine and sage and cook, while stirring, until the sauce has further thickened, about 2 minutes.

4. Add the onions and reduce heat to medium. Cook, while stirring frequently, until all of the onions are warmed through, about 6 minutes.

5. Whisk in the remaining butter, season with salt and pepper, and serve immediately.

INGREDIENTS:

2½ TABLESPOONS UNSALTED BUTTER

2 TABLESPOONS ALL-PURPOSE FLOUR

1½ CUPS VEGETABLE STOCK (SEE PAGE 562) OR CHICKEN STOCK (SEE PAGES 102–3)

½ CUP HEAVY CREAM, AT ROOM TEMPERATURE

½ CUP DRY WHITE WINE

¼ TEASPOON GROUND DRIED SAGE

1 LB. FROZEN PEARL ONIONS, THAWED AND DRAINED

SALT AND PEPPER, TO TASTE

CHARRED ONION PETALS

YIELD: 4 SERVINGS / ACTIVE TIME: 10 MINUTES / TOTAL TIME: 45 MINUTES

An easy-to-master and utterly beautiful preparation that makes for a stunning side dish. Make sure to use sweet onions, though, since the flavor of yellow onions will be too sharp. These are just as good cold, so don't hesitate to make a batch ahead of time.

1. Preheat the oven to 300°F.

2. Cut each onion in half lengthwise and remove the outer layer.

3. Place a 12-inch cast-iron skillet over high heat and add the vegetable oil. When the oil is shimmering, place the onions, cut side down, in the pan. Reduce heat to medium-low and cook until the onions are charred, about 20 minutes. They will smell burnt, but don't worry.

4. Place the skillet in the oven and roast until the onions are tender, 10 to 15 minutes. Remove the skillet from the oven and let the onions cool.

5. When the onions are cool enough to handle, use kitchen scissors to trim the tops and roots. Discard and separate the layers into individual petals. Season with salt and serve.

INGREDIENTS:

3 SWEET ONIONS (MAUI OR VIDALIA)

2 TABLESPOONS VEGETABLE OIL

FLAKY SEA SALT, TO TASTE

CREAMED KALE & SWISS CHARD

YIELD: 4 SERVINGS / ACTIVE TIME: 5 MINUTES / TOTAL TIME: 20 MINUTES

This dish is a brassica lover's dream, and it will change the mind of anyone who doesn't love their greens. The mustard powder pulls double duty here, adding a burst of flavor and helping to thicken the sauce. If you can find Rainbow chard, use that: the pretty red-and-yellow stems will make the dish Insta-worthy.

1. Place the coconut oil in a large cast-iron Dutch oven and warm over medium-high heat.

2. When the oil is shimmering, add the kale and stir to coat. Cook until the greens are wilted, about 5 minutes.

3. Add the mustard powder, cream, and water. Stir to incorporate, reduce the heat to medium-low, cover, and simmer for 5 minutes.

4. Remove the lid and stir in the Swiss chard. Cover again and simmer until the chard is wilted, about 2 minutes. Season with salt and serve.

INGREDIENTS:

2 TABLESPOONS COCONUT OIL

4 CUPS SHREDDED KALE LEAVES

2 TEASPOONS MUSTARD POWDER

1 CUP HEAVY CREAM

¼ CUP WATER

1 LARGE BUNCH OF SWISS CHARD, LEAVES AND STEMS CHOPPED

SALT, TO TASTE

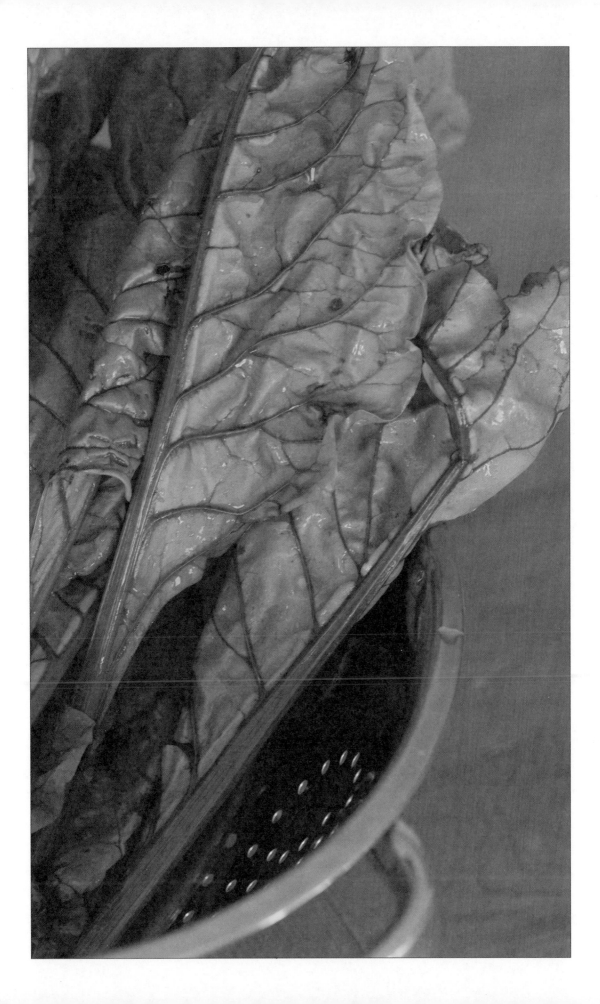

ROASTED GARLIC RADICCHIO

YIELD: 4 SERVINGS / ACTIVE TIME: 10 MINUTES / TOTAL TIME: 1 HOUR AND 30 MINUTES

If you like tart and bitter vegetables, this dish is for you. Just make sure the skillet is screaming hot before you add the radicchio, since you want it to be charred before adding the rest of the marinade.

1. Preheat the oven to 425°F.

2. Place the olive oil, garlic, rosemary, vinegar, anchovy (if using), salt, and pepper in a large bowl and stir to combine. Add the radicchio to the bowl and carefully toss to coat. Let the radicchio marinate for 1 hour.

3. Place a 12-inch cast-iron skillet over high heat for 10 minutes, until it is extremely hot. Using tongs, remove the radicchio from the marinade and arrange, cut side down, in the skillet. Let it sear for a few minutes.

4. Reduce the heat and pour the marinade over the radicchio. Place the skillet in the oven and roast until the radicchio is tender, about 20 minutes. Remove and garnish with the Parmesan before serving.

INGREDIENTS:

¼ CUP OLIVE OIL

8 GARLIC CLOVES, MINCED

2 TEASPOONS MINCED ROSEMARY LEAVES

¼ CUP BALSAMIC VINEGAR

1 ANCHOVY FILLET, SMASHED (OPTIONAL)

SALT AND PEPPER, TO TASTE

4 HEADS OF RADICCHIO, HALVED THROUGH THE ROOT

PARMESAN CHEESE, GRATED, FOR GARNISH

SPINACH & SHALLOTS

YIELD: 6 TO 8 SERVINGS / ACTIVE TIME: 10 MINUTES / TOTAL TIME: 10 MINUTES

Using mellow-flavored shallots instead of the usual garlic and onions keeps the spinach flavor bright in this quick-cooking dish. A splash of balsamic vinegar takes it over the top.

1. Place a 12-inch cast-iron skillet over medium-high heat. Add the olive oil and shallots and cook, while stirring, until shallots are translucent, about 2 minutes.

2. Add the spinach and cook, while stirring, until the leaves are covered by the oil and shallots, about 2 or 3 minutes. The spinach will start to wilt quickly. Reduce the heat and keep stirring so none of it burns. If desired, you can turn the heat to low and cover the skillet so the spinach steams.

3. When the spinach leaves are wilted and still bright green, splash them with the balsamic vinegar, shaking the pan to distribute. Season with salt and pepper and serve.

VARIATIONS: This dish works best with more mature spinach. Reserve baby spinach greens for salads and use the larger leaves for this dish. If you prefer a less onion-y dish, use two shallots instead of four.

INGREDIENTS:

3   TABLESPOONS OLIVE OIL

4   LARGE SHALLOTS, SLICED THIN

2   LBS. FRESH SPINACH, STEMMED, RINSED, AND THOROUGHLY DRIED

1   TABLESPOON BALSAMIC VINEGAR

     SALT AND PEPPER, TO TASTE

CRAZY GOOD CABBAGE

YIELD: 4 TO 6 SERVINGS / **ACTIVE TIME:** 15 MINUTES / **TOTAL TIME:** 45 MINUTES

This Southern-inspired dish is a colorful blend of pale green cabbage, bright green peppers, deep red tomatoes, and bright yellow corn—with a cayenne kick!

1. Place a 12-inch cast-iron skillet over medium-high heat and add the oil. Add the cabbage, bell pepper, and onion and cook, while stirring, until the onion becomes translucent, about 3 minutes. Add the tomatoes, corn, and cayenne and stir. Season with salt and pepper.

2. Cover, reduce the heat to low, and simmer until the cabbage is cooked through, about 30 minutes, while stirring occasionally. Season with salt and pepper and serve immediately.

INGREDIENTS:

2   TABLESPOONS OLIVE OIL

1   HEAD OF GREEN CABBAGE, CORED AND SHREDDED

1   GREEN BELL PEPPER, SEEDED AND DICED

1   YELLOW ONION, DICED

3   CUPS SEEDED AND CHOPPED TOMATOES

½   CUP CORN KERNELS

1   TEASPOON CAYENNE PEPPER

SALT AND PEPPER, TO TASTE

CARAWAY-SEED CABBAGE

YIELD: 4 TO 6 SERVINGS / ACTIVE TIME: 10 MINUTES / TOTAL TIME: 40 MINUTES

If you prefer a more Eastern European flavor to your cabbage, try this preparation.

1. Place a 12-inch cast-iron skillet over medium-high heat and add the oil. Add the cabbage, onion, and toasted caraway seeds and cook until the onion becomes translucent, about 3 minutes. Season with salt and pepper.

2. Cover, reduce the heat to low, and simmer until the cabbage is cooked through, about 30 minutes, while stirring occasionally. Serve hot and season with additional salt and pepper.

INGREDIENTS:

2   TABLESPOONS OLIVE OIL

1   HEAD OF GREEN CABBAGE, CORED AND SHREDDED

½   YELLOW ONION, DICED

1   TEASPOON CARAWAY SEEDS, TOASTED

SALT AND PEPPER, TO TASTE

CHARRED EGGPLANT *with* BONITO FLAKES

YIELD: 4 SERVINGS / ACTIVE TIME: 5 MINUTES / TOTAL TIME: 30 MINUTES

The trick to this incredible dish is to really char the eggplant, ensuring that it is very soft and has a light, smoky flavor. When paired with the bonito flakes (paper-thin flecks of dried fermented tuna, a key to the dashi broth that provides the base of a proper miso soup) and pickled onions, that smoke makes for a complex, flavor-packed dish that works as a side or a late lunch in the summer.

1. Preheat the broiler on your oven.

2. Place the eggplants in a 12-inch cast-iron skillet and place them under the broiler. Broil, while turning occasionally, until the eggplants have collapsed and are charred all over, about 10 minutes. Remove from the oven, transfer the eggplants to a large bowl, and cover with plastic. Let the eggplants steam for another 10 minutes.

3. Place the vinegar and sugar in a saucepan and bring to a simmer over medium heat. Add the onion and a large pinch of salt and cook until the onion is translucent, about 2 minutes. Remove from heat and set aside.

4. When the eggplants are cool enough to handle, peel off the skin, cut off the ends, and discard. Roughly chop the remaining flesh and return it to the large bowl. Add the lemon juice and olive oil, season with salt, and stir to combine.

5. Grate the Roma tomatoes into the bowl containing the eggplant. Use a slotted spoon to transfer the onion to the bowl. Add the arugula and toss to combine. Garnish with the bonito flakes and serve.

TIP: You can also serve this as a composed salad. To do that, spread the grated Roma tomatoes over four chilled salad plates. Top with the eggplant and sprinkle the onion and bonito flakes on top. Add the arugula, drizzle with olive oil, and serve.

INGREDIENTS:

2   LARGE EGGPLANTS

1   CUP CHAMPAGNE VINEGAR

½   CUP SUGAR

1   YELLOW ONION, SLICED INTO THIN HALF-MOONS

    SALT, TO TASTE

    JUICE OF 1 LEMON

¼   CUP OLIVE OIL

4   ROMA TOMATOES

2   LARGE HANDFULS OF WILD ARUGULA

1   CUP BONITO FLAKES, FOR GARNISH

WINTER TOMATOES *with* THYME

YIELD: 4 TO 6 SERVINGS / ACTIVE TIME: 5 MINUTES / TOTAL TIME: 1 HOUR

Chances are, the tomatoes in your area aren't at their peak during winter. That doesn't deter some people, though. For those stubborn folks, this slow-roasted version will provide the flavor they're after, which would be perfect alongside a baked fillet of fish.

1. Preheat the oven to 300°F.

2. Place the olive oil in a cast-iron Dutch oven and warm over medium-low heat. Add the tomatoes and cook, without stirring, for 3 minutes. Add the garlic and thyme and toss to coat.

3. Cover the Dutch oven and place it in the oven. Roast until the tomatoes and garlic are extremely tender, about 45 minutes. Remove and let cool.

4. Remove the sprigs of thyme and discard. Serve, or store in the olive oil for up to 2 months.

INGREDIENTS:

1	CUP OLIVE OIL
12	ROMA TOMATOES, SEEDED AND CHOPPED
12	WHOLE GARLIC CLOVES
6	SPRIGS OF THYME

STUFFED TOMATOES

YIELD: 6 SERVINGS / ACTIVE TIME: 1 HOUR / TOTAL TIME: 2 HOURS

If you want to make this without sausage, simply omit it, double the quantity of mushrooms, and, after sautéing the mushrooms and peppers, drain the excess liquid. You can also add toasted walnut pieces for additional flavor and fiber.

1. Preheat the oven to 375°F.

2. Cut off the tops of the tomatoes, and use a small paring knife or a serrated grapefruit spoon to scoop out the insides. Once hollowed, sprinkle salt on the insides and turn upside down on a plate covered with a paper towel to absorb the water. Let sit for about 30 minutes.

3. Heat a 12-inch cast-iron skillet over medium-high heat and cook the sausage, breaking it up with a wooden spoon as it cooks. Cook until there is no pink showing in the meat. When cooked, use a slotted spoon to transfer the sausage to a large bowl. In the sausage fat, cook the onion and garlic until the onion is translucent, about 4 minutes. Add the mushrooms and bell pepper and cook over medium heat, while stirring, until vegetables soften, about 10 minutes. Add red pepper flakes, if desired.

4. Add the mushroom mixture to the sausage and stir to combine. Then add the bread crumbs, sage, and Parmesan. Season with salt and pepper.

5. Wipe down the skillet and brush with olive oil. Position the tomatoes in the skillet, bottoms down. Start filling the tomatoes gently, dividing the filling between them. Cover the skillet with aluminum foil and put the skillet in the oven. Bake for about 30 minutes, remove the foil, and continue baking for another 10 to 15 minutes, until cooked through. Serve hot.

INGREDIENTS:

6   LARGE RIPE TOMATOES

    SALT AND PEPPER, TO TASTE

1   LB. SAUSAGE, CASINGS REMOVED

1   ONION, DICED

4   GARLIC CLOVES, MINCED

8   WHITE MUSHROOMS, STEMMED AND DICED

½   GREEN BELL PEPPER, SEEDED AND DICED

2   TEASPOONS RED PEPPER FLAKES (OPTIONAL)

2   CUPS PLAIN BREAD CRUMBS

2   TABLESPOONS DRIED SAGE

1   CUP GRATED PARMESAN CHEESE

    OLIVE OIL, AS NEEDED

FRIED ARTICHOKES *with* GREMOLATA

YIELD: 2 TO 4 SERVINGS / **ACTIVE TIME:** 20 MINUTES / **TOTAL TIME:** 30 MINUTES

This beautiful dish is one of the classics in Roman Jewish cuisine, where it is known as *carciofi alla giudia*. Like so many culinary cornerstones, it's simple: fry tender artichokes until crisp and dress with an Italian gremolata. The key is seasoning the artichokes with the correct amount of salt after they come out of the oil, so don't be afraid to experiment until you get it just right.

1. Place the lemon zest in a small bowl. Place the lemon juice in a separate bowl. Add the water to the lemon juice, stir to combine, and set aside.

2. Add the parsley and the minced garlic to the lemon zest, stir to combine, and set the gremolata aside.

3. Cut any large artichokes in half lengthwise. Place all of the artichokes in the lemon water. Line a baking sheet with paper towels and place it near the stovetop.

4. Add olive oil to a cast-iron Dutch oven until it is ½ inch deep. Warm over medium heat for 4 minutes and then drop in the whole garlic clove. Remove the garlic when the oil starts to bubble.

5. Drain the artichokes and pat dry. Working in three batches, drop the artichokes into the oil and fry, while turning occasionally, until golden brown, about 5 minutes. Carefully remove the fried artichokes and transfer them to the lined baking sheet. Sprinkle with salt, garnish with the gremolata, and serve.

INGREDIENTS:

- ZEST AND JUICE OF 2 LARGE LEMONS
- 2 CUPS WATER
- ½ CUP MINCED PARSLEY
- 7 GARLIC CLOVES, 6 MINCED, 1 WHOLE
- 3 LBS. BABY ARTICHOKES, TRIMMED
- OLIVE OIL, FOR FRYING
- SALT, TO TASTE

TRIMMING ARTICHOKES

Using a serrated bread knife, cut ¼ inch off the top to remove the spiky ends. Snap back the outer leaves until you get to the paler inner leaves. Small artichokes don't have a prickly center, so you don't need to do anything further. If you are using larger artichokes, use a spoon to remove the inner heart.

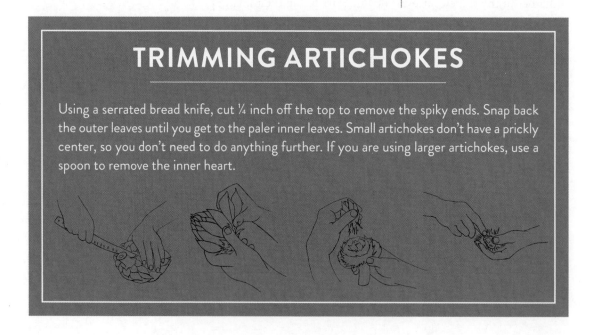

ROASTED SUNCHOKES

YIELD: 4 SERVINGS / ACTIVE TIME: 10 MINUTES / TOTAL TIME: 40 MINUTES

Slow roasting in a hot oven is what's required to draw out the sweet and nutty flavor of sunchokes—also known as Jerusalem artichokes. Adding a small amount of water to the pan is the key when slow-roasting vegetables, as it keeps them from drying out as they brown. Serve this alongside chicken, beef, rabbit, or lamb.

1. Preheat the oven to 500°F.

2. Place the sunchokes and olive oil in a large bowl and toss to coat. Season with salt and toss to coat.

3. Warm a 12-inch cast-iron skillet over high heat. When it is hot, add the sunchokes and water, place it in the oven, and roast for 20 minutes. Stir and then cook for another 15 minutes, until the sunchokes are well-browned and tender.

INGREDIENTS:

2   LBS. SUNCHOKES, SCRUBBED

1   TABLESPOON OLIVE OIL

    KOSHER SALT, TO TASTE

¼   CUP WATER

CREAMY SUCCOTASH

YIELD: 8 TO 10 SERVINGS / ACTIVE TIME: 30 MINUTES / TOTAL TIME: 1 HOUR

Take advantage of the season when fresh corn is plentiful to create this cookout classic. This uses a lot of corn and is a nice alternative to corn on the cob.

1. Bring a medium pot of salted water to a boil over high heat. Add the lima beans and reduce the heat. Cook until they are al dente, about 5 minutes. Drain and set aside.

2. Standing each ear up in the middle of a large baking dish, use a sharp knife to cut down the sides and remove all the kernels. With the kernels off, take the blade of a dull knife and press it along each side of the ears to "milk" the cob of its liquid. Discard the milked cobs.

3. Place the bacon in a nonstick skillet and cook over medium heat until it is crispy, about 8 minutes. Transfer to a paper towel–lined plate and let it drain. When cool enough to handle, chop the bacon into bite-sized pieces.

4. Place a 12-inch cast-iron skillet over medium heat. When hot, lower the heat and add the butter so it melts slowly. When melted, add the corn kernels and "milk" from the cobs and stir to coat the kernels with the butter. Increase the heat to medium-high and add the water and whole milk. Bring to a boil, while stirring constantly, and then reduce heat to low. Add the lima beans, salt, and pepper.

5. Add the flour, cherry tomatoes, and bacon pieces to the skillet, stir to incorporate, and cook over low heat until the sauce thickens. If it gets too thick, add some more whole milk. Serve hot.

TIP: You'll want to freeze some of this to enjoy in the dead of winter. It's easy. Allow the succotash to cool, put it in airtight containers, being sure to push all the air out, seal the container, and place in the freezer. Put the date it was cooked on the container so you remember.

INGREDIENTS:

- 4 CUPS FRESH OR FROZEN LIMA BEANS
- KOSHER SALT AND FRESHLY GROUND BLACK PEPPER, TO TASTE
- 12 EARS OF CORN, SHUCKED AND RINSED
- ½ LB. THICK-CUT BACON
- 3 TABLESPOONS UNSALTED BUTTER
- 1 CUP WATER, AT ROOM TEMPERATURE
- 1 CUP WHOLE MILK, PLUS MORE AS NEEDED
- 3 TABLESPOONS ALL-PURPOSE FLOUR
- 1 CUP CHERRY TOMATOES, HALVED

EDAMAME SUCCOTASH

YIELD: 4 TO 6 SERVINGS / ACTIVE TIME: 5 MINUTES / TOTAL TIME: 20 MINUTES

Everyone knows that "succotash" is fun to say, but many have never tried the dish that has proven to be such a lexical delight. Maybe that's because of the divisive lima beans that feature in traditional preparations. We decided to switch those out for protein-rich and bright edamame, making this side dish a welcome sight at any picnic or barbecue.

1. Place a 12-inch cast-iron skillet over medium heat, then add the bacon and cook until crispy, about 8 minutes. Remove from the pan and place on a paper towel–lined plate to drain. When it is cool enough to handle, crumble into bite-sized pieces.

2. Wipe the excess drippings from the skillet and add the onion. Cook over medium-high heat until it has softened, about 5 minutes. Add the corn, bell pepper, black beans (if using), and edamame and cook, while stirring often, until the corn is tender and bright yellow, about 4 minutes.

3. Add the butter and stir until it has melted and everything is evenly coated. Season with salt and pepper.

4. Add the marjoram or oregano, basil, and crumbled bacon, stir to incorporate, and serve.

INGREDIENTS:

4 SLICES OF THICK-CUT BACON

1 RED ONION, MINCED

KERNELS FROM 5 EARS OF CORN (ABOUT 4 CUPS)

1 RED BELL PEPPER, SEEDED AND DICED

1 CUP CANNED BLACK BEANS (OPTIONAL)

2 CUPS FRESH OR FROZEN EDAMAME

1 TABLESPOON UNSALTED BUTTER

SALT AND PEPPER, TO TASTE

1 TABLESPOON MINCED FRESH MARJORAM OR OREGANO

½ CUP CHOPPED FRESH BASIL

GREEN BEANS WITH BACON

YIELD: 4 SERVINGS / ACTIVE TIME: 10 MINUTES / TOTAL TIME: 15 MINUTES

As contemporary culture continually asserts, you can never go wrong with bacon. Smoky, salty, and buttery, the balance of flavors it possesses is unmatched. Here it is charged with lifting green beans to transcendent heights, a task it handles beautifully.

1. Place a cast-iron skillet over medium heat for 5 minutes, until it is hot. Add the bacon and cook until it is browned, about 6 minutes. Transfer to a paper towel–lined plate to drain. When cool enough to handle, crumble into bite-sized pieces.

2. Remove all but 2 tablespoons of the bacon drippings from the skillet. Add the green beans and sauté, while tossing to coat, for about 4 minutes. The green beans should be bright green and just tender. Remove from the skillet and season with salt and pepper.

3. Sprinkle the crumbled bacon on top and serve.

INGREDIENTS:

6   SLICES OF UNCURED BACON

2   CUPS TRIMMED GREEN BEANS

SALT AND PEPPER, TO TASTE

SHAVED RADISH & FENNEL SALAD
with IKURA *and* KETTLE POTATO CHIPS

YIELD: 4 SERVINGS / ACTIVE TIME: 10 MINUTES / TOTAL TIME: 30 MINUTES

Everyone thinks of salads as healthy, but that doesn't mean you can't make them a bit indulgent. This photogenic salad—try to find watermelon radishes for additional color—shows you how to do just that, adding fresh, golden potato chips and *ikura* (large salmon roe) for a surprisingly flavor-packed dish.

1. Place the orange juice, lemon juice, sugar, rice vinegar, shallot, and salt in a saucepan and bring to a boil over medium-high heat. Boil until the mixture starts to thicken, about 5 minutes. Remove from heat and let cool completely.

2. Place the mixture in the saucepan (which is also known as a gastrique) and mayonnaise in a mixing bowl and whisk to combine. Season to taste and set the dressing aside.

3. Place the radishes, fennel, cucumbers, and sliced shisho or basil in a salad bowl and toss to combine.

4. Divide the salad between 4 chilled plates. Drizzle with the dressing, top with the *ikura*, and serve with the Kettle Potato Chips.

KETTLE POTATO CHIPS

1. Add vegetable oil to a cast-iron skillet until it is 3 inches deep. Bring to 375°F over medium-high heat.

2. Use a mandoline to slice the potatoes into paper-thin slices.

3. Add the potatoes to the oil in batches and fry until golden brown. Transfer to a paper towel–lined plate to drain, sprinkle with salt, and serve.

INGREDIENTS:

1	CUP ORANGE JUICE
½	CUP FRESH LEMON JUICE
½	CUP SUGAR
2	TABLESPOONS RICE VINEGAR
1	SHALLOT, SLICED THIN
	SALT, TO TASTE
½	CUP MAYONNAISE
10	RADISHES, SLICED THIN
2	BULBS OF FENNEL, SLICED THIN
2	PERSIAN CUCUMBERS, SLICED THIN
½	CUP THINLY SLICED SHISHO OR BASIL LEAVES
½	CUP IKURA
	KETTLE POTATO CHIPS (SEE RECIPE), FOR SERVING

KETTLE POTATO CHIPS

	VEGETABLE OIL, FOR FRYING
2	YUKON GOLD POTATOES
	SALT, TO TASTE

ZUCCHINI SOUP

YIELD: 4 TO 6 SERVINGS / **ACTIVE TIME:** 10 MINUTES / **TOTAL TIME:** 45 MINUTES

The key to this little bit of heaven is browning the zucchini and onion so that the flavor really develops. Do that, and the intriguing, subtle flavor added by the dill seeds will really shine.

1. Place the butter in an enameled cast-iron Dutch oven and cook over medium heat until it starts to sizzle. Add the zucchini and onion and sauté until browned, about 8 minutes. Add the garlic, oregano, dill seeds, and parsley and sauté until just fragrant, about 2 minutes. Reduce the heat, cover the Dutch oven, and let the vegetables sweat for 5 minutes.

2. Remove the lid and add the stock or water, white pepper, broccoli, and rice. Season to taste and bring to a simmer. Simmer for another 25 minutes.

3. Remove from heat and let cool for a few minutes. Transfer to a blender and puree until smooth. Season to taste and garnish with Croutons or walnuts.

VEGETABLE STOCK

1. In a large stockpot, add the vegetable oil and the vegetables and cook over low heat until the moisture has evaporated. This allows the flavor of the vegetables to become concentrated.

2. Add the garlic, parsley, thyme, bay leaf, water, peppercorns, and salt. Raise heat to high and bring to a boil. Reduce heat and simmer for 2 hours. Skim fat and impurities from the top as the stock cooks.

3. When the stock has finished cooking, strain through a fine sieve or cheesecloth. Place the stock in the refrigerator to chill. Once cool, skim the fat layer from the top and discard. Use immediately, refrigerate, or freeze.

INGREDIENTS:

2	TABLESPOONS UNSALTED BUTTER
2	LARGE ZUCCHINI, CHOPPED
1	LARGE YELLOW ONION, CHOPPED
4	GARLIC CLOVES, MINCED
1	TABLESPOON DRIED OREGANO
1	TABLESPOON DILL SEEDS
2	TABLESPOONS DRIED PARSLEY
6	CUPS VEGETABLE STOCK (SEE RECIPE) OR WATER
1	TEASPOON WHITE PEPPER
2	CUPS BROCCOLI FLORETS
1	CUP BASMATI RICE
	SALT, TO TASTE
	CROUTONS (SEE PAGE 566), FOR GARNISH (OPTIONAL)
	WALNUTS, TOASTED AND CHOPPED, FOR GARNISH (OPTIONAL)

VEGETABLE STOCK

2	TABLESPOONS VEGETABLE OIL
2	LARGE LEEKS, TRIMMED AND RINSED WELL
2	LARGE CARROTS, PEELED AND SLICED
2	CELERY STALKS, SLICED
2	LARGE ONIONS, SLICED
3	GARLIC CLOVES, UNPEELED BUT SMASHED
2	SPRIGS OF PARSLEY
2	SPRIGS OF THYME
1	BAY LEAF
8	CUPS WATER
½	TEASPOON BLACK PEPPERCORNS
	SALT, TO TASTE

FIVE-ONION SOUP

YIELD: 4 TO 6 SERVINGS / ACTIVE TIME: 30 MINUTES / TOTAL TIME: 2 HOURS

We tend to think of fall and winter as the only seasons for soup, but this one should be a staple all year long. If you're like me and you enjoy a nice, cold stout, here's a perfect opportunity to crack one open.

1. Place the onions, garlic, and the stick of butter in a cast-iron Dutch oven and cook over medium heat until the onions get a rich, caramel color, about 30 to 40 minutes.

2. Add the flour and stir until it has been incorporated. Add the red wine to deglaze the pot, making sure to scrape the bottom with a wooden spoon to remove any bits that have started to stick. Add the thyme, stock, soy sauce, bay leaves, salt, and pepper, reduce the heat so that the soup gently simmers, and cook until the broth is thick enough to lightly coat a wooden spoon.

3. When the soup is close to finished, preheat your broiler and spread the softened butter on the slices of bread. Place the bread in the oven and toast until brown and crispy, about 5 minutes. Remove from the oven and set aside.

4. Ladle the soup into bowls and top each one with 1 piece of toast and 2 slices of cheese. Place the bowls under the broiler until the cheese is melted and bubbly.

TIPS: A quick way to peel cipollini onions is to submerge them in boiling water for a few minutes to loosen the skins. Then remove the tops and bottoms with a small knife and squeeze the onions out. If you want to make this soup vegetarian, use Vegetable Stock (see page 562) and add another tablespoon of dark soy sauce.

INGREDIENTS:

- 1 LB. WHITE ONIONS, SLICED THIN
- 1 LB. YELLOW ONIONS, SLICED THIN
- 1 LB. VIDALIA ONIONS, SLICED THIN
- ½ LB. SHALLOTS, SLICED THIN
- ½ LB. CIPOLLINI ONIONS, SLICED THIN
- 3 GARLIC CLOVES, SLICED THIN
- 1 STICK OF SALTED BUTTER, PLUS 6 TABLESPOONS, SOFTENED
- ¼ CUP ALL-PURPOSE FLOUR
- ½ CUP RED WINE (BURGUNDY IS RECOMMENDED)
- 2 TABLESPOONS FRESH THYME LEAVES
- 8 CUPS BEEF STOCK (SEE PAGE TK)
- 1 TABLESPOON DARK SOY SAUCE
- 2 BAY LEAVES
  SALT AND PEPPER, TO TASTE
- 6 PIECES OF SOURDOUGH BREAD, SLICED 1-INCH THICK
- 12 SLICES OF SWISS CHEESE

CREAMY CAULIFLOWER SOUP *with* JUNIPER SALT

YIELD: 4 TO 6 SERVINGS / ACTIVE TIME: 20 MINUTES / TOTAL TIME: 1 HOUR AND 15 MINUTES

An elegant soup that emerges from humble ingredients. Juniper—the defining element in gin—adds its fragrant touch to the earthy cauliflower here, drawing a typically hidden quality out of this pale brassica. If you end up with leftover juniper salt, sprinkle it on your next burger, or stir it into cream cheese and slather it on an everything bagel. This dish also freezes well, so don't hesitate to double the batch.

1. Preheat the oven to 400°F.

2. Place the juniper berries and salt in a mortar or spice grinder and grind until fine. Let the mixture sit for 10 minutes to give the oils from the juniper a chance to perfume the salt. Sift through a fine sieve and set aside.

3. Place the cauliflower and vegetable oil in a large bowl and toss to coat. Add half of the juniper salt and toss, adding more juniper salt as needed until all of the florets are coated. Place in a single layer on a foil-lined baking sheet, place in the oven, and roast until crispy and brown, about 45 minutes.

4. Place the butter in a cast-iron Dutch oven and melt over medium heat. Add 5 cups of the cauliflower, the stock or water, and the bay leaves and bring to a simmer. Let the soup simmer for 10 minutes.

5. Remove the bay leaves. Transfer the soup to a blender or use an immersion blender to puree the soup until it is velvety and smooth. Add the Crème Fraîche and white pepper, puree, and season with salt.

6. Ladle into warmed bowls and garnish with the remaining cauliflower and the Croutons.

CRÈME FRAÎCHE

Place the ingredients in a mason jar, cover, and let stand at room temperature for 12 hours. Store in the refrigerator for up to 1 month.

CROUTONS

1. Preheat the oven to 350°F.

2. Place the pieces of baguette, olive oil, salt, and pepper in a mixing bowl and toss to coat. Transfer the pieces of baguette to a foil-lined baking sheet and place in the oven. Bake, while turning over once, until crispy and browned on both sides, about 10 minutes.

INGREDIENTS:

- 10   **JUNIPER BERRIES**
- 2   **TABLESPOONS KOSHER SALT, PLUS MORE TO TASTE**
- 6   **CUPS CAULIFLOWER FLORETS**
- ¼   **CUP VEGETABLE OIL**
- 2   **TABLESPOONS UNSALTED BUTTER**
- 6   **CUPS CHICKEN STOCK (SEE PAGES 102–3) OR WATER**
- 2   **BAY LEAVES**
- 1   **CUP CRÈME FRAÎCHE (SEE RECIPE)**
- ¼   **TEASPOON WHITE PEPPER**

    CROUTONS (SEE RECIPE), FOR SERVING

CRÈME FRAÎCHE
- 1   **CUP HEAVY CREAM**
- 1   **TABLESPOON BUTTERMILK**

CROUTONS
- 1   **BAGUETTE, CUT INTO CUBES**
- 2   **TABLESPOONS OLIVE OIL**

    SALT AND PEPPER, TO TASTE

SPICED BUTTERMILK STEW *with* SPINACH DUMPLINGS

YIELD: 6 TO 8 SERVINGS / ACTIVE TIME: 15 MINUTES / TOTAL TIME: 30 MINUTES

It seems like any time a recipe calls for buttermilk, it's just a small amount, leaving reasonable cooks to wonder what to do with the rest of the container. This dish offers a solution for that delicious problem. Not only does it use buttermilk as a main ingredient, but it will also quickly become an all-time favorite dish. Like many Indian-inspired recipes, there are a lot of ingredients, but don't be daunted—the final result is well worth it. Traditionally, the dumplings are fried, but steaming them in the buttermilk provides a lightness that the dish is so much the better for.

1. Place half of the buttermilk, the chickpea flour, turmeric, and salt in a blender and puree until smooth. Set the mixture aside.

2. Place the vegetable oil in a cast-iron Dutch oven and warm over high heat. When the oil is shimmering, add the coriander and mustard seeds and cook, while stirring, until they start to pop.

3. Reduce the heat to medium and add the onions, garlic, ginger, amchoor, and serrano peppers. Sauté until slightly browned and then pour in the buttermilk mixture. Add the remaining buttermilk, reduce the heat so that the stew gently simmers, and prepare the dumplings.

4. To prepare the dumplings, place the spinach, serrano peppers (if using), salt, red pepper flakes, and chaat masala in a mixing bowl and stir to combine. Add the chickpea flour and stir to incorporate. The dough should be quite stiff.

5. Add tablespoons of the dough to the stew. When all of the dumplings have been added, cover the Dutch oven and cook for 10 minutes over low heat. Ladle into warmed bowls and serve.

NOTE: Amchoor is a sour powder made from the dried flesh of an unripe mango. Crucial to North Indian cuisine, it can be found at high-end grocery stores or online.

INGREDIENTS:

FOR THE STEW

8	CUPS BUTTERMILK
½	CUP CHICKPEA FLOUR
1	TABLESPOON TURMERIC
1	TEASPOON KOSHER SALT
1	TABLESPOON VEGETABLE OIL
1	TEASPOON CORIANDER SEEDS
1	TABLESPOON BLACK MUSTARD SEEDS
2	LARGE YELLOW ONIONS, SLICED INTO THIN HALF-MOONS
6	GARLIC CLOVES, MINCED
2	TABLESPOONS MINCED GINGER
1	TEASPOON AMCHOOR
2	SERRANO PEPPERS, SEEDED AND MINCED

FOR THE DUMPLINGS

2	CUPS SPINACH, COOKED, DRAINED, AND CHOPPED
2	GREEN SERRANO PEPPERS, SEEDED AND MINCED (OPTIONAL)
2	TEASPOONS KOSHER SALT
1	TEASPOON RED PEPPER FLAKES
1½	TEASPOONS CHAAT MASALA
1	CUP CHICKPEA FLOUR

RATATOUILLE

YIELD: 4 SERVINGS / ACTIVE TIME: 40 MINUTES / TOTAL TIME: 2 HOURS

There are variations on this dish—some insist that zucchini is a necessary ingredient—but this recipe calls for just eggplant, peppers, and tomatoes (and garlic, of course) for a simple, filling meal.

1. Heat half of the olive oil in a 12-inch cast-iron skillet over medium-high heat. Add the garlic and eggplant and cook, while stirring, until the pieces are coated with oil and just starting to sizzle, about 2 minutes. Reduce the heat slightly, add the peppers and remaining oil, and stir to combine. With the heat on medium, cover the skillet and let cook, stirring every few minutes to be sure vegetables aren't sticking to the bottom of the pan. If the mix seems too dry, add a little more olive oil. As the eggplant softens, the dish will regain moisture.

2. After about 15 minutes, when the eggplant and peppers are nearly soft, add the tomatoes and stir to combine. With the lid off, continue to cook the ratatouille, stirring occasionally, until the eggplant and peppers are soft and the tomatoes are wilted. Remove the skillet from heat, season with salt and pepper, and allow to sit for at least 1 hour. Reheat before serving.

VARIATION: If you want to make this with zucchini, choose a small one, and cut it into thin half-moons. Add the zucchini with the peppers.

INGREDIENTS:

- ⅓   CUP OLIVE OIL, PLUS MORE AS NEEDED
- 6   GARLIC CLOVES, MINCED
- 1   EGGPLANT, TRIMMED AND CUT INTO BITE-SIZED CUBES
- 2   BELL PEPPERS, SEEDED AND DICED
- 4   TOMATOES, SEEDED AND CHOPPED

   SALT AND PEPPER, TO TASTE

SKILLET EGGPLANT PARMESAN

YIELD: 4 SERVINGS / ACTIVE TIME: 20 MINUTES / TOTAL TIME: 1 HOUR

Gooey goodness straight from the skillet, rich with garlic, fresh mozzarella, and Parmesan cheese—and the eggplant isn't fried, so it's not too heavy.

1. Preheat the oven to 350°F.

2. Trim the top and bottom off the eggplant and slice the remainder into ¼-inch slices. Put the slices on paper towels in a single layer, sprinkle salt over them, and let stand for 15 minutes. Turn the slices over, sprinkle with salt, and let sit for another 15 minutes.

3. Rinse the eggplant and pat dry with paper towels.

4. Drizzle the olive oil over a baking sheet in preparation for the eggplant.

5. In a shallow bowl, combine the bread crumbs and Parmesan cheese. Put the beaten egg in another shallow bowl. Dip the slices of eggplant in egg, then in the bread crumb mixture, coating both sides. Put them on the baking sheet.

6. Bake in the oven for about 10 minutes, turn them over, and bake another 10 minutes. Remove the sheet from the oven.

7. Put a layer of marinara sauce in a 12-inch cast-iron skillet and stir in the pressed garlic. Lay the eggplant slices in the sauce, layering to fit. Top with the shredded mozzarella.

8. Put the skillet in the oven and bake for about 30 minutes, until the sauce is bubbling and the cheese is golden. Allow to cool for about 10 minutes and then serve with additional sauce, if desired.

INGREDIENTS:

1	LARGE EGGPLANT
	SALT, TO TASTE
2	TABLESPOONS OLIVE OIL
1	CUP ITALIAN-SEASONED BREAD CRUMBS
2	TABLESPOONS GRATED PARMESAN CHEESE
1	EGG, BEATEN
½	CUP MARINARA SAUCE, PLUS MORE FOR SERVING (ADDITIONAL IS OPTIONAL)
2	GARLIC CLOVES, PRESSED
½	LB. MOZZARELLA CHEESE, SHREDDED

VEGETABLE LO MEIN

YIELD: 4 TO 6 SERVINGS / ACTIVE TIME: 15 TO 25 MINUTES / TOTAL TIME: 30 MINUTES

This dish works either hot or cold, making it a perfect option for summertime, when a hot meal can be the last thing you want.

1. In a large mixing bowl, add the sesame oil, soy sauce, black vinegar, brown sugar, and fish sauce and whisk to combine. Set aside until the noodles have been cooked.

2. Place the vegetable oil, scallion whites, ginger, and garlic in a cast-iron Dutch oven and cook over high heat for 2 minutes. Add the mushrooms, onion, bean sprouts, and carrot and cook for 2 to 3 minutes, until the vegetables are cooked but still crisp. Remove the mixture from the pan and set aside to cool.

3. Wipe out the pot and bring 4 quarts of water to a boil. Add the noodles and cook for 5 to 7 minutes, until al dente. Drain and add the noodles to the mixing bowl containing the dressing. Toss to coat and add the vegetables and the scallion greens. Serve hot or refrigerate for up to 2 days.

TIPS: To keep this dish vegetarian, substitute 2 additional tablespoons of soy sauce for the fish sauce. If you're in need of protein, add ½ lb. of small shrimp to the pan while you are cooking the vegetables.

INGREDIENTS:

¼ CUP SESAME OIL

3 TABLESPOONS SOY SAUCE

2 TABLESPOONS BLACK VINEGAR

1 TABLESPOON BROWN SUGAR

3 TABLESPOONS FISH SAUCE

1 TABLESPOON VEGETABLE OIL

5-6 SCALLIONS, WHITES MINCED, GREENS CUT INTO 2-INCH PIECES

1 TABLESPOON MINCED GINGER

2 GARLIC CLOVES, MINCED

¼ LB. BUTTON MUSHROOMS, SLICED

½ WHITE ONION, SLICED

½ CUP BEAN SPROUTS

1 CARROT, CUT INTO MATCHSTICKS

2 LBS. LO MEIN NOODLES

DESSERTS

We have come to the end at last . . . dessert. The happiest course of any meal. A time to pause, sip some coffee, and reflect on the meal you just had.

We all know how blissful it can be, but I'm guessing that many don't have any idea how much more delicious some of your favorites can be when made in cast iron. It's just a dream. Close your eyes, and picture a dimly lit room with bananas bathed in a brief and flickering fire (see page 649), or imagine yourself on a beach in southern India, biting into a perfectly sweet and spicy mango drenched in lime-pepper syrup (see page 650). Bon appétit, lovers of sweet things. These decadent recipes are for you.

GLUTEN-FREE MACAROON BARS

YIELD: 8 SERVINGS / ACTIVE TIME: 15 MINUTES / TOTAL TIME: 45 MINUTES

The traditional method of scooping the macaroons onto a baking sheet is time-consuming and messy. With this version, just pour the confection into the skillet, bake, cool, slice, and eat.

1. Preheat the oven to 350°F. While the oven is preheating, put a 10-inch cast-iron skillet in the oven to warm it up.

2. In a large bowl, add the sugar, coconut, egg whites, vanilla, and salt. Stir to combine well.

3. When the oven is preheated, remove the skillet. Put the batter into the pan and put it back in the oven.

4. Bake for 20 to 30 minutes, until browned on top.

5. Remove the skillet from the oven and allow to cool for 30 minutes before serving. Slice into wedges and use a pie server to remove from the skillet.

INGREDIENTS:

1½	CUPS SUGAR
4	CUPS UNSWEETENED COCONUT FLAKES
4	EGG WHITES
2	TEASPOONS VANILLA EXTRACT
¼	TEASPOON SALT

BAKED CRUST

YIELD: 12-INCH CRUST / ACTIVE TIME: 20 MINUTES / TOTAL TIME: 2 HOURS

Many of the pies in this book call for a simple, single baked crust. It's fast and easy to put together and the result is delicious.

1. In a large bowl, combine the flour and salt. Add the stick of butter and work it into the flour mixture with a pastry blender or 2 knives until the dough resembles coarse meal. Add 3 tablespoons cold water to start, and, using your hands or a fork, work the dough, adding additional tablespoons of water until the dough just holds together when you gather it in your hands.

2. Working on a lightly floured surface, gather the dough and form it into a solid ball or disk. Wrap tightly in plastic wrap and refrigerate for about an hour. The dough can be refrigerated for a couple of days or frozen for a couple of months.

3. Preheat the oven to 450°F. Take the dough out of the refrigerator to allow it to warm up a bit, but work with it cold. Put the refrigerated dough on a lightly floured surface, and, with a lightly dusted rolling pin, flatten the dough into a circle, working to extend it to a 12-inch round.

4. Grease a 12-inch cast-iron skillet with the remaining tablespoon of butter.

5. Carefully position the crust in the skillet so it is evenly distributed, pressing it in lightly. Crimp the edges. Use a fork to prick the crust on the bottom and sides. Line with foil or parchment paper and fill with uncooked rice as a weight.

6. Bake for 10 to 12 minutes, until lightly browned. Transfer to a wire rack to cool before filling.

INGREDIENTS:

- 1¼ CUPS ALL-PURPOSE FLOUR, PLUS MORE FOR DUSTING
- ¼ TEASPOON SALT
- 1 STICK OF UNSALTED BUTTER, CHILLED AND CUT INTO SMALL PIECES, PLUS 1 TABLESPOON FOR GREASING THE SKILLET
- 4-6 TABLESPOONS ICE WATER

FLAKY PASTRY CRUST

YIELD: 12-INCH CRUSTS / ACTIVE TIME: 30 MINUTES / TOTAL TIME: 2 TO 3 HOURS

This is a traditional piecrust recipe, and while it's tempting to take a shortcut and use a mix or even a premade crust, there truly is nothing as delicious as a crust made from scratch. Once you get the hang of it, you'll find making the crust as enjoyable and therapeutic as indulging in the pie.

1. In a large bowl, combine the flour and salt. Add the shortening, and, using a fork, work it in until the mixture forms a very coarse meal. Add the stick of butter and work it into the dough with a pastry blender or your fingers until the butter is incorporated. Don't overwork the dough; there can be chunks of butter in it. Add 4 tablespoons cold water to start, and, using your hands or a fork, work the dough, adding additional tablespoons of water until the dough just holds together when you gather it in your hands.

2. Working on a lightly floured surface, gather the dough and form it into a solid ball. Separate into equal parts and form into disks. Wrap each tightly in plastic wrap and refrigerate for 30 to 60 minutes. Dough can be refrigerated for a couple of days or frozen for a couple of months.

3. Take the dough out of the refrigerator to allow it to warm up a bit, but work with it cold. Put the refrigerated dough on a lightly floured surface, and, with a lightly dusted rolling pin, flatten the dough into 2 circles, working to extend each to a 12-inch round.

4. Grease a 12-inch cast-iron skillet with the remaining tablespoon of butter.

5. Carefully position the crust in the skillet so it is evenly distributed, pressing it in lightly and allowing the dough to extend over the side.

6. If making a single-crust pie, crimp the edges as desired. If filling and adding a top crust, leave the extra dough so it can be crimped with the top crust. Fill the pie as directed, and then roll out the top crust so it is just bigger than the diameter of the top of the skillet. For an extra-flaky pastry crust, refrigerate the assembled pie for about 30 minutes before baking.

7. When ready to bake, cut a slit or hole in the middle of the top crust for heat and water vapor to escape. Brush the crust with milk, which will turn it a nice brown color. Bake as directed.

INGREDIENTS:

2½ CUPS ALL-PURPOSE FLOUR, PLUS MORE FOR DUSTING

1¼ TEASPOONS SALT

¼ CUP VEGETABLE SHORTENING

1 STICK OF UNSALTED BUTTER, CHILLED AND CUT INTO SMALL PIECES, PLUS 1 TABLESPOON FOR GREASING THE SKILLET

6-8 TABLESPOONS COLD WATER

SWEET & SAVORY CORNMEAL CRUST

YIELD: 10-INCH CRUST / **ACTIVE TIME:** 20 MINUTES / **TOTAL TIME:** 1 HOUR AND 30 MINUTES

A crust that includes cornmeal will have more texture and flavor than a crust made from solely all-purpose flour. The distinctive texture and flavor are the perfect complements to savory fillings when prepared without sugar, but this makes a great base for sweet pies as well.

1. In a large bowl, thoroughly combine the flour, cornmeal, sugar if making a sweet crust, and salt. Add the stick of butter and work it into the flour mixture with a pastry blender or your fingers to form a coarse meal. Add the egg and continue to blend until the dough comes together.

2. Shape into a disk, cover tightly with plastic wrap, and refrigerate for 30 minutes.

3. Preheat the oven to 375°F. Take the dough out of the refrigerator to allow it to warm up a bit, but work with it cold. Put the refrigerated dough on a lightly floured surface, and, with a lightly dusted rolling pin, flatten the dough into a circle, working to extend it to a 10-inch round.

4. Grease a 10-inch cast-iron skillet with the remaining tablespoon of butter.

5. Carefully position the crust in the skillet so it is evenly distributed, pressing it in lightly. Crimp the edges. Use a fork to prick the crust on the bottom and sides. Line with foil or parchment paper, and fill with uncooked rice as a weight.

6. Bake for 10 to 12 minutes, until lightly browned. Transfer to a wire rack to cool before filling.

INGREDIENTS:

- ¾ CUP ALL-PURPOSE FLOUR, PLUS MORE FOR DUSTING
- ¾ CUP YELLOW CORNMEAL
- 3 TABLESPOONS SUGAR (IF MAKING A SWEET CRUST)
- ½ TEASPOON SALT
- 1 STICK OF UNSALTED BUTTER, CHILLED AND CUT INTO SMALL PIECES, PLUS 1 TABLESPOON FOR GREASING THE SKILLET
- 1 EGG, LIGHTLY BEATEN

PECAN NUT CRUST

YIELD: 10-INCH CRUST / ACTIVE TIME: 30 MINUTES / TOTAL TIME: 45 MINUTES

So simple, elegant, and delicious, nut crusts are a great gluten-free alternative to traditional crusts. They can be used as a base for everything from creamy, earthy fillings like pumpkin to decadent chocolate cream and even frozen yogurt with fruit.

1. Preheat the oven to 400°F.

2. Put the pecan pieces in a food processor and pulse until you have a coarse, crumbly meal. Alternately, you can put the pieces in a large, thick plastic bag and mash them with a rolling pin or meat tenderizer.

3. Transfer the crushed nuts to a bowl and add the honey and 2 tablespoons of butter, mixing with a pastry blender, fork, or your fingers until a coarse meal is formed. There can be chunks of butter that remain.

4. Grease a 10-inch cast-iron skillet with the remaining butter. Transfer the nut mixture to the skillet and gently press it into the pan to form a crust.

5. Put the skillet on top of a cookie sheet to catch any oil that may splatter. Bake for 10 to 12 minutes, until browned and toasty. Remove from the oven and let cool completely on a wire rack.

VARIATIONS: For an almond-based crust, substitute 1½ cups raw almonds for the pecans; for a walnut-based crust, substitute 1½ cups raw walnut pieces for the pecans; for a hazelnut-based crust, use ¾ cup raw hazelnuts and ¾ cup almonds or pecans. Or use 1½ cups of a blend of these nuts.

INGREDIENTS:

- 1½ CUPS RAW PECANS
- 1½ TABLESPOONS HONEY
- 2 TABLESPOONS UNSALTED BUTTER, CHILLED AND CUT INTO SMALL PIECES, PLUS 1 TABLESPOON FOR GREASING THE SKILLET

GRAHAM CRACKER CRUST

YIELD: 10-INCH CRUST / ACTIVE TIME: 20 MINUTES / TOTAL TIME: 45 MINUTES

You can crush graham crackers to make this crust, or you can purchase graham cracker crumbs in the baked goods aisle of your grocery store. Either works, as the cracker is held together with butter and sugar. There are so many fillings that complement the flavor and texture of a graham cracker crust, so be sure to experiment and enjoy.

1. Preheat the oven to 375°F.

2. In a large bowl, add the graham cracker crumbs and sugar and stir to combine. Add the maple syrup and melted butter and stir to thoroughly combine.

3. Liberally grease a 10-inch cast-iron skillet with the tablespoon of room-temperature butter. Pour the dough into the skillet and lightly press into shape. Line with aluminum foil and fill with uncooked rice. Bake for 10 to 12 minutes, until golden.

4. Allow to cool on a wire rack before filling.

INGREDIENTS:

1½ CUPS GRAHAM CRACKER CRUMBS

2 TABLESPOONS SUGAR

1 TABLESPOON MAPLE SYRUP

5 TABLESPOONS UNSALTED BUTTER, MELTED, PLUS 1 TABLESPOON AT ROOM TEMPERATURE FOR GREASING THE SKILLET

PALEO PIECRUST

YIELD: 10-INCH CRUST / ACTIVE TIME: 15 MINUTES / TOTAL TIME: 1 HOUR AND 15 MINUTES

You can make any pie a "Paleo pie" with a few key ingredient swaps, starting with this perfect, Paleo-friendly piecrust.

1. Combine the flours, potato starch, xanthan gum, salt, and sugar. Work the fat into the flour.

2. When a crumbly dough forms, add the water 2 tablespoons at a time, working it with your fingers until it holds together.

3. Transfer to a lightly floured surface and form a disk. Wrap in plastic and refrigerate about 1 hour before rolling it out on a floured work surface.

NOTE: This piecrust does not need to be baked before being filled. Instead, it should be cooked at the same time as the filling.

INGREDIENTS:

½   CUP RICE FLOUR, PLUS MORE FOR DUSTING

½   CUP TAPIOCA FLOUR

½   CUP POTATO STARCH

2   TEASPOONS XANTHAN GUM

½   TEASPOON SALT

    DASH OF SUGAR

¼   CUP LARD, GHEE, OR COCONUT OIL

4-5   TABLESPOONS VERY COLD WATER

GLUTEN-FREE CRUST

YIELD: 10-INCH CRUST / **ACTIVE TIME:** 20 MINUTES / **TOTAL TIME:** 1 HOUR AND 30 MINUTES

Achieving flakiness with a gluten-free crust is tricky. This comes very close, and it's delicious, too. Double the recipe for a two-crust pie.

1. In a large bowl, combine the flour blend, sugar, xanthan gum, and salt. Add the 6 tablespoons of butter and work it into the flour mixture with a pastry blender or your fingers to form a coarse meal that includes whole bits of butter.

2. In a small bowl, whisk the egg and lemon juice together briskly until very foamy. Add to the dry ingredients and stir until the dough holds together. If dough isn't quite holding, add 1 tablespoon of cold water at a time until it does. Shape into a disk, wrap tightly in plastic wrap, and refrigerate for 30 to 60 minutes or overnight.

3. When ready to make the pie, take the dough out of the refrigerator and allow to rest at room temperature for about 10 minutes before rolling. Working on a flat surface dusted with gluten-free flour, roll the dough into a 10-inch round.

4. Grease a 10-inch cast-iron skillet with the remaining tablespoon of butter.

5. Carefully position the crust in the skillet so it is evenly distributed, pressing it in lightly. Crimp the edges. Fill and bake as directed.

INGREDIENTS:

- 1¼ CUPS GLUTEN-FREE MULTI-PURPOSE FLOUR BLEND, PLUS MORE FOR DUSTING
- 1 TABLESPOON SUGAR
- ½ TEASPOON XANTHAN GUM
- ½ TEASPOON SALT
- 6 TABLESPOONS UNSALTED BUTTER, CHILLED AND CUT INTO SMALL PIECES, PLUS 1 TABLESPOON FOR GREASING THE SKILLET
- 1 LARGE EGG
- 2 TEASPOONS FRESH LEMON JUICE
- 1-2 TABLESPOONS COLD WATER

BLUEBERRY PIE

YIELD: 6 TO 8 SERVINGS / ACTIVE TIME: 1 HOUR / TOTAL TIME: 2 HOURS

An incredibly easy way to capture the brief glory that is blueberry season. It's summer in a slice!

1. Preheat the oven to 350°F.

2. If using frozen blueberries, it's not necessary to thaw them completely. Put the blueberries in a large bowl and add the lemon juice, 1 cup of granulated sugar, and flour. Stir to combine.

3. Put a 10-inch cast-iron skillet over medium heat and melt the butter in it. Add the brown sugar and cook, while stirring constantly, until the brown sugar is dissolved, 1 or 2 minutes. Remove pan from heat.

4. Gently place one crust over the butter-and-sugar mixture. Fill with the blueberries and place the other crust over the blueberries, crimping the edges together.

5. Brush the top crust with the egg white and then sprinkle the remaining granulated sugar over it. Cut 4 or 5 slits in the middle.

6. Put the skillet in the oven and bake for 50 to 60 minutes, until the pie is golden brown and bubbly. Cover the outermost edge with aluminum foil in the last 10 minutes of baking to prevent it from burning.

7. Remove from the oven and allow to cool before serving.

TIP: If you feel like adding a decorative touch to your pie, cut your second crust into strips and lay them across the top to make a picture-perfect lattice crust.

INGREDIENTS:

- 4 CUPS FRESH OR FROZEN BLUEBERRIES
- 1 TABLESPOON FRESH LEMON JUICE
- 1 CUP OF GRANULATED SUGAR, PLUS 2 TABLESPOONS
- 3 TABLESPOONS ALL-PURPOSE FLOUR
- 1 STICK OF UNSALTED BUTTER
- 1 CUP LIGHT BROWN SUGAR
- 2 FLAKY PASTRY CRUSTS (SEE PAGE 580)
- 1 EGG WHITE

CHERRY PIE

YIELD: 4 TO 6 SERVINGS / **ACTIVE TIME:** 30 MINUTES / **TOTAL TIME:** 1 HOUR AND 30 MINUTES

Nothing heralds the true start of spring like cherry blossoms, and what better way to showcase that beautiful display than using the resulting fruits to make an irresistible pie?

1. Preheat oven to 350°F. Place the cherries, sugar, and lemon juice in a saucepan and cook, while stirring occasionally, over medium heat until the mixture is syrupy.

2. Combine the cornstarch and water in a small bowl and stir this mixture into the saucepan. Reduce heat to low and cook, while stirring, until the mixture is thick. Remove from heat, add the almond extract, and let cool.

3. When the cherry mixture has cooled, place the bottom crust in a greased cast-iron skillet and pour the cherry mixture into the crust. Top with the other crust, make a few slits in the top, and brush the top crust with the beaten egg.

4. Place the pie in the oven and bake until the top crust is golden brown, about 45 minutes. Remove and let cool before serving.

INGREDIENTS:

4   CUPS CHERRIES (DARK OR RAINIER PREFERRED), PITTED

2   CUPS SUGAR

2   TABLESPOONS FRESH LEMON JUICE

3   TABLESPOONS CORNSTARCH

1   TABLESPOON WATER

¼   TEASPOON ALMOND EXTRACT

2   FLAKY PASTRY CRUSTS (SEE PAGE 580)

1   EGG, BEATEN

YOGURT CUSTARD PIE
with BLACKBERRY PRESERVES

YIELD: 6 TO 8 SERVINGS / **ACTIVE TIME:** 1 HOUR / **TOTAL TIME:** 3 TO 24 HOURS

If you want a pie that's a bit healthier than the rich desserts featured in this chapter, this one's for you. Greek yogurt is thick and creamy and just a little tart, and makes a delicious, custardy filling. Put it in a nut crust and top with warmed preserves, and you have an easy, instant hit.

---

1. Preheat the oven to 350°F.

2. In a large bowl, whisk together the yogurt, eggs, sugar, lemon juice, and vanilla.

3. Working with the crust in a 10-inch cast-iron skillet, transfer the filling into the piecrust and distribute evenly.

4. Put the skillet in the oven and bake for 25 minutes, until the filling is just set. A toothpick inserted in the edge of the pie will come out clean, but the center can still look slightly undercooked.

5. Remove the skillet from the oven and allow the pie to cool for 5 to 10 minutes. Warm the preserves in a small saucepan or a microwave-safe bowl. Spread over the yogurt filling, add fresh berries for garnish, cover with plastic wrap, and refrigerate for at least 2 hours and up to a day before serving.

INGREDIENTS:

1   CUP LOW-FAT PLAIN GREEK YOGURT

2   EGGS, LIGHTLY BEATEN

¼   CUP SUGAR

3   TABLESPOONS FRESH LEMON JUICE

1   TEASPOON VANILLA EXTRACT

1   PECAN NUT CRUST (SEE PAGE 584)

½   CUP BLACKBERRY PRESERVES

    FRESH BERRIES, FOR GARNISH

PUMPKIN PIE

YIELD: 6 TO 8 SERVINGS / **ACTIVE TIME:** 30 MINUTES / **TOTAL TIME:** 1 HOUR AND 30 MINUTES

With the butter-and-sugar combo underneath the pie shell, the result is a crisp, sweet crust topped with an earthy, smooth pumpkin filling. It really works.

1. Preheat the oven to 400°F.

2. In a large bowl, combine the pumpkin puree, evaporated milk, eggs, sugar, salt, cinnamon, ginger, and nutmeg. Stir to combine thoroughly.

3. Put a 12-inch cast-iron skillet over medium heat and melt the butter in it. Add the brown sugar and cook, while stirring constantly, for 1 to 2 minutes, until the sugar is dissolved. Carefully remove pan from heat.

4. Place the piecrust over the sugar mixture. Fill with the pumpkin mixture.

5. Put the skillet in the oven and bake for 15 minutes, then reduce the heat to 325°F and bake for an additional 30 to 45 minutes, until the filling is firm and a toothpick inserted in the middle comes out clean. Don't overcook.

6. Remove the skillet from the oven and allow to cool before serving. Serve with fresh whipped cream.

INGREDIENTS:

- 1   (14 OZ.) CAN OF PUMPKIN PUREE (NOT PUMPKIN PIE FILLING)
- 1   (12 OZ.) CAN OF EVAPORATED MILK
- 2   EGGS, LIGHTLY BEATEN
- ½   CUP SUGAR
- ½   TEASPOON SALT
- 1   TEASPOON CINNAMON
- ¼   TEASPOON GROUND GINGER
- ¼   TEASPOON GROUND NUTMEG
- 1   TABLESPOON UNSALTED BUTTER
- 1   TABLESPOON LIGHT BROWN SUGAR
- 1   FLAKY PASTRY CRUST (SEE PAGE 580)

PECAN PIE

YIELD: 8 TO 10 SERVINGS / ACTIVE TIME: 30 MINUTES / TOTAL TIME: 1 HOUR AND 30 MINUTES

This simple dessert of nuts, eggs, sugar, and vanilla is associated with the South, especially Louisiana. Credit for its creation, however, is partly owed to the French, who used the newly discovered nut in a dessert during their early days in the territory.

1. Preheat the oven to 350°F.

2. In a large bowl, whisk the eggs until thoroughly combined. Add the corn syrup, sugar, melted butter, and vanilla. Whisk until combined, then stir in the pecan pieces.

3. Working with the crust in a 10-inch cast-iron skillet, transfer the filling into the piecrust, shaking the skillet gently so that the filling is distributed evenly.

4. Put the skillet in the oven and bake for about 1 hour or until a knife inserted in the center comes out clean. If the edge of the crust becomes overly brown, remove the skillet from the oven and put foil over the exposed crust until the filling is set.

5. Remove the skillet from the oven and allow to cool to room temperature before serving.

TIP: If you intend to remove the pie before serving, make sure you grease the skillet with butter or cooking spray before cooking. When the pie is cooked and completely cooled, it will be possible to slide the pie out with the help of a thin plastic spatula. However, greasing the pan in this manner will lend the bottom crust a slightly rough texture.

INGREDIENTS:

3 EGGS

1 CUP DARK CORN SYRUP

½ CUP SUGAR

4 TABLESPOONS UNSALTED BUTTER, MELTED

1 TEASPOON VANILLA EXTRACT

1 CUP PECAN HALVES OR BROKEN PIECES

1 FLAKY PASTRY CRUST (SEE PAGE 580)

CHOCOLATE & BOURBON PECAN PIE

YIELD: 8 TO 10 SERVINGS / **ACTIVE TIME:** 45 MINUTES / **TOTAL TIME:** 2 HOURS

Here's another step up in the pecan pie department. If you're looking to make a pie that will have your guests raving about your cooking, this is the one!

1. Preheat the oven to 350°F. Spread the pecan pieces on a baking sheet in a single layer. Bake for 6 to 10 minutes, checking often to make sure they don't burn. When fragrant, remove from oven and let cool. Chop pecans into small pieces and set aside.

2. Reduce oven temperature to 325°F.

3. Working with the crust in a 12-inch cast-iron skillet, sprinkle the toasted pecan pieces and chocolate chips evenly onto the crust.

4. In a saucepan over medium heat, combine the corn syrup, granulated sugar, light brown sugar, and bourbon. Stir to combine and cook, while stirring constantly, until the mixture just comes to a boil. Remove from heat.

5. In a large bowl, whisk the eggs until thoroughly combined. Add the melted butter, vanilla, and salt, and whisk to combine. Add about ¼ of the sugar-and-bourbon mixture to the egg mixture, whisking briskly to combine so the eggs don't curdle or cook. When thoroughly combined, continue to add the hot liquid to the egg mixture in small amounts, whisking to combine thoroughly after each addition until all of it is incorporated. Pour this mixture over the nuts and chocolate pieces and shake the skillet gently to distribute evenly.

6. Put the skillet in the oven and bake for 1 hour or until a knife inserted toward the middle comes out clean. If the edge of the crust becomes overly brown, remove the skillet from the oven and put aluminum foil over the exposed crust until the filling is set. Remove the skillet from the oven and allow to cool completely before serving.

INGREDIENTS:

1½ CUPS PECANS

1 FLAKY PASTRY CRUST (SEE PAGE 580)

6 OZ. SEMISWEET CHOCOLATE CHIPS

1 CUP DARK CORN SYRUP

⅓ CUP GRANULATED SUGAR

½ CUP FIRMLY PACKED LIGHT BROWN SUGAR

¼ CUP BOURBON

4 LARGE EGGS

4 TABLESPOONS UNSALTED BUTTER, MELTED

2 TEASPOONS VANILLA EXTRACT

½ TEASPOON TABLE SALT

CHOCOLATE & SALTED PISTACHIO PUDDING PIE

YIELD: 6 TO 8 SERVINGS / ACTIVE TIME: 1 HOUR / TOTAL TIME: 2 TO 24 HOURS

So easy to make, so good, and so colorful, too. Kids love this one. And guess what? So do adults.

1. Warm a 10-inch cast-iron skillet over low heat and then place 1 tablespoon of the butter into it.

2. In a large bowl, mix the cookie crumbs with the remaining butter until combined. Carefully remove the cast-iron skillet from the heat and press the cookie mixture into the bottom of the pan to form a crust. Allow to cool and set.

3. In a small microwave-safe bowl, microwave the chocolate in 15-second increments, removing to stir after each, until just melted. Stir in the sweetened condensed milk.

4. Pour the chocolate mixture over the crust. Sprinkle with half of the salted pistachio pieces. Refrigerate for about 30 minutes.

5. In a large bowl, whisk together the pudding mix and milk for about 3 minutes, until the mixture is smooth and thick. Put the pudding into the crust and spread evenly. Sprinkle with remaining pistachios. Add a layer of whipped topping, if desired.

6. Cover with plastic wrap and refrigerate for at least 1 hour and up to a day. When ready to serve, remove plastic wrap and sprinkle with additional salted pistachio pieces.

INGREDIENTS:

7   TABLESPOONS UNSALTED BUTTER, MELTED

8   OZ. VANILLA WAFER COOKIES, CRUSHED

2   OZ. SEMISWEET CHOCOLATE CHIPS

¼   CUP SWEETENED CONDENSED MILK

1   CUP SALTED, SHELLED PISTACHIO PIECES, PLUS MORE FOR TOPPING

2   (3.4 OZ.) BOXES OF INSTANT PISTACHIO PUDDING MIX

2   CUPS WHOLE MILK

1   CUP COOL WHIP OR WHIPPED CREAM, FOR TOPPING (OPTIONAL)

LEMON MERINGUE PIE

YIELD: 6 TO 8 SERVINGS / **ACTIVE TIME:** 1 HOUR / **TOTAL TIME:** 1 HOUR AND 30 MINUTES

This is one of my very favorite pies, and while there are several ways you can make it, this one is the best. Be sure to use fresh lemon juice, not the stuff that comes in a bottle. It makes a huge difference.

1. Preheat the oven to 400°F.

2. In a saucepan, combine the cornstarch, 1 cup of the sugar, and pinch of salt. Whisk to combine. Stir in the water, lemon zest, and lemon juice. Cook over medium heat, stirring constantly, until mixture comes to a boil. Remove the saucepan from heat.

3. Place the egg yolks in a bowl and add a spoonful of the hot lemon mixture. Stir rapidly to combine so the eggs don't cook or curdle. Add another spoonful of the lemon mixture and repeat. Transfer the tempered egg yolks to the saucepan and stir constantly to combine well.

4. Cook over medium heat, while stirring. Add the butter. Stir until butter is completely melted and the mixture has thickened, about 3 minutes.

5. Working with the crust in a 10-inch cast-iron skillet, transfer the filling into the piecrust.

6. In a large bowl, beat the egg whites and the remaining salt with an electric mixer on high until soft peaks form. Continue to beat, adding the remaining sugar 2 tablespoons at a time until all the sugar has been incorporated and stiff peaks start to form.

7. Spoon the meringue onto the lemon filling and spread to cover evenly.

8. Put the skillet in the oven for about 10 minutes, until the meringue is just golden.

9. Remove skillet and allow to cool completely before serving.

INGREDIENTS:

⅓ CUP CORNSTARCH

1½ CUPS SUGAR

¼ TEASPOON SALT, PLUS A PINCH

1½ CUPS WATER

ZEST OF 1 LEMON

½ CUP FRESH LEMON JUICE

4 EGGS, SEPARATED

1 TABLESPOON UNSALTED BUTTER

1 BAKED CRUST (SEE PAGE 579)

DOUBLE LEMON TART

YIELD: 6 TO 8 SERVINGS / ACTIVE TIME: 30 MINUTES / TOTAL TIME: 1 HOUR

Lemons are like sunshine—they brighten everything! Very thinly sliced lemons sit atop a lemon-drenched custard to make a dessert whose flavor shines from the first bite to the last.

1. Preheat the oven to 325°F.

2. In a medium bowl, combine the condensed milk, lemon juice, egg yolks, and vanilla. Working with the crust in a 10-inch cast-iron skillet, pour the filling into the crust. Top with the very thin slices of lemon, arranged in a decorative pattern.

3. Put the skillet in the oven and bake for about 15 to 20 minutes, until the liquid has set into a soft custard.

4. Remove the skillet from the oven and allow to cool completely before serving.

INGREDIENTS:

1 (14 OZ.) CAN OF SWEETENED CONDENSED MILK

½ CUP FRESH LEMON JUICE

4 LARGE EGG YOLKS

1 TABLESPOON VANILLA EXTRACT

1 GRAHAM CRACKER CRUST (SEE PAGE 586)

1 LEMON, SEEDED AND SLICED VERY THIN

FRENCH APPLE TART

YIELD: 6 TO 8 SERVINGS / **ACTIVE TIME:** 1 HOUR / **TOTAL TIME:** 2 TO 24 HOURS

Cast-iron skillets caramelize fruits to perfection. This recipe is the quintessential example. It's what the French call "tarte Tatin," and for them it's a national treasure.

1. To make the pastry, whisk together the flour, salt, and 1 tablespoon of sugar in a large bowl. Using your fingers, work 6 tablespoons of the butter into the flour mixture until you have coarse clumps. Sprinkle the ice water over the mixture and continue to work it with your hands until the dough just holds together. Shape it into a ball, wrap it in plastic wrap, and refrigerate it for at least 1 hour or overnight.

2. The tart starts in a 12-inch cast-iron skillet. Place the remaining pieces of butter evenly over the bottom of the skillet, then sprinkle the remaining sugar evenly over everything. Next, start placing the apple slices in a circular pattern, starting at the edge of the pan and working in. The slices should overlap and face the same direction. Place either 1 or 2 slices in the center when finished working around the outside. As the tart bakes, the slices will slide down a bit.

3. Place the skillet on the stove and turn the heat to high. Cook until the juices in the pan are a deep amber color, about 10 minutes. Remove from heat and turn the apples over. Place the skillet back over high heat, cook for another 5 minutes, and then turn off the heat.

4. Preheat the oven to 400°F and position a rack in the center.

5. Take the chilled dough out of the refrigerator and, working on a lightly floured surface, roll it out into a circle just big enough to cover the skillet (about 12 to 14 inches). Taking care not to burn your fingers on the hot skillet, drape the pastry over the apples and it in around the sides.

6. Put the skillet in the oven and bake for about 25 minutes, until the pastry is golden brown.

7. Remove the skillet from the oven and allow to cool for about 5 minutes. Find a plate that is an inch or 2 larger than the top of the skillet and place it over the top. You will be inverting the tart onto the plate. Be sure to use oven mitts or secure pot holders, as the skillet will be hot.

8. Holding the plate tightly against the top of the skillet, turn the skillet over so the plate is now on the bottom. If some of the apples are stuck to the bottom, gently remove them and place them on the tart. Allow to cool a few more minutes, or set aside until ready to serve. The tart is best served warm.

INGREDIENTS:

- 1   CUP ALL-PURPOSE FLOUR, PLUS MORE FOR DUSTING
- ½   TEASPOON SALT
- 1½   CUPS SUGAR, PLUS 1 TABLESPOON
- 2   STICKS UNSALTED BUTTER, CUT INTO SMALL PIECES
- 3   TABLESPOONS ICE WATER
- 8   APPLES, PEELED, CORED, AND SLICED

PEACH GALETTE

YIELD: 6 TO 8 SERVINGS / ACTIVE TIME: 45 MINUTES / TOTAL TIME: 1 HOUR AND 30 MINUTES

When peaches are ripe in the mid-to-late summer, this is a super-simple way to turn them into a great dessert. Smearing some peach jam on the crust before adding the fruit will intensify the flavor, and if you want something a little more "adult," consider adding some Amaretto or bourbon to the jam.

1. Preheat the oven to 400°F.

2. When rolling out the crust, keep in mind that it should be slightly larger than the bottom of the pan so that it can be folded over. Place the crust in a greased 10-inch cast-iron skillet.

3. In a large bowl, mix the peaches with the ½ cup of sugar, lemon juice, cornstarch, and salt. Stir well to coat all the fruit.

4. If using the Amaretto or bourbon, mix it with the jam in a small bowl before brushing or smearing the jam over the center of the crust.

5. Place the peaches in a mound in the center of the crust. Fold the edge of the crust over to cover about 1 inch of filling. Brush the crust with the beaten egg and sprinkle it with the remaining sugar.

6. Put the skillet in the oven and bake until the filling is bubbly, which is necessary for it to thicken, about 35 to 40 minutes.

7. Remove the skillet from the oven and let cool before serving.

INGREDIENTS:

1   FLAKY PASTRY CRUST (SEE PAGE 580)

3   CUPS FRESH PEACHES, PEELED (OPTIONAL), PITTED, AND SLICED

½   CUP SUGAR, PLUS 1 TABLESPOON

    JUICE OF ½ LEMON

3   TABLESPOONS CORNSTARCH

    PINCH OF SALT

1   TEASPOON AMARETTO OR BOURBON (OPTIONAL)

2   TABLESPOONS PEACH JAM

1   EGG, BEATEN

PLUM GALETTE

YIELD: 4 TO 6 SERVINGS / **ACTIVE TIME:** 40 MINUTES / **TOTAL TIME:** 1 HOUR AND 30 MINUTES

Here's another summer fruit–laden treat that is so easy to put together and tastes great! The flavor of the plums is definitely enhanced by the jam, and the whole thing is sublime when topped with ice cream and roasted and salted pumpkin seeds.

1. Preheat the oven to 400°F.

2. When rolling out the crust, keep in mind that it should be slightly larger than the bottom of the pan so that it can be folded over. Place the crust in a greased 10-inch cast-iron skillet.

3. In a large bowl, mix the plums with ½ cup of the sugar, lemon juice, cornstarch, and salt. Stir well to coat all the fruit.

4. Brush or smear the jam over the center of the crust. Place the plums in a mound in the center. Fold the edges of the crust over to cover about 1 inch of the filling. Brush the crust with the beaten egg and sprinkle it with the remaining sugar.

5. Put the skillet in the oven and bake until the filling is bubbly, which is necessary for it to thicken, about 35 to 40 minutes.

6. Remove the skillet from the oven and let cool before serving.

INGREDIENTS:

1   **FLAKY PASTRY CRUST (SEE PAGE 580)**

3   **CUPS FRESH PLUMS, PITTED AND SLICED**

½   **CUP SUGAR, PLUS 1 TABLESPOON**

    JUICE OF ½ LEMON

3   **TABLESPOONS CORNSTARCH**

    PINCH OF SALT

2   **TABLESPOONS BLACKBERRY JAM**

1   **EGG, BEATEN**

PINEAPPLE UPSIDE-DOWN CAKE

YIELD: 8 TO 10 SERVINGS / ACTIVE TIME: 1 HOUR / TOTAL TIME: 2 HOURS

This is another recipe that is cooked to perfection in cast-iron. In 1925, Dole sponsored a pineapple recipe contest, promising to publish winning recipes in a book. The company received over 50,000 recipes, and over 2,000 of them were for pineapple upside-down cake. It's been a classic of American cooking ever since.

1. Preheat the oven to 350°F.

2. Place a 10-inch cast-iron skillet over medium-high heat. Add the room-temperature butter, the juice from the can of pineapples, and the dark brown sugar. Stir continuously while the sugar melts, and continue stirring until the liquid boils and starts to thicken. Cook until the sauce darkens and gains the consistency of caramel.

3. Remove from heat and place the pineapple rings in the liquid, working from the outside in. If adding cherries, place a cherry in the center of each ring. Put the skillet in the oven while preparing the batter.

4. Beat the 4 tablespoons cold butter and light brown sugar with an electric mixer until light and creamy. Beat in the eggs one at a time, making sure the first is thoroughly incorporated before adding the next. Add the buttermilk and vanilla extract.

5. In a small bowl, whisk together the flour, baking powder, and salt. Combine the dry and wet mixtures and stir until combined but not overly smooth.

6. Remove the skillet from the oven and pour the batter over the pineapple rings. Return to the oven and bake for 45 minutes, until the cake is golden and a knife inserted in the center of the cake comes out clean.

7. Remove from the oven and let rest for about 10 minutes.

8. Find a plate that is an inch or two larger than the top of the skillet and place it over the top. You will be inverting the cake onto the plate. Be sure to use oven mitts or secure pot holders, as the skillet will be hot. Holding the plate tightly against the top of the skillet, turn the skillet over so the plate is on the bottom. If some of the pineapple is stuck to the bottom of the skillet, gently remove it and place it on the cake.

9. Allow to cool a few more minutes, or set aside until ready to serve. The cake is best served warm.

INGREDIENTS:

- 1 STICK OF UNSALTED BUTTER, ½ AT ROOM TEMPERATURE, ½ CHILLED
- 1 (20 OZ.) CAN OF PINEAPPLE RINGS, WITH THE JUICE
- ½ CUP DARK BROWN SUGAR
- MARASCHINO CHERRIES, AS NEEDED (OPTIONAL)
- 1 CUP LIGHT BROWN SUGAR
- 2 EGGS
- 1 CUP BUTTERMILK
- 1 TEASPOON VANILLA EXTRACT
- 1½ CUPS ALL-PURPOSE FLOUR
- 1½ TEASPOONS BAKING POWDER
- ½ TEASPOON SALT

ORANGE CAKE

YIELD: 6 TO 8 SERVINGS / **ACTIVE TIME:** 40 MINUTES / **TOTAL TIME:** 1 HOUR AND 30 MINUTES

When all your friends have flown south for the winter and you're listening to a forecast for snow, stop everything and make this cake. As it's cooling, take a fragrant bubble bath, wrap yourself in a fluffy robe, put on warm slippers, and have a piece of this cake with a glass of Champagne.

1. Preheat the oven to 350°F. Put a 12-inch cast-iron skillet in the oven as it warms.

2. In a large bowl, combine the sugar and orange zest, working them together so the oils from the zest permeate the sugar. Add the butter and beat until the mixture is light and fluffy. Add the eggs one at a time, stirring to combine thoroughly after each addition.

3. In the measuring cup holding the flour, add the baking powder and mix together. Alternate adding the flour mixture and the orange juice to the butter-sugar mixture and stir until thoroughly combined.

4. Remove the skillet from the oven using pot holders or oven mitts. Pour the batter into it.

5. Put the skillet in the oven and bake for about 30 to 35 minutes, until the top is golden, the cake springs to the touch, and a toothpick inserted in the middle comes out clean. Remove the skillet, let cool, and cut into wedges.

6. Serve with fresh whipped cream flavored with Grand Marnier liqueur and a glass of Champagne.

INGREDIENTS:

¾ **CUP SUGAR**

ZEST OF 2 ORANGES (ABOUT 2 TABLESPOONS)

1 **STICK OF UNSALTED BUTTER, CUT INTO SMALL PIECES**

3 **EGGS**

1½ **CUPS ALL-PURPOSE FLOUR**

1 **TEASPOON BAKING POWDER**

½ **CUP ORANGE JUICE (FRESHLY SQUEEZED PREFERRED)**

GRAND MARNIER WHIPPED CREAM, FOR SERVING

CHAMPAGNE, FOR SERVING

BASIC CARROT CAKE

YIELD: 8 SERVINGS / ACTIVE TIME: 20 MINUTES / TOTAL TIME: 1 HOUR

This recipe makes a delicious and moist carrot cake. It's especially tasty topped with an easy-to-make cream cheese frosting.

1. Preheat the oven to 350°F.

2. In a 10-inch cast-iron skillet, melt the butter over medium heat. When it's melted, add the carrots and raisins. Simmer over low to medium heat.

3. In a large bowl, combine the cake mix, water, oil, applesauce, and eggs. Stir to combine.

4. When the butter in the skillet is bubbling, turn off the heat and pour the cake batter over the carrot-and-raisin mixture.

5. Place the skillet in the oven and bake for 35 to 40 minutes, until the cake is browned on top and a toothpick inserted in the middle comes out clean.

6. Remove the skillet from the oven and allow the cake to cool for about 10 minutes. The skillet will still be hot. Put a large serving plate on the counter and, working quickly and purposefully, flip the skillet so the cake is inverted onto the plate. Allow to cool completely before applying the Easy Cream Cheese Frosting.

EASY CREAM CHEESE FROSTING

1. In a large bowl, combine all ingredients. With an electric mixer, beat on medium until well combined and smooth.

2. Spread over cooled cake.

INGREDIENTS:

- 1   STICK OF UNSALTED BUTTER
- 1   CUP JULIENNED CARROTS, FINELY CHOPPED
- 1½   CUPS GOLDEN RAISINS
- 1   (15.25 OZ.) BOX OF CARROT CAKE MIX
- ¾   CUP WATER
- ⅔   CUP VEGETABLE OIL
- 6   OZ. UNSWEETENED APPLESAUCE
- 4   EGGS
-   EASY CREAM CHEESE FROSTING (SEE BELOW)

EASY CREAM CHEESE FROSTING

- 6   OZ. CREAM CHEESE, AT ROOM TEMPERATURE
- 4   TABLESPOONS UNSALTED BUTTER, AT ROOM TEMPERATURE
- 1¼   CUPS CONFECTIONERS' SUGAR
- ½   TEASPOON VANILLA EXTRACT

DOUBLE CHOCOLATE DECADENCE CAKE

YIELD: 8 SERVINGS / ACTIVE TIME: 20 MINUTES / TOTAL TIME: 1 HOUR

When you are in the mood for a fudgy, quick chocolate cake, look no further than this recipe. It's so easy to make—and so addicting.

1. Preheat the oven to 350°F.

2. In a 10-inch cast-iron skillet, melt the butter over medium heat. When it's melted, add the chocolate chips. Reduce heat and cook until the chocolate is melted.

3. In a large bowl, combine the cake mix, water, oil, applesauce, and eggs. Stir to combine.

4. When the chocolate/butter mixture is melted and hot, but not bubbling, turn off the heat and pour the batter over the chocolate.

5. Place the skillet in the oven and bake for 35 to 40 minutes, until the cake is browned on the top and sides and a toothpick inserted in the middle comes out clean.

6. Remove the skillet from the oven and allow the cake to cool for about 10 minutes. The skillet will still be hot. Put a large serving plate on the counter and, working quickly and purposefully, flip the skillet so the cake is inverted onto the plate.

7. Allow to cool slightly before serving.

INGREDIENTS:

6	TABLESPOONS UNSALTED BUTTER
1	CUP SEMISWEET CHOCOLATE CHIPS
1	(15.25 OZ.) BOX OF CHOCOLATE CAKE MIX
1	CUP WATER
½	CUP VEGETABLE OIL
6	OZ. UNSWEETENED APPLESAUCE
4	EGGS

LEMON & RASPBERRY CAKE

YIELD: 6 TO 8 SERVINGS / **ACTIVE TIME:** 40 MINUTES / **TOTAL TIME:** 1 HOUR AND 30 MINUTES

Bright, beautiful, and as delicious to eat as it is to look at, this is a cake you'll find yourself making repeatedly in the summer. Serve it with fresh raspberries, blueberries, or blackberries and a dollop of whipped cream flavored with raspberry liqueur.

1. Preheat the oven to 350°F. Put a 10-inch cast-iron skillet in the oven as it warms up.

2. In a small bowl, gently mash the raspberries and sprinkle with the 1 tablespoon of sugar. Set aside.

3. In a large bowl, combine the remaining sugar and the lemon zest, working them together so the oils from the zest permeate the sugar. Add the butter and beat until the mixture is light and fluffy. Add the eggs one at a time, stirring to combine after each addition.

4. In the measuring cup holding the flour, add the baking powder and mix the ingredients together. While stirring, alternate adding the flour mixture and the sour cream to the butter-and-sugar mixture until thoroughly combined. Gently stir in the mashed raspberries. Be careful not to overmix.

5. Remove the skillet from the oven with pot holders or oven mitts and fill with the batter.

6. Put the skillet in the oven and bake for about 30 to 35 minutes, until the top is golden, the cake springs to the touch, and a toothpick inserted in the middle comes out clean. Remove the skillet, let cool, and cut into wedges.

INGREDIENTS:

½ CUP FRESH RASPBERRIES, OR FROZEN RASPBERRIES, THAWED AND DRAINED

1 CUP SUGAR, PLUS 1 TABLESPOON

ZEST OF 2 LEMONS (ABOUT 1 TABLESPOON)

6 TABLESPOONS UNSALTED BUTTER, CUT INTO SMALL PIECES

2 EGGS

1 CUP ALL-PURPOSE FLOUR

1 TEASPOON BAKING POWDER

½ CUP SOUR CREAM

GERMAN CHOCOLATE CAKE

YIELD: 8 SERVINGS / ACTIVE TIME: 20 MINUTES / TOTAL TIME: 1 HOUR

By adding some chocolate malt to a devil's food cake mix—and lots of yummy coconut—this cake takes on a distinctive flavor that's rich without being overly sweet. Which means you can put a layer of gooey Coconut-Pecan Frosting on it and really indulge.

1. Preheat the oven to 350°F.

2. In a 10-inch cast-iron skillet, melt the butter over low to medium heat.

3. In a large bowl, combine the cake mix, Ovaltine, coconut flakes, water, oil, applesauce, and eggs. Stir to combine.

4. Pour the batter over the butter. Place the skillet in the oven and bake for 25 to 30 minutes, until the cake is browned on the top and a toothpick inserted in the middle comes out clean.

5. Remove the skillet from the oven and allow the cake to cool for about 10 minutes. The skillet will still be hot. Put a large serving plate on the counter and, working quickly and purposefully, flip the skillet so the cake is inverted onto the plate. Allow the cake to cool an additional 15 to 20 minutes before applying the Coconut-Pecan Frosting, slicing, and serving.

COCONUT-PECAN FROSTING

1. In a large saucepan, combine the evaporated milk, sugar, egg yolk, butter, and vanilla. Cook over medium heat, stirring frequently, until thickened, about 10 to 12 minutes. Add the coconut and pecans and stir to combine. Remove the saucepan from heat and let cool, while stirring occasionally. Spread over the top of the cooled cake.

INGREDIENTS:

- 1   STICK OF UNSALTED BUTTER
- 1   (15.25 OZ.) BOX OF DEVIL'S FOOD CAKE MIX
- ⅓   CUP CHOCOLATE OVALTINE
- 1   CUP UNSWEETENED COCONUT FLAKES
- 1   CUP WATER
- ½   CUP VEGETABLE OIL
- 6   OZ. UNSWEETENED APPLESAUCE
- 4   EGGS
-      COCONUT-PECAN FROSTING (SEE RECIPE)

COCONUT-PECAN FROSTING

- ½   CUP EVAPORATED MILK
- ½   CUP SUGAR
- 1   EGG YOLK
- 4   TABLESPOONS UNSALTED BUTTER, CUT INTO SMALL PIECES
- ½   TEASPOON VANILLA EXTRACT
- ½   CUP SWEETENED COCONUT FLAKES
- ½   CUP PECANS, CHOPPED

CARAMEL RAISIN SPICE CAKE

YIELD: 8 SERVINGS / **ACTIVE TIME:** 20 MINUTES / **TOTAL TIME:** 1 HOUR

It's so much fun to shop for add-ins to cake mixes! When I discovered caramel raisins, I couldn't resist adding them to a spice cake mix along with some chopped nuts. See if your family enjoys it as much as mine did (if they're a little reticent, draw them in by adding a scoop of butter pecan ice cream).

1. Preheat the oven to 350°F.

2. In a 10-inch cast-iron skillet, melt the butter over low to medium heat.

3. In a large bowl, combine the cake mix, caramel raisins, nuts, water, oil, applesauce, and eggs. Stir to combine.

4. When the butter in the skillet is hot, pour the batter over it.

5. Place the skillet in the oven and bake for 30 minutes, until the top of the cake is browned and a toothpick inserted in the middle comes out clean.

6. Remove the skillet from the oven and allow the cake to cool for about 10 minutes. The skillet will still be hot. Put a large serving plate on the counter and, working quickly and purposefully, flip the skillet so the cake is inverted onto the plate. Allow the cake to cool an additional 15 to 20 minutes before serving.

INGREDIENTS:

1   STICK OF UNSALTED BUTTER

1   (15.25 OZ.) BOX OF SPICE CAKE MIX

1   (7 OZ.) PACKAGE OF CARAMEL RAISINS

½   CUP WALNUTS, ALMONDS, OR PECANS, CHOPPED

1   CUP WATER

½   CUP VEGETABLE OIL

6   OZ. UNSWEETENED APPLESAUCE

4   EGGS

PRALINE RED VELVET CAKE

YIELD: 8 SERVINGS / ACTIVE TIME: 20 MINUTES / TOTAL TIME: 1 HOUR

This cake verges on the elegant—there's something about red velvet that looks exotic and special—and it can be served with no regrets at a dinner party. The butter-brown sugar-pecan topping is crunchy and delicious.

1. Preheat the oven to 350°F.

2. In a 10-inch cast-iron skillet, melt the butter over medium heat. When thoroughly melted, sprinkle the brown sugar over it, then distribute the chopped pecans evenly over the mixture. Lower the heat but continue to cook until the butter is just bubbling.

3. In a large bowl, combine the cake mix, water, oil, applesauce, and eggs. Stir to combine.

4. Turn off the heat and pour the batter into the skillet.

5. Place the skillet in the oven and bake 35 to 40 minutes, until the cake is golden brown on the top and a toothpick inserted in the middle comes out clean.

6. Remove the skillet and allow the cake to cool for about 15 minutes. Run a spatula around the edges and toward the bottom to loosen any sugar or nuts. Put a large serving plate on the counter and, working quickly and purposefully, flip the skillet so the cake is inverted onto the plate. Cool to room temperature before serving.

INGREDIENTS:

1	STICK OF UNSALTED BUTTER
½	CUP DARK BROWN SUGAR
1	CUP PECANS, CHOPPED
1	(15.25 OZ.) BOX OF RED VELVET CAKE MIX
1	CUP WATER
½	CUP VEGETABLE OIL
6	OZ. UNSWEETENED APPLESAUCE
4	EGGS

SOCKERKAKA

YIELD: 12 SERVINGS / ACTIVE TIME: 25 MINUTES / TOTAL TIME: 1 HOUR AND 20 MINUTES

This fragrant cake was adapted from *The Great Scandinavian Baking Book*, and it requires a 12-cup cast-iron fluted tube pan to give the exterior crumb the proper burnish. Serve plain or top slices with sliced citrus, a cinnamon-rich applesauce, or lightly sweetened whipped cream.

1. Preheat the oven to 350°F.

2. Spray a cast-iron fluted tube pan with nonstick cooking spray.

3. Place the flour, sugar, baking powder, cardamom, orange zest, and salt in a large bowl and whisk to combine.

4. Place the eggs, yogurt, and milk in another bowl and stir to combine. Add the wet mixture to the dry mixture and stir with a wooden spoon until just combined.

5. Pour the batter into the prepared pan and bake until a toothpick inserted into the center of the cake comes out clean, about 55 minutes. Immediately remove the cake from the pan and let it cool on a wire rack. Let cool completely before slicing and dusting with the confectioners' sugar.

INGREDIENTS:

2	CUPS ALL-PURPOSE FLOUR
1¼	CUPS SUGAR
2	TEASPOONS BAKING POWDER
2	TABLESPOONS CARDAMOM
	ZEST OF 1 LARGE ORANGE
½	TEASPOON SALT
3	LARGE EGGS
1	CUP PLAIN YOGURT
½	CUP WHOLE MILK
	CONFECTIONERS' SUGAR, FOR DUSTING

DUTCH APPLE BABY

YIELD: 4 SERVINGS / ACTIVE TIME: 45 MINUTES / TOTAL TIME: 1 HOUR AND 15 MINUTES

This is a classic cast-iron skillet recipe for a pastry that puffs up in the oven. It is reminiscent of the recipe for David Eyre's Pancake (see page 72).

1. Preheat the oven to 425°F and position a rack in the middle.

2. Cut the apples into slices. Heat a 10-inch cast-iron skillet over medium-high heat. Add the butter and apples and cook, while stirring, for 3 to 4 minutes, until the apples soften. Add the ¼ cup of sugar and cinnamon and continue cooking for another 3 or 4 minutes. Distribute the apples evenly over the bottom of the skillet and remove from heat.

3. In a large bowl, mix the remaining sugar, flour, and salt together. In a smaller bowl, whisk together the milk, eggs, and vanilla or almond extract. Add the wet ingredients to the dry ingredients and stir to combine. Pour the batter over the apples.

4. Place the skillet in the oven and bake for 15 to 20 minutes, until the "baby" is puffy and browned on the top.

5. Remove the skillet from the oven and allow to cool for a few minutes. Run a knife along the edge of the skillet to loosen the dessert. Put a plate over the skillet and, using oven mitts or pot holders, flip the skillet over so the dessert is transferred to the plate. Serve warm with a dusting of confectioners' sugar.

INGREDIENTS:

- 2   FIRM, SEMI-TART APPLES (MUTSU OR GOLDEN DELICIOUS), PEELED AND CORED
- 4   TABLESPOONS UNSALTED BUTTER
- ¼   CUP SUGAR, PLUS 3 TABLESPOONS
- 1   TABLESPOON CINNAMON
- ¾   CUP ALL-PURPOSE FLOUR
- ¼   TEASPOON SALT
- ¾   CUP WHOLE MILK
- 4   EGGS
- 1   TEASPOON VANILLA OR ALMOND EXTRACT

   CONFECTIONERS' SUGAR, FOR DUSTING

SOPAIPILLAS

YIELD: 24 SOPAIPILLAS / ACTIVE TIME: 25 MINUTES / TOTAL TIME: 45 MINUTES

This fried, puffed pastry, which is popular in New Mexico and parts of South America, is sweet, simple, and utterly addictive.

1. Place the flour, baking powder, salt, and sugar in the bowl of a stand mixer and whisk to combine.

2. Turn the mixer on low speed and slowly drizzle in the warm water. Beat until a soft, smooth dough forms, about 8 minutes. Cover the bowl and let the dough rest for 20 minutes.

3. Place a cast-iron Dutch oven over medium-high heat for 2 minutes. Add oil or lard until it is 2 inches deep. Reduce the heat to medium-low.

4. Divide the dough in half and pat each piece into a rectangle. Cut each rectangle into 12 squares and roll each square to ⅛ inch thick.

5. Raise the heat under the Dutch oven to medium and heat for 4 minutes. Working in batches of three, place the squares in the oil and use tongs to gently submerge each sopaipilla until they are puffy and golden, about 1 minute. Transfer to a paper towel–lined tray and continue until all of the squares have been fried. Serve immediately with confectioners' sugar, cinnamon, and honey.

INGREDIENTS:

3 CUPS SELF-RISING FLOUR

1½ TEASPOONS BAKING POWDER

1 TEASPOON SALT

1 TEASPOON SUGAR

1 CUP WARM WATER (110°F)

VEGETABLE OIL OR LARD, FOR FRYING

CONFECTIONERS' SUGAR, FOR SERVING

CINNAMON, FOR SERVING

HONEY, FOR SERVING

COCONUT PUDDING PANCAKES

YIELD: 30 PANCAKES / ACTIVE TIME: 20 MINUTES / TOTAL TIME: 20 MINUTES

This is a very popular Thai street food that is known as *khanom krok*, or "candy bowl," because of the shape and sweetness. The traditional toppings are green onion and corn, making it both sweet and savory, but you can also add cooked taro or diced pumpkin for an authentic bite. The biggest challenge will be gaining control of the heat—too hot and the outside burns, too cool and it won't crisp properly.

1. Place the coconut milk, 1 cup of the rice flour, coconut flakes, the 1 tablespoon of sugar, and the salt in a bowl and whisk vigorously to combine, making sure that the sugar dissolves. Set the mixture aside.

2. Place the cream of coconut, remaining rice flour, remaining sugar, and tapioca starch or cornstarch in another bowl and whisk to combine, making sure that the starch dissolves.

3. Transfer both mixtures to separate pitchers (or measuring cups with spouts) for easy pouring.

4. Place a cast-iron takoyaki pan or aebleskiver pan over medium heat and coat each well with a drop of the vegetable oil.

5. Fill each well two-thirds of the way with the coconut milk mixture. Let that set for about 1 minute. If using, top with the corn and green onions. Add a layer of the cream of coconut mixture, cover the pan, and let the cakes steam for 5 minutes, until they are fairly solid.

6. Carefully lift a cake out of the well, invert it, and top with another one to make a sphere. Set the sphere aside and repeat with the remaining half-moons.

7. Repeat until all of the mixtures have been used and serve immediately.

TIP: Rice flour can be found in most well-stocked markets. We prefer seeking out Thai rice flour, but the Japanese brand Mochiko is widely available and is a good alternative.

INGREDIENTS:

- 1½ CUPS COCONUT MILK
- 1½ CUPS RICE FLOUR
- ½ CUP SWEETENED COCONUT FLAKES
- ¼ CUP SUGAR, PLUS 1 TABLESPOON
- ½ TEASPOON KOSHER SALT
- 1 CUP CREAM OF COCONUT
- ½ TABLESPOON TAPIOCA STARCH OR CORNSTARCH
- 2 TABLESPOONS VEGETABLE OIL
- ¼ CUP CORN (OPTIONAL)
- 2 GREEN ONIONS, SLICED THIN (OPTIONAL)

THE BEST SKILLET BROWNIES

YIELD: 6 TO 8 SERVINGS / ACTIVE TIME: 40 MINUTES / TOTAL TIME: 1 HOUR AND 30 MINUTES

If you're serious about brownies, you'll love this recipe. When shopping for the ingredients, remember that the better the chocolate, the better the taste and texture of the brownie. What gets baked up in the cast-iron skillet is a gooey yet crunchy confection that is heaven in every bite. Don't even slice them up—serve them right out of the skillet (when cool enough). Just be sure to have friends and family around when you do, as you may be tempted to eat the whole pan by yourself.

1. Preheat the oven to 350°F.

2. In a microwave-safe bowl, microwave 9 tablespoons of the butter and chopped chocolate pieces together, cooking in 15-second increments and stirring after each, until the butter and chocolate are just melted together and smooth.

3. In a large bowl, add the sugar and eggs and whisk to combine. Add the vanilla and stir to combine. Working in batches, start mixing the melted chocolate into the mixture, stirring vigorously to combine after each addition. In a small bowl, mix the flour, cocoa powder, and salt. Gently fold the dry mixture into the chocolate mixture. Next, fold in the chocolate chips.

4. Over medium heat, melt the remaining butter in a 10-inch cast-iron skillet. When melted, pour in the batter. Place the skillet in the oven and bake for about 30 minutes or until a toothpick inserted in the center comes out with a few moist crumbs. It may need a couple more minutes, but be careful not to overbake this or you'll lose the gooeyness that makes these brownies so great. When the brownies are ready, remove the skillet from the oven and allow to cool for about 10 minutes.

5. Dig right in, or scoop into bowls and serve with your favorite ice cream.

VARIATION: To give the brownies a refreshing zing, add ½ teaspoon of peppermint extract and 1½ cups of chopped York Peppermint Patties to the batter.

INGREDIENTS:

- 10 **TABLESPOONS UNSALTED BUTTER**
- ½ **LB. SEMISWEET CHOCOLATE, COARSELY CHOPPED**
- 1 **CUP SUGAR**
- 3 **EGGS, AT ROOM TEMPERATURE**
- 1 **TEASPOON VANILLA EXTRACT**
- ½ **CUP ALL-PURPOSE FLOUR, PLUS 2 TABLESPOONS**
- 2 **TABLESPOONS UNSWEETENED COCOA POWDER**
- ¼ **TEASPOON SALT**
- 1 **CUP SEMISWEET CHOCOLATE CHIPS**

  VANILLA ICE CREAM, FOR SERVING (OPTIONAL)

GIANT CHOCOLATE CHIP COOKIE

YIELD: 6 TO 8 SERVINGS / **ACTIVE TIME:** 20 MINUTES / **TOTAL TIME:** 45 MINUTES

Yes, your cast-iron skillet is also a great baking sheet—just smaller, and with sides. So why not bake a giant cookie in it?

1. Preheat oven to 375°F. Place a 12-inch cast-iron skillet in the oven while making the batter.

2. In a large bowl, beat the butter and sugars together until light and fluffy. Add the eggs one at a time, being sure to combine each one thoroughly before proceeding to the next. Stir in the vanilla.

3. Dissolve the baking soda in the hot water and add to the batter with the salt. Stir in the flour and chocolate chips.

4. Remove the skillet from the oven and put the batter in it, smoothing the top with a rubber spatula.

5. Put the skillet in the oven and bake for about 15 minutes, until golden. Serve with ice cream.

INGREDIENTS:

- 2 STICKS OF UNSALTED BUTTER, SOFTENED
- ½ CUP GRANULATED SUGAR
- 1 CUP BROWN SUGAR
- 2 EGGS
- 2 TEASPOONS VANILLA EXTRACT
- 1 TEASPOON BAKING SODA
- 2 TEASPOONS HOT WATER (120°F)
- ½ TEASPOON SALT
- 2½ CUPS ALL-PURPOSE FLOUR
- 2 CUPS SEMISWEET CHOCOLATE CHIPS
- ICE CREAM, FOR SERVING

CLASSIC SHORTBREAD WEDGES

YIELD: 6 TO 8 SERVINGS / **ACTIVE TIME:** 25 MINUTES / **TOTAL TIME:** 1 HOUR

Shortbread is wonderfully simple to prepare and so, so yummy. The butter shines through in each flaky bite. These wedges are the perfect late-afternoon pick-me-up when served with coffee, tea, or hot chocolate.

1. Preheat the oven to 300°F. Place a 12-inch cast-iron skillet in the oven while making the dough.

2. In a large bowl, combine the flour, salt, and sugar, whisking to combine.

3. Cut the butter into slices and add to the flour mixture. The best way to work it into the flour is with your hands. As it starts to come together, add the vanilla extract. Work the mixture until it resembles coarse meal.

4. Gather the dough into a ball. On a lightly floured surface, roll it out into a circle that's just smaller than the surface of the skillet. Slice the round into 8 wedges.

5. Remove the skillet from the oven and place the wedges in it to recreate the circle of dough. Bake for about 45 minutes or until the shortbread is a pale golden color. Remove the skillet from the oven and allow to cool for about 10 minutes before transferring the cookies to a plate.

INGREDIENTS:

1   CUP ALL-PURPOSE FLOUR, PLUS MORE FOR DUSTING

¼   TEASPOON SALT

¼   CUP SUGAR

1   STICK OF UNSALTED BUTTER, CHILLED

½   TEASPOON VANILLA EXTRACT

WALNUT BREAD PUDDING

YIELD: 4 TO 6 SERVINGS / ACTIVE TIME: 45 MINUTES / TOTAL TIME: 2 HOURS

If you want a super-simple, irresistible recipe for no-fail bread pudding, look no further. The addition of toasted pecan pieces sets this dish apart. The better the quality of the ice cream, the tastier the bread pudding will be and the better it will set up.

INGREDIENTS:

- ½ CUP WALNUTS, CHOPPED
- 4 TABLESPOONS UNSALTED BUTTER
- 4 CUPS DAY-OLD BREAD PIECES
- ½ CUP RAISINS
- 2 EGGS
- ¼ CUP RUM
- 1 PINT OF VANILLA ICE CREAM, SOFTENED

1. Place a 10-inch cast-iron skillet over medium-high heat. When hot, add the chopped walnuts. Shake the walnuts in the skillet while they cook. You want them to toast but not brown or burn. This should take just a few minutes.

2. When toasted, transfer the walnuts to a plate and allow to cool.

3. Reduce heat to low, add the butter to the skillet, and let it melt. Add the bread pieces and raisins to the skillet and distribute evenly. Sprinkle the walnuts over the bread.

4. In a bowl, whisk the eggs and the rum together. Add the softened ice cream and stir just enough to combine. Pour this mixture over the bread and nuts. Shake the skillet gently to distribute the liquid evenly.

5. Cover with aluminum foil, put in a cool place, and allow the mixture to rest for about 30 minutes so that the bread cubes can soak up the liquid.

6. Preheat the oven to 350°F.

7. Uncover the skillet and bake until the bread pudding is set and the edges are slightly browned, about 40 minutes. Use pot holders or oven mitts to take the skillet out of the oven. Allow to cool for 5 to 10 minutes before serving.

VARIATION: Make a pretty and patriotic red, white, and blue bread pudding by substituting strawberry ice cream for the vanilla and sprinkling fresh or frozen blueberries over the bread pieces before the skillet goes in the oven.

STRAWBERRY RHUBARB CRISP

YIELD: 4 SERVINGS / ACTIVE TIME: 30 MINUTES / TOTAL TIME: 1 HOUR

This magnificent combo traditionally appears in a pie, but this crisp allows you to enjoy it without all of the fuss.

1. Preheat the oven to 450°F.

2. In a bowl, combine the rhubarb pieces, strawberries, granulated sugar, and the 2 teaspoons of flour, and toss to coat the fruit. Transfer to a 10-inch cast-iron skillet.

3. In another bowl, add the butter and brown sugar and work the mixture with a fork or pastry blender. Add the oats, hazelnuts (if using), and remaining flour and continue to work the mixture until it is a coarse meal. Sprinkle it over the fruit in the skillet.

4. Put the skillet in the oven and bake for about 30 minutes, until the topping is golden and the fruit is bubbly. Serve warm with whipped cream or ice cream.

INGREDIENTS:

1½ CUPS CHOPPED RHUBARB

1½ CUPS HULLED AND SLICED STRAWBERRIES

2 TABLESPOONS GRANULATED SUGAR

⅓ CUP ALL-PURPOSE FLOUR, PLUS 2 TEASPOONS

4 TABLESPOONS UNSALTED BUTTER, CHILLED AND CUT INTO PIECES

¼ CUP DARK BROWN SUGAR

¾ CUP QUICK-COOKING OATS

¼ CUP CHOPPED HAZELNUTS (OPTIONAL)

WHIPPED CREAM, FOR SERVING (OPTIONAL)

ICE CREAM, FOR SERVING (OPTIONAL)

APPLE & PEAR CRUMBLE

YIELD: 4 TO 6 SERVINGS / **ACTIVE TIME:** 30 MINUTES / **TOTAL TIME:** 45 MINUTES

The tart pop of the Cortland apples and the sweet softness of the red pears give this dish a wonderful balance, and adding freshly grated ginger to the topping really sets it apart.

1. To prepare the topping, place all of the ingredients in a large mixing bowl and use a fork to mash the butter and other ingredients together. Continue until the topping is a collection of pea-sized pieces. Place the bowl in the refrigerator.

2. To prepare the filling, preheat the oven to 350°F.

3. Place an 8-inch cast-iron skillet over medium heat. Add the butter. Place the salt, brown sugar, and tapioca starch or cornstarch in a bowl and stir to combine.

4. Once the butter has melted, put the apple slices in the pan in one even layer, working from the outside toward the center. Cook for 5 to 7 minutes.

5. Sprinkle half of the brown sugar mixture over the apples.

6. Utilizing the same technique you used for the apple slices, layer all of the pear slices in the skillet. Sprinkle the remaining brown sugar mixture on top. Top with any remaining apple slices.

7. Combine the vanilla extract, almond extract, and lemon juice in a bowl and pour over all of the fruit.

8. Remove the topping from the refrigerator and spread in an even layer on top of the fruit. Cover the skillet with foil, place in the oven, and bake for 15 minutes.

9. Remove the foil and bake for another 20 minutes.

10. If you would like the crisp to set, turn the oven off and open the door slightly. Let the skillet rest in the oven for another 20 minutes. Or remove the skillet, top the crisp with your favorite ice cream or whipped cream, and serve.

INGREDIENTS:

FOR THE TOPPING

½ CUP WHOLE WHEAT FLOUR

1 STICK OF UNSALTED BUTTER, CUT INTO SMALL PIECES

½ CUP OATS

½ CUP BROWN SUGAR

¼ CUP GRANULATED SUGAR

1 TABLESPOON GRATED GINGER

½ TEASPOON CINNAMON

½ TEASPOON NUTMEG

½ TEASPOON KOSHER SALT

FOR THE FILLING

2 TABLESPOONS UNSALTED BUTTER

PINCH OF KOSHER SALT

2 TABLESPOONS BROWN SUGAR

2 TABLESPOONS TAPIOCA STARCH OR CORNSTARCH

3 CORTLAND APPLES, EACH PEELED, QUARTERED, AND CUT INTO 20 EVEN SLICES

3 RED PEARS, EACH PEELED, QUARTERED, AND CUT INTO 16 EVEN SLICES

1 TABLESPOON VANILLA EXTRACT

1 TABLESPOON ALMOND EXTRACT

JUICE OF ½ LEMON

ICE CREAM, FOR SERVING (OPTIONAL)

WHIPPED CREAM, FOR SERVING (OPTIONAL)

PEACH CRISP

YIELD: 4 TO 6 SERVINGS / **ACTIVE TIME:** 30 MINUTES / **TOTAL TIME:** 1 HOUR AND 30 MINUTES

When you've got ripe peaches to work with, you want to find as many recipes as possible to use them in. This one is so quick and easy, it just may rise to the top of that list.

1. Preheat the oven to 350°F.

2. In a bowl, combine the peach slices with ¼ cup of the granulated sugar and 1 or 2 tablespoons of the flour. The amount of flour you use will depend on how juicy the peaches are—more juice means more flour. Let the peaches sit while you make the topping. If there's juice left in the bowl after sitting, add another tablespoon of flour.

3. In another bowl, make the topping. Blend the remaining flour, the remaining granulated sugar, salt, and the brown sugar together, and add the butter, using a fork to combine. When somewhat mixed and crumbly, add the oats and stir to incorporate.

4. Put the peaches in a 10-inch cast-iron skillet and add the topping in an even layer.

5. Put the skillet in the oven and bake for about 1 hour, until the topping is golden and the peaches are bubbling. If it doesn't look crispy enough, turn the oven up to 375°F and continue to bake, checking every 5 minutes until it looks just right. Be careful not to burn the topping.

6. Serve warm with fresh whipped cream and a sprinkling of toasted nuts.

INGREDIENTS:

- 5-6 PEACHES, PITTED AND SLICED
- ¾ CUP GRANULATED SUGAR
- ¾ CUP ALL-PURPOSE FLOUR, PLUS 1 TO 2 TABLESPOONS
- ¼ TEASPOON SALT
- ¼ CUP DARK BROWN SUGAR
- 1 STICK OF UNSALTED BUTTER, CHILLED AND CUT INTO SMALL PIECES
- ½ CUP QUICK-COOKING OATS (NOT INSTANT)
- WHIPPED CREAM, FOR SERVING
- TOASTED PECANS OR WALNUTS, FOR SERVING

BANANAS FLAMBÉ

YIELD: 4 SERVINGS / **ACTIVE TIME:** 15 MINUTES / **TOTAL TIME:** 20 MINUTES

This may well be the perfect dessert. It comes together in a snap, doesn't require any hard-to-find ingredients, and tastes like heaven. If you really want to make a show of it, dim the lights before you add the rum and let your guests "ooh" and "ahh" as you expertly flambé your dish.

1. Place the pat of butter in a 12-inch cast-iron skillet and melt it over medium-high heat. Swirl to make sure the melted butter coats the bottom of the pan.

2. Place the bananas, cut side down, in the skillet and let them cook, undisturbed, until they start to caramelize.

3. Place the nutmeg, granulated sugar, brown sugar, water, and nuts in a mixing bowl and whisk to combine. Carefully pour the mixture over the bananas.

4. Tilt the pan away from you and add the rum. The alcohol will ignite and burn for about 10 seconds before going out. Cook until the sauce is thick and sticky. Serve immediately with vanilla ice cream.

INGREDIENTS:

1 STICK OF UNSALTED BUTTER, MELTED, PLUS 1 PAT

4 BANANAS, PEELED AND SLICED LENGTHWISE

1 TEASPOON GROUND NUTMEG

¾ CUP GRANULATED SUGAR

2 TEASPOONS BROWN SUGAR

½ CUP WATER

½ CUP PECANS OR WALNUTS, TOASTED AND CHOPPED

½ CUP RUM

VANILLA ICE CREAM, FOR SERVING

MANGO *with* LIME-PEPPER SYRUP

YIELD: 4 SERVINGS / ACTIVE TIME: 15 MINUTES / TOTAL TIME: 15 MINUTES

Make this recipe when mangoes are at their most ripe and fragrant. Paired with floral yuzu juice and sweet honey, it's an ideal finish to any Asian-inspired meal. If your pan is well seasoned, don't worry about the acid from the mangoes.

1. Place a dry 10-inch cast-iron skillet over high heat. Add the mango and cook, while turning once, until it is slightly charred, about 3 minutes (depending on how juicy it is).

2. Reduce the heat to low and add the honey, lime zest, lime juice, yuzu or lemon juice, and peppercorns. Cook, while stirring to coat the mangoes, until the honey is melted.

3. Remove from heat and let cool slightly. Remove the mangoes with a slotted spoon and leave the peppercorns in the skillet. Divide the mangoes between 4 small dishes.

4. Top with a dollop of the yogurt, drizzle with additional honey, and serve immediately.

INGREDIENTS:

FLESH OF 2 LARGE MANGOES, DICED

¾ CUP HONEY, PLUS MORE FOR DRIZZLING

ZEST AND JUICE OF 2 LIMES

2 TABLESPOONS FRESH YUZU OR LEMON JUICE

8 WHOLE BLACK PEPPERCORNS

1 CUP GREEK YOGURT, STIRRED

BAKED APPLES

YIELD: 4 SERVINGS / **ACTIVE TIME:** 30 MINUTES / **TOTAL TIME:** 50 MINUTES

These are easy to make and are delicious served warm or at room temperature the next day. Of course, they're best with a side of vanilla ice cream.

1. Preheat the oven to 350°F.

2. Cut the tops off of the apples. Remove as much of the core as you can without cutting the apple in half and then replace the tops.

3. Place a 12-inch cast-iron skillet over medium-high heat. Add the butter and let it melt. Place the apples in the skillet. Add the water from the center so that it distributes evenly around the apples. Drizzle maple syrup or honey over the top of each apple.

4. Put the skillet in the oven and cook for about 20 minutes, or until apples are soft. Drizzle with additional maple syrup or honey, if desired.

VARIATION: Using apple cider instead of water will enable you to reduce the juices in the pan into a concentrated, flavorful sauce.

INGREDIENTS:

4   FIRM APPLES

2   TABLESPOONS UNSALTED BUTTER

½   CUP WATER

   MAPLE SYRUP OR HONEY, TO TASTE

CHERRY CLAFOUTI

YIELD: 4 TO 6 SERVINGS / **ACTIVE TIME:** 20 MINUTES / **TOTAL TIME:** 45 MINUTES

A French specialty that originated in the Limousin region of France, clafouti served as a vehicle for the sour morello cherries that grew there. This dessert is so delicious that it is now known around the world. There is some debate about whether the pits should be removed from the cherries, but Julia Child left them in, believing that they added a nutty flavor. With that kind of authority behind you, how can you go wrong?

1. Place 8 tablespoons of the butter in a microwave-safe bowl and microwave until melted. Preheat the oven to 400°F.

2. In a large bowl, mix together 6 tablespoons of the melted butter, ½ cup of the sugar, the flour, salt, vanilla, eggs, and milk until all ingredients are blended and smooth. Set aside.

3. Put 2 tablespoons of the melted butter in a 12-inch cast-iron skillet and put the skillet in the oven to heat up.

4. Transfer the skillet to the stovetop and add the remaining butter. When it is melted, put ½ cup of the sugar in the skillet and shake it so it distributes evenly. Add the cherries. Pour the batter over the cherries, sprinkle with the last 2 teaspoons of sugar, and put the skillet back in the oven. Bake for about 30 minutes, until the topping is golden brown and set in the center.

5. Dust with confectioners' sugar if desired, and serve warm—and be sure to let everyone know that the cherries contain pits.

INGREDIENTS:

- 10 TABLESPOONS UNSALTED BUTTER
- 1 CUP SUGAR, PLUS 2 TEASPOONS
- ⅔ CUP ALL-PURPOSE FLOUR
- ½ TEASPOON SALT
- 1 TEASPOON VANILLA EXTRACT
- 3 EGGS, BEATEN
- 1 CUP WHOLE MILK
- 3 CUPS RIPE CHERRIES, WITH PITS

  CONFECTIONERS' SUGAR, FOR DUSTING (OPTIONAL)

APPLE PIE

YIELD: 6 TO 8 SERVINGS / ACTIVE TIME: 30 MINUTES / TOTAL TIME: 1 HOUR AND 30 MINUTES

Apple pie is an American classic that bundles the tastes of fall into a single dish, perfect for enjoying with a spoonful of vanilla ice cream and a warm cup of coffee as the weather starts to turn towards winter.

1. Preheat the oven to 350°F.

2. In a large bowl, toss the apples with the cinnamon, sugar, and lemon juice.

3. Place a 12-inch cast-iron skillet over medium heat and melt the butter in it. Add the brown sugar and cook, while stirring constantly, until the sugar is dissolved, about 1 to 2 minutes. Carefully remove pan from heat.

4. Place one of the crusts over the butter-and-sugar mixture in the skillet. Fill with the apple mixture and place the other crust over the apples. Crimp the edges to seal.

5. Brush the top crust with the egg white and cut 4 or 5 slits in the middle.

6. Place the skillet in the oven and bake until the pie is golden brown and the filling is bubbly, about 1 hour. Cover the outermost edge with aluminum foil in the last 10 minutes of baking to prevent it from burning.

7. Remove from the oven and let cool before serving. Serve with whipped cream or ice cream.

TIP: You can flavor whipped cream with liqueur for an especially delicious topping. Beat heavy cream until soft peaks start to form. Add about ¼ cup sugar and continue beating until stiff peaks form. Gently beat in ¼ cup of liqueur, such as apple brandy or Cointreau. Serve immediately or cover with plastic wrap and refrigerate until ready to serve.

INGREDIENTS:

6   **GRANNY SMITH APPLES, PEELED, CORED, AND SLICED**

1   **TEASPOON GROUND CINNAMON**

¾   **CUP SUGAR**

1   **TEASPOON FRESH LEMON JUICE**

1   **TABLESPOON UNSALTED BUTTER**

1   **TABLESPOON LIGHT BROWN SUGAR**

2   **FLAKY PASTRY CRUSTS (SEE PAGE 580)**

1   **EGG WHITE**

   WHIPPED CREAM, FOR SERVING (OPTIONAL)

   VANILLA ICE CREAM, FOR SERVING (OPTIONAL)

GRAPE PIE

YIELD: 6 TO 8 SERVINGS / ACTIVE TIME: 1 HOUR / TOTAL TIME: 1 HOUR AND 30 MINUTES

This refreshing twist on a tarte Tatin is sure to steal the show on any dinner table spread. Sliced grapes make for beautiful presentation, and the taste is just as nice.

1. Preheat the oven to 350°F.

2. In a small bowl, combine the lemon curd, lemon juice, and lemon zest. Set aside.

3. Put a 12-inch cast-iron skillet over medium heat and melt the butter in it. Add the brown sugar and cook, while stirring constantly, until the sugar is dissolved. Carefully remove pan from heat.

4. Place the piecrust over the butter-and-sugar mixture. Spread the lemon curd mixture over the piecrust. Place the grape halves in a decorative pattern on top of the lemon curd, skin-side up. Sprinkle the granulated sugar over the top.

5. Put the skillet in the oven and bake until the filling is set, about 45 to 50 minutes.

6. Remove the skillet from the oven and let cool before serving.

INGREDIENTS:

1   (10 OZ.) JAR OF LEMON CURD

1   TABLESPOON FRESH LEMON JUICE

1   TEASPOON LEMON ZEST

1   TABLESPOON UNSALTED BUTTER

1   TABLESPOON LIGHT BROWN SUGAR

1   FLAKY PASTRY CRUST (SEE PAGE 580)

2-3   CUPS SEEDLESS GRAPES (GREEN, RED, OR A COMBINATION), HALVED

2   TABLESPOONS GRANULATED SUGAR

BLUEBERRY *&* BANANA BREAD PUDDING

YIELD: 4 TO 6 SERVINGS / ACTIVE TIME: 1 HOUR / TOTAL TIME: 2 HOURS

This delicious bread pudding, which features some buttermilk to balance out the sweetness of the rum caramel, is one of the best places for scraps of leftover bread to find a home.

1. Place the banana, eggs, and brown sugar in a mixing bowl and beat with a handheld mixer on medium-high until the mixture is smooth and creamy.

2. Place the cream, milk, buttermilk, vanilla, and salt in a separate bowl and whisk to combine. Pour this mixture into the banana-and-egg mixture and beat until combined.

3. Place the pieces of bread in the bowl and toss until all the pieces are coated. Let the bread soak until the majority of the liquid has been absorbed, 30 to 45 minutes.

4. Preheat the oven to 375°F and grease a 12-inch cast-iron skillet. Add the blueberries to the soaked bread and stir until evenly distributed. Pour the mixture into the skillet, cover with foil, and place in the oven. Bake for 25 minutes, remove the foil, and bake for an additional 20 minutes.

5. While the bread pudding is in the oven, prepare the rum caramel. Place the sugar and ¼ cup of rum in a small saucepan and cook over medium heat until the mixture acquires an amber color. Reduce the heat and add the heavy cream, stirring constantly to incorporate it. Add the remaining rum, butter, and salt, remove from heat, and pour into a heatproof mixing bowl.

6. To prepare the whipped cream, place all of the ingredients in a mixing bowl and beat with a handheld mixer until stiff peaks are just about to form.

7. Remove the bread pudding from the oven, drizzle with the rum caramel, and top with the whipped cream.

INGREDIENTS:

FOR THE BREAD PUDDING

1	BANANA
3	EGGS
¾	CUP PACKED BROWN SUGAR
½	CUP HEAVY CREAM
½	CUP WHOLE MILK
¼	CUP BUTTERMILK
1½	TEASPOONS VANILLA EXTRACT
½	TEASPOON SALT
6	CUPS SOURDOUGH BREAD PIECES
1½	CUPS BLUEBERRIES

FOR THE RUM CARAMEL

½	CUP SUGAR
¼	CUP DARK RUM, PLUS 2 TABLESPOONS
¼	CUP HEAVY CREAM, WARMED
1	TABLESPOON UNSALTED BUTTER
1	TEASPOON SALT

FOR THE WHIPPED CREAM

1	CUP HEAVY CREAM
2	TABLESPOONS CONFECTIONERS' SUGAR
½	TEASPOON SALT

HONEY-GINGER FROZEN YOGURT
with CARAMELIZED PLUMS

YIELD: 4 SERVINGS / ACTIVE TIME: 15 MINUTES / TOTAL TIME: 4 HOURS AND 30 MINUTES

Ginger, honey, and plums are incredibly complementary to one another, and frozen yogurt is the perfect vehicle for this powerful trio.

1. Place the yogurt, evaporated milk, vanilla, ginger, corn syrup, salt, and honey in a mixing bowl and stir to combine. Pour the mixture into an ice cream maker and churn until the desired texture has been reached. Transfer to the freezer and freeze for at least 4 hours.

2. When ready to serve, place the sugar in a bowl and dip the pieces of plum into it until they are completely coated.

3. Place the butter in a 12-inch cast-iron skillet and melt over medium heat. Add the pieces of plum and cook until golden brown all over, about 5 minutes.

4. Scoop the frozen yogurt into bowls and top with the caramelized plums.

INGREDIENTS:

2½ CUPS GREEK YOGURT

½ CUP EVAPORATED MILK

¼ TEASPOON VANILLA EXTRACT

1 TEASPOON GRATED GINGER

2 TABLESPOONS LIGHT CORN SYRUP

½ TEASPOON SALT

⅓ CUP HONEY

½ CUP SUGAR

2 PLUMS, PITTED AND CHOPPED INTO ½-INCH PIECES

4 TABLESPOONS UNSALTED BUTTER

GINGERBREAD MADELEINES

YIELD: 16 MADELEINES / ACTIVE TIME: 25 MINUTES / TOTAL TIME: 3 HOURS

The hunt for sweet treats never stops around Christmastime, and this seasonal take on a classic French pastry, the madeleine, has the potential to become a beloved tradition in your home.

1. Place the butter in a small skillet and cook over medium heat until lightly brown. Remove from heat and let cool to room temperature.

2. Place the butter and the brown sugar in the bowl of a stand mixer fitted with the whisk attachment. Beat on high speed until light and frothy. Lower the speed, add the eggs one at a time, and beat until incorporated. Add the ginger, vanilla, molasses, and milk and beat until incorporated.

3. Sift the flours and baking powder into a bowl. Add the salt, cloves, nutmeg, and cinnamon and stir to combine.

4. Gradually add the dry mixture to the wet mixture and beat until the dry mixture has been thoroughly incorporated. Transfer the dough to the refrigerator and chill for 2 hours.

5. Preheat the oven to 375°F and brush each shell-shaped depression in a cast-iron madeleine pan with butter. Place the pan in the freezer for at least 10 minutes.

6. Remove the pan from the freezer and the batter from the refrigerator. Fill each "shell" two-thirds of the way with batter, place the pan in the oven, and bake until a toothpick inserted into the center of a cookie comes out clean, about 12 minutes. Remove from the oven and place the cookies on a wire rack to cool slightly. Serve warm or at room temperature.

INGREDIENTS:

- 5 TABLESPOONS UNSALTED BUTTER, PLUS MORE FOR THE PAN
- ½ CUP BROWN SUGAR
- 2 EGGS
- 1 TABLESPOON MINCED GINGER
- 1¼ TEASPOONS VANILLA EXTRACT
- 1½ TABLESPOONS MOLASSES
- ⅓ CUP WHOLE MILK
- ½ CUP ALL-PURPOSE FLOUR
- ½ CUP CAKE FLOUR
- ¼ TEASPOON BAKING POWDER
- 1½ TEASPOONS SALT
- ¼ TEASPOON GROUND CLOVES
- ¼ TEASPOON NUTMEG
- 1 TEASPOON CINNAMON

PEACH BISCUIT COBBLER

YIELD: 4 TO 6 SERVINGS / ACTIVE TIME: 30 MINUTES / TOTAL TIME: 1 HOUR

Just like strawberries and rhubarb say early summer, a fresh peach cobbler says late summer. Use ripe fruit and plenty of it and you may end up making this every night while peaches are in season.

1. Preheat oven to 400°F.

2. In a bowl, combine the peach slices with the sugar and flour. The amount of flour you use will depend on how juicy the peaches are; more juice means more flour. Put the mixture in a 12-inch cast-iron skillet and bake for 10 minutes.

3. Remove the skillet from the oven and drop spoonfuls of the biscuit dough on top, making sure they are evenly distributed. Sprinkle the cinnamon on top and return the skillet to the oven.

4. Bake for about 15 minutes, until the biscuits are golden brown and the peaches are bubbling. Make sure not to burn the topping.

5. Serve warm with fresh whipped cream or ice cream.

INGREDIENTS:

- 5-6 PEACHES, PITTED AND SLICED, SKIN REMOVED IF DESIRED
- ¼ CUP SUGAR
- 1-2 TABLESPOONS ALL-PURPOSE FLOUR

  DOUGH FROM BISCUITS (SEE PAGE 116) OR 1 (26.5 OZ.) PACKAGE OF FROZEN BISCUITS
- 1 TEASPOON CINNAMON

  WHIPPED CREAM, FOR SERVING (OPTIONAL)

  VANILLA ICE CREAM, FOR SERVING (OPTIONAL)

OATMEAL BUTTERSCOTCH COOKIE BARS

YIELD: 8 TO 10 SERVINGS / **ACTIVE TIME:** 20 MINUTES / **TOTAL TIME:** 45 MINUTES

Sure, you've heard of oatmeal raisin cookies, but the slightly savory taste of butterscotch works incredibly well with an oatmeal base. Who knows, you may even find yourself swearing off raisins all together.

1. Preheat the oven to 350°F and place a 12-inch cast-iron skillet in the oven as it warms up.

2. Place the flour, oatmeal, baking soda, and salt in a mixing bowl and stir to combine.

3. In a large bowl, add the butter and sugars and beat until light and creamy. Add the egg and vanilla and beat to incorporate. Add the flour mixture, stir to incorporate, and then fold in the butterscotch chips.

4. Remove the skillet from the oven and pour the batter into it. Smooth the top with a rubber spatula.

5. Place the skillet in the oven and bake until the cookie is golden brown and cooked through, about 20 minutes. Remove the skillet from the oven and let cool for 10 minutes before slicing into eight to 10 wedges.

VARIATION: Substitute toffee chips for the butterscotch chips.

INGREDIENTS:

1¼ CUPS ALL-PURPOSE FLOUR

2 CUPS QUICK-COOKING OATMEAL

1 TEASPOON BAKING SODA

½ TEASPOON SALT

1½ STICKS OF UNSALTED BUTTER, SOFTENED

½ CUP DARK BROWN SUGAR

½ CUP GRANULATED SUGAR

1 EGG

½ TEASPOON VANILLA EXTRACT

1½ CUPS BUTTERSCOTCH CHIPS

PEANUT BUTTER PIE

YIELD: 8 TO 10 SERVINGS / ACTIVE TIME: 30 MINUTES / TOTAL TIME: 1 HOUR AND 30 MINUTES

Yes, this pie tastes as amazing as it sounds. If you're looking for a "peanut butter cup" kind of experience, you can also bathe the top in chocolate when the pie is cool. Try it, you'll love it.

1. Preheat the oven to 350°F.

2. Place the eggs in a large mixing bowl and beat until thoroughly combined. Add the corn syrup and sugar and whisk until the sugar has dissolved. Add the peanut butter and vanilla and whisk until the mixture is smooth. Take care not to overwork the mixture.

3. Working with the crust in a 10-inch cast-iron skillet, transfer the mixture into the crust and sprinkle the salted peanuts on top.

4. Put the skillet in the oven and bake until a knife inserted in the center comes out clean, about 1 hour. If the edge of the crust is browning too much, remove the skillet from the oven and put aluminum foil over the exposed crust until the filling is set. Remove the skillet from the oven and allow to cool completely.

5. If you'd like to top with chocolate, put the chocolate chips in a microwave-safe bowl and microwave in 15-second increments, removing to stir after each, until pieces are just melted. Drizzle over the cooled pie and refrigerate until the chocolate hardens. Garnish with pecans or walnuts and top with whipped cream, if desired.

INGREDIENTS:

3 EGGS

1 CUP DARK CORN SYRUP

½ CUP SUGAR

½ CUP CREAMY ALL-NATURAL PEANUT BUTTER (WITH NO ADDED SUGAR)

½ TEASPOON VANILLA EXTRACT

1 GRAHAM CRACKER CRUST (SEE PAGE 586), MADE WITH CHOCOLATE GRAHAM CRACKERS

1 CUP HIGH-QUALITY SALTED PEANUTS

6 OZ. SEMISWEET CHOCOLATE CHIPS, FOR TOPPING (OPTIONAL)

PECANS OR WALNUTS, FOR GARNISH (OPTIONAL)

WHIPPED CREAM, FOR SERVING (OPTIONAL)

CHOCOLATE CHEESECAKE TART

YIELD: 6 TO 8 SERVINGS / ACTIVE TIME: 40 MINUTES / TOTAL TIME: 1 HOUR AND 30 MINUTES

There's something so decadent about cheesecake; it's fantastic in a cookie crust, and this one is enhanced with cocoa powder and a dash of Kahlúa.

1. Preheat the oven to 350°F.

2. Place the cookies in a food processor and blitz until they are crumbs. If you don't have a food processor, you can also put the cookies in a resealable plastic bag and use a rolling pin to crush them.

3. Put the crumbs in a bowl and add the unsweetened cocoa powder and the Kahlúa. Stir in 6 tablespoons of the butter. Grease a 10-inch cast-iron skillet with the remaining butter. Press the cookie crumb mixture into the skillet. The crust should go about halfway up the side of the skillet.

4. Place in the oven and bake until the crust is firm, about 10 minutes. Remove the skillet from the oven and let cool. Reduce oven temperature to 325°F.

5. In a large bowl, add the cream cheese, sugar, sweetened cocoa powder, vanilla, and eggs and stir until thoroughly combined. Scrape the cream cheese mixture into the cooled crust.

6. Place the skillet in the oven and bake until the filling is set, about 40 minutes.

7. Remove the skillet from the oven and let cool. Place in the refrigerator for 1 hour before serving.

INGREDIENTS:

- 8-10 OREOS, FILLING SCRAPED OFF
- 1 TABLESPOON UNSWEETENED COCOA POWDER
- 2 TABLESPOONS KAHLÚA OR COFFEE LIQUEUR
- 1 STICK OF UNSALTED BUTTER, MELTED
- 2 (8 OZ.) PACKAGES OF CREAM CHEESE, SOFTENED
- 1 CUP SUGAR
- 1 TABLESPOON SWEETENED COCOA POWDER
- ½ TEASPOON VANILLA EXTRACT
- 2 EGGS

KEY LIME CHIFFON PIE

YIELD: 6 TO 8 SERVINGS / ACTIVE TIME: 30 MINUTES / TOTAL TIME: 2 HOURS

A fluffier version of a classic key lime pie. The cloud-like consistency is the perfect complement to the tangy taste of key limes. Make sure not to omit the lime zest from the recipe.

1. Place the cream in a mixing bowl and beat with a handheld mixer on high until peaks start to form. Add the sugar and beat until stiff peaks form.

2. In a small saucepan, place the lime juice, lime zest, and gelatin and stir until gelatin is dissolved. Cook over medium heat, while stirring constantly, until the mixture begins to thicken, 3 to 5 minutes. Do not let it come to a boil. Remove from heat and let cool briefly before stirring in the sweetened condensed milk.

3. Fold the warmed mixture into the cream-and-sugar mixture and stir until the mixture is smooth and just combined.

4. Working with the crust in a 10-inch cast-iron skillet, transfer the filling into the piecrust. Cover with plastic wrap and refrigerate until set, about 45 minutes. Garnish with whipped cream, the reserved key lime zest, and key lime wheels.

INGREDIENTS:

- 2 CUPS HEAVY CREAM
- ¼ CUP SUGAR
- ⅓ CUP FRESH KEY LIME JUICE
- ZEST FROM 4 KEY LIMES, 1 TEASPOON RESERVED FOR GARNISH
- 1 PACKET OF UNFLAVORED GELATIN
- ½ CUP SWEETENED CONDENSED MILK
- 1 GRAHAM CRACKER CRUST (SEE PAGE 586)
- WHIPPED CREAM, FOR GARNISH
- KEY LIME WHEELS, FOR GARNISH

MIXED BERRY PIE

YIELD: 6 TO 8 SERVINGS / **ACTIVE TIME:** 30 MINUTES / **TOTAL TIME:** 1 HOUR AND 30 MINUTES

The cornmeal crust helps give this pie texture, since the berries soften as they cook. It's always best to use fresh fruit, but if one of the ones called for here isn't in season, frozen fruit that has been thawed will work fine.

1. Preheat oven to 375°F.

2. In a large bowl, toss the berries with the lemon juice, brown sugar, and cornstarch until they are evenly coated. Transfer the mixture to a large saucepan and cook over medium heat until the fruit starts to break down, about 3 minutes.

3. Working with the crust in a 10-inch cast-iron skillet, scrape the fruit and resulting juices into the piecrust.

4. Place the preserves in a small bowl and stir until they start to liquefy. Drizzle over the top of the pie.

5. Place the skillet in the oven and bake until the filling starts to bubble, 30 to 40 minutes.

6. Remove the skillet from the oven and let cool before serving. Serve with whipped cream.

INGREDIENTS:

1½ CUPS FRESH BLUEBERRIES

1 CUP FRESH BLACKBERRIES

1 CUP FRESH RASPBERRIES

1½ CUPS HULLED AND HALVED FRESH STRAWBERRIES

1 TABLESPOON FRESH LEMON JUICE

½ CUP LIGHT BROWN SUGAR

2 TABLESPOONS CORNSTARCH

1 SWEET & SAVORY CORNMEAL CRUST (SEE PAGE 583)

½ CUP UNSWEETENED RASPBERRY PRESERVES

WHIPPED CREAM, FOR SERVING

NECTARINE & RASPBERRY GALETTE

YIELD: 4 TO 6 SERVINGS / **ACTIVE TIME:** 40 MINUTES / **TOTAL TIME:** 1 HOUR AND 30 MINUTES

The tangy nectarine is a wonderful complement to the raspberries in this striking galette, which somehow tastes even better than it looks.

1. Preheat the oven to 400°F.

2. Place the crust in a 10-inch cast-iron skillet.

3. In a large bowl, place the fruit, the ½ cup of sugar, lemon juice, lemon zest, cornstarch, and salt. Stir until the fruit is evenly coated.

4. Place the fruit mixture on the crust, making sure to leave 1 inch of crust open along the edge. Fold the edge of the crust over the filling, brush the crust with the beaten egg, and sprinkle the remaining sugar on top.

5. Place the skillet in the oven and bake until the filling is bubbly, about 35 minutes.

6. Remove the skillet from the oven and let cool before serving.

INGREDIENTS:

- 1 FLAKY PASTRY CRUST (SEE PAGE 580)
- 1½ CUPS PITTED AND SLICED FRESH NECTARINES
- 1½ CUPS FRESH RASPBERRIES
- ½ CUP SUGAR, PLUS 1 TABLESPOON
-   JUICE OF ½ LEMON
- 1 TEASPOON LEMON ZEST
- 3 TABLESPOONS CORNSTARCH
-   PINCH OF SALT
- 1 EGG, BEATEN

CHOCOLATE & ESPRESSO CREAM PIE

YIELD: 6 TO 8 SERVINGS / ACTIVE TIME: 45 MINUTES / TOTAL TIME: 2 HOURS

For those of us who love the combination of chocolate and coffee, this pie is a winner. The espresso adds an earthiness that draws an unexpected element out of the chocolate. If the chocolate Graham Cracker Crust seems like too much, use a Baked Crust (see page 579) instead.

1. Place 2 cups of the heavy cream in a saucepan and warm over medium heat. Add the chocolate chips and stir until melted. Add the vanilla, espresso powder or coffee, and salt and stir until they have been incorporated. Remove from heat and set aside.

2. Place the remaining cream in a mixing bowl and beat with a handheld mixer on high speed until it forms stiff peaks. Fold the whipped cream into the chocolate-espresso mixture.

3. Working with the crust in a 10-inch cast-iron skillet, transfer the filling to the piecrust and smooth the top with a rubber spatula. Cover with plastic wrap and refrigerate for at least 1 hour before serving. When ready to serve, top the pie with toasted slivered almonds, if desired.

INGREDIENTS:

3½ CUPS HEAVY CREAM

¾ LB. SEMISWEET CHOCOLATE CHIPS

1 TEASPOON VANILLA EXTRACT

1 TABLESPOON INSTANT ESPRESSO POWDER OR COFFEE

PINCH OF SALT

1 GRAHAM CRACKER CRUST (SEE PAGE 586), MADE WITH CHOCOLATE GRAHAM CRACKERS

½ CUP SLIVERED ALMONDS, TOASTED (OPTIONAL)

PEANUT BUTTER COOKIE BARS

YIELD: 6 TO 8 SERVINGS / **ACTIVE TIME:** 20 MINUTES / **TOTAL TIME:** 45 MINUTES

You can use creamy or chunky, traditional or all-natural peanut butter here. Just keep in mind that natural peanut butter needs to be stirred before you measure it out.

1. Preheat the oven to 350°F. Place a 10-inch cast-iron skillet in the oven as it warms.

2. In a bowl, whisk together the flour, baking soda, and salt.

3. In a separate bowl, add the butter and sugars and beat with a handheld mixer until light and creamy. Add the egg and vanilla and beat until incorporated. Incorporate the flour mixture and then stir in the peanut butter.

4. Remove the skillet from the oven and pour the batter into it. Smooth the top with a rubber spatula.

5. Place the skillet in the oven and bake until golden brown and cooked through, about 20 minutes. Remove the skillet from the oven and let cool for 10 minutes before slicing into wedges.

VARIATIONS: Substitute an equal quantity of almond butter or cashew butter for the peanut butter, or experiment with a blend of nut butters.

INGREDIENTS:

- 1½ CUPS ALL-PURPOSE FLOUR
- 1 TEASPOON BAKING SODA
  DASH OF SALT
- 1 STICK OF UNSALTED BUTTER, SOFTENED
- ½ CUP DARK BROWN SUGAR
- ½ CUP GRANULATED SUGAR
- 1 EGG
- ½ TEASPOON VANILLA EXTRACT
- ½ CUP PEANUT BUTTER

CARAMELIZED PINEAPPLE

YIELD: 6 TO 8 SERVINGS / **ACTIVE TIME:** 30 MINUTES / **TOTAL TIME:** 30 MINUTES

Experience the wonder that is the caramelized, crispy outside and the juicy inside of seared pineapple. It's like a fruit steak fresh off the grill.

1. Preheat the oven to 200°F and place a parchment-lined baking sheet in the oven. Warm a 10-inch cast-iron skillet over medium-high heat.

2. Add the butter, brown sugar, and rum to the skillet and stir until the butter is melted and starting to bubble.

3. Working in batches, place the pineapple in the skillet and cook until caramelized on both sides and warmed through, about 2 minutes per side.

4. Transfer the cooked pineapple to the baking sheet in the oven until all of the slices have been cooked.

VARIATIONS: This is delicious on its own, but there are plenty of ways to incorporate the pineapple into a fancier dessert. Put a scoop of vanilla ice cream in the hole in the center of each slice and top with a sprig of mint. Cut the pineapple into cubes and toss with chunks of mango or cantaloupe. Sprinkle shredded coconut over the slices of pineapple, or use it as a topping for pound cake.

INGREDIENTS:

4   TABLESPOONS UNSALTED BUTTER

½   CUP DARK BROWN SUGAR

¼   CUP DARK RUM

1   FRESH PINEAPPLE, PEELED, CORED, AND CUT INTO ½-INCH SLICES

KIWI-STRAWBERRY TART

YIELD: 6 TO 8 SERVINGS / **ACTIVE TIME:** 1 HOUR AND 30 MINUTES / **TOTAL TIME:** 4 HOURS

One of those desserts that always catches your eye in the display case at a high-end grocery store. When you make it yourself, you'll find that it's quite simple and looks just as impressive as store-bought.

1. Place the softened cream cheese and the sugar in a large mixing bowl and beat until the mixture is very smooth. Add the vanilla and stir to incorporate.

2. In a separate bowl, add the cream and beat with a handheld mixer on high until stiff peaks start to form. Fold the cream into the cream cheese mixture and beat until fully incorporated.

3. Working with the crust in a 10-inch cast-iron skillet, transfer the mixture into the piecrust and use a rubber spatula to evenly distribute.

4. Arrange the strawberries and kiwi slices on top, working from the outer edge to the center and alternating between the strawberries and kiwi. Cover with plastic wrap and refrigerate until set, about 1 hour.

5. Place the jam and the water in a small saucepan and cook over low heat until the jam has liquefied. Remove pan from heat, let cool slightly, and then brush the mixture over the surface of the tart. Place in the refrigerator and chill for at least 2 hours before serving.

INGREDIENTS:

½   CUP CREAM CHEESE, AT ROOM TEMPERATURE

½   CUP SUGAR

1   TEASPOON VANILLA EXTRACT

1   CUP HEAVY CREAM

1   BAKED CRUST (SEE PAGE 579)

1½   CUPS HULLED AND HALVED FRESH STRAWBERRIES

3   KIWIS, PEELED AND SLICED

3   TABLESPOONS SEEDLESS STRAWBERRY JAM

1   TABLESPOON WATER

INDUSTRY INSIDERS

Cooking with cast iron is a long-held tradition the world over, as this book makes clear. Because it is cookware made to last, and through generations has been treated with the care and reverence of any other family heirloom, there is no shortage of vintage examples waiting to be discovered at thrift stores and garage sales. Luckily, if you're not a collector, or not inclined to refurbish rusted skillets, the number of cast-iron cookware makers active today means there is a wealth of brand-new options that come in all shapes, sizes, and colors, at all price points.

What follows is by no means an exhaustive list of companies that make cast-iron pots and pans, but it is a representative sampling of producers both big and small, well established and just getting started. All of these makers have distinct approaches to what they do, though they all share an appreciation for honoring the past by infusing it with contemporary elements.

LODGE

If you don't know Lodge, you don't know cast iron. While other cast-iron producers in Tennessee closed their doors decades ago, Lodge is still going strong after 123 years and has experienced a steady rise in popularity, leading them to open a new foundry in November 2017. Their company is as dependable as their cast iron, surviving both world wars and the Great Depression. They have dedicated themselves to putting cast iron at the center of kitchens across America, and, with their wide distribution and commitment to quality, they've been largely successful. Their cast iron is well made and affordable, not to mention designed in a way that makes each of the company's pre-seasoned offerings archetypal.

In 1896, in South Pittsburg, Tennessee, Joseph Lodge founded the Blacklock Foundry, named after Lodge's minister friend. After a fire in 1910 burned the foundry to the ground, the company reopened three months later under the name Lodge Manufacturing Company; obviously, the name had staying power. Thanks to sound business practices; the ingenuity to pivot and create the cast-iron garden decorations that carried Lodge through the Great Depression; and a dedication to producing high-quality products, Lodge maintained their popularity. They were

eventually forced to switch from hand-pour foundry operations to an automated molding system to keep up with the growing demand for their products. Today, their products continue to hold up to their long history, and their pre-seasoned offerings have made entering the world of cast iron easier than ever.

Pre-seasoning wasn't always the industry standard for cast iron. From the start, Lodge's products were sold freshly cast and gray, with a clear layer of carnauba wax to keep them from rusting during transport. Each pan came with a brief description on how to season and maintain a cast-iron skillet, but, intimidated by the seemingly complicated instructions for caring for cast iron, many consumers either found their own way of seasoning their skillets or gave up on this incredible cookware out of frustration. In 2002, Lodge became the first-ever US cookware manufacturer to sell seasoned cast iron, and their popularity took off from there—to the point that unseasoned cast-iron pans were officially discontinued by Lodge in 2007.

Today, Lodge offers one of the largest arrays of cast-iron products on the market, from skillets ranging from 3½ inches to a whopping 17 inches, to Dutch ovens, camp ovens, enamel-coated cast-iron cookware, grill pans, baking pans, woks, and more. Their record distribution numbers have earned them a place on the shelves of popular retailers across the country.

It would be an understatement to call Lodge the "gateway cookware" for cast iron, as their products' general accessibility and simple design make them ideal for anyone looking to jump into the world of cast iron for the first time. But the new skillet purchased for a first apartment will doubtless become an heirloom. Once you purchase a Lodge product, you won't be satisfied until everything in your kitchen has their signature teardrop handle and gorgeous pre-seasoned burnish.

Lodge takes great strides to make sure their mark on the environment is as small as possible. From energy-saving measures to cardboard and foundry-sand recycling and repurposing, Lodge believes that both the environment and cast-iron cookware should last for generations.

LODGE PORK ROULADE *with* TOMATOES *and* PESTO

YIELD: 4 SERVINGS / ACTIVE TIME: 20 MINUTES / TOTAL TIME: 35 MINUTES

Liven up your next kitchen adventure with this pork roulade. Cherry tomatoes provide a bright pop of color on the plate (and on the palate) and are softened by the smooth, nutty flavor of an easy homemade pesto.

1. Preheat the oven to 350°F.

2. Butterfly the pork loin. Cut along the equator and be careful not to slice it all the way through. Lay the tenderloin open and gently pound it until both halves are ½-inch thick.

3. Spread the Homemade Pesto over the pork loin and sprinkle the tomatoes on top. Roll up the pork loin so that it maintains its length and tie with kitchen twine. Rub the olive oil over the outside, season with the salt and pepper, and sprinkle any remaining tomatoes on top.

4. Warm a 12-inch cast-iron skillet over medium-high heat. Add the pork loin and sear, while turning, until it is browned all over, 1 to 2 minutes. Transfer the skillet to the oven and roast until cooked through, about 10 minutes. Remove from the oven and let rest for 10 minutes before removing the twine and slicing the roulade.

HOMEMADE PESTO

1. Place the pine nuts, Parmesan cheese, garlic, salt, and basil in a food processor and pulse until combined, about 1 minute.

2. With the food processor running, slowly add olive oil until the pesto becomes smooth.

INGREDIENTS:

	2-LB. PORK LOIN
½	CUP HOMEMADE PESTO (SEE RECIPE)
¼	CUP CHERRY TOMATOES, QUARTERED
	KITCHEN TWINE, AS NEEDED
2	TABLESPOONS OLIVE OIL
½	TEASPOON SALT
½	TEASPOON CRACKED PEPPER
	FRESH BASIL LEAVES, SLICED THIN, FOR GARNISH

HOMEMADE PESTO

½	CUP TOASTED PINE NUTS
¾	CUP GRATED PARMESAN CHEESE
3	GARLIC CLOVES, MINCED
1	TEASPOON SALT
5	CUPS FRESH BASIL LEAVES
⅓-⅔	CUP OLIVE OIL

LODGE DRUNKEN RICE NOODLES *with* PORK

YIELD: 2 TO 4 SERVINGS / ACTIVE TIME: 20 MINUTES / TOTAL TIME: 40 MINUTES

This fragrant stir-fry calls for an entire cup of fresh basil to complement the spicy bird's eye chilies and the savory pork.

1. Place the noodles in a baking dish, cover with hot water, and let sit for 10 minutes. Drain and set the noodles aside. Place the pork and 2 tablespoons of the soy sauce in a mixing bowl and let marinate for 5 minutes.

2. Warm a 12-inch cast-iron skillet over medium-high heat for 5 minutes. When the skillet is very hot, add the oil. When it starts to shimmer, add the garlic and chilies and cook, while stirring, until the garlic starts to brown, about 2 minutes.

3. Add the pork and cook, while stirring, until it is cooked through, 4 to 6 minutes. Add the drained noodles, remaining soy sauce, fish sauce, oyster sauce, sugar, white pepper, and water. Cook, while stirring constantly, until noodles are almost soft, 5 to 8 minutes.

4. Stir in the bell pepper and snow peas and cook for 2 to 3 minutes. Turn off the heat, stir in the basil, and serve immediately.

INGREDIENTS:

½ (14 OZ.) PACKAGE OF RICE NOODLES

2 BONELESS PORK CHOPS, SLICED THIN

6 TABLESPOONS SOY SAUCE

¼ CUP CANOLA OIL

4 GARLIC CLOVES, CHOPPED

2 BIRD'S EYE CHILIES, CHOPPED

1 TABLESPOON FISH SAUCE

1 TABLESPOON OYSTER SAUCE

3 TABLESPOONS SUGAR

1 TEASPOON WHITE PEPPER

½ CUP WATER

1 RED BELL PEPPER, SEEDED AND SLICED INTO ¼-INCH STRIPS

1 CUP SNOW PEAS, TRIMMED AND HALVED

1 CUP FRESH BASIL, OR TO TASTE

LODGE NEW ENGLAND POT PIE

YIELD: 6 SERVINGS / ACTIVE TIME: 10 MINUTES / TOTAL TIME: 35 MINUTES

All-American chicken pot pie most likely comes to us via an early New England stew that was made with a sturdy biscuit crust and baked in a heavy cast-iron pot or casserole dish. The original pie probably contained neither peas nor mushrooms, but we think their addition accounts at least in part for the dish's popular and long-lasting appeal all over the country.

1. Preheat the oven to 425°F and grease a 2-quart cast-iron casserole dish with butter.

2. To make the filling, place the butter in the casserole dish and melt over medium heat. Add the onions, celery, and carrot and cook, while stirring, until the vegetables soften, about 5 minutes. Stir in the chicken, peas, and mushrooms, season with salt and pepper, and set aside.

3. In a heavy saucepan, melt the shortening over medium heat, sprinkle the flour over the top, and stir constantly for 3 minutes, taking care not to let the roux color. Remove from heat and gradually add the broth and half-and-half, stirring constantly until well-combined. Place the pan back over medium heat and cook, while stirring constantly, until the sauce thickens. Pour over the mixture in the casserole dish.

4. To make the biscuit crust, whisk the flour, baking powder, and salt together. Add the shortening and work the mixture with a pastry blender or your fingers until the mixture resembles a coarse meal. Add the milk and stir just until the dough forms a ball. Transfer to a lightly floured work surface, knead about 8 times, then pat the dough out until it is about ⅓-inch thick.

5. Cut the dough to fit the top of the casserole dish, drape it over the filling, and crimp the edge to seal. Cut a few vents in the top with a sharp knife and bake until the crust is nicely browned and juices are bubbling up through the vents, about 25 minutes.

INGREDIENTS:

FOR THE FILLING

- 2 TABLESPOONS UNSALTED BUTTER, PLUS MORE FOR THE CASSEROLE DISH
- 2 ONIONS, DICED
- 1 CELERY STALK, DICED
- 1 LARGE CARROT, DICED
- 3 CUPS DICED COOKED CHICKEN
- 1½ CUPS FRESH OR FROZEN GREEN PEAS
- 1 CUP DICED MUSHROOMS
- SALT AND FRESHLY GROUND BLACK PEPPER, TO TASTE
- ¼ CUP VEGETABLE SHORTENING
- ¼ CUP ALL-PURPOSE FLOUR
- 1½ CUPS CHICKEN BROTH
- 1 CUP HALF-AND-HALF

FOR THE BISCUIT CRUST

- 2 CUPS ALL-PURPOSE FLOUR, PLUS MORE FOR DUSTING
- 1 TABLESPOON BAKING POWDER
- ½ TEASPOON SALT
- ¼ CUP VEGETABLE SHORTENING, CHILLED
- 1 CUP WHOLE MILK

LODGE BRAISED LAMB *with* CARROTS

YIELD: 4 TO 6 SERVINGS / ACTIVE TIME: 20 MINUTES / TOTAL TIME: 3 HOURS AND 10 MINUTES

Braised lamb? Count us in! Garnish this dish of lamb and carrots with seasoned apples for some extra flair. Serve over polenta for a mouthwatering meal.

1. Season the lamb with the allspice, salt, and pepper. Place the oil in a cast-iron Dutch oven and warm over medium-high heat. Add the lamb and cook, while turning, until browned all over, about 12 minutes. Remove from the pot and set aside.

2. Add the carrots and shallots to the pot and cook until the carrots start to soften, about 5 minutes. Add the rosemary and cook until it is fragrant, about 2 minutes.

3. Deglaze the pot with the 1 cup of balsamic vinegar, return the lamb to the pot, and add water until three-quarters of the lamb shanks are submerged. Place the lid on the Dutch oven, reduce the heat to medium-low, and cook until the lamb is extremely tender, about 2½ hours.

4. Place the apple slices in a bowl with the remaining vinegar and toss to coat. Season with salt and pepper. Serve the lamb shanks, either on the bone or off, over the polenta and garnish with the apples.

INGREDIENTS:

- 2 (1½ LB.) LAMB SHANKS
- 1 TEASPOON ALLSPICE
- SALT AND FRESHLY GROUND BLACK PEPPER, TO TASTE
- ¼ CUP OLIVE OIL
- 3 CARROTS, PEELED AND CHOPPED
- 4 SHALLOTS, HALVED
- ¼ CUP MINCED FRESH ROSEMARY LEAVES
- 1 CUP BALSAMIC VINEGAR, PLUS 2 TABLESPOONS
- 2-3 CUPS WATER
- 1 RED APPLE, CORED AND SLICED, FOR GARNISH
- POLENTA, FOR SERVING

LODGE FRIED CATFISH *and*
TENNESSEE TARTAR SAUCE

YIELD: 8 SERVINGS / ACTIVE TIME: 15 MINUTES / TOTAL TIME: 35 MINUTES

Friends and family will love this quick and easy fried catfish recipe, especially when it's served with some delicious Tennessee tartar sauce! Pro tip: When you add oil to a Dutch oven, fill it no more than halfway up the side of the pot, because when you add food to the oil, the level will rise.

1. Season the catfish with salt and pepper, place it in a baking dish, and cover with the buttermilk. Chill in the refrigerator.

2. Place the baking powder, cayenne pepper, cornmeal, flour, garlic powder, a pinch of salt, and a pinch of pepper in a mixing bowl and whisk to combine. Set the mixture aside.

3. Add the oil to a cast-iron Dutch oven until it fills the pot halfway. Bring to 350°F over medium-high heat. While the oil is heating up, prepare the tartar sauce. Place all of the ingredients in a mixing bowl, stir to combine, cover with plastic wrap, and store in the refrigerator until ready to serve.

4. Remove the catfish from the refrigerator, shake off any excess buttermilk, and dip each piece into the cornmeal mixture. Shake off any excess.

5. Working in batches, place the catfish in the oil and fry, while turning over halfway, until golden brown all over, about 8 minutes. Place the cooked pieces on a paper towel–lined plate. When all of the catfish has been cooked, serve with the tartar sauce.

INGREDIENTS:

FOR THE CATFISH

4 LBS. CATFISH FILLETS, HALVED

2 CUPS BUTTERMILK

SALT AND PEPPER, TO TASTE

1 TABLESPOON BAKING POWDER

¼ TEASPOON CAYENNE PEPPER

2 CUPS YELLOW CORNMEAL

3 TABLESPOONS ALL-PURPOSE FLOUR

1 TEASPOON GARLIC POWDER

VEGETABLE OIL, FOR FRYING

FOR THE TARTAR SAUCE

1 CUP MAYONNAISE

½ TEASPOON HOT SAUCE

1 TABLESPOON SWEET-AND-SPICY RELISH

¼ TEASPOON GARLIC POWDER

1 TABLESPOON MINCED ONION

2 TABLESPOONS FRESH LEMON JUICE

SALT AND PEPPER, TO TASTE

LODGE PORK MEATBALLS *with* KALE

YIELD: 4 SERVINGS / ACTIVE TIME: 20 MINUTES / TOTAL TIME: 40 MINUTES

These heavenly meatballs get packed with sautéed kale and Parmesan before getting crisped up in olive oil spiked with rosemary.

1. Place the rosemary and olive oil in a 12-inch cast-iron skillet and warm over medium heat. Fry the rosemary until it is crispy, about 5 minutes. Transfer the rosemary to a paper towel–lined plate and season with salt. Strain the oil through a fine sieve and set aside.

2. Place 2 tablespoons of the infused oil and the kale in the skillet and sauté over medium-high heat until the kale starts to wilt, about 4 minutes. Transfer the kale to a bowl, season with salt, and let cool completely. When the kale is cool, mince one-third of it and set the remainder aside.

3. Place the ground pork, Parmesan, half of the soy sauce, the onion powder, and the minced kale in a mixing bowl, season with salt, and work the mixture with your hands to combine. Warm the skillet over medium heat, take a small piece of the mixture, place it in the skillet, and cook until cooked through. Taste and season the mixture accordingly. Form 2-tablespoon portions of the mixture into balls.

4. Place the remaining infused olive oil in the skillet and warm over medium heat. Working in batches if necessary, add the meatballs to the skillet and cook until they are golden brown all over, about 6 to 8 minutes. Remove the cooked meatballs from the pan and set them aside. When all of the meatballs have been cooked, add the mushrooms, cook until they are golden brown, and then deglaze the pan with the remaining soy sauce. Add the reserved kale and the meatballs, stir to combine, and cook until everything is warmed through. Garnish with the fried rosemary leaves and the shaved Parmesan and serve immediately.

INGREDIENTS:

- 3   SPRIGS OF ROSEMARY
- 6   TABLESPOONS OLIVE OIL
-      SALT AND PEPPER, TO TASTE
- 1   SMALL BUNCH OF KALE, STEMMED AND CHOPPED
- 10   OZ. GROUND PORK
- ¼   CUP GRATED PARMESAN CHEESE, PLUS SHAVED PARMESAN CHEESE FOR GARNISH
- ¼   CUP SOY SAUCE
- ½   TEASPOON ONION POWDER
- 10   OZ. BABY BELLA MUSHROOMS, STEMMED AND SLICED

LODGE SPOON ROLLS

YIELD: 14 ROLLS / **ACTIVE TIME:** 10 TO 15 MINUTES / **TOTAL TIME:** 30 TO 35 MINUTES

The cast-iron mini cake pan is the perfect baking vessel for these homemade spoon rolls, a recipe passed down through generations of the Lodge family.

1. Preheat the oven to 400°F. Grease the wells of 2 cast-iron mini cake pans or cast-iron muffin pans.

2. In a large bowl, dissolve the yeast in the warm water and let the mixture sit until it starts to foam.

3. Add the remaining ingredients and stir until a smooth batter forms.

4. Spoon the batter into the prepared pans, filling each well half-way to two-thirds full. Any unused batter will keep in an airtight container in the refrigerator for up to 1 week.

5. Place the rolls in the oven and bake until they are puffy and golden brown, about 20 minutes. Remove from the oven, invert the pans to turn the rolls out onto a wire rack, and briefly cool before serving.

INGREDIENTS:

1	(¼ OZ.) PACKET OF ACTIVE DRY YEAST
2	CUPS LUKEWARM WATER (90°F)
¼	CUP SUGAR
1	LARGE EGG, BEATEN
1½	STICKS OF UNSALTED BUTTER, MELTED
4	CUPS SELF-RISING FLOUR

LODGE CHOCOLATE OLIVE OIL CAKES

YIELD: 7 SERVINGS / ACTIVE TIME: 20 MINUTES / TOTAL TIME: 35 MINUTES

Want to know the secret ingredient that makes this cake light and fluffy? Vinegar! While it may be tart on its own, its addition to the batter elevates the texture of this rich chocolate cake so that you won't feel too guilty having just one more piece.

1. Preheat oven to 350°F and grease the wells of a cast-iron mini cake pan with olive oil.

2. Place the flour, ¾ cup of cocoa powder, 1½ cups of coconut sugar, baking soda, and salt in a large bowl and whisk until combined. Add ½ cup of the olive oil, the water, and the vinegar and whisk until no lumps remain and all of the ingredients have just been incorporated. Fill the wells halfway with the batter, place the pan in the oven, and bake until a toothpick inserted into the center of each cake comes out clean, 15 to 20 minutes.

3. While the cakes are baking, place the chocolate chips and the remaining cocoa powder, coconut sugar, and olive oil in a double boiler and warm, while stirring, until the chocolate is melted and the mixture is smooth. Keep warm.

4. Remove the cakes from the oven and gently invert the pan to turn the cakes out onto a wire rack. Let them cool briefly before topping with the chocolate glaze, sea salt, and fresh berries. You can do this prior to serving or tableside.

NOTE: If you don't have a double boiler, place the ingredients for the glaze in a heatproof mixing bowl and bring 1 inch of water to boil in a saucepan. Place the bowl over the saucepan, use a thick towel to hold the bowl steady, and stir with your other hand until the chocolate is melted and the mixture is smooth.

INGREDIENTS:

- ¾ CUP OLIVE OIL, PLUS MORE FOR THE CAKE PANS
- 1½ CUPS ALL-PURPOSE FLOUR
- ¾ CUP UNSWEETENED COCOA POWDER, PLUS 2 TABLESPOONS
- 1½ CUPS COCONUT SUGAR, PLUS 2 TABLESPOONS
- 1½ TEASPOONS BAKING SODA
- 1 TEASPOON SALT
- 1½ CUPS WATER
- 1 TABLESPOON APPLE CIDER VINEGAR
- 1 CUP DARK CHOCOLATE CHIPS
- FLAKY SEA SALT, FOR TOPPING
- FRESH BERRIES, FOR TOPPING

LE CREUSET

What began as a flame-colored enameled cast-iron cocotte produced in Fresnoy-le-Grand, France, in 1925 has since grown to be one of the largest collections of enameled cast iron on the market alongside the brand's stainless steel, nonstick, and stoneware options. The Le Creuset product line covers the whole kitchen, and with an array of beautiful colors and designs to choose from, this cookware is sure to leave you drooling over more than just your next meal.

Le Creuset was founded on the idea that cooking is at the heart of every celebration. With the cultural shift that took cooking from something behind closed doors to the joyful axis around which a household revolves, Le Creuset proved that cookware could be both functional and beautiful. Their production focuses on sand-casting their cookware, then the finished products are coated with two layers of chip-resistant enamel made to last a lifetime. With a constantly adapting product line that has been improved and updated over the course of 90 years, Le Creuset puts new meaning behind the term "legacy cookware."

Its popularity in the United States owes a nod of recognition to Julia Child, who not only introduced Americans to French cooking techniques but also introduced much of the cookware now considered standard for all kitchens. Her iconic "soup pot" (a 6-quart "La Mama" Le Creuset pot introduced in 1973) soon came to be found in almost every modern kitchen in America. Child's soup pot now holds a place of honor in the National Museum of American History.

Le Creuset cast-iron products are given the true artisan treatment before making it to the store. Each piece of cookware is individually cast, and inspected following each stage of development. Their enamel comes in all the colors of the rainbow in addition to the classic flame color that put Le Creuset on the map, and with an increasing number of skillets, pans, pots, Dutch ovens, and even flower pots to choose from, Le Creuset caters to every home chef looking to invest in quality products.

Not only can their cast-iron cookware be used on and in almost any type of stove, including outdoor grills, their specialty-made recessed lids keep moisture inside the pan to make sure recipes cook perfectly every time. And, as a bonus that comes with most enameled cast iron, Le Creuset pans are dishwasher-safe, meaning you don't have to worry about using soap to clean the stubborn remnants of that casserole.

Whether you're looking for a way to spice up your kitchen or want to invest in a set of cast-iron cookware that will last for generations, Le Creuset's dedication to details and design ensures that each of their pieces are unique, durable, and breathtaking.

NETHERTON FOUNDRY

Tucked into the town of South Shropshire, which was at the center of the Industrial Revolution in England, the family-owned Netherton Foundry produces some of the highest quality cast-iron cookware in the country. The bridge featured in the company's logo serves as an homage to Shropshire ironmaster Abraham Darby, the creator of the world's first iron bridge and the inspiration behind the company's ethos. Netherton Foundry is driven by the same yearning for ingenuity and innovation as the craftspeople who preceded the company in the town. Their mission is simple, yet profound: to build products with provenance.

A core belief held by Netherton Foundry is the importance of supporting independent retailers. They want their products to be handled and sold by real people, those who can help customers truly understand and appreciate the products that interest them. They trust that independent retailers provide the best experience for everybody involved and deliver an essential function within the goods industry.

Netherton Foundry's motives are rooted in conservation and efficiency, but, above all, they look to stay loyal to their roots. Over 75 percent of their creations are made from resources obtained in Shropshire and the surrounding counties, in an effort to both raise up the businesses and people around them and create as little impact on the planet as possible. They accomplish this by materializing goods that may live a long life out of supplies they believe in.

To further their commitment to sustainability, Netherton Foundry is able to trace the origin of their cast and iron sheet metal through tools provided by their suppliers. Not only does this save material that would have ended up in a landfill but it also saves tremendous amounts of energy, given that no additional iron ore must be mined in order to create the bowls and pans that they are known for. If you appreciate a thoughtful supplier who is committed to creating both impeccable cookware and a culture of responsibility to their environment and local providers, look no further than Netherton Foundry.

STARGAZER

Like many recently founded cast-iron cookware makers, Stargazer's origin story begins with the search for the perfect skillet, a fascination with vintage cookware, and the passion to fuse history with the present. After being dissatisfied with what the market had to offer, founder Peter Huntley, a designer by trade, spent a year hunting down old cast-iron cookware in order to restore it, use it, and devise a plan for how to make what he considered the perfect skillet. In 2015, Huntley, along with his friends Luke Trovato and Dan Stefan, launched Stargazer in Cherry Hill, New Jersey.

Stargazer's sturdy 10½-inch and 12-inch lightweight skillets are offered with a choice of either a bare or seasoned finish, and they both feature a forked handle that keeps it cooler than the pan. Every element of the cookware is made in the United States, even the packaging. And the company's commitment to the US is also found in their always-on-offer 15 percent military discount for all veterans and active service members.

Clearly, Stargazer knows what it's doing, because in 2017 the company moved into a 7,000 square-foot headquarters in Allentown, Pennsylvania, the heart of the famed Lehigh Valley. Such growth over a short period of time is always noteworthy. In the case of Stargazer, however, it is additionally remarkable considering that they only sell their products to customers directly; as their website says: "No wholesalers or distributors, no middlemen, no unnecessary markups. It's a little more work for us but a lot more value for you."

STARGAZER CHICKEN TAMALE CASSEROLE

YIELD: 4 TO 6 SERVINGS / **ACTIVE TIME:** 15 MINUTES / **TOTAL TIME:** 45 MINUTES

When the founders of Stargazer started making cookware, they wanted it to be accessible to everyone. That philosophy is reflected in this old-school chicken casserole recipe they developed and we adapted. It's got a hint of Mexican flair in a very American dish. To make it even quicker, try using a rotisserie chicken from the supermarket.

1. Preheat your oven to 400°F.

2. In a blender, add the tomatoes, chipotle, adobo sauce, garlic, and 1 teaspoon of the salt and puree until smooth. Set aside.

3. Place the oil in a 12-inch cast-iron skillet and warm over medium heat. When the oil starts to shimmer, add the chicken, stir to coat, and cook until slightly browned, about 8 minutes.

4. Reduce the heat to low, add the pureed tomato mixture, and let simmer for 6 minutes.

5. Remove the mixture from the pan and set aside. Wipe out the pan, then add 2 tablespoons of the butter and swirl to coat the whole pan.

6. Meanwhile, in a large bowl, whisk together the cornmeal, flour, sugar, remaining salt, and baking powder. Whisk in the egg, remaining butter, buttermilk, cream, and corn. Pour the batter into the hot skillet, place in the oven, and bake until set, about 20 minutes.

7. Remove from the oven and top the corn bread with the chicken mixture and the cheese. Bake until the cheese is melted and starts to brown, about 12 minutes.

8. Remove from the oven and garnish with the cilantro, green onion, avocado, jalapeño, and red onion.

INGREDIENTS:

- 2 LARGE TOMATOES, DICED
- 1 CHIPOTLE EN ADOBO
- SAUCE FROM (7 OZ.) CAN OF CHIPOTLES EN ADOBO
- 2 GARLIC CLOVES, CHOPPED
- 1½ TEASPOONS KOSHER SALT
- 2 TABLESPOONS VEGETABLE OIL
- 1½ LBS. BONELESS, SKINLESS CHICKEN BREASTS OR THIGHS, CHOPPED INTO BITE-SIZED PIECES
- 6 TABLESPOONS UNSALTED BUTTER, MELTED
- 1 CUP YELLOW CORNMEAL
- 1 CUP ALL-PURPOSE FLOUR
- 2 TABLESPOONS SUGAR
- 1 TABLESPOON BAKING POWDER
- 1 LARGE EGG
- ⅓ CUP BUTTERMILK
- ¼ CUP HEAVY CREAM
- 1 CUP CORN (FROZEN OR CANNED)
- 2 CUPS SHREDDED PEPPER JACK CHEESE
- 1 CUP CHOPPED CILANTRO, FOR GARNISH
- 2 GREEN ONIONS, SLICED THIN, FOR GARNISH
- FLESH FROM 1 AVOCADO, SLICED, FOR GARNISH
- SLICED JALAPEÑOS, TO TASTE, FOR GARNISH
- ½ RED ONION, DICED, FOR GARNISH

FERLEON

As a company, Ferleon has only been around for a little over 2 years, but their history stretches back to the heyday of cast iron. Founded in 2017 as a spin-off from Dovre, a bare and enameled high-grade cast-iron stove and fireplace maker that has been around for over 80 years, Ferleon gets its name from both Leon Gehem, the founder of the first Belgian Dovre factory, and *fer* the French word for iron, a meeting of the old and new that represents their products as a whole. While their cookware is designed to match the classics, their methods are anything but traditional.

Ferleon's line of stylish, durable cookware is a testament to their innovative entrepreneurship and passion for quality. Each Ferleon cast-iron piece is made in Belgium, and each and every piece is made to last a lifetime. Their design goal is to create functional, fashionable cast-iron cookware that matches every lifestyle, kitchen design, and aesthetic. This goal to harmonize cooking and taste in all of their products shows in their extensive lineup of cast-iron skillets, Dutch ovens, pots, pans, and even patio cookers, as well as enameled options. And with a thicker base than the average cast-iron cook-

ware, their products are perfect for induction cooking (as well as nearly any other cooking surface)—with no need to worry about scalding the food or damaging the pan.

Their enameled cast iron comes in classic colorways that will add a touch of class to any kitchen, be it modern or rustic. As with any piece of cast iron, their cookware is made to evenly transfer heat across the entire surface of the cookware, making the entire line ideal for cooking just about anything you can imagine. For Ferleon, creativity is one of the main assets of a good piece of cast iron, and their hope is that their products will help "give your imagination free range over the kitchen." In order to attain this goal, they take steps to ensure their products are top of the line from cast to packing.

At the Ferleon foundry in Weelde, Belgium, each cast-iron piece is crafted using a green sand block-mold technique that uses finer-grain sands than those used by other foundries to provide the most accurate cast for each mold. Then the raw iron is heated to 2,732°F and poured into the molds. Once cooled, each mold is removed, the cast iron is sanded, and the final product is prepared for either seasoning or enameling depending on the type of cast iron. Their casting process combines a mix of high-end technology with manual craftsmanship for strikingly consistent end results. Plus, not only are their pans 100 percent recyclable, Ferleon reuses their foundry sands to help further reduce impact on the environment.

With a commitment to eco-friendliness and high-quality products that are free from cadmium, a harmful substance found in some low-quality enamels, Ferleon products are made to stand up to the wear and tear of everyday use.

FINEX

The first time you see a FINEX pan, you may find yourself at a loss for words. FINEX took the versatility of cast iron and updated it for the modern world, all while staying true to the history of this resilient cookware. Their skillets are, in a word, unique: the octagonal design and coiled handle stand out immediately. FINEX offers a full line of cast-iron cookware, from skillets and grill pans to Dutch ovens and sauce pots, all in their signature octagonal design.

Based in Portland, Oregon, FINEX draws inspiration from their collection of vintage cast iron, and is constantly innovating and perfecting their methods. Their goal is simple: People eat with their eyes, so why not produce cast-iron cookware that is as delightful to look at as to use? FINEX believes that the best way to make cookware that lasts is to do it the old-fashioned way. The design principle behind every item of cookware is simple: it has to be functional, it has to be beautiful, and it has to last a lifetime. As they joke on their website, their business model is a little outdated. Each and every piece of cookware is treated like an artisan product, and the results are stunning.

FINEX doesn't just produce new cast iron, they produce old designs with a new flair. Each of their skillet and Dutch oven lids has a set of basting rims to ensure that moisture is distributed evenly throughout the pan, and their octagonal lids are made to completely seal the cookware, including the multiple pour spouts on every skillet. Their octagonal design is a result of something more than just learning from the past. When looking to create their first skillet, the team at FINEX approached professional chefs and home cooks and asked their opinions about the most frustrating part of cooking with cast iron. The answer: trying to get a spatula into the rounded pan without ruining what they were cooking. This led to the creation of their unmistakable octagonal design.

Every FINEX piece is worked by hand from pour to polish, and everything from the skillet to the endcap is made to age like a fine wine. When it comes to their seasoning process, attention to detail is everything. Each cast-iron product is seasoned with flaxseed oil to ensure the smooth, nonstick surface cast iron is known for, which means that their products are ready to cook with no matter when (or where) you use them. However, nearly as amazing as the end result of the seasoning is the process by which these pans get their deep, dark finish. FINEX has a no-waste seasoning process that is unlike any other in the US and possibly in the world.

When looking for a seasoning method that wouldn't leave behind odd residue or result in piles of waste—both of the flaxseed oil and of the materials used to ensure the smooth finish—the production team at FINEX came up with the perfect solution: birdseed. Each and every FINEX pan is placed in a tumbler filled with flaxseed oil–soaked bird seed, which coats the pans for 5 to 6 minutes. The result is a perfectly seasoned pan with no gaps, smears, or residual marks left behind. And once the flaxseed oil–soaked birdseed has done its job, it is shipped off to a local chicken farm to help feed the chickens, a truly no-waste process. They've been using this method for about 4 years now, and not only has it decreased the amount of oil needed to season their pans, the local chicken farmer couldn't be happier.

FINEX PUMPKIN SPICE DROP DOUGHNUTS

YIELD: 2 TO 4 SERVINGS / **ACTIVE TIME:** 10 MINUTES / **TOTAL TIME:** 25 MINUTES

These doughnuts might not have holes, but that doesn't mean they're not decadently delicious!

1. Add vegetable oil to a cast-iron Dutch oven until it is 2" deep. Heat the oil to 365°F.

2. In a mixing bowl, add the flour, brown sugar, baking powder, salt, cinnamon, and nutmeg. Whisk to combine.

3. In a separate bowl, add the egg, pumpkin, and milk and whisk to combine. Add the butter and vanilla and whisk to incorporate.

4. Add the wet mixture to the dry mixture and stir to combine. Drop teaspoons of the dough into the hot oil until there are five or six in the Dutch oven. Fry, while turning, until golden brown, 3 to 4 minutes.

5. With a slotted spoon, transfer the cooked doughnuts to a paper towel–lined plate to drain.

6. When all of the doughnuts are cooked, roll them in cinnamon sugar or dust with confectioners' sugar.

INGREDIENTS:

	VEGETABLE OIL, FOR FRYING
2	CUPS ALL-PURPOSE FLOUR
⅓	CUP PACKED BROWN SUGAR
2½	TEASPOONS BAKING POWDER
¼	TEASPOON SALT
¾	TEASPOON GROUND CINNAMON
¼	TEASPOON GROUND NUTMEG
1	LARGE EGG
1	CUP CANNED PUMPKIN
3	TABLESPOONS MILK
2	TABLESPOONS UNSALTED BUTTER, MELTED
1	TEASPOON VANILLA EXTRACT
½	CUP CINNAMON SUGAR (OPTIONAL)
½	CUP CONFECTIONERS' SUGAR (OPTIONAL)

FINEX BACON & MOLASSES CORN BREAD

YIELD: 8 SERVINGS / ACTIVE TIME: 10 MINUTES / TOTAL TIME: 50 MINUTES

There might be a million different kinds of corn bread out there, and most of them cook better in cast iron. This recipe, from Portland chef B. J. Smith, is no exception. Sweeter and more cake-like than traditional Southern corn breads, it nonetheless nods to those roots by including a hint of molasses and a couple cups of buttermilk. While it cooks well in any FINEX cast-iron skillet, we made it in our 10-inch skillet and recommend that size as a great place to start.

1. Preheat the oven to 350°F. Place the flour, cornmeal, sugar, and salt in a mixing bowl and whisk to combine.

2. Melt the butter in a 10-inch cast-iron skillet.

3. In a separate bowl, combine the baking powder with the buttermilk. Add the melted butter, eggs, honey, and molasses.

4. Add the dry mixture to the wet mixture and stir until there are no lumps in the batter.

5. Pour the batter into the skillet and top with the bacon lardons.

6. Place in the oven and bake until golden brown and a toothpick inserted into the center comes out clean, 30 to 35 minutes. Remove from the oven and let cool for 10 minutes before serving.

INGREDIENTS:

- 2 CUPS ALL-PURPOSE FLOUR
- 2 CUPS CORNMEAL
- 1¼ CUPS SUGAR
- 1 TEASPOON SALT
- 2 STICKS OF UNSALTED BUTTER
- 1 TEASPOON BAKING POWDER
- 2 CUPS BUTTERMILK
- 4 EGGS
- 1 TABLESPOON HONEY
- 1 TABLESPOON MOLASSES
- 4 OZ. BACON LARDONS

FINEX ESPRESSO-RUBBED ROASTED PORK TENDERLOIN
with SOUR CHERRY GLAZE *and* SUCCOTASH

YIELD: 4 SERVINGS / ACTIVE TIME: 15 MINUTES / TOTAL TIME: 35 MINUTES

Executive Chef Mike Garaghty from Wüsthof Knives put FINEX's cast-iron skillets to work when he crafted this delicious recipe. Espresso goes well on just about any protein, but it's especially delicious with pork tenderloin. As Chef Mike mentioned, "Pork tenderloin is an open canvas—you have to bring the flavor to it." Without a doubt, this rub does the trick. Give it a try!

1. Preheat oven to 400°F. Remove the skin and any excess fat from the tenderloins. Rub the tenderloins with a generous amount of olive oil.

2. Combine the espresso powder, ancho chili powder, paprika, brown sugar, salt, and pepper in a small bowl. Rub the pork tenderloins with the mixture, covering as much of the surface as possible. Warm a 12-inch cast-iron skillet over medium heat. Add enough olive oil to coat the bottom. When the oil starts to shimmer, add the tenderloins and sear on all sides, about 5 minutes total.

3. Place the skillet in the oven and roast until the internal temperature of the tenderloins is 145°F, about 15 minutes. Remove from the oven, place the tenderloins on a cutting board, loosely tent with foil, and let them sit for 10 to 15 minutes.

4. Slice the pork into medallions and place them over the Succotash in the skillet. Drizzle the Sour Cherry Glaze on top and serve.

SUCCOTASH

1. While the tenderloins are resting, place the bacon in the skillet and cook over medium heat until crispy. Transfer the bacon to a paper towel–lined plate to drain and leave the rendered fat in the skillet. When the bacon is cool enough to handle, chop into bite-sized pieces.

2. Add the bell pepper, onion, and garlic to the skillet and cook until they have softened, about 5 minutes. Add the corn, lima beans (or edamame), and greens and cook until the greens are wilted, about 3 minutes. Add the tomatoes and wine, stir to combine, and cook until the tomatoes are warmed through. Add the chopped bacon and season with salt and pepper.

SOUR CHERRY GLAZE

Place all of the ingredients in a saucepan and bring to a boil over medium-high heat. Reduce the heat and simmer until the mixture has thickened and reduced by half.

INGREDIENTS:

- 2 (1½ LB.) PORK TENDERLOINS
  OLIVE OIL, AS NEEDED
- 1 TABLESPOON INSTANT ESPRESSO POWDER
- 1 TABLESPOON ANCHO CHILI POWDER
- 1 TABLESPOON PAPRIKA
- 1 TABLESPOON BROWN SUGAR
- 1 TEASPOON KOSHER SALT
  GROUND BLACK PEPPER, TO TASTE
  SUCCOTASH (SEE RECIPE)
  SOUR CHERRY GLAZE (SEE RECIPE)

SUCCOTASH
- 4 STRIPS OF THICK-CUT BACON, CHOPPED
- 1 RED BELL PEPPER, DICED
- 1 SWEET ONION, DICED
- 1-2 GARLIC CLOVES, MINCED
- ¾ LB. SWEET CORN
- ¾ LB. FROZEN LIMA BEANS OR EDAMAME
- 3 CUPS BABY SPINACH OR BABY KALE (OR MIXTURE OF THE TWO)
- 1 CUP GRAPE TOMATOES
- ¼ CUP WHITE WINE
  KOSHER SALT AND GROUND BLACK PEPPER, TO TASTE

SOUR CHERRY GLAZE
- 1 CUP SOUR CHERRY PRESERVES
- ¼ CUP CHICKEN STOCK (SEE PAGES 102–3)
- 2 TABLESPOONS SOY SAUCE
- 2 TABLESPOONS SPICY BROWN MUSTARD

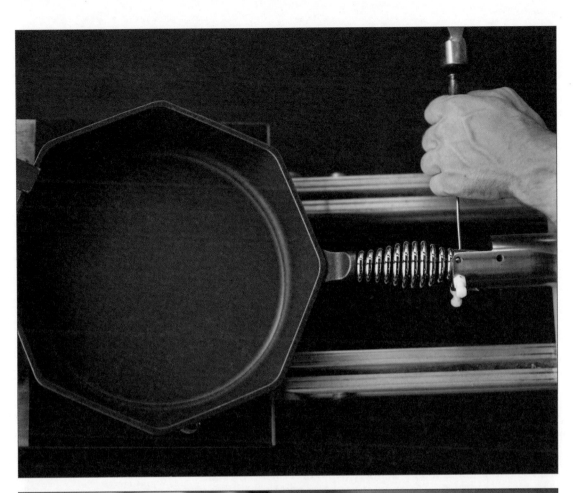

FINEX BIBINGKA (FILIPINO COCONUT-RICE CAKE)

YIELD: 8 SERVINGS / ACTIVE TIME: 35 MINUTES / TOTAL TIME: 1 HOUR AND 15 MINUTES

Bibingka is a popular breakfast or *merienda* (snack) food. Traditionally, it's placed in a banana leaf–lined terra-cotta pot and baked in a clay oven with preheated coals. In this instance, chef Carlo Lamagna replaced the terra-cotta pot with a 10-inch FINEX cast-iron skillet and baked it over a wood fire.

1. Preheat oven to 375°F.

2. Cut the banana leaf into squares and line a 10-inch cast-iron skillet with them, overlapping the squares. Trim any pieces that rise above the lip of the pan.

3. Combine the rice flour, sugar, baking powder, and salt in one bowl and the milk, coconut milk, eggs, and melted butter in another.

4. Combine the mixtures, stir until fully incorporated, and let the batter sit for 20 minutes to fully hydrate the flour. If using salted egg, chop and add to the batter.

5. Pour the batter into the banana leaf–lined skillet, place in the oven, and bake until a toothpick inserted into the center comes out clean, about 30 minutes. Remove and let cool slightly.

6. When the cake has cooled, grate the cheese on top. If using cured egg yolk, grate over the top with the cheese.

INGREDIENTS:

1	BANANA LEAF, WASHED AND DRIED
1	CUP SWEET RICE FLOUR
¾	CUP SUGAR
3	TEASPOONS BAKING POWDER
½	TEASPOON SALT
1	CUP WHOLE MILK
½	CUP COCONUT MILK
3	LARGE EGGS
3	TABLESPOONS UNSALTED BUTTER, MELTED AND BROWNED
	SALTED EGG OR CURED EGG YOLK, FOR GARNISH
	PARMESAN CHEESE OR EDAM CHEESE, FOR GARNISH

FINEX STRAWBERRY GINGERBREAD DUTCH BABY
with VANILLA CRÈME FRAÎCHE

YIELD: 8 SERVINGS / ACTIVE TIME: 15 MINUTES / TOTAL TIME: 50 MINUTES

Don't let the name fool you—this fluffy, eggy pancake has nothing to do with babies, but it is an essential cast-iron sweet treat.

1. Preheat the oven to 400°F. Crack the eggs into a food processor and blend for around 2 minutes, until the mixture is very smooth and pale. Add the brown sugar, flour, spices, salt, crème fraîche, and milk and continue to blend until the mixture is once again very smooth.

2. Place the cultured butter in a 12-inch cast-iron skillet. Place the skillet in the oven for 5 minutes, or until the butter has melted and begun to brown. Remove the skillet from the oven and swirl the butter around to coat the bottom and sides. Pour the batter into the pan and return it to the oven.

3. Bake for about 7 minutes, then sprinkle half of the strawberries and almonds onto the batter. Continue to bake until the batter has climbed the sides of the pan and the edges are golden brown, 15 to 20 minutes.

4. Remove from the oven and top with the remaining strawberries and almonds, and all of the basil. Cut into slices and top each serving with additional crème fraîche.

INGREDIENTS:

4   EGGS

2   TABLESPOONS DARK BROWN SUGAR

⅔   CUP ALL-PURPOSE FLOUR

¾   TEASPOON CINNAMON

½   TEASPOON GINGER

½   TEASPOON NUTMEG

¼   TEASPOON CLOVES

¼   TEASPOON KOSHER SALT

1   TABLESPOON VERMONT CREAMERY VANILLA CRÈME FRAÎCHE, PLUS MORE FOR TOPPING

⅔   CUP WHOLE MILK

3   TABLESPOONS VERMONT CREAMERY CULTURED BUTTER

1   QUART OF STRAWBERRIES, HULLED AND SLICED

⅓   CUP SLICED ALMONDS

2-3   BASIL LEAVES, SLICED THIN

IITTALA

Nordic living is the design base that Iittala is built upon. In the company's words: "[D]esign is a human issue. It is a way of looking forward." When purchasing cast iron from Iittala, you are making a commitment to love and use a piece born of thoughtful refinement. It is very possible that your children, and your children's children, will create dishes for their loved ones using the same tools you have invested in and cared for. Iittala's dedication to quality craftsmanship is evident in their products; on top of their new designs, there are also items that have been available for over 80 years.

Iittala started as a glass factory in 1881 in a village of the same name in southern Finland. The primary function of the small factory was to produce a variety of handmade glassware. While other producers were following the trend of intricately decorated dinnerware, Iittala made the bold and unique decision to buck the norm. They used Scandinavian design to create functional objects that not only served their purpose but were aesthetically pleasing without spilling into over embellishment. Designer Alvar Aalto had a vision of breaking the mold of rigid, geometric forms and allowing his creations to take on the form of organic, living beings in their own right.

Led by innovators of design like Alvar Aalto, Aino Aalto, and Kaj Franck, Iittala struck gold during the 1930s and 1940s. These artists held a deeply felt belief that their work should be available to everyone while still being created with care, purpose, and deliberate thought.

They gave birth to the design philosophy that Iittala still holds dear to this day: to push the boundaries and to give people tools of beauty and functionality.

The crux of Iittala as a brand lies within their belief of objects as "distinctive, combinable, and multifunctional, with lasting design that inspires individual use and expression." Rather than merely another article to utilize, their pieces are intended to enrich the kitchen experience. Each piece is meant to mesh with others in harmony without compromising the present design of a kitchen. No matter the series, Iittala's pieces flow with one another to create a tangible sense of symmetry and subtle cohesion.

While their design sense may appear modest and straightforward, there is a massive amount of accrued skill and knowledge that is necessary to bring these pieces to life. Experts across various professions work hand-in-hand during the production process to shepherd an object to completion. These craftspeople are the heart of Iittala.

NEST HOMEWARE

The Nest Homeware story is one of creativity, perseverance, and, surprisingly, a Kickstarter success that propelled the company out of the realm of founder Matt Cavallaro's imagination and into the manufacturing world. The cast-iron cookware Nest produces will take your breath away. The smooth, lightly seasoned surfaces give way to a side-wall thinness that matches that of the renowned Griswold pans of the past. Each of these pans looks like they could have been picked from a cherry tree and set on your table, ready to use.

After graduating from the Industrial Design program at the Rhode Island School of Design, Cavallaro began designing his first prototypes in 2013, and the idea of cast iron grew from there. Cavallaro's own fascination with combining functionality and gorgeous cookware led to his first cherry branch–inspired handle. His seamless blending of natural aesthetics and durable cast iron grew into Nest Homeware, a down-to-earth cast iron production company that puts quality and creativity before quantity. And with the help of a Kickstarter campaign that gained 235 backers and raised almost $36,000, the rest is history. For Cavallaro, the real purpose of Nest Homeware is to design meaningful objects that bring warmth and sustenance to family and friends.

Nest Homeware cookware is double-seasoned with flaxseed oil, giving it a bronze sheen that, with time and use, darkens into that trademark cast-iron black. Their cast-iron products are lighter than many others on the market, with a 9-inch cast-iron skillet that weighs only 4½ pounds, and their cherry tree branch–inspired handles are gorgeous to look at while still being long enough to keep your hands cooler for longer while you're cooking. They offer two skillets, a 4½-inch and a 9-inch, as well as a 3.5-quart Dutch oven with a gorgeous golden-toned handle on the lid.

Nest Homeware marks a real resurgence in artisan cast-iron cookware and has helped to harken back to a time where quality cookware was the centerpiece of homes and meals alike. While their products cannot be found in most retail stores at this time, they can be purchased directly from their website, where Cavallaro also maintains a blog about the creative process behind his designs.

KRAMPOUZ

Founded in 1945 in Pouldreuzic, France, Krampouz produced the first electric crepe maker on the market in response to a request from the founder's family. Before that time, the only way to make crepes was on a cast-iron griddle placed over a fireplace or woodstove. Once word got out about this new way to make crepes, requests started pouring in from all over Brittany. After making a trip to New York in 1966, then visiting London, Brussels, Athens, and countless other international cities, Krampouz soon came to distribute their cookware all over the globe.

Their company name comes from the Breton word meaning "pancake," but their cookware has a universal appeal. The company's motto is no matter the recipe or location—from okonomiyaki in Japan, chapati in India, tortillas in Mexico, or pancakes in England—crepes can be found in many forms all around the globe. While they've branched out into cast-iron waffle makers, panini presses, and, of course, standard kitchen grills, the crepe makers still hold an honored position in Krampouz's product line.

Krampouz listens to its customers and adjusts their products to provide the best cooking experience, whether for one of their industrial griddles or those designed for home use. By taking in customer feedback on every product, they've developed their easy-clean system, automatic heat regulation on their griddles, and their patented "Easy Crêp" system for their cast-iron crepe makers.

Krampouz prides themselves on their three standards of design: quality, reliability, and durability. In order to meet these standards, each product is designed out of recyclable materials to produce 100-percent sustainable products that will last for decades. With a goal of producing zero pollution, their manufacturing line generates no CO_2 or waste water, and they work closely with local suppliers to keep their products eco-friendly. And, of course, by designing products that will last for years, Krampouz also helps their customers keep the environment in mind when it comes to their cookware choices.

With a commitment to high-quality products and 100-percent sustainable development, if you find yourself craving a perfectly cooked, delicious crepe, a Krampouz crepe maker is a must-have.

SMITHEY IRONWARE

Founded in Charleston, South Carolina, and still made in America, the Smithey Ironware Company is the result of a passion for quality vintage cast iron. Founder Isaac Morton established the company in 2014 with a single 10-inch skillet that honored the classic style of heirloom pieces with modern technology and processes. Today, the company designs and manufactures an entire line of premium cast-iron cookware at its workshop in North Charleston.

Smithey works with a handful of family-owned US foundries to cast its cookware. After casting, the raw iron skillets have a surface finish similar to heavy-grit sandpaper. They are then shipped to Smithey's workshop, where each casting is transformed by hand and machine into elegant cookware pieces through multiple processes that include grinding, polishing, and machining.

Smithey currently features a cookware lineup that consists of three sizes of skillet: 8-inch, 10-inch, and 12-inch. In addition, the company makes a limited number of 12-inch hand-forged carbon steel skillets in collaboration with a world-renowned blacksmith in Charleston. Smithey expects to continue to add to its lineup of premium cookware inspired by vintage design.

MILO

Milo was founded in 2018 to bring heritage-quality cast iron into homes everywhere. Inspired by the qualities of French enameled cookware—excellent heat retention and distribution, durability and dishwasher safety, beautiful finish and the patina it develops—but frustrated by the high pricing, Milo sought a way to produce enameled cast-iron products without an overwhelming price tag. Milo holds to the idea that cast iron has been around for centuries and shouldn't be treated like a luxury item.

After 2 years of relentless testing and product development, they created their enameled cast-iron line, perfect for home cooks everywhere. After their products were released to the market, they sold out in the first month, and the line has continued to receive overwhelming support from customers. And with Milo's commitment to premium kitchenware at a fraction of the cost of other makers' wares, their popularity continues to grow.

By offering their products directly to consumers, Milo has taken high-quality cookware out of the aspirational realm and allowed everyone a chance to experience—and taste—the wonders of cast-iron cooking. Their cookware holds its own besides the big names (and is made using the same method as their competitors) and these well-designed tools offer the consistency you would expect from high-end cookware for almost a quarter of the price.

Easy to use, easy to care for, and impossible to resist, once you get your hands on a piece of Milo cookware, you're sure to be hooked.

MILO WILD MUSHROOM RISOTTO

YIELD: 4 SERVINGS / **ACTIVE TIME**: 40 MINUTES / **TOTAL TIME**: 40 MINUTES

Thanks to the even heat distribution offered by cast iron, a number of those notoriously difficult dishes have been brought to heel. This mushroom risotto is one of them.

1. Warm a 12-inch cast-iron skillet over medium heat as you prepare the mushrooms. Remove all of the rough, woody stems and add them to a microwave-safe bowl large enough to hold the broth. Chop the mushroom caps into a mix of thin slices and small cubes.

2. Add the olive oil to the skillet and swirl to coat the bottom of the pan. When it is almost smoking, add the mushroom caps, raise the heat to medium-high, and cook, while stirring occasionally, until the mushrooms' moisture has evaporated and they start to brown, about 10 minutes. You might need to do this in two batches.

3. While the mushrooms brown, pour the chicken broth over the mushroom stems, and heat for a couple minutes in the microwave until boiling. Remove from the microwave and let the mixture sit. You can also do this on the stove in a saucepan.

4. When the mushrooms are a little brown around the edges, add the onion and cook until it is translucent, about 3 minutes.

5. Add the garlic and a small pinch of salt. Cook, while stirring, until the garlic is just starting to soften, about 3 minutes. Add the rice and stir it around so it gets coated with the oil. Sauté the rice until it starts to warm and begins to look opaque.

6. Add the wine and gently stir until it's almost totally evaporated. Lower the heat to medium-low and ladle in about a cup of the mushroom-and-chicken broth. Stir vigorously to release the rice's starch.

7. Once the first bit of stock is almost gone, ladle in another cup. Repeat this stock-and-stirring process until all the broth is gone (you can discard the mushroom stems). Once the risotto reaches the right consistency and texture (we like it just a bit chewy, and a little loose), turn off the heat. It's okay if you have broth left in the skillet, or if you need to add a bit of extra water to thin it out.

8. Add the thyme, Parmesan, and butter and stir until everything is creamy. Serve immediately.

INGREDIENTS:

2   LBS. MUSHROOMS

¼   CUP OLIVE OIL

8-10   CUPS CHICKEN BROTH (HOMEMADE IS BEST, OR STORE-BOUGHT LOW-SODIUM)

1   YELLOW ONION, MINCED

2-3   GARLIC CLOVES, MINCED

  SALT, TO TASTE

1½   CUPS ARBORIO RICE

½   CUP DRY WHITE WINE

  WATER, AS NEEDED

  LEAVES FROM 2 SPRIGS OF THYME, CHOPPED (OR 1 TEASPOON DRIED THYME)

1   CUP GRATED PARMESAN CHEESE, OR TO TASTE

2   TABLESPOONS UNSALTED BUTTER, OR TO TASTE

BOROUGH FURNACE

Borough Furnace is a design studio and metal casting workshop in Owego, New York, known for beautiful, high-performance cooking tools made with care. Founded in 2011, it is a family-owned business owned by partners John Truex and Liz Seru.

"We initially raised seed money on Kickstarter to set up a micro-foundry to self-produce two sizes of cast-iron skillets as our initial offerings," says Seru. "Our first workshop in Syracuse used traditional foundry techniques updated for environmental sustainability. John built our first set of machinery, including our furnace, nicknamed 'the Skilletron,' that ran on waste vegetable oil collected from local restaurants. All of our source material was, and continues to be, recycled iron. In keeping with our mission to consume as little as possible, the sand from our molds is broken up and reused, creating very little waste.

"In the interim eight years, we've since expanded that hand-built workshop into our current incarnation, a 20,000–square foot factory in Owego. Central to our growth has been our personal commitment to environmental sustainability. Our furnace is now powered by electricity, and we're running it on wind-offsets as we work toward financing an on-site solar array and battery bank to run our full operation.

"Our line of cast-iron cookware borrows the best aspects of the classic American skillet design, but with contemporary updates. Features include gently sloped sides, for ease of use with a spatula, and balanced large handles to move the pans easily from the oven to the table. The long handle on our frying skillets stays cool to the touch on the cooktop and can be held barehanded. We hand-sand the surface of our skillets smooth and then give them a micro-texture for optimal oil adhesion. The oils and fats in your food are what make cast iron naturally nonstick, and our finish is optimized for this seasoning to build easily through cooking. We've expanded our initial offerings to include oven-to-table bakeware and a Dutch oven, which has the distinction of being the only enameled cast iron made in the United States.

"When we started Borough Furnace, we were the only US producer of cast iron other than Lodge. We started describing our products as 'hand-cast and finished' to highlight our small-scale foundry practice and the intimate way in which our products are made. Our design and craftsmanship have been recognized in the *New York Times*, the *Wall Street Journal*, *Saveur*, *Food & Wine*, *GQ*, *Wired*, and *Raw Craft with Anthony Bourdain*, amongst others. Christopher Kimball of *America's Test Kitchen* memorably called us the 'the Tiffany of cast-iron cookware.' We feel that our success stems from the deep connection between design, craft, and production. Because we are able to machine our own tooling and we make our own castings, we can prototype our products endlessly—taking them home, cooking with them, and making refinements until the details are just perfect."

TRAMONTINA

Tramontina was founded in Brazil in 1911 by Valentin Tramontina as a family company. Nestled into the small town of Carlos Barbosa, Valentin and his wife, Elisa De Cecco, built a modest wooden house that would become the base of their iron operations. They began by producing cookware for the local community and developed a reputation as hardworking, committed, and honest creators.

In 1939, after almost three decades of dedication, Valentin passed away, and it was time for Elisa to take up the mantle of leading the company. Her life revolved solely around maintaining the quality that the Tramontina brand was known for and ensuring fair wages for her employees. For Elisa, this meant working around the clock, delivering products door-to-door in the community. After continuing the good name and faith of the brand for another decade, her son, Ivo, took over the day-to-day operations. Together with his business partner, Ruy J. Scomazzon, Ivo began the new generation of Tramontina.

By 1986, Tramontina had expanded their business to the United States, with their new presence centered in Houston, Texas. As a satellite expansion of the company, they began selling knives exclusively. They focused on curating an assembly of like-minded and dedicated employees in the US throughout the 2000s and were able to expand their product availability.

Tramontina doubled down on the company's commitment to expanding the brand in the US by reopening a shuttered aluminum factory in Manitowoc, Wisconsin. Their effort helped to rehabilitate a community of hardworking labor-ers, allowing them to uphold their collective character as skilled craftspeople. Tramontina is proud to have been a positive influence in each community they have impacted, focusing heavily on lifting up locals and providing high-quality products along the way. They attribute their success not only to their committed employees but also to the steadfast communities that support them.

Tramontina strives for excellence in all facets of their production and are always pursuing new design concepts to push the boundaries of what they can offer. Their products are sold not only online through all major online retailers but also in numerous US housewares stores.

The cast iron produced by Tramontina is meant to last a lifetime and beyond; their goal is to pass down culinary traditions from generation to generation. This doesn't mean that their cast iron is traditional by any means; the sleek design and enamel coating reinforce the idea that these implements are manufactured for a modern kitchen. In their own words: "Each piece comes with a vibrant, gradated porcelain enamel exterior finish, offering an elegant kitchen to table serving option. The heavy-gauge cast-iron interior is coated with an easy-to-clean porcelain enamel finish, while the sturdy side handles make transport easy. The self-basting condensation ridges on the lid uniformly collect and direct vapors onto food, producing moist and savory dishes and making this cookware perfect for slow-cooking recipes, braised meats, baked dishes, and even for frying."

MARQUETTE CASTINGS

This family-owned and -operated casting business started out with a goal: relearn how to make thin, smooth cast-iron cookware in the modern day, and with the Steckling brothers behind the helm, they've accomplished this goal with flying colors. Eric, Kurt, Karl, and Jason Steckling are the definition of "do-it-yourself," and, according to their website, they have been makers since before being a "maker" was a thing. With their past projects ranging from kids' picnic tables to toothbrush heads, and taking them through fields like woodworking, electronics, and a little bit of everything else, innovation and creativity were the modus operandi for these siblings long before they turned to cast iron.

Frustrated by how many of the nonstick pans he had received as wedding gifts were falling apart, Eric started to look for alternatives to contemporary cookware. "I remember really being sick of nonstick cookware," Eric says. "You reach a point where you know you have to throw this pan away, but you hold off. Maybe it's not broken, maybe I can use it one more time. That debate really stuck with me." Inspired to create a set of pans that would last for years, Eric began to turn his talent for innovation toward the cast-iron market, and in 2015 the Steckling brothers started Marquette Castings, with their headquarters located in Royal Oak, Michigan.

But it was not all smooth sailing from there. Eric found himself going from one foundry to another, carrying the 6-inch Griswold skillet that inspired him to invest in cast iron. "All these advances in technology and yet we've lost the casting information," Eric explains. "We would show the skillet to foundries and they all said, 'We can't do that. No one can do that.'" After jumping between four cast-iron foundries, they finally settled on the investment-casting method for their products, and the results were almost instantaneous. After years of trying to find the right start for their products, Marquette Castings shipped out their first Michigan-made skillet in the fall of 2018.

The investment casting process for cast iron has been around for generations. Investment casting is a lost-wax process, meaning the skillets are first cast in wax and a tree is assembled out of the castings. Then the tree is coated in an exterior shell made of ceramic "slurry" and sand. This process is repeated multiple times until a shell is formed, then the wax is melted out. The shells are heated at close to 1,700°F, and molten metal is poured inside. Once the metal has cooled, the shells are broken and six cast-iron skillets are removed from the metal trees. The skillets then go on to polishing, grinding, and, of course, seasoning before being shipped out. While this process takes more time than other casting processes, the results are well worth the added effort, leading to some of the most striking pieces of cast-iron cookware on the market.

Currently offering 10½-inch and 13-inch cast-iron skillets, Marquette Castings prides themselves on their skillets' 2½-millimeter walls and smooth finish. Along with their carbon-steel line of products, they are currently working on creating an enameled cast-iron line, hoping to bring the enameling industry back to the US. If their goal was to help restart traditional cast-iron cookware after the Teflon craze, they have been successful. When asked about what makes buying cast iron worthwhile, Eric responds, "If you have a suit you're only going to wear once or twice, then it's not worth it. But if you wear suits every day, then you should get a nice suit. The same investment works for cast iron, because this is cookware that lasts for generations, not just ten uses."

MORE MAKERS

These smaller companies might not have the profile of Lodge and Le Creuset, but that doesn't mean they don't make quality cast-iron cookware.

Best Duty – The premier South African manufacturer of *potjie* pots and Dutch ovens or bake pots. Their cast-iron products come in a wide variety of sizes, from 3 quarts to a monster 75-quart kettle that weighs in at 170 pounds.

Bristow Iron Works – This Canadian company makes a beautiful array of skillets, cauldrons, and pots as well as more esoteric items like loaf pans, an aebleskiver pan, and a cast-iron batard pan for making crusty bread. They also make dinner bells and a convertible tripod for campfire cooking.

Cousances – Originally a foundry in northern France, Cousances began production in 1553. The historic company existed for centuries before it was purchased by Le Creuset in 1957. The company still sporadically reissues some of the Cousances line in limited editions that are available online or at select retail outlets.

Guro Cast Iron – Established in 2007 in Japan, Guro makes cast-iron pans and enameled cast-iron pots. They pre-season all of their cookware with soy oil as a nod to their commitment to eco-friendly, non-chemical production processes.

Iwachu – This company, based in Morioka, Japan, was founded in 1902. Iwachu is an incredibly popular and well-known manufacturer of classic *tetsubin* teakettles and covetable art gallery–worthy skillets, sukiyaki pots, soup pots, and casseroles.

Kamasada – This 100-plus-year-old company sells their *nanbu tekki* housewares and art objects in museum gift shops and shops that are curated as if they were museums. Designer Nobuho Miya has won numerous awards for his thoughtfully made two-handled pans, rice cookers, and *yonabe* pots.

Skeppshult – Another design-focused company, Skeppshult was founded in Sweden in 1906. They create skillets with wooden handles, and a few pots come with glass lids as well. The products all have a very sleek and decidedly modern Scandinavian aesthetic.

Zishta – This Indian company offers a range of cookware aimed to reinvent and reinvigorate cooking practices while supporting traditional iron artisans from Tamil Nadu, in the foothills of the Western Ghats mountains. It's a feel-good company that is worth supporting.

CAST IRON CARE AND KEEPING

Cast iron is the original nonstick cookware. But whether you are using a pre-seasoned pan or a vintage one, some care and keeping are called for in order to maintain that nonstick quality. Luckily, it really isn't very hard, and a little effort at the start of your relationship with a piece of cast-iron cookware will save you a great deal of time in the long run. The pages that follow detail how best to season, clean, and store your cookware so that not only is it conditioned to help you make the best food possible, it'll be kept in tip-top condition so you can pass it along to a friend or family member one day.

SEASONING A NEW PAN

A cast-iron pan is metal that has been poured into a mold and formed into a shape that allows you to cook food, hence why they are called cast-iron pans. Across the world, in every culture, humans have cooked in metal vessels that can withstand direct heat since we figured out how to extract metal from the earth. At first, they were rudimentary cauldrons, but over time they evolved into myriad shapes and sizes. For the most part, once the basic and most necessary shapes were created, the innovation in this field ended. Today, we have more understanding of the science and the benefits of casting cookware, but for the most part nothing has changed in the last few hundred years.

So, you have this pan. It's made from a raw material that needs to be seasoned to create a non-stick coating that acts as a defense against rusting. Many people have decided that the coating process and the maintenance of the seasoning is somehow difficult. It isn't. It's simple. What makes it complicated is that the general directions can be very detailed. But as with anything, it's better to have more information than not enough.

The steps to seasoning your new cast-iron cookware are simple:

1. Wash it with warm, soapy water, using an abrasive sponge to really scrub it. If it just came from the store, it should be relatively clean, but you want to make sure there is no dust or debris.

2. Dry the pan thoroughly with a clean cloth. It's best to do this immediately and to make sure it's absolutely dry before you move

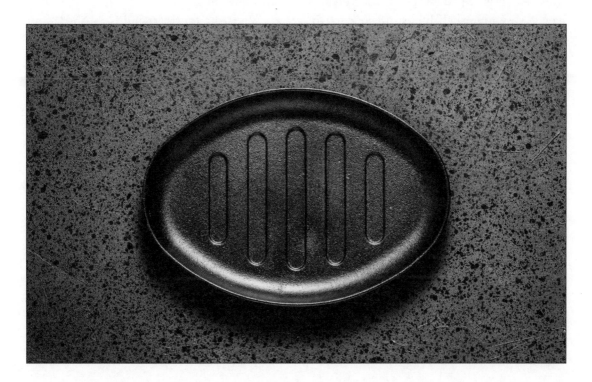

COCONUT FLAKE SEASONING

Founded in 2017 by Chef Lalita Kaewsawang in Santa Cruz, California, HANLOH specializes in Thai food catering and pop-up events. Kaewsawang also uses an interesting alternative technique for seasoning cast iron (especially useful for your aebleskiver or khanom krok pan, with its multiple wells). The idea is to fill your cast-iron pan with raw coconut flakes and bake it at 350°F for 1½ hours. Once the cast iron is out of the oven, discard the coconut, wipe the pan to remove any excess oil, and use as you would any other seasoned piece of cookware.

on to the next step: put it on the stove top over a low flame for a few minutes. It really needs to be dry.

3. Using a clean cloth (or your fingers), coat the entire pan—inside and out, including the handle—with a thin layer of oil, making sure to really rub it in. The pan should absorb the oil and it should not seem at all greasy. Ideally, you want to use flaxseed oil, but vegetable oil works too. Flaxseed oil is expensive and doesn't have a very long shelf life, so make sure to refrigerate what remains of the bottle and use it within 6 months (it's great in salad dressings and smoothies).

4. Place a baking sheet or just a large piece of foil on the lower rack in your oven; this will prevent any drips from causing a mess later.

Place the oiled pan, upside down, on the upper rack and heat the oven to 450°F. Let it bake for 30 minutes. During this time, it may get a little smoky, so make sure to have the vent on or a window open.

5. Remove the pan from the oven and let it cool completely. This should take about 45 minutes.

6. Repeat Steps 3 to 5 three times. Yes, that says three times.

When the fourth round is finished, your pan is seasoned. When it's cooled, wipe it again with a clean cloth. The oil will have chemically reacted to the heat and become polymerized, so the surfaces will be dark black and slightly shiny.

Use and enjoy your pan!

STRIPPING OLD SEASONING

When purchasing secondhand cast iron, even if it isn't rusty, you probably want to strip the old seasoning. You don't know what the seasoning on your newfound treasure has previously been through, and it may not have been done correctly. Sellers sometimes hastily oil up a pan so that it has a nice sheen for display, but it may not have been oil you should cook with

and may be difficult to clean afterward.

A good soak in a bath of 1 part white vinegar and 1 part water will strip seasoning, and you don't need a scrubbing pad or steel wool; a regular plastic scrub brush or sponge will work just fine. Following the directions on store-bought cast-iron or oven cleaners that advertise stripping will also do the trick.

MAINTAINING YOUR CAST-IRON COOKWARE

Now you've put in the effort to season your cast iron. So how do you care for these pots and pans between uses?

They are happiest when they are stored in a dry place. For most people, that means leaving them on the cooktop at all times. You can also hang them on a rack, store them in the oven, or stack them in a drawer or cupboard, making sure to place a piece of felt or a paper towel in between each pan. This protects the pan from dust and potential chipping, scratching, or cracking.

Almost every time you use your cast-iron cookware, you'll be adding more fat and baking in the seasoning even further. This is the most important thing you can do for your pan: use it. There are a few other things to keep in mind that will keep that pan looking good and in rotation:

1. If you have a vegetarian in the house, it's nice to set one or two pans aside for your non-animal protein cooking. Many people dedicate one pan just for cooking fish. You would be hard-pressed to notice that your pan is holding onto any odors, but you may not want to mingle the different types of fat.

2. If you keep kosher, you already know the deal. You'll want to have different pans for meat and dairy recipes.

3. You've heard it over and over that you should never use soap on your cast-iron pans. While for the most part that's true, it doesn't mean you can never do it. You just want to only do it once in a great while. If you've properly seasoned the pan, there isn't much that can truly remove all of that polymerized oil. What you absolutely don't want to do is soak the pan or leave it wet. Iron rusts very quickly, even when it's properly seasoned, and you don't want to deal with that, so make sure to wipe out and dry off your pan whenever you use it.

4. When you're cleaning your pan, avoid overly abrasive things like steel wool. A stiff plastic brush is perfect for scrubbing, but ideally you just want to use your dishcloth or sponge.

5. As tempting as it may be, don't try to use high heat or direct flames to clean your pans. The debris will for sure turn to ash, but the cleanup is going to be a lot of work, and you will have to re-season the pan. That said, you can simmer a bit of water in the pan, over high heat, to remove any burnt matter.

THE "NO" LIST FOR CAST IRON

In order to keep your cast iron in the best possible shape for a lifetime, you should follow some rules. These are relatively basic and will become second nature the longer you have your pans:

1. The dishwasher is no place for cast iron. Ever.
2. Never leave your cast iron soaking in water.
3. Always dry your cast iron completely after washing.
4. Never leave your cast iron outdoors.
5. Never store food in cast iron cookware.

ABOUT PRE-SEASONED AND ENAMELED CAST IRON

PRE-SEASONED CAST IRON

Several manufacturers, including Lodge, sell pans that have been pre-seasoned. What that means is that the pan has been heat-treated with oil to create a seasoned layer. When you get it home, you should still wash it gently with warm, soapy water and dry it completely before using for the first time. Like all pan seasoning, it will still need to be re-seasoned when it seems to be wearing off. That will depend on how often you use the pan, how often you cook with oil—frying is a great way to keep your pans seasoned—and how vigorously you clean it. How does one determine that it is time to re-season?

1. Food starts to stick to the surface.
2. The surface seems dull.

It's that simple. Treat a pan that was purchased with seasoning the same way you would a pan that you seasoned yourself after the first year of use.

ENAMELED CAST IRON

When we talk about cast-iron cookware in this book, we're mostly referring to raw, seasoned iron. The matte black kind. But that isn't the only game in town. Enameled cast-iron pots and pans have been coated with a very durable outer layer of enamel and come in a rainbow of colors. The original enameled cast-iron pans, created at the end of the seventeenth century, were designed to create a smooth cooking surface. Enameled cast iron has lower thermal conductivity than raw cast iron, so it heats more slowly, and doesn't retain heat as long. The enameled surface doesn't ever need to be seasoned, but you need to be more conscious of possible chipping, discoloration, and pitting. Never use enameled cast iron over a campfire. An enameled pot or pan will cost more than raw cast iron, but you are paying for craftsmanship and, usually, a lifetime warranty. It doesn't rust, but it may chip if you use metal utensils. It also does not add iron to your diet, which for some people is a benefit of using cast iron. Enameled cast iron is an easier material to maintain in the long run and is a good choice for cooking acidic foods, too.

ACCESSORIES AND TOOLS

Beyond all the pots and pans, there are plenty of accessories designed to help clean, protect, and maintain your cast-iron cookware.

GRILL PAN SCRAPER

If you're buying a cast-iron grill pan, you absolutely need this indispensable little tool. It's a square piece of thick plastic that acts like a comb and gets the nitty-gritty cleanup job done in a snap. It is critical for getting down into the grooves and making sure the pan stays clean between uses.

DUTCH OVEN TOTE BAG

Seek out durable, padded bags that are sized to fit your cast-iron Dutch oven. They smartly have handles, making them easy to transport. These are great if you're going to be heading to the outdoors or just to a BBQ at your neighbor's house. They clean up easily, but we like to have a plastic trash bag in there, too, in case the pan can't be cleaned thoroughly before you take it home or to its next campsite.

SCRUBBING BRUSH

A stiff, rounded plastic scrubbing brush is key for maintaining your cast-iron pan. A good brush will help remove debris without damaging that well-established seasoning on the surface of the pan. They need to be replaced periodically when the bristles bend or discolor, so buy a few at a time and you'll never be caught in a pinch.

HANDLE COVERS

You can purchase handle covers made from silicone, leather, or thick fabric (such as terrycloth) for your long-handled pans, or pick out smaller options for loop handles. Due to the fact that your cast-iron pan almost certainly has been forged as one piece, the handles will get hot, and these items are helpful for avoiding burns.

TRIVET

Not only is it great to cook with cast-iron cookware, but it is also attractive enough to use as a serving dish. But whether it's coming off the stove or out of the oven, the hot dish can't just be set on the table. A trivet is a small, usually round, heatproof object that you can safely place your hot pans on to prevent burning surfaces. Trivets come in thousands of colors, styles, and designs. Some are more utilitarian and some are perfectly suited to be on the dining table. You can also find custom and heritage trivets that are worth collecting.

RESTORING CAST-IRON COOKWARE

Cast iron is basically indestructible, but it can rust. Rust is an iron oxide. That means it's a chemical compound composed of iron and oxygen, similar to the way water is a chemical compound made of hydrogen and oxygen. Rust is flaky, friable (easily crumbled), and reddish orange. When iron has rusted, the rust will, in time, corrode and disintegrate your pan (which might make for a cool science experiment, but it's not the best way to utilize your cookware). The real reason you want to get rid of rust is that it will cause pitting and unevenness. If your pan's surface is affected, your food can't lay flat, which will lead to uneven cooking. It can also impact the flavor, and you definitely don't want that.

If you find your pan has taken this unfortunate turn, or you've discovered an old, long-ignored skillet that you just had to own, don't despair. If the piece is pitted or cracked, best to recycle it. But if it's just rusted, your pan can be revived, and there are several methods to do just that.

STEEL WOOL AND ELBOW GREASE

This is the best method if you want to do something manually, have a lot of patience, and want the satisfaction of knowing you did it all by hand. It can also be oddly cathartic, like taking a boxing class (and it requires pretty much the same amount of upper body strength). The steps are easy. Wash and scrub the pan to remove any loose debris. Dry it completely. Using a hearty amount of baking soda and coarse kosher salt, scrub with steel wool. Keep going. Add a splash of distilled white vinegar and more baking soda. Wipe often. Is it clean yet? If it is, congratulations! If not, keep going. When it's really clean, season it again. And then be sure to take care of it; you put in a lot of work.

OVEN CLEANER

This method is good in terms of intensity, but it does require using lye-based oven cleaner, which isn't something you want to breathe in. It does work, though. To get started, wash and scrub the pan to remove any loose debris. Dry completely. Put on a pair of heavy-duty gloves to protect your hands. In a very well-ventilated room (or better yet, outdoors), spray the pan all over with oven cleaner. Now you have two choices. You can place the pan in a plastic bag, seal the bag, and wait 24 hours before scrubbing again. Or place the pan in your oven (no plastic bag!) and turn on the self-cleaning cycle. If your oven needs a cleaning, this option cleans two things at once. When it's done and the pan is cool, scrub again. Re-season and enjoy.

COLA

Does it work? Mostly. Is it silly? Yes. Cola has phosphoric acid, which is corrosive to iron, meaning it both cleans the rust off and creates more. If you really want to do this, though (and it is a fun experiment), simply submerge your pan in cola for 2 to 3 days, checking frequently after the first day. When the rust can be wiped off, clean the pan immediately and make sure no cola stays behind—if it does, it will cause the pan to rust again. Then re-season immediately.

MOLASSES

Pretty much the same as cola, except stickier and much more expensive. What makes it work is that molasses has cyclic hydroxamic acids and chelating agents—scientific words that mean you can soak a pan in an 8:1 solution of water and molasses for a few days before wiping it off completely and re-seasoning your pan.

DISTILLED WHITE VINEGAR

Another method that technically works, but it's slow and can actually cause more rusting. If you choose to do this, submerge the pan in distilled white vinegar for 2 hours, clean it, and re-season.

RUST REMOVER (LIKE METAL RESCUE BRAND)

This is a water-based chelating agent that contains no acid and is safe on all surfaces, even skin. Simply submerge your pan in the solution—following the directions on the bottle—and wipe off any remaining rust. It's like magic. There's really no reason to use any other method.

IMPOSTER ALERT!

Or, How to Spot Fake Cast Iron
in a Collector's World

That Lodge pan sitting on your stove top is most likely the real thing. You probably got it from your parents or grandparents, or at a cookware store on Main Street. But that doesn't mean that all pots and pans that purport to be the real deal are. With the increased popularity of vintage cast-iron cookware, a new collector needs to have some tools and do a lot of research before making any major investments. When it comes to spotting a fake (and yes, strange as it might seem, this is a real thing) there are several simple steps you can take before investing your money in what may be a forgery.

First and foremost, pick it up. Cast iron is heavy. Even the newfangled brands that have tinkered with technology to lighten things up still have a bit of heft. So, does the pan in your hand have some oomph? If so, it's most likely cast iron. Another excellent giveaway is rust. Is it rusty? Then it's cast iron.

Second, turn that beauty over and inspect the bottom. Does it have a logo of a brand you've heard of, or more importantly, the one you're looking for or hoping to find? If it's collectible, it may also have a serial number and the name of the city where it was cast. These are good signs, but you need to keep going. If the piece looks older, but the imprinted logo is really crisp, take a hard pass. It may be a reproduction. Is there a line or groove on the bottom of the skillet? This is called "bottom gating"

technology, and neither Erie nor Griswold ever used it.

Third, is that bad boy all one piece? Meaning—was it cast? Yes, some brands (FINEX, for example) are not all one piece, but anything collectible should be. The handle should not be screwed on. That's not what you want.

Fourth, is it small? Like, perhaps made for a tea party? Chances are that's not real, and it's definitely not for cooking in.

Fifth, does it seem too good to be true? Trust yourself here. There are not a lot of genuine pans floating around priced at $2. With the internet, shop owners can and do research their merchandise before sticking on that price tag, so while a thrift store or garage sale may have something worth picking up for cheap, you need to have your skeptical glasses on when the prices fall to the unbelievable bargain level.

Lastly, do your research. There are some pans out there that have been tagged on numerous sites for being fakes.

This list could go on for days, but the main thing to concern yourself with is whether the piece appears to have been cast well. As you learn more about each brand, you will find lots of specific examples of fraudulent pieces. Then again, if you happen to like the way it looks and feels and aren't in sticker shock over the price, you can just buy it anyway. It's your money and it'll be your pan.

APPENDIX

OUTDOOR COOKING

Using cast-iron cookware outdoors is rustic and satisfying. It's also a bit of an art, and not quite as simple as just having the right tools. There are several things you need to factor in before tackling it for the first time. Once you've mastered the basics, though, you'll be off and running and won't ever need to look back.

Any time you're considering cooking outdoors the absolute first thing to do is make sure the surroundings are perfectly safe. If you'll be cooking in a public area like a park or campground, you need to seek out and check all posted signs and make sure fires are allowed, and, if so, that it hasn't been designated a "high fire risk" day. If your area doesn't issue fire warnings, use your best judgment. Additionally, take a look and see if there are any major hazards. There should be no dry material within 10 feet of where you'll be building the fire. The area around your firepit or campfire should be cleared of any debris or otherwise flammable materials.

If you're making your own pit, dig your hole 1 foot deep and 2 to 3 feet across and encircle the pit with rocks. If you're using an existing pit or grill, make sure there is no debris or trash that needs to be removed. Other users may not have been as conscientious or courteous as you.

You are now ready to build a fire.

WHAT YOU'LL NEED TO BUILD A FIRE
- Charcoal or firewood
- A shovel
- A charcoal chimney starter
- A long lighter or matches
- Heavy gloves
- A bucket of water

Please note that while using lighter fluid makes starting a fire easier, it doesn't make it better; the preferred method is the tried-and-true combination of fire and wood. Lighter fluid has fumes and is not ideal to travel with.

FIREWOOD

Only use firewood that you have purchased from a reputable source, or collect wood from the immediate area where you will be cooking. Always make sure you are burning nontoxic woods (and never poison oak), and remember that using non-native wood can have serious ecological impact through the inadvertent relocation of insects and diseases.

OUTDOOR COOKING FOOD SAFETY

The food you are going to cook outdoors needs to be kept fresh until your fire is ready. Make sure any perishable food you decide to bring to a campsite is kept on ice. According to the USDA: "Bacteria grow most rapidly in the range of temperatures between 40°F and 140°F, doubling in number in as little as 20 minutes. This range of temperatures is often called the Danger Zone. Never leave food out of refrigeration over 2 hours."

IF USING WOOD

Collect a combination of dry and cured small twigs—or tinder (not the app!)—dry leaves, medium branches, and larger logs. Make sure your wood is cut or broken to fit in the pit.

Put the twigs and leaves in the center of your firepit. Now you want to build a cone sculpture. It should be about 2 feet tall.

Using a long match or stick lighter, carefully ignite the leaves at the bottom of the cone from a few angles. As the fire builds and burns, carefully add larger pieces of wood to keep it going. Never leave your fire unattended.

IF USING CHARCOAL

Loosely wad up a few pieces of paper and place a charcoal chimney starter on top, in the center of your firepit. Fill the chimney almost to the top with charcoal. Using a long match or stick lighter, light the paper on fire from the bottom.

The coals will be red-hot (500°F or so) and covered with a light layer of white ash in about 15 minutes. When they're ready, pour the coals into the center of your pit or grill. Place the empty chimney someplace safe to cool.

Once your fire is lit and has had a while to burn down (you never want to cook over flames that are shooting up) you're ready to cook. Keep in mind that cooking over a fire takes longer than

cooking over a stove and requires more attention.

Now you have to decide: Do you want to cook on a grate or use a tripod? A grate is best if you will be using a pan or Dutch oven. A tripod is the only choice if you're using a round-bottomed cauldron or a Dutch oven with a hanging loop handle (that part is essential). You also have the option of cooking directly on the fire, which is best done with three-legged cauldrons or a skillet. Lastly, you can bury a Dutch oven into the embers directly.

To set up a grate for cooking, make sure it is as level as possible, and that it will not fall over. It should be sturdy enough to hold all of the cookware you plan on placing on it. Set the grate over the fire using gloved hands and tongs.

Tripods have three legs and a sturdy chain that hangs from the center. Set it up prior to building your fire. Make sure it is very stable and that it can handle the weight of a full Dutch oven. You can purchase tripods at well-equipped camping stores; alternately, there are kits available online.

The heat of the fire can't be regulated, but you can determine where the hotter and cooler spots are. The edges of the fire will of course be cooler, so place most of your pots and pans to the side. With this method, you will need to keep an eye on everything. Also, the higher up

OUTDOOR CAST-IRON COOKING AROUND THE WORLD

While the image of cowboys cooking beans in a cast-iron pot is part of American mythology, it's not the only way people have cooked outdoors through the ages. Most iron-producing cultures have a variation on griddles and skewers for cooking over fire, but in a few spots, things have evolved.

In Argentina, the cowboy is a *gaucho*, and the cooking is done with a *chapa*, a large table that can be placed directly over a fire and used like a large griddle.

The second most popular Argentine tool is an iron cross, which is pretty much exactly what it sounds like: a large cross attached to a base that tilts over a roaring fire. Its only real use is for cooking whole animals.

The Japanese hibachi is a versatile, portable coal grill that is used for cooking small pieces of meat and vegetables and can be used as a cooktop for heating small saucepans and kettles.

In India, breads like chapati are made by street vendors who place the rolled-out dough directly on charcoal held in cast-iron cauldrons.

your pot or pan is, the further it is from the heat and the less chance there will be burning.

The best meals cooked over a campfire are the ones that have only a few ingredients, all of which come to life when kissed by fire.

To make the most of your experience, try to do all of the prep work for your meal before you head out. Have all of the ingredients, tools, and equipment you will need ready to go. Aluminum foil can be a lifesaver, too. Never leave a roll behind when you're heading to the great outdoors.

METHODS

SKILLET
Using a skillet over a campfire is almost primal. To do so, you can place it on a grate while wearing a heavy mitt. No matter what you're cooking, you'll need a small amount of fat in a hot pan, the product—a sausage, a freshly caught and cleaned fish, or even some nice vegetables—seasoning (salt at the very least), and heat. This also works for Dutch ovens. For baking, try simple stir-and-pour cakes to start.

SUSPENDED DUTCH OVEN
This is the ideal method for making campfire baked beans, chili, stews, and soups. You will need at least one-third of the vessel to have liquid

(stock, broth, wine, water, etc.), then you're free to fill the rest with your selections of vegetables, protein, beans, hearty grains, and seasonings. As your meal cooks, make sure to stir periodically.

COAL-TOP OVEN
Many Dutch ovens have a distinct lip on the lid. This feature was designed for you to place hot coals on top—using very long, strong tongs. This creates more of an oven atmosphere within the pot. For this method, place the oven on a grate or heat plate. Fill with your food and cover the lid with coals. To determine how many coals you'll need to maintain heat, multiply the size of your Dutch oven by 2, then put one-third of the

coals below and two-thirds on top. For a 12-inch Dutch oven, you will want around eight coals underneath and 16 on top, evenly spaced.

You will also need to rotate the pot occasionally, since the heat of your fire will be uneven.

When you need to lift the lid, you may want to consider using a Dutch oven lid lifter. This contraption, which allows you to pick up the lid from the center of a burning-hot fire, is totally worth the investment.

CLEANUP

When you have removed all of the food from your vessel, add a bit of water. When the water has cooled slightly, use a good stiff brush or scrubbing pad to clean it. Rinse and dry as thoroughly as possible. Your cast iron will rust out in nature just as easily as at home.

What you never want to do when you are outdoors is use salt to clean your pans. It's still effective, but it's not easy to dispose of large amounts. Throwing salt on the ground or in a freshwater lake or river can kill plants and animals.

When you're done with your firepit, you need to make sure there's no danger of it reigniting and check that you haven't littered or polluted the area. Here are the seven steps you should follow to extinguish a campfire. They are based on the USDA Forest Service guidelines:

1. Drown the campfire with water.

2. Mix the ashes and any partially burned sticks and embers in with the soil.

3. Stir the ashes, embers, partially burned sticks, and soil with a small shovel, making sure everything is wet.

4. Using a bare hand, feel everything, making sure it is completely cool. If not, add more water.

5. When you think you are done, wait a few minutes and check again that everything is cool and wet.

6. Inspect the area and make sure there are no sparks or embers. It only takes one to start a fire.

7. "If it's too hot to touch, it is too hot to leave."

Erwin E. Smith, photographer, *JA chuck-wagon, getting dinner. Texas,* ca. 1907. Photograph. Library of Congress, Prints and Photographs Division, Washington, DC.

Cowboys at Lunch, postcard by the Detroit Publishing Company, ca. 1898–1931. The New York Public Library, The Miriam and Ira D. Wallach Division of Art, Prints and Photographs: Photography Division.

APPENDIX

CHUCK WAGONS: THE ORIGINAL FOOD TRUCKS

Trends can be cyclical, meaning that what is in fashion will fall out of fashion before rising again. The ubiquity of cast-iron cookware in kitchens today certainly fits this pattern, though the advent of cast-iron cookware had nothing to do with being trendy and everything to do with practicality. And while the interest in cooking with cast iron has greatly been bolstered by cable television and social media, it is way more than a fad; it is a return to fundamentals, an embrace of tradition. Chuck wagons, if you think of food trucks kitted out with cast-iron Dutch ovens and skillets as an updated version, have also undergone a revival of late.

The chuck wagon isn't some Hollywood invention. It was thought up in 1866 by Texas rancher Charles Goodnight, who figured that if he could offer cowboys better food than the dried meats and hard biscuits they typically carried, and more of it, then he would have a leg up on other ranchers when it came to enticing cowboys to join his cattle drives, which could last for several months. Starting with a Studebaker army wagon, Goodnight crafted a mobile kitchen outfitted with storage compartments, including a "chuck" box on the back of the wagon; its hinged top opened up to create a table. The cast-iron Dutch oven went in the boot with other heavy items; sturdy canvas or cowhide called the "possum belly" hung beneath the wagon and held wood and cow chips for the fire; and a water barrel and coffee grinder were bolted to the wagon's side. Had other mobile kitchens been used before this? Probably. But Goodnight's take coincided with a watershed moment in post–Civil War America. The chuck wagon, with its central role in these far-reaching cattle drives, became an iconic symbol of life on the range, alongside images of dust-covered, tired men lounging on the ground after a long day in the saddle, waiting for food being prepared in cast-iron cookware.

The chuck wagon was run by a "cookie," second in importance only to the trail boss on a drive; not only did a cookie feed the cowboys, he also served as a barber, dentist, and banker. Chuck wagons also carried the cowboys' bedrolls. It was

Richard E. Ahlborn, photographer, *Buckaroo Breakfast at Chuck Wagon (Chuck Wheelock),* July 1978. Photograph. Library of Congress, Paradise Valley Folklife Project Collection, Washington, DC.

Alexander Lambert, photographer, *Lunch at Chuck Wagon,* ca. 1905. Stereograph. Library of Congress, Prints and Photographs Division, Washington, DC.

essentially a general store and a communal hub for as long as the drive went on (the goal of most drives was to move herds of cattle overland to railroads that could then transport the cattle to processing facilities in a city like Chicago).

By virtue of being on a cattle drive, beef was easy to come by on the range, though cowboys also hunted wild game and fished when possible in order to add some variety to the meals doled out at the chuck wagon. Staples that a cookie kept on hand included nonperishable items like salt, brown sugar, flour, beans, rice, salt pork, cornmeal, dried fruit, baking powder, baking soda, syrup, and coffee. Sourdough breads were common as well, and many cookies kept the starters on them at all times. Skillet gravies were made using bacon grease. In the December 2015 *True West Magazine* article "Cowboy Grub," Texas cowboy WH Thomas is reported to have said of the nourishment on a late nineteenth-century cattle drive: "Eating around a chuck wagon is the best eating in the world. Nothing special, but good solid food like whistle berries, beef, sow belly strips, and some of the best sop in the world can be made from the grease you get from fried sowbelly. . . . If everything was favorable, you could depend on a slice of pie two or three times a week, sometimes more."

Because cattle drives spurred the Texas economy after the Civil War, on May 26, 2005, the state's legislature passed a resolution decreeing the chuck wagon as the official vehicle of Texas: "Whereas, the chuck wagon has been important in Texas since the great cattle drives that lasted from the end of the Civil War to the mid-1880s; during that period, approximately 10 million head of cattle were driven along trails all the way from Texas to railheads in Kansas, Missouri, Wyoming, and Canada." If not for all that cast iron rattling around as chuck wagons rolled across the western United States, cowboys would not have been able to stay healthy out in the elements, a shift that could have jeopardized the ranchers' investments, and, ultimately, disrupted the delivery of beef to the rest of North America.

Today, there is probably at least one restaurant or food-related business, if not several, in every state with a name that includes "cast-iron." When the term is used, it is meant to signal durability and authenticity. It doesn't matter if skillet bread is being made or a Japanese omelette. These chefs follow the tremendous example set by the chuck wagon: that cast-iron cookware is designed to produce delicious food virtually anywhere.

Cowboys eating out on the range, chuck wagon in background, ca. 1880–1910. Photograph. Library of Congress, Photographs and Prints Division, Washington, DC.

Cowboys eating out on the range, chuck wagon in background, ca. 1880–1910. Photograph. Library of Congress, Photographs and Prints Division, Washington, DC.

METRIC EQUIVALENTS

WEIGHTS

1 ounce = 28 grams
2 ounces = 57 grams
4 ounces (¼ pound) = 113 grams
8 ounces (½ pound) = 227 grams
16 ounces (1 pound) = 454 grams

VOLUME MEASURES

⅛ teaspoon = 0.6 ml
¼ teaspoon = 1.23 ml
½ teaspoon = 2.5 ml
1 teaspoon = 5 ml
1 tablespoon (3 teaspoons) = ½ fluid ounce = 15 ml
2 tablespoons = 1 fluid ounce = 29.5 ml
¼ cup (4 tablespoons) = 2 fluid ounces = 59 ml
⅓ cup (5⅓ tablespoons) = 2.7 fluid ounces = 80 ml
½ cup (8 tablespoons) = 4 fluid ounces = 120 ml
⅔ cup (10⅔ tablespoons) = 5.4 fluid ounces = 160 ml
¾ cup (12 tablespoons) = 6 fluid ounces = 180 ml
1 cup (16 tablespoons) = 8 fluid ounces = 240 ml

TEMPERATURE EQUIVALENTS

°F	°C	Gas Mark
225	110	¼
250	130	½
275	140	1
300	150	2
325	170	3
350	180	4
375	190	5
400	200	6
425	220	7
450	230	8
475	240	9
500	250	10

RESOURCES

These books were of immense help when putting together *Cast Iron*.

Donald B. Wagner
Iron and Steel in Ancient China
(E.J. Brill, 1996)

Dominique DeVito
The Complete Cast-Iron Cookbook
(Cider Mill Press, 2018)

Dominique DeVito
*Cast Iron Cookware: The Care &
Keeping Handbook*
(Cider Mill Press, 2017)

Shane Hetherington
One Pot, Big Pot
(Cider Mill Press, 2018)

**Keith Sarasin &
Chris Viaud**
The Farmers Dinner
(Cider Mill Press, 2019)

Derek Bissonnette
Soup
(Cider Mill Press, 2018)

IMAGE CREDITS

Page 15, courtesy of Museum of New Zealand; pages 19-39, courtesy of United States Patent and Trademark Office; pages 78, 100, 120, 122, 125, 127, 204, 207, 250, 253, 289, 291, 303, 304, 324, 331, 339, 348, 369, 378, 387, 392, 395, 396, 403, 415, 424, 447, 455, 456, 480, 484, 495, 496, 503, 564, 592, 660, 663, 664, courtesy of Cider Mill Press; pages 691-695, 698, 701, 704 courtesy of Lodge Cast Iron; page 706, courtesy of Le Creuset; page 710, courtesy of Stargazer Cast Iron; pages 713-717, courtesy of Ferleon Cookware; pages 718, 721-722, 725, courtesy of FINEX; pages 732-733, courtesy of Smithey Ironware; pages 734-736, courtesy of Milo; pages 739-741, courtesy of Borough Furnace; page 744, courtesy of Marquette Castings; pages 766-769, courtesy Library of Congress.

All other images used under official license from Shutterstock.com.

INDEX

ABOUT THE AUTHOR

Rachael Narins is a chef, instructor, and cookbook author who enjoys sharing her knowledge with others. This is her second book about cast iron. She resides in Los Angeles.